MOON

T0304567

San Miguel de Allende

JULIE MEADE

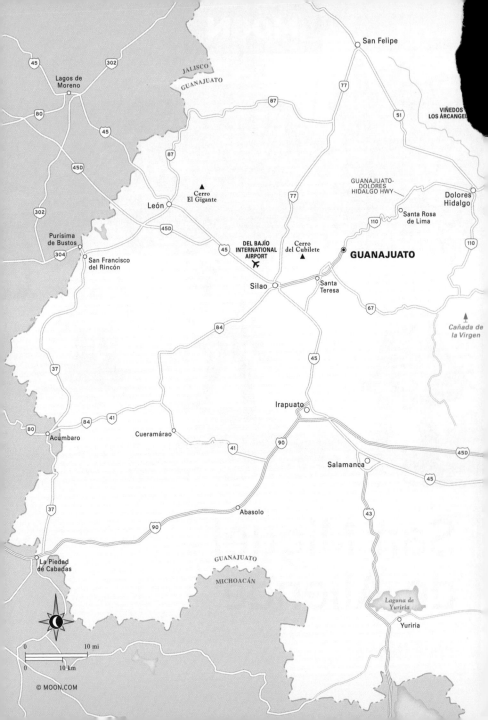

SAN MIGUEL DE ALLENDE REGION

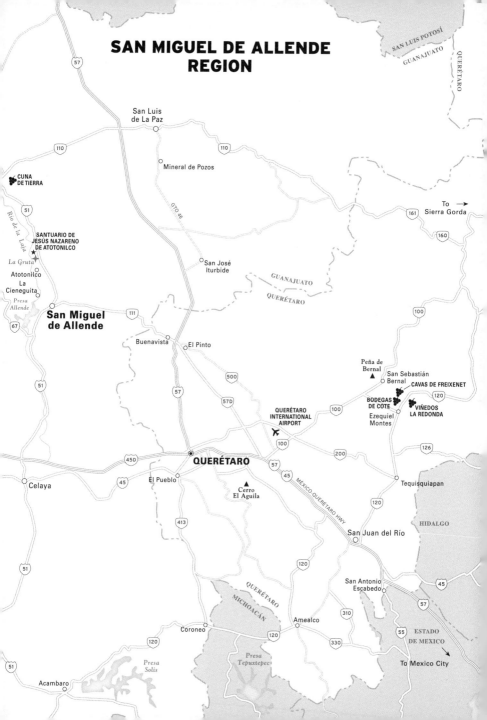

SAN LUIS POTOSÍ

GUANAJUATO

QUERÉTARO

57

110

San Luis de La Paz

110

110

Mineral de Pozos

CUNA DE TIERRA

GTO 46

To → Sierra Gorda

161

160

51

Río de la Laja

SANTUARIO DE JESÚS NAZARENO DE ATOTONILCO

La Gruta

San José Iturbide

GUANAJUATO

QUERÉTARO

100

Atotonilco

La Cieneguita

Presa Allende

67

San Miguel de Allende

111

Buenavista

El Pinto

Peña de Bernal

San Sebastián Bernal

CAVAS DE FREIXENET

51

500

57

BODEGAS DE COTE

VIÑEDOS LA REDONDA

120

57D

Ezequiel Montes

QUERÉTARO INTERNATIONAL AIRPORT

100

100

126

45D

QUERÉTARO

57

200

Celaya

45

El Pueblo

45

Cerro El Aguila

MÉXICO-QUERÉTARO HWY

Tequisquiapan

120

HIDALGO

413

San Juan del Río

120

51

San Antonio Escabedo

45

QUERÉTARO

MICHOACÁN

Amealco

310

57

55

ESTADO DE MEXICO

120

Coroneo

120

330

To Mexico City

51

Presa Solis

Presa Tepuxtepec

Acambaro

Contents

San Miguel de Allende

San Miguel de Allende

As evening falls across the Sierra de Guanajuato, the brilliant blue skies above San Miguel de Allende warm to a rosy pink. Birds streak over chapel domes while clanging iron bells herald the end of the day. As the dry air drops to a pleasant chill, mariachis tune their instruments and sidewalks hum with diners, gallerygoers, and revelers. For generations, moments like these have charmed visitors to San Miguel, one of Mexico's most beloved destinations.

San Miguel de Allende is located in Mexico's semiarid central highlands, a gateway between the vast northern deserts and bustling southern states. Built with the spoils of the colonial-era silver trade, San Miguel and its neighboring cities—Guanajuato and Querétaro—are some of the country's most splendid, renowned for their fine baroque architecture and historic city centers. The region is also known as the cradle of Mexican independence, and it is here that national heroes like Miguel Hidalgo and Ignacio Allende raised the call to arms against the Spanish crown, igniting the country in war.

San Miguel is a quintessentially Mexican place, where tacos and tamales are standard fare, the midday siesta is respected, and religious festivals are frequent, ritualistic, and raucous. Yet tradition and modernity are intertwined in San Miguel today, where a large expatriate population and a spate of boutique hotels and concept shops have brought a sleek patina to a town once known for its quaintness. Here you'll find a mix of cultures and people: the modern art gallery and the antique apothecary, the French bistros and the buzzing taco stands, the young art students and the foreign retirees. This joyous conviviality is precisely what makes San Miguel de Allende such a rewarding place to visit, spend a season, or settle down.

colorful facades of San Miguel de Allende

10 TOP
EXPERIENCES

1 Relaxing in the **jardín,** San Miguel's charming central square, beneath the pink sandstone towers of the Parroquia de San Miguel Arcángel (page 41).

2 Admiring **historic architecture,** from spectacular baroque churches to well-preserved colonial-era mansions (page 25).

3 **Shopping for traditional craftwork** at the many design shops and boutiques in San Miguel de Allende (page 76).

4 Soaking up the healing properties of the crystal clear **hot springs near Atotonilco** (page 62).

5 Celebrating art and artists in San Miguel de Allende's cozy, fun, and inclusive **gallery scene** (page 64).

6 Attending the **Festival Internacional Cervantino** in Guanajuato (page 145).

7 Experiencing the countryside on a walk through **El Charco del Ingenio** (page 49), a guided tour to the **Cañada de la Virgen** archaeological site (page 54), or a **horseback ride** at a working ranch (page 58).

8 Delving into the story of **Mexican independence** at famous historical sites throughout the Bajío region (page 28).

9 **Taking a class** at one of the many art, culture, and language schools in San Miguel de Allende and Guanajuato (pages 85 and 149).

10 Savoring the traditional and contemporary flavors of the Bajío's growing **food and wine scene** (page 32).

Planning Your Trip

WHERE TO GO

San Miguel de Allende

San Miguel de Allende is a small colonial town, known for its beautiful light, charming atmosphere, and artsy expatriate community. Irresistibly romantic yet surprisingly modern, San Miguel offers a little something for everyone, whether you are an artist, a history buff, or just looking for a great place to relax. Tour colonial-era architecture, visit contemporary **art galleries,** shop for **traditional crafts,** or linger over coffee in a sidewalk café. Visit the nearby **hot springs** for a relaxing afternoon in the desert, or take a **horseback ride** through the countryside.

Guanajuato

Guanajuato is one of Mexico's historic silver cities, built with the wealth of New Spain's lucrative mineral mines. It boasts a magnificent mix of baroque, neoclassical, and contemporary **art and architecture** as well as one of the world's most unusual urban maps. Here the centro histórico was built within a steep ravine; automobile traffic passes through underground tunnels while pedestrians navigate a dizzying mess of hills and alleyways above. Home to a prestigious public university, Guanajuato is a spirited **college town** with a youthful atmosphere and an impressive tradition in the arts; it's particularly well-known for the spectacular Festival Internacional Cervantino, an international performing arts festival held every fall.

Querétaro

Querétaro is a handsome, bustling city that is generally overlooked by tourists despite its important role in Mexican history and its remarkably well-preserved centro histórico, filled with sunny plazas and ornate baroque mansions, convents, and churches. A popular choice for Mexico City natives looking to relocate to a safer and more low-key metropolis,

© MOON.COM

trees lining a Querétaro walkway

Querétaro has a cosmopolitan side, with some great **restaurants, galleries,** and **museums,** yet it remains old-fashioned and unpretentious all the same. From Querétaro, visit the charming country towns of Tequisquiapan and San Sebastián Bernal and its eponymous monolith, stopping at one of the wineries or cheese producers along the way.

WHEN TO GO

San Miguel de Allende and the surrounding region are **year-round destinations,** though climate and costs vary depending on the season you choose to visit.

High Season

North American winter is typically the international tourist high season in San Miguel de Allende, when the region is cool, dry, and sunny. Additionally, from **December through April,** large numbers of part-time residents from the United States and Canada arrive for their annual sojourn in San Miguel. As a result, hotel prices tend to be higher from **November through April.**

Shoulder Season

Throughout the region, the weather heats up significantly during the month of **May.** May is the one month when tourism is a bit more sluggish; it picks up again when the **rainy season** begins, around mid-June. With the rains, the climate cools off pleasantly, making it a nice time to visit. Although hotels and restaurants aren't quite as full during the summer as they are during the winter, there is still considerable tourism to the region. **Summer** is also a popular time for college students to take language classes or volunteer in San Miguel or Guanajuato.

Festivals and Holidays

Another thing to keep in mind when planning

your trip to San Miguel de Allende, Guanajuato, or other nearby towns is that these destinations are popular with national tourists as well as international tourists, with national tourism surging at different times during the year. On the weekends, San Miguel is often thronged with families from Monterrey or León, while big national holidays can transform the city with crowds of revelers. You will need to make advance hotel reservations if you plan to visit San Miguel de Allende during Holy Week in the spring, Independence Day weekend in September, Día de Muertos in November, or the Christmas season in December, or if you plan to visit Guanajuato in October, when the city hosts the annual Festival Internacional Cervantino.

BEFORE YOU GO

Passports and Visas

Since 2008, all foreign visitors must have a **valid passport** to enter Mexico. At the port of entry, immigration officials issue each visitor a six-month **temporary tourist permit,** or tourist card. You must keep your stamped tourist card and return it at the airport when you check in for your flight out of the country. If you enter by car, you must stop at an immigration office at the border to pick up your tourist card and, likewise, return it to immigration officials on your way home.

Transportation

San Miguel de Allende, Guanajuato, and other towns in northern Guanajuato state can be accessed by air via León's **Del Bajío International Airport** (BJX). Equidistant to San Miguel de Allende is the **Querétaro International Airport** (QRO), about half an hour outside

If You Have . . .

- **A LONG WEEKEND:** Book a hotel in downtown San Miguel de Allende, and spend the weekend exploring the centro histórico.

- **ONE WEEK:** Follow the "Best of San Miguel" itinerary, allowing for a travel day at the beginning and end of the trip.

- **ONE MONTH:** Make San Miguel de Allende your home base, and plan trips to the cities of Guanajuato, Querétaro, Mineral de Pozos, and Dolores Hidalgo.

- **A WINTER:** With a season in San Miguel, you can do it all: make friends, take a class, attend concerts, soak in the hot springs, and plan weekend trips throughout the region.

Querétaro. Most travelers arrive in **León,** which offers more international flights than Querétaro, though both ports are about 90 minutes from San Miguel de Allende. The city of Guanajuato is about half an hour from the BJX terminal. Several tour operators offer shuttle service to and from the airport to San Miguel de Allende. For some travelers, it is easiest to book flights to **Mexico City** and then use ground transportation, which can also be arranged via tour operators in San Miguel de Allende.

There is plenty of **bus service** to and from the region, which is located in the very center of Mexico, including frequent departures to San Miguel de Allende, Guanajuato, and Querétaro from Mexico City. There is also frequent service between Bajío cities, including frequent first- and second-class departures to Querétaro and Guanajuato from San Miguel.

BEST OF
San Miguel de Allende

The perfect place for a getaway, San Miguel de Allende unites recreation, relaxation, and culture. In five days, you can see the city's historic sights, visit the countryside, eat memorable meals at rooftop restaurants and patio cafés, even take a day trip—and still have time to relax, soak in the hot springs, and thumb through a novel. The key is to plan, but not excessively: In this charming little town, you'll often encounter your most memorable moments by chance.

Day 1

Every tour of San Miguel de Allende should begin in the **jardín,** the city's heart both geographically and spiritually. The always-busy plaza is quietest in the mornings, though loyally attended by newspaper vendors and flocks of pudgy pigeons. Take a moment to admire the pink sandstone spires of the **Parroquia de San Miguel Arcángel,** San Miguel's singular neo-Gothic church, then walk a few blocks west for a delicious breakfast and coffee at **Lavanda,** a deservedly popular half-day café.

Now it's time to perfect the art of the not-totally-aimless wander through the centro histórico, San Miguel's 500-year-old downtown district. You might begin at the **Centro Cultural Ignacio Ramírez "El Nigromante"** (also known as Bellas Artes), an art school and exhibition space, then visit the adjoining Templo de la Inmaculada Concepción, San Miguel's largest domed church. From there, it's an easy 10-minute stroll east along Mesones toward the Templo de San Francisco and the Oratorio San Felipe Neri, two gorgeous baroque temples.

Just around the corner from San Felipe Neri, the **Mercado Ignacio Ramírez** is a traditional food and flower market on Colegio, adjoined by the Mercado de Artesanía, an open-air craft market that fills a descending alleyway, all the way to the street Relox. Wander through the markets, then head north along Relox toward the jardin. If you need a snack, pick up a savory bean-and-chorizo empanada at **La Colmena,** a traditional Mexican bakery that has been in operation for over 100 years.

Spend a leisurely afternoon browsing the many small **boutiques and galleries** in the centro histórico, all located just a few blocks from one another. Start on the street Recreo, where you'll find gorgeous handwoven Oaxacan textiles at Juana Cata and contemporary Mexican art at Galeria Nudo. Continue south on Recreo to visit Casa Diana, a gallery showcasing work by artist Pedro Friedeberg and the concept shop Atemporal, beside Parque Juárez. Follow up the visual feast with a fine dinner at **The Restaurant,** one of nicest eateries in town and a truly beautiful one to boot, located in an open-air patio with Moorish details.

Day 2

Now that you've got the lay of the land, give yourself the luxury of a lazy morning, lingering over coffee at **La Cabra Iluminada,** a modern café with a wonderful vegan breakfast menu. When you are ready to get moving, take a taxi to **El Charco del Ingenio,** the botanical gardens and ecological preserve located east of the city center. Spend some time amid the flowering

El Charco del Ingenio

cactus and mesquite trees along El Charco's winding nature trails, framed by sweeping views of the city below.

Catch a taxi back to the centro to have ceviche and pisco sours at **La Parada,** an airy Peruvian restaurant located on the southern end of Recreo street. From La Parada, you're just one block north of **El Chorro,** the site of San Miguel's founding. Enjoy a stroll along El Chorro's shady terraces, then walk one block east for a respite in **Parque Juárez,** listening to the cries of snowy egrets and the giggles of local children while relaxing on an old iron bench. From the park, stroll along Cardo to the Ancha de San Antonio to visit the **Instituto Allende,** an impressive 18th-century mansion that is now home to the city's oldest art school, as well as several shops and galleries.

Double back to Cardo to watch the sunset from **Luna Rooftop Tapas Bar,** an open-air lounge on the top floor of the luxury Rosewood Hotel. There are delicious tapas on the menu here, but hold off: You're just a block away from **Tostévere,** a local favorite for small plates and cocktails, a perfect place for dinner.

Day 3

Rise early to have a delicious Mexican breakfast at **Raíces,** then join anthropologist Albert Coffee for a tour of the wonderful **Cañada de la Virgen** archaeological site, just outside San Miguel de Allende. Alternatively, you can explore the Mexican countryside on a half-day horseback ride with the spirited cowboys at family-owned **Rancho Xotolar.** Both Albert Coffee and Rancho Xotolar provide transportation to and from San Miguel de Allende, passing the Presa Allende (Allende Reservoir) and small towns along the way.

After a morning of fresh air and sunshine, take it easy with a quick, economical lunch right in the center of town at **Carnitas Apolo XI.** From there, you might retire for a well-deserved siesta, or get a scoop of mango ice from **Nieves Las Monjas,** which you can take to the jardín to watch the afternoon crowd mill about.

That evening, make it a point to attend an art opening, a live music performance, or a film screening at a local gallery, a venue like **Mama Mía,** or the Teatro Santa Ana, a nonprofit performing arts space in the **Biblioteca de San Miguel.** There's almost always something happening in San Miguel, and it's fun to rub elbows with locals at these well-attended events. Afterward, keep up the spirited mood at **El Manantial,** an atmospheric old cantina that serves strong drinks and some of the best fish tacos in town.

Day 4

By the time you've spent a few days in San Miguel, you've likely fallen in step with the city's easygoing rhythm. Now it's time to pick up the pace in **Guanajuato,** a lively college town just an hour-and-a-half drive northwest of San Miguel. Start your tour in the **Jardín de la Unión,** the city's music-filled central plaza, then cross the street to visit the **Templo de San Diego Alcantará,** which has numerous large-format oil paintings from the 17th century through the post-independence era, many by anonymous artists. Back outside, walk north toward the Plaza de la Paz, following Avenida Juárez until you arrive at the atmospheric **Mercado Hidalgo.** Grab a snack in the market, then head to the interesting regional museum inside the historic **Alhóndiga de Granaditas,** just a block away.

Have an artfully prepared lunch at modern-Mexican restaurant **Mestizo,** then spend the afternoon popping into museums, galleries, and shops along Positos Street; a highlight is the **Museo Casa Diego Rivera,** the childhood home of the famous muralist. Continue wandering toward the center of town, checking out the fine art galleries and climbing the iconic staircase on the main campus of the Universidad de Guanajuato.

Before heading back to San Miguel de Allende, relax with a shot of tequila at **Bar Tradicional Luna,** where you'll get a front-row view of the mariachi bands strolling the **Jardín de la Unión** plaza.

Templo de San Diego Alcantará and the Jardin de la Unión

Day 5

It's worth getting an early start to visit the hot springs while the air is still cool and there aren't big crowds in the pools. Just a 15-minute drive from downtown San Miguel, flower-filled **La Gruta** is the best-known spot for soaking, but there are several other bathing pools along the highway to Dolores Hidalgo. Before taking off, have your taxi stop for coffee and pastries at **Panina,** an excellent bakery and breakfast spot in the San Antonio neighborhood.

Head back to San Miguel for a relaxing lunch at **Bennu,** a serene courtyard restaurant that's known for its chewy sourdough-crust pizzas. Continue relaxing with a spa treatment or a siesta—or simply grab a book or a journal and head to **Ki'bok** to spend a few hours with a delicious coffee in a relaxed atmosphere.

Wrap up the day in classic San Miguel style: on a rooftop with a view. Just beside the jardín, stylish **La Azotea** is a deservedly popular place for cocktails, snacks, and sunsets, with beautiful views of downtown. For one final bite, head to **Don Taco Tequila,** where you can start planning your next trip to San Miguel over a plate of creative vegan tacos and a mezcal cocktail. Crash to sleep amid the clang of church bells.

Historic Architecture

During the 17th and 18th centuries, the silver trade brought prosperity to the towns and settlements along the Camino Real de Tierra Adentro, a route that ran from the northern reaches of New Spain's territory to Mexico City. Working with some of Mexico's most celebrated architects and artists, wealthy families built haciendas, churches, and other buildings in the cities of the Bajío, which continue to dazzle visitors today. Though taking cues from the Old World, the artisans who built these cities brought their own inventive flourishes to the work, adding unique elements to traditional European design.

Mexican Baroque

Downtown San Miguel de Allende, Guanajuato, and Querétaro are often compared to the Old World, and for good reason: During the colonial era, Mexican architecture followed trends from Spain, where baroque was the dominant aesthetic. An evolution of the classical style favored during the Renaissance, baroque architecture is characterized by its elaborate ornamentation, dramatic use of light, and monumental facades.

Where to Find It

- In San Miguel, the **Casa de Allende** is an example of baroque civil architecture, built in the 18th century by one of the city's prominent families (page 44).

- In Guanajuato, the **Templo de San Roque** (page 133) and the **Basílica de Nuestra Señora de Guanajuato** (page 129) are two beautiful representations of the baroque style.

- The impressive baroque altarpieces in the **Templo y Ex-Convento de Santa Rosa de Viterbo** in Querétaro have been partially destroyed, but along with the building's interesting facade, they provide a wonderful example of inventive Mexican baroque (page 174).

Churrigueresque

During the late 1600s, Spanish architect José Benito de Churriguera developed a style of ornamentation, called churrigueresque, that was a more elaborate offshoot of baroque design. Influenced by Churriguera's florid aesthetic, Mexican architects began to incorporate more extravagant embellishments onto the facades of 18th-century churches.

Where to Find It

- In San Miguel, visit the **Templo de San Francisco** for a fine example of early-18th-century churrigueresque ornamentation. You can see the direct influence of Churriguera's style in the elaborately carved sandstone columns (page 49).

- In Guanajuato's Valenciana neighborhood, the astonishingly detailed sandstone relief on the **Templo de San Cayetano** is known throughout the country as one of the most beautiful representations of churrigueresque ornamentation (page 137).

1: Templo de San Francisco 2: Museo Gene Byron

Gothic Revival

In Northern Europe, the mid-1700s saw a resurgent interest in medieval architecture, known as the Gothic Revival. Gaining popularity in the Western Hemisphere in the 1800s, this style borrowed from traditional Gothic design and aesthetics.

Where to Find It

- In San Miguel, there is one unmistakable neo-Gothic structure: the pink sandstone facade on the famous **Parroquia de San Miguel Arcángel,** inspired by Gothic cathedrals in Europe. Its towering spires and pointed arches are distinct trademarks of the style, though the design of the parroquia is largely original (page 44).

Neoclassical

During the late 1700s, classical architecture also experienced a revival worldwide. Typified by its clean lines and symmetry, neoclassical design often employs large arches, columns, and pilasters.

Where to Find It

- In Guanajuato, there are many striking neoclassical buildings downtown, from the austere **Alhóndiga de Granaditas** (page 135) to the impressive columned facade of **Teatro Juárez** (page 127).

- In Querétaro, the elaborate **Fuente de Neptuno,** built in 1797, is neoclassical in style (page 173).

- Also note the massive neoclassical altarpieces in many of San Miguel's churches—including the **Templo de la Inmaculada Concepción**

1: Templo de San Roque in Guanajuato
2: Templo y Ex-Convento de Santa Rosa de Viterbo 3: the Fuente de Neptuno, outside the Templo de Santa Clara

(page 46) and the **Parroquia de San Miguel Arcángel** (page 44).

become cities in their own right. In downtown San Miguel, many present-day individual homes were once part of larger family estates.

The Hacienda

The hacienda—a large estate overseen by a Spanish family—was a major influence on Bajío architecture. Throughout the region, small towns, such as Dolores Hidalgo, were often founded as haciendas, eventually growing large enough to

Where to Find It

- For a glimpse into the lifestyle of 17th- and 18th-century haciendas, visit the **Ex-Hacienda San Gabriel de Barrera** (page 138) or the **Museo Gene Byron** (page 139) in Guanajuato.

3

Independent Spirit

Mexico's war for independence officially began in the small town of Dolores, where popular pastor and rebel leader Miguel Hidalgo raised the first battle cry against the Spanish crown on September 16, 1810. San Miguel de Allende, Querétaro, and Guanajuato also played major roles in the fight for independence. Today the Bajío region, which celebrated 200 years of independence in 2010, boasts historic sites scattered throughout the major cities.

CASA DE ALLENDE

The seeds of independence were sown in early-19th-century San Miguel. At his home on the town square, Ignacio Allende held secret meetings to plan a revolt against the Spanish crown. Today his home is the **Casa de Allende** (page 44), a museum chronicling the life and times of the city's most famous insurgent.

CASA DE LA CORREGIDORA

Querétaro's corregidor (mayor) was a coconspirator against the Spanish crown, often meeting in secret with Allende and Hidalgo.

The mayor's wife, Josefa Ortiz de Domínguez, was instrumental in saving the independence movement from being quashed: After the Spanish uncovered the independence plot, Ortiz de Domínguez sent warning to the conspirators, saving them from capture. The Domínguez home is today known as the **Casa de la Corregidora** (page 173).

PARROQUIA DE NUESTRA SEÑORA DE LOS DOLORES

Once Allende and his coconspirators realized that their plot had been uncovered, they launched their revolt. Father Miguel rang the bell in the **Parroquia de Nuestra Señora de los Dolores** (page 80) to summon his forces. In front of a crowd, Father Hidalgo and the Mexican army declared independence from Spain, in the early morning hours of September 16, 1810.

Today the bell from the parish in Dolores hangs in Mexico City's Palacio Nacional, where the president re-enacts Hidalgo's independence cry—known as the Grito de Dolores—on the night of September 15 each year.

SANTUARIO DE JESÚS NAZARENO DE ATOTONILCO

From Dolores, Father Miguel Hidalgo rode with his cavalry to the **Santuario de Jesús Nazareno de Atotonilco** (page 53), where he pulled down a banner bearing an image of the Virgen de Guadalupe, which became the new flag for the insurgent army. To this day, the virgin's image is a symbol of Mexican culture.

LA ALHÓNDIGA DE GRANADITAS

Though San Miguel and Celaya quickly fell to the insurgent army, Guanajuato's royalist leaders resisted. The first major battle in the war—and one of its bloodiest—took place at **La Alhóndiga de Granaditas** (page 135).

Here an Indigenous miner nicknamed El Pípila became a hero of the independence movement, leading the rebels to victory. (Months later, Spanish forces would capture Allende and Hidalgo and hang their severed heads from the corners of the Alhóndiga.)

OTHER INDEPENDENCE SITES

In addition to historical sites, there are many Bajío streets and parks named after independence heroes, as well as monuments to the independence movement.

Note the pretty **Plaza de la Corregidora** (page 176) in Querétaro and Guanajuato's titanic **monument to El Pípila** (page 125), as well as the statue to El Pípila at the southern entrance to San Miguel de Allende, among many other tributes to the region's war heroes.

Above: statue of independence hero Ignacio Allende

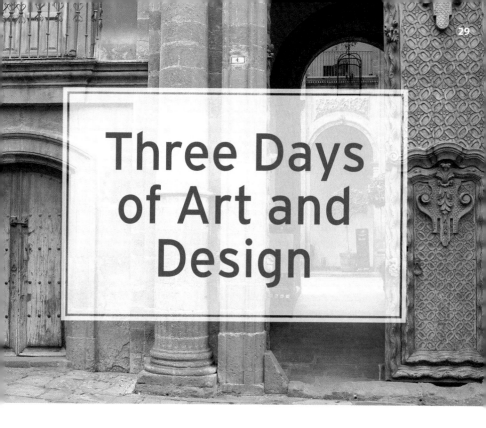

Three Days of Art and Design

San Miguel de Allende has a long tradition of excellence in architecture, the arts, and design. This small city is home to an eclectic, entertaining mix of design shops, artist-run galleries, and contemporary boutique hotels, which contrast delightfully with the grand colonial-era architecture and old-fashioned ambience in the city center.

Thursday: Tradition and Modernity

San Miguel is a wonderful place to learn about Mexico's unique traditions in handcraft, with many well-curated shops that elevate craft to fine-art status. Start with a joyous approach to popular craft at **La Esquina: Museo del Jugete Popular Mexicano,** a lovely two-floor museum that showcases the fine craftsmanship and creativity behind traditional Mexican toys. It's almost impossible to resist picking something up at their delightful on-site gift shop. From there,

it's a short walk to the small showroom of **Juana Cata** on Recreo, which specializes in huipiles, embroidered blouses, hand-loomed shawls, and other rare and beautiful textiles from the state of Oaxaca.

Cross the jardín to visit the gallery and gift shop at the **Casa del Mayorazgo de la Canal.** Set inside an impressive colonial-era mansion, it represents top-quality artisan work, in addition to selling a nice collection of books about Mexican craft traditions. Just a block north on Mesones, **La Calaca** is a wonderful little shop that specializes in antique and one-of-a-kind artisan pieces, including ceremonial masks.

Now that you've had a thorough introduction to traditional craft, check out the city's contemporary art scene. In the heart of downtown, **Galeria Nudo** and **Galeria Noel Cayetano** are good spots to see new work by Mexican artists, while the impressive interiors and design studio **Tao,** on the street Sollano, has an avant-garde feel. Close the day at **Bekeb,** a stylish rooftop cocktail bar whose distinctive drinks marry tradition and modernity.

Friday: Behind Closed Doors

As beautiful as they are from the outside, San Miguel's grand old homes are often more stunning behind their towering rust- and ochre-colored facades. Today you'll get a peek inside, starting with breakfast at **Posada Corazón,** a quiet guest house and breakfast-only restaurant, set inside the living areas of a rambling 1960s-era mansion on Aldama.

At noon, join the weekly **House and Garden Tour,** run by the Biblioteca de San Miguel de Allende, which will take you (and a large group of fellow visitors) inside several of the city's most splendid houses. Though the itinerary changes frequently, the tour often includes properties that have been featured in magazines and coffee-table books.

In the evening, continue the theme of peeking behind closed doors with a flight of tequila at the reservations-only **Obsidian Bar** at La Casa Dragones. Set inside a historic 17th century mansion, this ultra-contemporary bar opened in 2023, a one-of-a-kind setting to enjoy a guided tasting of Casa Dragones premium spirits.

Saturday: Superlative Shopping

Saturday's agenda is for the serious shopper. Start the day at the wonderfully curated boutique **Mixta,** where the eclectic collection of furniture, clothing, jewelry, original art, and accessories includes work by some interesting contemporary Mexican designers.

Just a couple blocks east, there are several fun boutiques and a lovely showroom for furniture line **Namuh** in **Cuna Quince,** a little shopping plaza in a historic building on Cuna de Allende. From there, head east to upscale clothier **Recreo,** on the street of the same name, where a line of beautiful, high-quality wraps, shawls, and ponchos blend classic Mexican aesthetics with a contemporary, luxe look.

Next, walk about 15 minutes north of the centro to the **Fábrica La Aurora,** a large art and shopping center in a converted turn-of-the-20th-century textile factory. With dozens of galleries, studios, and shops tucked into unexpected nooks and crannies, you'll find nearly endless visual inspiration in the goods on offer—from Italian linens at La Bottega di Casa to Mexican antiques at atmospheric La Buhardilla. The space itself is enchanting, with an old-style industrial feeling, largely left intact despite the factory's reinvention as a shopping center. You could spend the whole afternoon exploring its labyrinthine hallways, chockablock with art studios, design shops, and galleries. If you're lucky, you've come on a Saturday when the Fábrica La Aurora is hosting an **Art Walk.** If so, you can expect to see a flurry of attendees wandering through the space and sipping from little cups of cheap Chilean wine in the galleries.

Hidden Gems for Art Lovers

Art is everywhere in San Miguel de Allende, including in some rather unusual places. While visiting galleries and design shops is a must, there are some hidden treasures of the local art scene as well.

HOMECOMING FOR THE HAND

In 2021, celebrated surrealist artist Pedro Friedeberg returned to his longtime home of San Miguel de Allende to inaugurate the installation of a six-ton replica of *Mano-Silla (Hand Chair)*, his most famed sculptural piece, at the **Bajada del Chorro,** the beautiful tree-filled site of San Miguel's founding (page 51).

UNFINISHED MASTERPIECE

One of the most famous artists, activists, and thinkers of 20th-century Mexico, David Alfaro Siqueiros was invited to San Miguel in the 1940s to work with students on a mural dedicated to Ignacio Allenge, in the art school that is today the **Centro Cultural Ignacio Ramírez "El Nigromante."**

After a falling-out with the school's director, Siqueiros departed abruptly, leaving the mural unfinished—but nonetheless incredibly interesting to see, as it offers insight into Siqueiros's unique approach to composition. You can see the piece at the Sala Siqueiros, on the first floor of the cultural center (page 46).

AT THE VINEYARD

In addition to making some artful whites and reds, family-run winery **Dos Búhos** operates an international artist-in-residence program at their vineyard. If you come for lunch or a tasting, ask the staff to show you to a small screening room on-site where video-art installations are shown. You'll also find a big collection of local art in their tasting room, chapel, and gardens (page 100).

COLORFUL STREETS

Through a neighborhood project called Muros en Blanco (Blank Walls) launched in 2013, the **Guadalupe neighborhood,** just north of the city center, now has murals on almost every street in the neighborhood, including a long strip along Canción India. Tip: Pick up a juice or coffee at Guadalupe eatery **Deli Q** to sip while you tour the area on foot (page 96).

SLEEPER HIT

Hotel Matilda's excellent in-house art collection includes well-known names in modern and contemporary Mexican art, from Diego Rivera to Bosco Sodi (page 111).

THE BUG, THE BAR, THE GALLERY

With local artists as longtime patrons, **La Cucaracha,** San Miguel's legendary dive bar, has a collection of haphazardly hung art on the walls of the otherwise no-frills space (page 102). (The bar has also been known to host an art exhibition.)

The Bajío Palate

Mexico's color and creativity are reflected in its wonderful food. Every region in the country is distinguished by its own culinary traditions, as well as ingredients native to the land. In San Miguel de Allende and the surrounding area, several well-known local products and dishes are worth seeking out on a trip to the region. In addition, the growing organic and natural food movement, as well as a burgeoning wine industry, have made the Bajío a new culinary destination. If you want to get a taste of the region, here are some foods to try.

Nopal

Nopal, or prickly pear cactus, is a popular vegetable throughout Mexico and abundant in the highlands around San Miguel. It is often sliced and served as a stuffing in gorditas or grilled whole and served with cheese. One tasty stew served throughout the region features chopped nopal with garbanzo beans and cilantro.

Find nopal in San Miguel alongside eggs in salsa at **Raíces** (page 98), as a grilled side dish at **Don Taco Tequila** (page 90), and at the **Mercado Ignacio Ramírez** (page 95), where you can buy it both fresh and prepared in salad.

Xoconostle

Throughout Mexico, the tuna (prickly pear fruit) is consumed whole or blended into ice cream and aguas. In the Bajío, a type of sour tuna called xoconostle is used in regional dishes as well as in sweets, where it takes on a pleasingly tart flavor.

Try a tangy xoconostle-mezcal cocktail at wonderful **Casa Mercedes Restaurante** (page 155) in Guanajuato.

Queso Ranchero and Other Local Cheeses

Called queso fresco in other parts of Mexico, the Bajío's delicious queso ranchero is a fresh, white, salty cheese, often crumbled atop enchiladas or guacamole. Look for queso ranchero at supermarkets, at San Miguel's **Mercado de Martes** (page 101), or at the **Mercado de la Cruz** (page 177) in Querétaro.

In recent years, small and artisanal cheesemakers have been cropping up around the Bajío. Many, like **Cava Bocanegra** (page 201) in Querétaro, have country stores where you can pick up their products (or take a tour of the ranch or cheese-making facilities). In San Miguel de Allende, drop by **Luna de Queso** (page 98) for a large and excellent selection of Mexican-made cheese and dairy, alongside an excellent all-day café for dining.

Cajeta

Cajeta, caramelized milk candy, is a specialty of Celaya, a small industrial city just an hour east of San Miguel. Created with a mix of scalded goat and cow milk, cajeta sauce is served in crepes and on ice cream or slathered onto wafers. You can also find cajeta candy rolled in nuts.

Try some at Guanajuato sweet shop **La Catrina** (page 149), or order a scoop of cajeta-flavored ice cream in the town square in **Dolores Hidalgo** (page 80). For excellent cajeta and other traditional sweets, stop into **Dulces Bernal** (page 208), in the state of Querétaro.

Wine

The Bajío's nascent wine industry has been growing rapidly since the 2010s. If you'd like to taste some local wines, schedule a tasting at one of the new wineries near San Miguel de Allende, like **Dos Búhos** (page 100), or in Querétaro state, like **Bodegas de Cote** (page 204). In San Miguel de Allende, you'll find interesting local and natural wines to sip at cozy bar **Xoler** (page 104).

Mezcal

The most famous varieties of mezcal come from the state of Oaxaca, though the spirit is produced throughout Mexico.

Mezcal produced in the state of Guanajuato, like the brand Jaral de Berrio, is served at bars and cantinas like **El Manantial** (page 101) and **San Mezcal** (page 105).

Mixiote

Popular here and in the Valley of Mexico, mixiotes are slow-cooked meats (typically rabbit, chicken, lamb, and pork) wrapped in maguey leaves and steamed in an underground pit.

While in San Miguel, you can order mixiotes at the rooftop restaurant **La Posadita** (page 90) or at ultra-low-key **El Pato Barbacoa y Mixiotes** (page 99). For something different, try the duck mixiote at upscale Mexican restaurant **La Doña** (page 91) or the delicious mushroom mixiotes at vegan restaurant **Don Taco Tequila** (page 90).

Gorditas

Gorditas are thick corn flatbreads, grilled and stuffed with fillings like cheese, chile peppers, chicken, or beans. Gorditas are sold by street vendors and in market stalls throughout the region. You'll find freshly made gorditas with a range of savory fillings on street corners throughout Guanajuato and San Miguel de Allende.

Try the Querétaro-style gordita at the **Mercado de la Cruz** (page 177) in Querétaro.

Enchiladas Mineras

A hearty meal suited to a hungry laborer, these cheese-stuffed "miner's enchiladas" are bathed in guajillo chile sauce and topped with a generous serving of sautéed potatoes, carrots, and cheese. Fill your stomach with this regional specialty at **Truco 7** (page 152) in Guanajuato.

Very similar to enchiladas mineras, enchiladas queretanas are also bathed in a guajillo sauce; find them at **La Cenaduria** (page 189) in Querétaro.

San Miguel de Allende

San Miguel de Allende is a town of a thousand picture postcards, renowned for its baroque architecture and sparkling blue skies.

You can hardly turn a corner without finding a splendid scene before you. On one block, there is a crumbling stone chapel, its iron bells hanging crookedly in the belfry. On another, a flower seller stacks bushels of roses atop an 18th-century fountain. Along the winding streets of the centro histórico (historical district), vines of magenta bougainvillea spill over the walls of colonial residences. Throughout the winter and spring, the setting sun throws a scarlet blanket across the sky, as white egrets streak across the sky. It is precisely when everything seems too beautiful to believe that you stumble upon something

Highlights

Look for ★ to find recommended sights, activities, dining, and lodging.

★ **Parroquia de San Miguel Arcángel and El Jardín:** San Miguel's iconic parish church is a symbol of the town and one of the most original architectural sights in Mexico, located right on the charming central square, or jardín (pages 41 and 44).

★ **El Charco del Ingenio:** An expansive nature preserve and botanical garden, El Charco offers sweeping views of the city, charming nature trails, and excellent bird-watching along a dramatic canyon ridge (page 49).

★ **Fábrica La Aurora:** This turn-of-the-20th-century textile factory has been refashioned as an art and design center, with galleries, shops, and studios, plus restaurants and cafés (page 51).

★ **Parque Juárez:** Spend a peaceful afternoon in the shade of fan palms and jacarandas in this historic and family-friendly urban park (page 51).

★ **El Chorro:** Located at the site of San Miguel's founding, the cascading terraces of El Chorro are among the most enchanting spots in town (page 51).

★ **Santuario de Jesús Nazareno de Atotonilco:** One of the finest churches in all of Mexico, the enigmatic sanctuary in Atotonilco has been a site of religious retreat and refuge since the 18th century (page 53).

★ **Cañada de la Virgen:** See another side of Mexican history at this small but fascinating archaeological site, located within an expansive nature preserve just outside San Miguel de Allende (page 54).

★ **Horseback Riding in the Countryside:** Visit a charming family-owned ranch for spectacular half- or full-day horseback rides through the countryside near the Cañada de la Virgen (page 58).

★ **La Gruta:** Take a morning soak at La Gruta, one of several bathing spots near San Miguel de Allende, where thermal pools are surrounded by lush gardens (page 62).

new: an old wooden doorway, a wedding party led by a flower-wreathed donkey, an unexpected burst of fireworks over the star-lit skyline.

Beautiful as it is, San Miguel de Allende is much more than an attractive facade. Warm, accepting, and amiable, it's a place of living culture and community. On the weekends, the sidewalks are pleasantly humming with diners, revelers, and families. Mariachi musicians fill the central jardín. Crowds spill from the doors of overstuffed galleries, where local artists host exhibitions fueled by glasses of cheap vino tinto (red wine). Join the crowd and you'll quickly learn that there are no tourists in San Miguel. Everyone's a local in this welcoming city, where cultures and people mix as easily as tequila and lime.

Since the early 2000s, San Miguel has steadily become bigger and more cosmopolitan. The cozy ambience that once defined the town has largely disappeared, and there is now a diversity of things to do, see, eat, and experience to rival many big cities. Today San Miguel has restaurants serving formal tasting menus, chic mezcal bars, and rooftop lounges with New York City price tags—as well as sprawling residential developments and big-box stores near the city center. Luxury and design-centric boutique hotels, once a rarity in a town known for its quaint bed-and-breakfasts and family-run inns, have cropped up throughout the city, while high-end shops and food halls now fill many colonial-era mansions.

Since the 1940s, San Miguel has been home to a community of expatriates from across the world, predominantly the United States and Canada. Many of the city's first foreign residents came to study art and ended up making San Miguel their permanent home. Today the city draws foreigners of every ilk who come to live their dreams. For some, it's a place to escape and relax, while others come to start a new career or open a business. Expatriates are joined by thousands of Mexicans who have come to San Miguel from across the country, many opening businesses and buying homes.

What makes San Miguel so remarkable is its capacity to accept change yet never lose hold of its character. As the suburbs expand, prices rise, and gluten-free cookies become as ubiquitous as tamales, San Miguel is still a convivial and welcoming place, defined by culture and traditions, both old and new.

PLANNING YOUR TIME

Even as San Miguel de Allende grows, almost everything there is to do, see, eat, and experience happens in the 10 square blocks around the central square. If you have just **a day or two** in town, plan to spend your time in the centro histórico. In a couple of easy days, you can visit many of the beautiful monuments that have made San Miguel famous, fit in some quality shopping, and eat in a few of the city's best restaurants. If your time is short, a **guided walking tour** can provide an interesting introduction to San Miguel's sights and history, leaving the afternoon free for an independent ramble. Strolling around the centro, you will stumble upon little alleyways barely fit for cars, gurgling fountains, and small stone chapels. Even the quiet residential streets are charming, with rows of rust-colored houses draped with flowers.

If you plan to spend **more than a couple of days** in San Miguel de Allende, a day trip to the bustling university town of Guanajuato makes an excellent complement to the laid-back vibe in San Miguel. In addition to its unique student-friendly atmosphere, Guanajuato's historic sights and architecture are among Mexico's most splendid. It's also worth spending time in the beautiful **countryside** around San Miguel, which has become increasingly accessible to visitors in recent years. Plan a day horseback riding, wine tasting, visiting the hot springs, or touring the Cañada de la Virgen archeological site—or just take a taxi to one of the many country restaurants that have sprung up around town.

As many residents of San Miguel will tell you, the longer you stay, the better it gets. If you come to town for **a longer sojourn,** there are plenty of off-the-beaten-track places to visit, enough restaurants to fill up weeks, and new friends to be made within the local crowd. Consider enrolling in an art or Spanish-language class or volunteering with a local organization.

With all there is to do, see, and eat, planning your time in San Miguel de Allende may feel overwhelming, but keep this in mind: Visiting San Miguel is just as much about downtime as it is about sightseeing. With a friendly, small-town atmosphere and year-round sunny weather, it's the perfect place to unwind, either on a bench in the town square or on the patio of your bed-and-breakfast. Don't worry about fitting it all in. Instead, take it easy and enjoy the relaxed rhythm of the days in this charming little town.

ORIENTATION

Built along a hillside, San Miguel de Allende is generally flat and walkable, with a few gentle slopes and staircases to navigate between major sites and neighborhoods. The city's topography is most challenging for pedestrians in the residential neighborhoods east of the central plaza, which are built along a steep slope and border a large natural arroyo that slices through the northeast of town. The Presa Allende, a large public reservoir, occupies a swath of land just west of town, and is surrounded by several small suburban communities.

For the San Miguel novice, navigation can be a bit frustrating, if also a bit amusing and folkloric. When in doubt, look for the spires of the parroquia (church) in the town square, or just ask a local for directions. People in San Miguel are famously friendly, and most will gladly help you find what you are looking for.

Centro Histórico

Like most Mexican cities, San Miguel de Allende is organized around a town square—the plaza principal, or as it is known to most residents, **jardín.** The blocks surrounding the town square, known as the centro histórico, constitute the oldest, busiest, and most important district in the city. Here you'll find the Parroquia de San Miguel Arcángel, government buildings, banks, and the highest concentration of shops, bars, and restaurants. You will also find many of San Miguel's most interesting sights just a stone's throw away from each other.

Although city streets form a loose grid around the jardín, the names of these streets change as they cross the plaza from east to west and north to south. For example, Calle San Francisco runs directly into the plaza from the east, changing its name to Canal as it exits to the west. Even streets that don't run directly through the plaza will often take new names as they change latitude. To make everything more complicated, many of these streets have changed their names during the course of history. In many cases, the former street name is still posted on the corner!

Guadalupe and Aurora

Most visitors to San Miguel de Allende make at least one excursion north of the centro to visit the **Fábrica La Aurora** in the Aurora neighborhood. To the southwest of the Aurora, the Guadalupe neighborhood is known for its street art and murals, as well as some highly recommended places to eat, like Hierba Santa and Deli Q.

Parque Juárez

The cobblestone streets around leafy Parque Juárez, south of the jardín, are among the city's most beautiful. Though technically part of the centro histórico, Parque Juárez has its own distinct feeling. Vacation rentals and hotels in this area—like **Casa de Liza** (and **Santa Mónica**)—are among the city's most coveted.

San Miguel de Allende

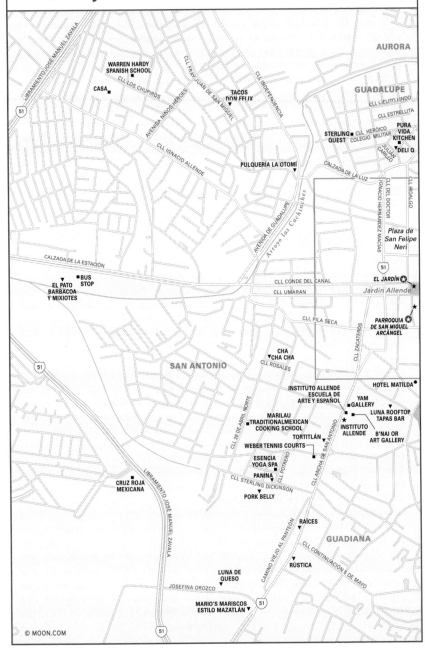

AURORA

WARREN HARDY
SPANISH SCHOOL

GUADALUPE

CASA

CLL LOS CHUPIROS

CLL CIELITO LINDO

CLL FRAY JUAN DE SAN MIGUEL

CLL INDEPENDENCIA

CLL ESTRELLITA

TACOS
DON FELIX

AVENIDA NIÑOS HÉROES

STERLING
QUEST

PURA
VIDA
KITCHEN

CLL HEROICO
COLEGIO MILITAR

DELI Q

JULIAN
CARILLO

CLL IGNACIO ALLENDE

PULQUERÍA LA OTOMÍ

CALZADA DE LA LUZ

AVENIDA DE GUADALUPE

Arroyo las Cachinches

CLL DEL DOCTOR

IGNACIO HERNÁNDEZ MACÍAS

CLL HIDALGO

Plaza de
San Felipe
Neri

CALZADA DE LA ESTACIÓN

51

BUS
STOP

EL JARDÍN ✪

CLL CONDE DEL CANAL

EL PATO
BARBACOA
Y MIXIOTES

Jardín Allende

CLL UMARAN

CLL PILA SECA

PARROQUIA
DE SAN MIGUEL
ARCÁNGEL ✪

51

CLL ZACATEROS

CHA
CHA CHA

SAN ANTONIO

CLL ROSALES

HOTEL MATILDA

INSTITUTO ALLENDE
ESCUELA DE
ARTE Y ESPAÑOL

YAM
GALLERY

CLL 28 DE ABRIL NORTE

LUNA ROOFTOP
TAPAS BAR

MARILAU
TRADITIONALMEXICAN
COOKING SCHOOL

INSTITUTO
ALLENDE

B'NAI OR
ART GALLERY

CLL ANCHA DE SAN ANTONIO

TORTITLÁN

WEBER TENNIS COURTS

ESENCIA
YOGA SPA

CLL POTRERO

PANINA

CRUZ ROJA
MEXICANA

CLL STERLING DICKINSON

LIBRAMIENTO JOSÉ MANUEL ZAVALA

PORK BELLY

RAÍCES

GUADIANA

CAMINO VIEJO AL PANTEÓN

CLL CONTINUACIÓN 5 DE MAYO

RÚSTICA

LUNA DE
QUESO

JOSEFINA OROZCO

51

MARIO'S MARISCOS
ESTILO MAZATLÁN

51

© MOON.COM

51

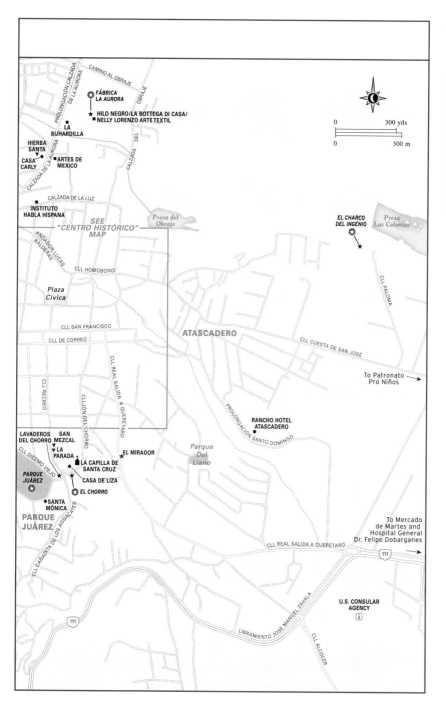

CAMINO AL OBRAJE

PROLONGACIÓN CALZADA DE LA AURORA

FÁBRICA LA AURORA

★ HILO NEGRO/LA BOTTEGA DI CASA/
■ NELLY LORENZO ARTE TEXTIL

■ LA BUHARDILLA

HIERBA SANTA

CASA CARLY ■ ARTES DE MEXICO

CALZADA DE LA AURORA

CALZADA DEL OBRAJE

0   300 yds

0   300 m

CALZADA DE LA LUZ

■ INSTITUTO HABLA HISPANA

SEE "CENTRO HISTÓRICO" MAP

Presa del Obraje

EL CHARCO DEL INGENIO

Presa Las Colonias

ANDADOR LUCAS BALDERAS

CLL HOMOBONO

CLL PALOMA

Plaza Cívica

CLL SAN FRANCISCO

CLL DE CORREO

ATASCADERO

CLL CUESTA DE SAN JOSÉ

CLL RECREO

CLL REAL SALIDA A QUERÉTARO

CLLJÓN DEL CHORRO

To Patronato Pro Niños

PROLONGACIÓN SANTO DOMINGO

RANCHO HOTEL ATASCADERO

LAVADEROS DEL CHORRO

SAN MEZCAL

▼ LA PARADA

EL MIRADOR

Parque Del Llano

CLL DIEZMO VIEJO

▲ LA CAPILLA DE SANTA CRUZ

PARQUE JUÁREZ

CASA DE LIZA

EL CHORRO

● SANTA MÓNICA

PARQUE JUÁREZ

CLL CAÑADITA DE LOS AGUACATES

To Mercado de Martes and Hospital General Dr. Felipe Dobarganes

CLL REAL SALIDA A QUERÉTARO

111

111

U.S. CONSULAR AGENCY

LIBRAMIENTO JOSÉ MANUEL ZAVALA

CLL ALCOCER

San Antonio

A pretty church and plaza are at the center of this attractive residential neighborhood southwest of the centro histórico. Many visitors come here to visit the restaurants like **Panina, Pork Belly,** or **Cha Cha Cha,** to play a set at **Weber Tennis Courts,** or to visit local businesses, like **Esencia Yoga Spa.**

Guadiana

Just south of the Parque Juárez neighborhood, the Guadiana is a quiet residential area with a central location, close to the **Salida a Celaya.** There's a nice park in the neighborhood, but you won't find many sights or activities in this quiet corner of San Miguel.

Atascadero

Built along the hillside to the east above the centro histórico, this historic neighborhood is one of San Miguel's most beautiful, with cobbled streets and old leafy trees. It can be a nice place to stay, either at the old-fashioned **Rancho Hotel Atascadero** or in a vacation home rental.

San Miguel de Allende Countryside

As San Miguel de Allende grows, activities in the outlying suburbs and surrounding countryside have proliferated. Things to do outside town include wine tasting, hiking, eating at country restaurants, and visiting the hot springs, among other experiences. Many of the most popular options are located north of San Miguel de Allende, near the community of Atotonilco and on the highway toward Dolores Hidalgo. Most of these destinations can be easily accessed via taxi or Uber, though renting a car can also be a good option if you'd like to visit multiple places outside of town.

There are wineries, ranches, and miles and miles of beautiful open space to the west between San Miguel de Allende and the city of Guanajuato. Worth noting here is the wonderful Cañada de la Virgen archeological site, located off Highway 51 to Guanajuato, past the Presa Allende. This area is also popular for horseback rides at one of the working ranches along the route.

Exiting San Miguel de Allende from the east, toward the city of Querétaro, a growing number of wineries, restaurants, and other destinations are worth seeking out, mostly near the highway and around the community of Jalpan. The area is largely rural, and public transportation is more limited; however, it is easy to access destinations here via car, ride-hailing service, or taxi.

HISTORY

In 1542 Franciscan friar Juan de San Miguel arrived in the Laja River Valley, where he founded the mission town of San Miguel Arcángel near an existing native settlement. Inconsistent water sources and native resistance to colonization made the mission hard to maintain, and between 1548 and 1549, French friar Bernardo Cossin moved the settlement to Izcuinapan, site of a natural spring known today as El Chorro.

In the mid-16th century, the discovery of silver veins near the cities of Zacatecas and Guanajuato changed the course of history for this small settlement—it became a strategic protective town along the Camino Real de Tierra Adentro (Royal Inland Route) to Mexico City. By the 17th century, San Miguel had grown to a small city of 15,000. Wealthy residents built luxurious homes around the town's main plaza, in addition to commissioning churches and monuments from some of the country's most famous architects and artists.

In the 18th century, changes to Spanish governance of the colonies affected the silver trade, tobacco farming, and other regional industries, while the seeds of independence were being sown across the region. In San Miguel, Ignacio Allende and criollo leaders began to plot for Mexican independence from Spain. When the fight for independence began in 1810, San Miguel fell peacefully to the newly formed Mexican army, but the town was ruinously sacked. A year later, Allende was captured and executed by the Spanish forces.

After the War of Independence ended, San Miguel was largely destroyed. Silver production dropped and the city went into decline. By 1821, there were only 5,000 residents. The town was renamed San Miguel de Allende in 1826.

Sleepy, rural, and largely forgotten until the early 20th century, San Miguel de Allende was declared a national monument in 1926.

Shortly thereafter, Latin America's first art school, La Escuela Universitaria de Bellas Artes, opened in an 18th-century cloister downtown. After World War II, a handful of Americans came to study at the school under the GI Bill. Many never left. In 2008 the entire downtown district of San Miguel de Allende was named a World Heritage Site by the United Nations.

Sights

Located on the Camino Real de Tierra Adentro (Royal Inland Route), San Miguel de Allende grew rapidly during the 17th and 18th centuries, when it benefited greatly from the wealth of the colonial-era silver trade. Today San Miguel's centro histórico is a unique example of city planning from that era, with an unusual mix of architectural styles. In particular, the town is recognized for its fine 18th-century Mexican baroque buildings. In 1926 San Miguel de Allende was declared a national monument by the Mexican government, a designation that, among other things, prohibits the construction of tall buildings or other structures that would compromise the city's historic downtown. As a result, the center of San Miguel has been remarkably well preserved, even as the city expands around it.

Most of San Miguel de Allende's historic architecture is religious, with beautiful churches, chapels, and convents crammed into the narrow streets of the centro histórico. Many of these old churches are still used for religious services, though visitors and tourists are welcome to go inside. When entering a church, be respectful by speaking in a low voice and not using the flash on your camera. If a mass or ceremony is in progress, observe before entering. Tourists sometimes wander into churches during more personal events, like funerals, which are best left to the family. If you would like to avoid religious services altogether, most churches do not hold mass

1pm-5pm, though note that some also close their doors to the public at this time.

CENTRO HISTÓRICO

TOP EXPERIENCE

★ El Jardín

Plaza Principal s/n; no tel.; 24 hours

The town square—officially called the **plaza principal** but known to all as the jardín—is the heart and soul of San Miguel de Allende, surrounded by colonial-era mansions and bordered to the south by the parroquia. From dawn to dusk, the jardín is filled with a pleasant crowd of locals and tourists resting their legs on iron benches, walking their dogs, or stopping for a chat in the shade of the many well-manicured laurel trees. Above them, hundreds of happy birds tweet away the afternoon, while balloon sellers and fruit vendors make a slow turn through the crowds, tempting the children who've come to play there. Sit on a bench to soak up the sun with an ice cream or watch people go by.

Those who've traveled in other parts of Mexico often wonder why San Miguel's square is referred to as the jardín, not the zócalo. Generally, the term "zócalo" refers to a central plaza adjoining a cathedral. Despite its multitiered opulence, San Miguel's parroquia is not a cathedral but a parish church. The cathedral and the seat of the bishop overseeing San Miguel de Allende's parish

Centro Histórico

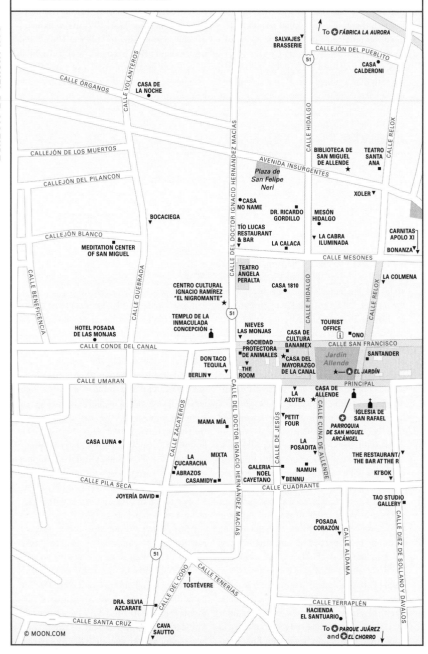

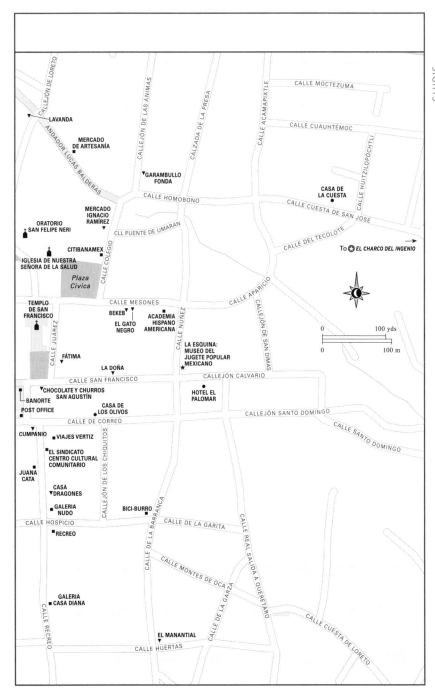

CALLEJÓN DE LORETO

CALLE MOCTEZUMA

CALLE ACAMAPIXTLE

CALLE CUAUHTÉMOC

CALLEJÓN DE LAS ÁNIMAS

CALZADA DE LA PRESA

CALLE HUITZILOPOCHTLI

ANDADOR LUCAS BALDERAS

LAVANDA

MERCADO DE ARTESANÍA

GARAMBULLO FONDA

CASA DE LA CUESTA

CALLE HOMOBONO

CALLE CUESTA DE SAN JOSÉ

ORATORIO SAN FELIPE NERI

MERCADO IGNACIO RAMÍREZ

CLL PUENTE DE UMARAN

CALLE DEL TECOLOTE

CITIBANAMEX

CALLE COLEGIO

To ☾ EL CHARCO DEL INGENIO

IGLESIA DE NUESTRA SEÑORA DE LA SALUD

Plaza Cívica

CALLE APARICIO

TEMPLO DE SAN FRANCISCO

CALLE MESONES

0   100 yds

CALLE JUAREZ

BEKEB

EL GATO NEGRO

ACADEMIA HISPANO AMERICANA

CALLE NÚÑEZ

CALLEJÓN DE SAN DIMAS

0   100 m

FÁTIMA

LA ESQUINA: MUSEO DEL JUGETE POPULAR MEXICANO

LA DOÑA

CALLE SAN FRANCISCO

CALLEJÓN CALVARIO

CHOCOLATE Y CHURROS SAN AGUSTÍN

HOTEL EL PALOMAR

BANORTE

CASA DE LOS OLIVOS

POST OFFICE

CALLEJÓN SANTO DOMINGO

CALLE DE CORREO

CALLE SANTO DOMINGO

CUMPANIO

VIAJES VERTIZ

EL SINDICATO CENTRO CULTURAL COMUNITARIO

CALLEJÓN DE LOS CHIQUITOS

JUANA CATA

CASA DRAGONES

GALERIA NUDO

BICI-BURRO

CALLE HOSPICIO

CALLE DE LA BARRANCA

CALLE DE LA GARITA

CALLE REAL SALIDA A QUERÉTARO

RECREO

CALLE MONTES DE OCA

CALLE DE LA GARZA

GALERIA CASA DIANA

CALLE RECREO

CALLE CUESTA DE LORETO

EL MANANTIAL

CALLE HUERTAS

are in the city of Celaya, about an hour south of San Miguel.

★ Parroquia de San Miguel Arcángel

Plaza Principal s/n; tel. 415/152-4197; www.
sanmiguelarcangelsma.org; generally 7am-2pm and
4pm-9pm daily

The neo-Gothic sandstone towers of the Parroquia de San Miguel Arcángel are the rosy crown of the city. The building itself was constructed in the 16th century and, as old photographs corroborate, was large but rather unspectacular. In the 19th century, the church's facade received a complete renovation at the hands of an imaginative architect, Zeferino Gutiérrez. According to local history, this self-taught draftsman based his design for the parish on prints of the Gothic cathedral in Cologne, Germany. No matter what Gutiérrez had in mind, the results are entirely original, with cascading bricks of pink sandstone surrounding the peaked archways of the parish, concluding in three pointed bell towersWhile the exterior of the parroquia is elaborate, the interior's design is spare and neoclassical; towering stone columns flank the altar and chapels, some gilded. There is a carved statue of the eponymous San Miguel Arcángel on the altar; but in the east transept is a more notable sculpture of Jesus, carved from cane bark and highlighted by a backdrop of turquoise Byzantine mosaic and aging murals.

Today the Parroquia de San Miguel Arcángel is still the parish seat (parroquia means parish church), mass is held here daily, and weddings take place almost every weekend. On days of celebration, the four iron bells of the parroquia are manually rung from the towers. When you hear their merry cacophony, look for the figures between the narrow arches, spinning the bells in circles.

Iglesia de San Rafael

Plaza Principal s/n; tel. 415/152-4197; generally 8am-8pm daily

Also known as the **Santa Escuela,** the small and often overlooked Iglesia de San Rafael shares its courtyard entrance with the parroquia. Inside, the church is a wash of aqua, with turquoise tile floors and painted blue ceilings. Large oil paintings and wooden saints line the walls, some in rather dramatic dioramas. A particularly nice oil painting hangs to the left of the neoclassical altar depicting San Miguel. Above the Iglesia de San Rafael, a brick bell tower rings out the time every 15 minutes.

Casa de Allende

Cuna de Allende 1; tel. 415/152-2499; www.inah.gob.mx;
9am-5pm Tues.-Sun.; US$3, free Sun.

A famous hero in Mexico's War of Independence from Spain, Ignacio Allende was born to a prominent family of San Miguel el Grande in 1769. His family's home, an opulent colonial-era mansion on the southeast corner of the central square, is now the **Museo Histórico de San Miguel.** The museum is commonly known as Casa de Allende. Allende famously hosted secret meetings with co-conspirators here. Today the space is dedicated to the history of the town and to the life of its most famous former resident.

During the 17th century, the first floor of a colonial mansion was generally reserved for servants' activities and quarters. The museum dedicates these rooms to the history of San Miguel de Allende, from its founding through the independence. The rooms contain a few nice artifacts from the colonial era and informational videos, all in Spanish. Upstairs, the Allende family's living quarters have been restored and re-created. The replica of the kitchen is particularly interesting, since it deviates so greatly from the modern version. It is also worth noting that there were no bathrooms in the opulent Allende home, though a toilet did exist near the horse stables in the pretty back patio.

1: Casa del Mayorazgo de la Canal 2: the spires of the Oratorio San Felipe Neri rising over San Miguel's skyline

Casa del Mayorazgo de la Canal

Canal 4; no tel.; https://fomentoculturalbanamex.org; 9am-6pm Mon.-Fri., 10am-6pm Sat.-Sun.; free

A wealthy businessman from Mexico City, Don Manuel Tomás de Canal moved to San Miguel in 1732. He bought numerous haciendas in the region, took control of San Miguel's textile industry, and made major investments in buildings and infrastructure throughout the city. He is remembered as one of San Miguel's most generous benefactors. In addition to the money that Canal spent on religious and municipal projects, he spent thousands of pesos lavishly refurbishing his magnificent mansion, which still stands on the corner of Canal and Hidalgo on San Miguel's central square. His home, the Casa del Mayorazgo de la Canal, is one of the most spectacular examples of 17th-century civil architecture in the region. Its massive red facade runs along the side of the jardín, where a row of balcony windows from the family's living quarters overlook the parroquia. Take note of the elaborately carved wooden doorways on the north side of the building, flanked by towering stone columns. The niche above them holds a stone figure of Our Lady of Loreto and the family coat of arms.

Today the Casa del Mayorazgo de la Canal is home to a free art gallery and cultural center, owned and operated by Citibanamex's cultural foundation. Visitors can see the inside the home's impressive inner courtyard and back patio, where soaring archways separate the first floor from the second. Several exhibition spaces are dedicated to rotating exhibits of work by important Mexican and international artists, as well as the history of San Miguel. There are guided tours of the space (in Spanish) every day at noon and 4pm, Tuesday-Saturday, and noon on Sunday. In addition, the foundation runs a small but beautifully curated gift shop, featuring high-quality Mexican crafts, as well as a selection of books from the foundation's publishing imprint.

Templo de la Inmaculada Concepción

esq. Canal y Hernández Macías s/n; generally 9am-6pm daily

The massive dome that dominates San Miguel's skyline belongs to the Templo de la Inmaculada Concepción, more widely known as **Las Monjas.** According to local history, it was originally commissioned and funded by a young nun and heiress, Josefina Lina de la Canal y Hervas, as a church and nunnery (hence its popular name, Las Monjas, "the nuns"). The first child of Manuel Tomás de Canal, Josefa was a devout Catholic and a close confidante of Father Luis Felipe Neri de Alfaro. After spending a week at his religious retreat in Atotonilco, Josefa decided to spend her entire inherited fortune building a lavish new temple and religious convent for an order of nuns in San Miguel. Construction on the massive building began in 1755, though funds ran out before its conclusion in 1842. Josefa died in 1770, at age 33.

This massive church is one of San Miguel's most iconic structures. Although the temple's architect is unknown, the dome was said to be a copy of Les Invalides in Paris. At night, this massive structure often out-glitters the Parroquia de San Miguel Arcángel, with a ring of bright lights illuminating the dome and the parade of stone saints that surrounds it. Pass through the worn wooden doors of the church to admire the massive dome from the inside, where it illuminates a towering neoclassical altar, with numerous niches containing life-size statues of saints. On your way out, note the large conch shell that is embedded into the stone column as a receptacle for holy water.

Centro Cultural Ignacio Ramírez "El Nigromante"

Hernández Macías 75; tel. 415/152-0289; http:// elnigromante.inba.gob.mx; office 10am-3pm and 4pm-6pm Mon.-Fri., galleries and installations 10am-6pm Mon.-Sat., 10am-2pm Sun.; free

The large stone building adjoining the Templo de la Inmaculada Concepción was once the cloister for the temple's order of nuns. Today, it is the Centro Cultural Ignacio Ramírez "El Nigromante," popularly known as **Bellas Artes.** Owned and managed by Mexico's Instituto Nacional de Bellas Artes (National Fine Arts Institute), Bellas Artes is both a small art school and a cultural center. Although this building was constructed for religious purposes, the center's namesake, Ignacio Ramírez, was an outspoken writer, thinker, lawyer, and atheist born in San Miguel de Allende during the early 19th century. Among other notable achievements, Ramírez defended the rights of Indigenous peoples in independent Mexico and served on the country's supreme court.

Bellas Artes is one of the most peaceful places in downtown San Miguel. The school's lovely courtyard is filled with swaying reeds of bamboo, blooming orange trees, and a lovely old stone fountain. Beneath the arcades that surround the courtyard, there are several exhibition spaces open to the public, showing work by local artists as well as itinerant exhibitions from across the country. Notably, one of the back salons contains an incomplete mural by famous postrevolutionary artist David Alfaro Siqueiros, painted in 1948. On both the first and second floors, the school's enchanting classrooms are housed in the tiny rooms of the former cloister; each is dedicated to a discipline, such as ceramics, oil painting, guitar, and piano.

Biblioteca de San Miguel de Allende

Insurgentes 25; tel. 415/152-0293; http://bibliotecasma. com; 10am-7pm Mon.-Fri., 10am-2pm Sat.

A nonprofit organization with a long history and deep roots in the local community, the Biblioteca de San Miguel de Allende (Library of San Miguel de Allende), formerly known as the Biblioteca Pública, is home to a large bilingual lending library, a nice open-air café, and a small theater. As a part of its mission to serve the community, the library manages a scholarship program for local children, as well as free art and music classes, a

language exchange program, summer programs for local children, and other educational opportunities.

For many expatriates, the library is something of a social hub, where people come together to lend a hand, have a cappuccino at the on-site **Café Santa Ana** (Relox 50; 9am-5pm Mon.-Fri., 9am-2pm Sat.; $5), take a class, or see a speaker or documentary in the **Teatro Santa Ana** (Relox 50; https://teatrosantaana. org; open during events only; $10-30).

The used bookshop **Tesoros** (https://labibliotecapublica.org/tienda-tesoros; 10am-5pm Mon.-Fri., 10am-2pm Sat.) at the library's entrance supports the organization's social programs, as do frequent book sales, fundraising events, and the weekly House and Garden Tour. Check the library's corkboard for information about upcoming programs.

Oratorio San Felipe Neri

Insurgentes s/n; tel. 415/152-0521; generally 9am-6pm daily

During the 18th century, the congregation of San Felipe Neri was rapidly gaining popularity throughout New Spain. In San Miguel de Allende, the congregation constructed the beautiful Oratorio San Felipe Neri in 1714, along with a school, the Colegio San Francisco de Sales. The pink sandstone facade of the oratorio is delicately carved and represents the beginning of a shift in architectural aesthetic, from baroque to churrigueresque. Above the facade, the church has five beautiful bell towers, which were recently restored. The unpainted pink sandstone tower to the northwest of the church is particularly lovely.

Inside the oratory, delicate pink frescoes on the ceiling, old tiled walls, and worn floors reflect the church's long history. As in the majority of baroque churches in San Miguel, most of the original paintings and altarpieces in the oratorio were lost or looted; however, several of the original 18th-century wooden saints and retablos are still on the walls of the nave. In the 19th century, the famous architect of the parroquia, Zeferino Gutiérrez, designed the building's neoclassical altar. As

Guided Tours

A guided tour can be an excellent introduction to San Miguel's sights and history. In many cases, your hotel or bed-and-breakfast can help organize a tour or experience during your stay in San Miguel. In addition, here are a few of the most popular and longest-running tour options in town.

PATRONATO PRO NIÑOS WALKING TOUR

tel. 415/152-7796; https://historicalwalkingtour.org; US$25

Patronato Pro Niños, a local nonprofit organization, offers highly recommended cultural walking tours of San Miguel de Allende's centro histórico with knowledgeable English-speaking Mexican tour guides. Tours depart from the jardín every Monday, Wednesday, and Friday at 9:45am, cover about 10 blocks, and last about 2.5 hours. They can also arrange private tours for small groups, with a focus on different aspects of San Miguel's architecture and history. All the proceeds from the tour benefit Patronato Pro Niños' medical and dental services program, which provides free or very low-cost medical care to 2,500 children in the San Miguel area, as well as dental services to over 9,000 children.

HOUSE AND GARDEN TOUR

Biblioteca de San Miguel de Allende, Insurgentes 25; tel. 415/152-0293; noon Fri.; US$30 pp

Ever wondered what's behind those old wooden doors and big stucco facades? You're not alone. One of the most popular activities in town, the weekly House and Garden Tour gives participants a chance to peek inside several historic and lavishly decorated homes in San Miguel de Allende. Drawing from a roster of over 300 historic homes in San Miguel, the lineup changes weekly, but it usually includes at least four properties. The tour departs from the nonprofit Biblioteca de San Miguel de Allende (Library of San Miguel de Allende) every Friday at noon in large buses. You must buy tickets in advance at the library shop (10am-5pm Mon.-Thurs., 10am-2pm Sat). The Biblioteca also offers cultural tours to Dolores Hidalgo, Guanajuato, and the Peña de Bernal. All proceeds support the Biblioteca's social and educational programs.

GLOBO SAN MIGUEL

www.globosanmiguel.com; starting at $185 pp

You must rise at dawn for this once-in-a-lifetime aerial tour of San Miguel, but gliding above town (and sometimes above the cloud line) in a hot air balloon is worth setting an alarm for. During the roughly hourlong flight, you'll have an unparalleled bird's-eye view of downtown San Miguel and the surrounding countryside as the sun comes up. Globo San Miguel has been in business for more than 25 years, and they've got their operations down pat—from coordinating the early morning pickup to hiring the licensed pilots who fly their balloons each morning. For larger parties, Globo San Miguel can arrange to have several balloons take off at once.

you walk out, look up at the beautiful gilded organ above the entryway. On occasion, the oratory will host organ concerts with this unique instrument.

You will have to make an extra effort if you want to visit the chapel **Santa Casa de Loreto** and the adjoining **Camarín de la Virgen,** a jewel of colonial architecture located in the precept to the left of the oratory's altar. Commissioned and paid for by Don Manuel Tomás de Canal in the 18th century,

this elaborate gilded chapel is possibly San Miguel's finest historic structure. The chapel is not normally open to the public. However, the priests do occasionally unlock the chapel's old iron doors during morning and evening masses.

Iglesia de Nuestra Señora de la Salud

Church of Our Lady of Health, Plaza Cívica s/n; no tel.; generally 9am-6pm daily

Just to the east of the oratorio and overlooking

the Plaza Cívica, the Iglesia de Nuestra Señora de la Salud is distinguished by the scalloped stone dome that presides over the church's curved entryway. An influential figure in San Miguel de Allende, Father Luis Felipe Neri de Alfaro erected this church in the 17th century as an accompaniment to the adjoining school, San Francisco de Sales. The school was an important institution in San Miguel de Allende, teaching philosophical thought to many of the young criollo heirs who would oversee the town and, eventually, instigate the independence movement.

Inside the Iglesia de Nuestra Señora de la Salud, the altar surrounds an azure-dressed Virgin Mary in a gilded glass box. Like the oratory, this small church was looted, and most of its original pieces were destroyed. But to the right of the altar, there is still a beautiful collection of 17th-century oil paintings depicting the Stations of the Cross, some punctured or damaged.

Outside, the **Plaza Cívica** is a popular place to sit in the shade, and it is occasionally the site of crafts or book fairs (during late October, there is a large market selling crafts, candies, and candles for Día de Muertos altarpieces). For many years, the Plaza Cívica was also the site of San Miguel de Allende's municipal market.

Templo de San Francisco

San Francisco s/n, esq. con Juárez; tel. 415/152-0947; 10am-2pm and 4pm-7:30pm Mon.-Sat., hours vary Sun.

The many pigeons perched on the stone facade of the Templo de San Francisco—despite the city's attempts to ward them off with chicken wire—have found plenty of places to nest amid the ornate carvings of this church's churrigueresque entryway. A fine example of Mexican baroque architecture, this church was constructed at the end of the 18th century. The principal facade is the site's most striking feature, with cascading sandstone columns carefully carved with saints and figures. Walk east around the church to get a sense of its size and grandeur. There is another less ornate but also beautiful facade on its eastern wall. Above it, the church's large dome towers over Calle

Mesones. In contrast to its ornate exterior, the Templo de San Francisco's interior is austere, with very high ceilings and glass chandeliers, a neoclassical altar, and walls lined with rows of wooden saints and dark retablos.

Directly to the east and adjoining the same small plaza as the Templo de San Francisco, the **Capilla de la Tercera Orden** is a far simpler Franciscan church. Like its neighbor, it was constructed in the 18th century, though it appears much older. The lovely, crumbling belfry that tops this old stone building has recently been restored and repainted, and it wears its age handsomely.

TOP EXPERIENCE

★ El Charco del Ingenio

Paloma s/n; tel. 415/103-8090; https://elcharco.org.mx; 9am-5pm daily; US$3

San Miguel de Allende's unique botanical garden, El Charco del Ingenio, is located along the ridge of a canyon overlooking the city center. Bring a hat and good walking shoes to explore the rustic and meandering footpaths within this ecological preserve, which covers more than 40 hectares (100 acres) of natural habitat along the canyon's edge and the shores of a small reservoir. With admission, staffers will give you a map to the grounds; a highlight is the covered conservatory, which houses a rare and weird collection of cacti and succulents. It's a wonderful place to simply walk and wander, though there are also excellent guided tours in English, which depart every Tuesday and Thursday at 10am and last about two hours (US$8). Additionally, El Charco del Ingenio frequently hosts special events, such as full moon ceremonies, nature talks, yoga classes, or traditional temazcal steam baths. At the small café and gift store at the entrance, visitors can support the project by purchasing live cacti, books, or handicrafts made in local villages.

Getting There

El Charco del Ingenio is located about 3 km (1.8 mi) east of San Miguel's central square,

or jardín, on the edge of the largely residential Balcones neighborhood. Because it is a steep uphill climb from the center of town to El Charco, most visitors arrive via taxi or Uber (US$4). Once there, the site can be explored on foot; it is also wheelchair accessible.

GUADALUPE AND AURORA
★ Fábrica La Aurora

Calzada de la Aurora s/n, Col. Aurora; tel. 415/152-1312; www.fabricalaaurora.com; generally 9am-11pm Mon.-Sat., 10am-5pm Sun., hours vary by shop

Some of the older residents of San Miguel remember the cry of the steam-generated whistle that sounded every morning from the Fábrica La Aurora. Until the early 1990s, the Fábrica La Aurora was one of Mexico's largest textile factories and the single biggest employer in the town of San Miguel. After cotton imports began flooding the Mexican market, domestic production was greatly affected. The factory closed in 1991, and the space was converted to a warehouse. A few years later, some local artists and designers began to express interest in renting the old factory rooms as studios and workspaces. The first shops and studios opened in 2001. The project quickly grew, and today the former factory houses more than 35 studios, galleries, design shops, antiques dealers, boutiques, restaurants, and a café. Many of San Miguel's most beloved artists and exhibition spaces are located in the Aurora. Its unique ambience is perfect for strolling and passing a morning.

Typical of turn-of-the-20th-century constructions, the factory's long sandstone facade, concrete floors, and industrial architecture provide a contrasting (yet complementary) backdrop to modern art and design. Wandering around the corridors, you can see some of the old equipment from the factory's former days in textile production, and old photographs of the space line the walls of the principal hallway. Hours vary by shop, so visit during the morning or early afternoon, Monday through Saturday, to see the most spaces open.

PARQUE JUÁREZ
★ Parque Benito Juárez

Aldama and Diezmo Viejo

A few blocks south of the central square, beloved Parque Benito Juárez is one of the greenest spots in San Miguel de Allende. Take a stroll along the park's old curving walkways, admiring the old stone fountains and the wild, tropical vegetation that flourishes everywhere. Throughout the day, you'll find teenage couples holding hands, ambitious joggers, seniors reading the paper, exuberant Zumba classes, or dogs and their owners wandering along the shaded footpaths. Bring a book and stake out a spot on one of the weathered stone benches, or simply enjoy the people-watching. The park is also a favorite nesting spot for white egrets, and the birds in the trees above can become surprisingly noisy.

★ El Chorro

Bajada del Chorro

After its founding on the banks of the Río Laja, the settlement of San Miguel de los Chichimecas moved to the hill of Izcuinapan, site of a copious natural spring. According to local legend, the Purépecha people from Michoacán had originally discovered the spring after their xoloitzcuintle dogs dug up water along the hillside. Today the site of San Miguel's founding is a verdant corner of the city known as El Chorro (the spring). On the hillside, San Miguel's **Casa de la Cultura El Chorro** (Bajada del Chorro 4) is a cultural center that offers art, dance, and music classes to local children. Though classrooms aren't generally open to the public, you can walk along the exterior arcades and sometimes see classes in action after school hours or during the summer. In 2021, the city government installed the sculpture *Mano-Silla* on one of the terraces at El Chorro, just below the Casa de la Cultura. An oversize hand shaped like a chair,

1: El Charco del Ingenio 2: Fábrica La Aurora 3: Parque Benito Juárez 4: The cultural center at El Chorro is one of the most enchanting spots in San Miguel de Allende.

San Miguel de Allende Countryside

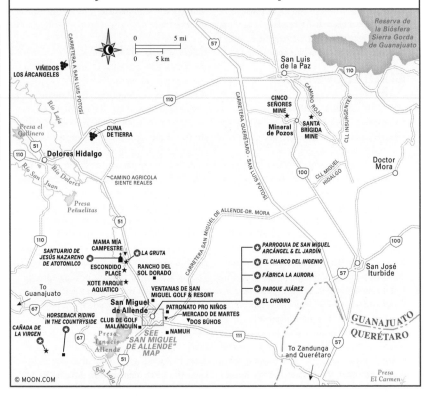

© MOON.COM

Mano-Silla is the iconic work by famed artist Pedro Friedeberg, who lived in San Miguel for many years.

In the shade of breezy trees, El Chorro is among the most beautiful spots in town. The steep hill leading up to the Casa de la Cultura is lined with cascading patios and winding staircases, a lovely place to rest amid the lush foliage and the sound of squabbling egrets. Just to the north, a stone staircase leads you to a pretty plaza and **La Capilla de Santa Cruz del Chorro** (Callejón del Chorro 56; generally closed to the public), a 16th-century church and one of the oldest structures in San Miguel de Allende. From there, you can huff and puff up the tiny pedestrian alleyway La Bajada del Chorro, an enchanting, if challenging, ascent to the Salida a Querétaro.

Just below El Chorro, take notice of the row of the **Lavaderos del Chorro,** the red lavaderos públicos (public washtubs) that surround a small plaza below the hillside. For years, the natural spring fed water into these washtubs, where local families came to do their laundry. According to some historians, these washtubs were among the municipal projects financed by Manuel de la Canal in the 18th century.

El Mirador

Salida a Querétaro and Piedras Chinas; 24 hours; free

If you have a set of wheels, taxi fare, or strong legs for walking, follow the Salida a Querétaro uphill to El Mirador, a small outlook with panoramic views of the city below. From here, you can see the river valley stretching beyond the town, including the large reservoir beyond the city and the distant Sierra de Guanajuato. The bust of Pedro Vargas, a famous singer and actor from Mexico's golden age of cinema, presides over the mirador. Vargas was born in San Miguel; his former home adjoins this small plaza.

SAN ANTONIO
Instituto Allende

Ancha de San Antonio 20; tel. 415/152-0226; www. institutoallende.com; generally 11am-6pm daily, though individual business hours vary

Originally built in 1735 by the wealthy de la Canal family as their country residence, this massive stone building was later occupied by Carmelite nuns. The entire building became an art school in the 1950s, when Peruvian painter Felipe Cossío del Pomar moved his academy from its original location in the ex-convent at the Templo de la Inmaculada Concepción to this colonial-era mansion. The art school, now a part of the Unviersidad de Guanajuato, is located in the back, while the front of the building, including its beautiful stone courtyard, is a nice commercial plaza with a comfortable café, colorful murals, and several good galleries—though note that the space is frequently closed for private events and weddings.

SAN MIGUEL DE ALLENDE COUNTRYSIDE
★ Santuario de Jesús Nazareno de Atotonilco

Plaza Principal s/n; 8am-6pm daily

Located in the small community of Atotonilco, the magnificent Santuario de Jesús Nazareno de Atotonilco is one of the finest examples of baroque art and architecture in Mexico. The majority of the church was constructed between 1740 and 1776, beginning with the facade, the main nave, and several adjoining chapels. After its construction, the artist Miguel Antonio Martínez de Pocasangre spent more than 30 years painting the walls and ceiling of the nave with detailed religious histories and personages. As you walk through the creaky entryway into the church, the visual stimulation from floor-to-ceiling murals is momentarily overwhelming. One could easily spend hours examining the many unusual figures and strange histories related on the sanctuary's walls.

In 2008 the United Nations named the Santuario de Atotonilco a World Heritage Site, together with San Miguel de Allende's downtown. Thereafter, the church underwent a massive restoration project. Now it is easier to appreciate the incredible masterwork inside the church, as Martínez's frescoes have been nicely restored.

In addition to its historical and architectural significance, the Santuario de Atotonilco is an important pilgrimage destination for Mexican Catholics throughout the region. In particular, many come to see and give thanks to the wooden figure of **El Señor de la Columna,** widely revered for its ability to perform miracles. The santuario also continues to serve as a religious retreat of the most austere variety, with dorm dwellers sleeping on cold stone floors and often subjecting themselves to corporal punishment. On some days, the plaza in front of the church is packed with pilgrims and vendors, some of whom sell rough twine ropes for self-flagellation and real crowns of thorns. Other days, the town is as quiet as history, with nothing but the sound of wind whipping dust into the air.

Guided Tours

There are occasionally Spanish-speaking tour guides at the church's entryway who can help illuminate the fantastic meaning behind the elaborate painting. The **Biblioteca de San Miguel** can arrange cultural tours to Atotonilco, while **Bici-Burro** will take you there on bicycle via country roads.

Getting There

The Santuario is located in the community of Atotonilco, about 14 km (9 mi) north of San Miguel de Allende, east off Highway 51 to Dolores Hidalgo. It takes about 20 minutes to reach Atotonilco by car or taxi.

★ Cañada de la Virgen

Carretera Guanajuato-San Miguel s/n, Carretera Federal 51, Km 10+800; 10am-6pm Tues.-Sat.; US$4 adults, US$1 seniors and children

To get a taste of Mexico's grand pre-Hispanic history, visit the interesting local archaeological site known as the Cañada de la Virgen, about 30-40 minutes southeast of San Miguel de Allende. Opened to the public in 2011 after a preliminary excavation and study, the ruins of this pre-Columbian city are believed to be tied to the Panteca people of the greater Toltec empire, who once lived along the floodplain of the Laja River. Occupied around AD 540-1000, the site contains five groups of monuments, including a 15-m (50-ft) temple-pyramid and a large sunken plaza. Here, as in many Mesoamerican cities, the main architectural structures were constructed to align with the sun's path. Archaeological study of the site is ongoing, and plans for more extensive excavation of the area are underway.

The Cañada de la Virgen is operated by the Instituto Nacional de Antropología e Historia (INAH), Mexico's bureau of history and anthropology, and the site itself is located on federally protected land.

Planning Your Visit

- All visitors to the Cañada de la Virgen must be accompanied by a guide licensed by the state of Guanajuato. The service is included in the cost of a ticket, though note that tours are only given in Spanish. Tours to the site depart hourly 10am-4pm. On weekends or holidays, tour groups may fill up (the number of people allowed at the ruins is limited), in which case, you could

be required to wait up to an hour for the next tour.

- Visitors are shuttled by van from the main parking lot to the entrance to the ruins. From there, visitors must walk about a kilometer uphill to the site.

- Note that backpacks and food are not permitted, and there are no food stalls or vendors on-site. Have a good breakfast before you head out. Water, good walking shoes, and sunscreen are necessities.

Guided English-Language Tours

For excellent, authoritative English-language tours of the site, contact **Albert Coffee Archaeotours** (tel. and WhatsApp 55/1184-5639; www.albertcoffeetours.com; US$59 pp). Albert Coffee is a professional anthropologist and Guanajuato-state-certified tour guide who worked on the ruins' excavation. Coffee is passionate and knowledgeable about Mesoamerican cultures and provides a rich and detailed explanation of the different structures at the site, as well as an introduction to local ecology, Mesoamerican history, and local customs. Generally departing in the morning, tours include transportation to and from downtown San Miguel and entrance fees to the site.

Getting There and Around

The Cañada de la Virgen is just over 24 km (15 mi) west from San Miguel de Allende. To get there, take the highway toward Celaya until you reach the turnoff to Highway 51. From there, follow the signs toward Guanajuato, passing the Ignacio Allende reservoir and then the community of Agustín González. Shortly thereafter you'll see signs for the archeological site. There is a parking lot and ticket office at the main entrance, just off the highway; from there, a van will take you to the archaeological site.

1: Santuario de Jesús Nazareno de Atotonilco
2: Cañada de la Virgen archeological site

Mineral de Pozos

Mineral de Pozos

For a taste of Old Mexico, the entire city of Pozos is a sight in itself. Here the windswept dirt roads are lined with crumbling adobe houses, stray dogs mill through the sleepy central plaza, and the desert landscape is stark and beautiful. The mines, both sorrowful and majestic, are among the most interesting places to visit in the Bajío region.

Not far from San Miguel de Allende, travelers have begun to take notice of this unusual destination, and the romance of a desert ghost town has convinced some artists and expatriates to settle down here permanently.

SIGHTS

Plaza Principal

Plaza Principal s/n; 24 hours; free

Plaza Principal is a lovely little square equipped with a cantina on one corner and a church on the other. On the weekends, there are many more tourists in town, and vendors arrive in the square to sell pan de dulce (sweet bread), roasted corn, aguas frescas, and other small snacks.

Cinco Señores Mine

9am-4pm daily; US$5, guided tours $8

Cinco Señores Mine offers a fascinating glimpse into the splendor of Pozos's former wealth and prestige. You can wander among roofless buildings, crumbling porticoes from 19th-century offices, huge stone tubs filled with moss-rich water, and the dark mouths of numerous abandoned mine shafts. Within the site, there are several of the wells, or pozos, for which the city is famous. Use care when walking near the edge of wells and mines, as the ground can be uneven, and some shafts are only minimally marked.

To reach Cinco Señores, head west up Manuel Doblado from the main square. Continue one block past the Plaza Zaragosa (only about three large blocks from the square), and then veer left on a dirt road. There is a small admission fee, and guides for hire (Spanish only).

Santa Brígida Mine

11am-6pm daily; $5

Santa Brígida Mine, the very first mining camp in Pozos, is located just outside the city center. Uniquely in the region, Santa Brígida was mined by Indigenous people before it came under Spanish control. Watch your step everywhere around Pozos, and especially in the mining camp. The mouth of the mine is uneven and gravelly, plunging deep into the earth. In addition to the mine, there are several deep wells around the mining camp. Keep a close eye on dogs and children!

To reach the Santa Brígida Mine, follow Highway 46 through town north toward San Luis de la Paz. Just as the pavement begins, take a right on a large, unmarked dirt road. At the first major fork, go left (or north) toward the mine. After about 1 km (0.6 mi), you will see the smokestacks in the distance. Park near the large red and white building. There may be a watchman charging a modest entry fee.

FOOD AND ACCOMMODATIONS

Posada de las Minas
Manuel Doblado 1; tel. 442/293-0213; https://hotelposadadelasminas.com.mx; US$60-120
Posada de las Minas is the largest establishment in Pozos, with eight pretty guest rooms housed in a restored 19th-century mansion.

Downstairs, the in-house restaurant (8:30am-10pm daily; US$15) is set in a wildly pleasant courtyard. Mexican specialties like guacamole, enchiladas, and stuffed peppers are the best dishes here (and are appropriately accompanied by a nice list of tequilas by the glass), though they also serve a range of sandwiches, burgers, fish, and pastas. The food is decent, the service is attentive, if a bit slow, and the atmosphere is casually luxurious.

SHOPPING

Casa del Venado Azul
Centenario 34; tel. 468/101-0558; 9am-6pm daily
Casa del Venado Azul is a long-running workshop, healing center, and guest house that first opened in 1995. Inside you'll find a series of patios that showcase the workshop's handmade percussion instruments, based on pre-Hispanic designs, including drums, flutes, and shakers, many quite original. They sell a small range of craftwork in addition to instruments, and offer temezcal and other native healing ceremonies.

Camino de Piedra
Leandro Valle 13; tel. 442/202-2024; 10am-6pm daily
Camino de Piedra is owned by a family of artisans who create instruments based on pre-Hispanic designs, including rain sticks, whistles, percussive gourds, conch shells, seed rattles, and flutes. Everything you see was created by the shop's artisans, and many of the pieces are beautifully carved and handpainted as well.

SERVICES

Although the atmosphere can feel rather posh for a ghost town, Pozos offers very little to the visitor in terms of services. There are no banks or ATMs in town, so you must bring cash with you. It has no tourist office, no local publications, and no taxis. Sometimes even phone service and electricity can be unexpectedly cut off, so be prepared for anything when visiting Pozos.

GETTING THERE AND AROUND

The best way to get to Mineral de Pozos is in a car. To get to Pozos from San Miguel de Allende, follow the Salida a Querétaro out of the city. Arriving at the traffic circle, head east, following the signs toward Doctor Mora and Los Rodríguez. Follow this two-lane highway through Los Rodríguez (watch out for speed bumps!), crossing over Highway 57 on an overpass. About 8 km (5 mi) from the highway, you will reach an intersection indicating the turnoff for Pozos and San Luis de la Paz; turn north toward these cities. About 16 km (10 mi) down the road, the highway turns to dirt, and you have arrived in Pozos.

Sports and Recreation

With its leisurely pace, near-perfect climate, and breathtaking architecture, it is easy to give in to San Miguel's relaxing atmosphere—except that it's so hard to sit still! There is always something to do in San Miguel, whether it's horseback riding through desert canyons or soaking away the morning in natural hot springs. Taking the time to explore the peaceful, cactus-filled, starkly beautiful semiarid landscape around San Miguel de Allende may be one of the most memorable parts of a trip to the area—and a pleasing contrast to the vibrant colors and bustling activity downtown.

YOGA, MEDITATION, AND SPAS
Centro Histórico
Meditation Center of San Miguel
Callejón Blanco 4; tel. 415/156-1950; www.
meditationsma.org; free (donations welcomed)
The friendly nonprofit Meditation Center of San Miguel provides three sitting meditation sessions Monday-Friday, at 8am, 8:50am, and 5:30pm, plus a single session on Saturday at 10am. There are also occasional talks and classes offered in the center's peaceful main room, overlooking a small courtyard garden. The center is Buddhist-oriented, though nondenominational, and participants are welcome to practice any form of still, silent mediation.

Essential Spa and Watsu
cell tel. 415/114-8469; www.essentialmassageandwatsu.
com; 9am-9pm daily, by appointment; treatments
starting at US$50
David Galitzky, the owner of Essential Spa, is a highly recommended and licensed massage therapist specializing in watsu, a form of aquatic body work. In addition to watsu, David and his colleagues offer excellent well-priced treatments, including reflexology, deep tissue massage, and craniosacral therapy.

San Antonio
Esencia Yoga Spa
Portrero 13, Col. San Antonio; tel. 415/152-5421; www.
esenciayogaspa.com; 10am-6pm Mon.-Sat.; massage
starting at US$30 for 30 minutes
The low-key, positive-vibes atmosphere at Esencia Yoga Spa feels pleasantly in tune with the ambience in San Miguel de Allende. The simple spa rooms are comfortable but not fancy, and therapists are warm and experienced. Well-priced spa treatments and therapies include reflexology, deep-tissue massage, manicures and pedicures, facials, and reiki. In addition, the spa has a large yoga room for a weekly lineup of vinyasa, hot yoga, and flow classes (starting at US$17/class, with multiple class packages available), most taught in both English and Spanish.

TOP EXPERIENCE

★ HORSEBACK RIDING
San Miguel de Allende Countryside
Rancho Xotolar
tel. 415/154-6275; cell tel. 415/105-2622; www.
xotolarranch.com; from US$150 pp
There is no better way to experience the beauty and spirit of the Mexican countryside west of San Miguel de Allende than on a horseback ride at this wonderful working ranch, which has been owned by the same family for generations. On an unforgettable day for riders of any level, Rancho Xotolar's expert cowboys and well-trained horses will lead you across mesquite-studded grasslands, down the edge of a canyon, and along a rocky riverbed, which during the summer rainy season is often rushing with water. All rides include transport to and from San Miguel, as well as a delicious ranch lunch, with fresh cheese, grilled nopales (prickly pear cactus), handmade tortillas, and other traditional country dishes. In addition to the

Mind, Body, Spirit

For many, San Miguel isn't a traditional tourist destination, where sightseeing and recreation are the priority. Instead it's a place to relax, learn, and spend some time off the grid. For dharma bums, burgeoning artists, or stressed-out city types looking for a respite, San Miguel is a wonderful place for a low-key retreat.

MIND

- Start writing your memoirs in a workshop with the **San Miguel Literary Sala** (page 87) or learn to express yourself in paint through a class at the **Instituto Allende** (page 53).

- Attend a talk with a local author at the **Café Santa Ana** at the Biblioteca Pública (page 47).

- Participate in a still and **silent meditation** session at the welcoming **Meditation Center of San Miguel** (page 58).

Esencia Yoga Spa

BODY

- Book a massage at **Essential Spa and Watsu** (page 58).

- Join a yoga class at **Esencia Yoga Spa** (page 58) or **Rancho del Sol Dorado** (page 60).

- Soak in the covered pools at **La Gruta,** where the natural warm water is believed to have healing properties (page 62).

- Just down the road, **Escondido Place** has a series of progressively warmer pools, filled daily by natural springs, as well as cold-water pools (page 63).

- Take a self-guided walk around the Presa Allende (Allende reservoir) or get your heart beating on a rigorous Sunday expedition with the **San Miguel Hiking Group** (page 60).

SPIRIT

- Connect with the outdoors at **El Charco del Ingenio.** San Miguel's unique botanical gardens and nature preserve is a peaceful place to spend a few hours wandering and reflecting under the Mexican sun. They also host frequent special events, like temazcal steam baths, morning **yoga** sessions, and **wildlife workshops** (page 49).

- Join the volunteers cleaning up the Allende reservoir or maintaining the Parque Juárez pollinator garden through the **Sociedad Audubon de México** (page 61).

- Visit the **Cañada de la Virgen,** a small but beautiful archaeological site located within an expansive ecological reserve (page 54).

breathtaking scenery, one of the best aspects of the day is getting to meet the family who runs the ranch and see their operations first-hand. Xotolar also offers combination day trips with horseback riding on the ranch followed by a tour of the Cañada de la Virgen.

Coyote Canyon Adventures

tel. 415/154-4193 or 415/121-0340; www. coyotecanyonadventures.com; from US$160 pp

A friendly family-run tour group, Coyote Canyon Adventures leads half-day and full-day horseback riding tours in the beautiful ranchland near the Cañada de la Virgen ecological preserve, west of San Miguel de Allende. The day of your scheduled outing, someone from the team will pick you and your group up in San Miguel and take you out to the country. Beautiful scenery and fun but manageable rides suitable for any skill level characterize this tour group. While horseback riding is Coyote Canyon's specialty, they also offer adventure sports like rappelling, hiking and camping tours, biking, and nature walks. Prices start at about US$160 per person for a half-day ride.

Rancho del Sol Dorado

El Sol Dorado Km 5.5; tel. 415/101-3858; www. ranchodelsoldorado.com; from US$100 pp

Located north of San Miguel de Allende, off the highway to Querétaro, this gorgeous luxury ranch and guest house is the place to go for a relaxing day in the country, surrounded by prickly pear and mesquite trees. Guided horseback rides of 1-2 hours start at US$100 and explore the surrounding countryside, though there are other ways to enjoy the ranch, including weekly on-site yoga classes or a dip in the beautiful heated pool, which is available for day use. For a more thorough respite, the rustic-chic guest rooms, located in former stables, start at about US$220/night. The entire property can also be rented for a wedding, special event, or retreat. Taxis from San Miguel run about US$14 to Rancho del Sol Dorado.

HIKING AND BIKING
San Miguel Hiking Group

www.sanmiguelhiking.com; info@sanmiguelhiking.com; by donation

What began as an informal group of hikers meeting up on Sunday mornings is now

horseback riding with Rancho Xotolar

an established hiking club, with weekly volunteer-led hikes that benefit local organizations supporting rural families and the natural environment. The group leads moderate to difficult hikes throughout the region, which require a decent level of fitness and agility to complete. Fill out the form on their website to join a hike, though note that there is generally a wait list for new hikers. If you aren't able to join a Sunday morning excursion, you can download the group's free hiking guide online, which includes a number of easy-to-access hikes around the reservoir and just outside town, as well as contact information for licensed hiking guides in the area.

Sociedad Audubon de México

tel. 415/119-4671; www.audubonmexico.org; audubondemexico@gmail.com; US$11

Mexico's only Audubon chapter, Sociedad Audubon de México is an active volunteer-run organization that hosts monthly birding walks on the third Saturday of every month (US$11 pp), departing early morning from the Instituto Allende. Though locations change, the walks will often take you to the shores of the Río Laja or the area around the Allende dam, where you can spot ducks, shovelers, hawks, kites, egrets, and many other beautiful bird species. There are numerous other ways to get involved with the organization, like helping maintain the pollinator garden in Parque Juárez on Thursday mornings or volunteering to remove parasitic species from local trees. Learn more about volunteer opportunities on their website, or reach out directly via email.

Bici-Burro

Hospicio 1; WhatsApp 415/100-6507; www.bici-burro. com; 9am-2pm and 4pm-7pm Mon.-Fri., 9am-2pm Sat.; US$110

Bici-Burro is a family-run bike shop and tour operator leading off-road biking trips in the countryside around San Miguel de Allende.

Some of the bicycle tours will take you along the former silver route (which was used to bring goods to and from San Miguel during the colonial era) and out to the beautiful Santuario de Atotonilco. It is a great way to see the countryside while also checking out some of San Miguel's cultural sights. A half-day tour runs about US$110 per person, including a tour guide and the rental of an aluminum mountain bike, helmet, and gloves.

SPORTS AND FITNESS
San Antonio
Weber Tennis Courts

Callejón de San Antonio 12, Col. San Antonio; www. sanmigueltennis.com; 11am-6pm Mon.-Thurs., 1pm-6pm Fri.-Sat, 10am-1pm Sun., hours vary; from US$14/hour single

Long-standing favorite Weber Tennis Courts has three clay tennis courts popular with locals, both Mexican and expatriate, which you can use for about US$14 per hour for a singles match; additional players are about US$7 per hour. Courts are open to the public by reservation (email or in-person), though walk-ins are also welcome. If you want to improve your backhand, Weber will also help set up private lessons.

San Miguel de Allende Countryside
Ventanas de San Miguel Golf & Resort

Carretera San Miguel Allende-Dolores Hidalgo, Km 1.5; tel. 415/688-0061 ext. 105; www. clubventanasdesanmiguel.com; 7am-5:30pm Mon.-Fri., 7am-4:30pm Sat.-Sun.; US$175 Mon.-Fri., US$200 Sat.-Sun.

Located north of San Miguel de Allende, the Ventanas de San Miguel Golf & Resort has an 18-hole Nick Faldo-designed Championship Course at par 70. The course hosts several annual golf tournaments, with daily greens fees for the public as well as membership options. Private classes are also available with a golf pro throughout the week.

Hot Springs and Swimming

La Gruta hot springs

In the region surrounding the town of Atotonilco (about 13 km/8 mi from downtown San Miguel), volcanic activity under the earth has produced copious natural, nonsulfurous hot springs. Many locals believe the water has healing properties, and after a dip you may agree. If you want to try the hot springs, there are a number of low-key places to enjoy this amazing natural resource. No matter where you choose to soak, don't forget to bring a towel! Besides cafés and snack shops, there are few services at most of these family-style swimming spots.

★ LA GRUTA

Carretera San Miguel Allende-Dolores Hidalgo, Km 10; tel. 415/185-2162; https://lagruta-spa.com.mx; 7am-5pm Wed.-Sun.; US$14

La Gruta is the most popular bathing spot near San Miguel. From the warmest outdoor pool, you can swim down a covered hallway to a domed cave that is filled with even warmer water, fed directly from the spring. (This is the gruta, or grotto, for which the spot is named.) After a dip, you

Club de Golf Malanquín

Carretera San Miguel-Celaya, Km 3; tel. 415/152-0516 or 415/154-8210; www.malanquin.com.mx; 6:30am-9pm Tues.-Sat., 7am-7pm Sun.; US$120 Mon.-Fri., US$150 Sat.-Sun.

San Miguel's oldest course, Club de Golf Malanquín maintains a well-groomed nine-hole golf course right on the western edge of town. During the weekdays, greens fees are accessible; they also offer temporary memberships, for those who'd like to play multiple times or take advantage of the club's other facilities. If you want to practice your stroke, highly recommended golf pros offer beginning, intermediate, and advanced golf clinics throughout the week. Membership allows access to the club's tennis courts, swimming pool, steam bath, newly renovated clubhouse, restaurant, and coffee shop.

can relax in the pretty gardens, which are shaded by fig trees and dotted with picnic tables and recliners. La Gruta's small café serves breakfast and lunch—fruit, scrambled eggs, chilaquiles, quesadillas, guacamole, and the like—plus juice, soft drinks, beer, and margaritas. For the most Zen experience, get there early in the morning, when the pools are just filling up with water and few people have arrived.

ESCONDIDO PLACE

Carretera San Miguel Allende-Dolores Hidalgo, Km 10; tel. 415/185-2202; http://escondidoplace.com; 8am-5pm daily; US$14

Every morning, water is pumped into the barrel-shaped caves that cover several adjoining pools at Escondido Place, filling them with steam. It's a gorgeous and peaceful setting for a soak. There are also several outdoor pools, a small snack bar, and a picnic area with outdoor grills on-site. Though the gardens are beautiful and the pools are warm, Escondido is less popular with locals than La Gruta, so crowds are not a big problem and early birds often have the place to themselves.

XOTE PARQUE AQUATICO

Carretera San Miguel Allende-Dolores Hidalgo, Km 5.5; tel. 415/155-8330; www.xote.com.mx; 10am-5:30pm daily; US$14 adults, US$7 children, $7 seniors

Family-friendly Xote is a water park, not a relaxation center. This large, hilltop spot caters to children; not only is there a large swimming pool at the park's summit, there are several high-speed waterslides, plus a playground for children. Summer afternoons can become overwhelmingly crowded, when Xote also allows families to camp on the grounds. Once children are taller than 1.35 m (4 ft, 4 in), they must pay adult prices.

GETTING THERE

Xote, Escondido Place, and La Gruta are located between San Miguel de Allende and Atotonilco, off the highway to Dolores Hidalgo (Mexico 51). Closest to San Miguel, Xote is just over 2 km (1.2 mi) north of San Miguel, at the Camino a Xote, which runs east off the highway (look for the billboard on the highway indicating the exit after crossing the railroad tracks). Escondido Place is also located off a country road on the east side of the highway, about 10 km (6 mi) from San Miguel. La Gruta is less than 0.5 km (0.3 mi) farther north, and the entrance is marked by a giant billboard. There is no direct bus service to the hot springs, so it is best to drive or take a taxi.

Entertainment and Events

Since the early 20th century, San Miguel has been home to a community of artists and writers, both national and international. Today there are many small galleries, some artist-run, where new exhibitions open seemingly every weekend, often drawing overflowing crowds. Live music, dance, and even theater are performed at a few city venues. Jazz music is universally popular, and a few cool DJ bars make San Miguel a semi-chic destination for weekenders.

LIVE MUSIC

Live music plays an important role in Mexican culture. In San Miguel de Allende, marimba musicians play jubilantly on busy avenues for

Celebrate the Visual Arts

Following independence from Spain and the decline of the silver trade, San Miguel de Allende was largely abandoned—though even time and the elements could not destroy the beauty of its baroque churches and colonial-era mansions. The crumbling, romantic atmosphere began to attract Mexican and Latin American bohemians to then-sleepy San Miguel de Allende, which developed a reputation as an artist enclave.

Though now removed from its bohemian roots, San Miguel continues to be a mecca for visual artists, and dozens of artist studios and artist-run galleries are scattered around town, in addition to a never-ending slate of arts-related events taking place at public institutions, galleries, and other more unusual venues. Here are some of the best places to go.

OUTSTANDING INSTITUTIONS

Two institutions worth noting are the **Casa del Mayorazgo de la Canal** (page 46), a cultural center and exhibition space in the city's grandest colonial-era mansion, and the **Centro Cultural Ignacio Ramírez "El Nigromante"** (page 46), also called Bellas Artes, an art school and cultural center with several public galleries.

When visiting the latter, it's worth seeking out the unfinished mural by Mexican master **David Alfaro Siqueiros,** located in one of Bellas Artes' back salons.

GALLERIES

There are dozens of art galleries throughout San Miguel, some amateur but enthusiastically run, others professional and representing well-known names in art.

One of the best, **Yam Gallery** often shows work by local artists, as well as talent from around Mexico and Latin America (page 84).

Another spot worth seeking out is **Noel Cayetano Arte Contemporáneo,** which is run by a well-known Oaxacan gallerist and represents a number of well-known Mexican artists, chiefly painters, sculptors, and printmakers (page 83).

PUBLIC ART

There are numerous sculptures by local artists beneath the trees of the beautiful **Parque Juárez** (page 51) and an iconic sculpture by Pedro Friedeberg just below the **Casa de la Cultura El Chorro** (page 51).

The **Guadalupe neighborhood,** just north of the centro histórico, is known for its many colorful murals. Stroll along the street Margarito Ledesma to see a few.

EVENTS

Art openings at local galleries are often fun and well-attended events. During an art walk at the **Fábrica La Aurora,** most galleries and artist studios stay open late and serve refreshments. It's a good opportunity to talk with working artists in town while enjoying a glass of wine and a night under the stars (page 51).

tips from passersby, while merry marching bands accompany wedding parties as they make their way out of a chapel. Roving guitarists play songs by request in San Miguel's restaurants, and norteño trios entertain the taco rush at the weekly Mercado de Martes. In the jardín, mariachis make the rounds in the evenings, their joyous sound floating over the centro.

Many of San Miguel de Allende's popular restaurants have live musicians accompanying the dinner crowd, while others schedule special musical events with local talent. The guitarist Gil Gutiérrez is one of San Miguel's best known performers, who often plays ticketed events. Pianist Gabriel Hernández and guitarist Severo Barrera are both excellent musicians whom you can see at the dinner hour at local restaurants. Live DJs are also a major draw at bars like the Bar at the R, Pulquería La Otomí, El Manantial, or at restaurants like La Doña.

Throughout the year, there are frequent live music and dance performances in the jardín, sponsored by the municipal and state government. These free concerts really run the gamut, from lively traditional dance performances to wailing rock shows by San Miguel teenagers. Sometimes wonderful, sometimes painful, most performances in the town square draw a multigenerational crowd. To see what's coming up, you can check the monthly schedule in the jardín, which is usually posted beneath the arcades on all four corners of the square.

Centro Histórico
Teatro Santa Ana
Relox 50; tel. 415/121-4583, WhatsApp 415/216-5443; https://teatrosantaana.org; US$10-30
Located within the Biblioteca Pública, this intimate performing arts venue hosts an ongoing series of speakers, book readings, movie screenings, and live music events. The changing lineup may include a classical guitar concert, a traditional Mexican dance performance, a documentary film, or a talk with a San Miguel de Allende-based author. Proceeds benefit the Biblioteca's social programs. Upcoming shows can be viewed and tickets can be purchased via their website.

Teatro Ángela Peralta
Mesones 82; tel. 415/152-2200; open during events; tickets starting at $10
The neoclassical Teatro Ángela Peralta was built at the end of the 19th century. The sandstone facade was restored during the 1980s, but the building is basically unchanged since its construction. Its namesake, Ángela Peralta, was a famous opera singer of her day, and she personally inaugurated the theater with a

concert on May 20, 1873. Since then, the theater has been one of San Miguel's most important venues for music and performance. Though not open to the public on a regular basis, the theater opens its doors frequently for concerts and events, from flamenco shows to opera. It is one of the major venues for the annual Festival Internacional de Música San Miguel de Allende in July, which features a wonderful two-week program of classical music ensembles.

San Miguel de Allende Countryside
Mama Mía
Hernández Macías 91; tel. 415/152-2063; https://mamamia.com.mx; 8am-midnight Sun.-Thurs., 8am-3am Fri.-Sat.; entrées US$18, no cover
When family-friendly Italian restaurant and music venue Mama Mía moved from its longtime location on Umarán to a new spot on Hernández Macías, it brought its warm service, homestyle recipes, and lineup of excellent musicians with it. Now located in the gorgeous tree-filled patio of a historic mansion north of town, Mama Mia continues its long tradition of hosting live music every night of the week, in addition to brunch shows on Saturdays and Sundays. There's no cover, but you should plan to dine while the music is on. Incorporating produce from the family's ranch in Atotonilco, the food is homemade-tasting Italian fare—pastas, lasagna, pizzas, salads—along with a range of meats and chicken, and there's a full bar, wine, and a housemade line of tasty craft beer on tap.

Zandunga
Carretera a Jalpa s/n, Jalpa; reservations WhatsApp 415/153-5098 or info@zandunga.net; Sun. 1pm-5pm; $45 cover for food and music
Located off a beautiful country road in the hamlet of Jalpa, this Sundays-only music venue is the best place to see (and dance to) live music in San Miguel de Allende, and is owned by celebrated guitarist Gil Gutiérrez and his family. Zandunga's two-set Sunday shows feature Gil himself and a changing

lineup of excellent international musicians from Mexico, Cuba, Venezuela, and beyond. The dance floor gets going over the course of the afternoon; when you want to rest your legs, there are great views of the stage from any table. The ticket price includes a generous lunch buffet with made-to-order tacos, quesadillas, elotes, and ice cream, plus a cash bar with excellent mezcal margaritas. You must purchase tickets in advance via WhatsApp, email, or in person at Hernández Macías 129 (10am-3pm Mon., Wed., and Fri.). Though most taxi drivers will know the venue's location, you can follow the map on their Instagram page to get there.

ART MUSEUMS

For a town of its size, San Miguel has built a strong reputation for its commitment to the visual arts, boasting numerous art schools, a surprising number of galleries, and a slew of working artists, both newbies and professionals. Notably, there is great interest in the visual arts throughout every sector of the community. Here, even coffee shops, dive bars, and real estate offices are known to host an art exhibition or two.

Centro Histórico
Centro Cultural Ignacio Ramírez "El Nigromante"

Hernández Macías 75; tel. 415/152-0289; http://elnigromante.inba.gob.mx; 10am-6pm Tues.-Sun.; free

You'll mostly see art hanging in private galleries in San Miguel de Allende, but there are several nice public exhibition spaces on the first floor of the government-run Centro Cultural Ignacio Ramírez "El Nigromante." These galleries often feature one or several individual and collective shows of work by local artists, in addition to interesting exhibitions from artists across Mexico. In 2023, for example, the galleries held a retrospective of work by late Mexican artist Luis Nishizawa and a playful show of new work from children's book illustrator Monique Zepeda. The galleries are free and open to the public.

La Esquina: Museo del Juguete Popular Mexicano

Nuñez 40; tel. 415/152-2602; www.museolaesquina.org.mx; 10am-6pm Tues.-Sat., 11am-4pm Sun.; US$5 adults, US$2 children under 12, seniors, students, and teachers

An enchanting little museum located in a beautifully renovated colonial home, La

countryside views at Zandunga music venue

Esquina: Museo del Jugete Popular Mexicano is dedicated entirely to traditional Mexican toys. Behind the museum's glass display cases, the permanent collection includes a wide range of antique and contemporary toys, including painted papier-mâché dolls, cornhusk figurines, clay whistles, little wooden chairs, toy planes and automobiles, wool stuffed animals, toy instruments, and many other lovely and imaginative designs. There are also changing exhibitions on the top floor dedicated to regional toy designs from different Mexican states. The light and colorful space is appropriate for kids (plus they get a discount on the admission cost), but visitors of any age will enjoy the diversity and imagination of traditional toy design from across Mexico.

FESTIVALS AND EVENTS

Many people in San Miguel de Allende claim that this small town has more municipal festivals than any other city in Mexico. While that may or may not be true, it is easy enough to believe. In San Miguel barely a day goes by that does not celebrate a patron saint, a beloved chapel, or a revolutionary hero. Every neighborhood has its own annual party, and on any given night loud fireworks crackle through the sky in celebration.

In addition to the near-constant festivities rumbling through San Miguel's neighborhoods, there are several important events and dozens of popular celebrations that take place every year, with much anticipation and fanfare. San Miguel enthusiastically participates in every national holiday, from Cinco de Mayo to Constitution Day. You'll also see plenty of festivities during the numerous unofficial but incredibly important holidays like May 10—Mother's Day.

Visiting during one of San Miguel's festivals can be a memorable experience; however, you should plan ahead if you want to visit during the most popular dates, especially the weeks around Semana Santa and Día de la Independencia.

January
El Día de los Reyes Magos
Jan. 6

On El Día de los Reyes Magos, or Three Kings' Day, children receive gifts from the reyes magos (the three wise men) and families get together to share a rosca de reyes, a delicious wreath-shaped sweet bread topped with crystallized fruit and sugar; during the first week of the year, you'll see them in every bakery in town. This family gathering is also the informal end of the holiday season, which is sometimes dubbed "Guadalupe Reyes," as it spans from the Día de la Virgen de Guadalupe, on December 12, to El Día de los Reyes Magos, on January 6.

If you pick up a rosca (and you should!), be aware before you take a bite: There are plastic figurines representing baby Jesus baked inside. Traditionally, the person who finds a baby in their slice of bread is appointed godmother or godfather to the baby Jesus in the family's nativity scene. The "godparent" is responsible for dressing the baby Jesus and taking him to the church for blessing on February 2, the day of La Candelaria, and then inviting friends and family to their home for a traditional dinner of tamales, atole, and hot chocolate.

Ignacio Allende's Birthday
Jan. 21

While not a national holiday, Ignacio Allende's birthday is celebrated in San Miguel on January 21. The life and achievements of San Miguel's native son are recognized with a parade downtown put on by local schoolchildren.

February
El Día de La Candelaria
Feb. 2

On February 2, El Día de la Candelaria (Candlemas), families take the baby Jesus doll from their nativity scene to be blessed in church before it is stored away until next Christmas. On the same day, families gather for tamales, atole, and hot chocolate, traditionally at the home of whoever found the

Avoid the Crowds

Forget about the high season and low season. San Miguel is now a popular destination year-round. The bustling feeling can be part of the fun, especially during one of the city's popular festivals, but here are a few tips to maximize your time in San Miguel.

CONSULT THE CALENDAR

San Miguel attracts tourists throughout the year, with the largest number of foreign visitors coming to town between December and April, the traditional high season in central Mexico. National visitors and day-trippers flock to San Miguel year-round, and their numbers surge even higher during Holy Week, Independence Day, and December, as well as Mexican holidays and three-day weekends. September is a particularly busy month for Mexican visitors to San Miguel, with Independence Day festivals followed shortly thereafter by El Día de San Miguel Árcangel, the city's biggest festival. If you are visiting during a busy weekend, book ahead for hotels, restaurants, and spa treatments, whenever possible.

CONSIDER A WEEKDAY VISIT

In some cases, hotels may raise their rates 10-15 percent on the weekends (especially Saturdays) and during peak holidays. Restaurants and other attractions are often less crowded on weekdays too.

TAKE A WALK

If you find yourself in town during an especially busy weekend, a quick taxi ride to **El Charco del Ingenio** will get you fresh air, space, and a respite from the bustle of downtown (page 49).

PLAN A COUNTRY WEEKEND

San Miguel's jardín and the blocks that surround it are often flooded with local tourists on the weekends, making Saturday and Sunday a good time to explore the countryside with horseback riding, wine tasting, hiking, or biking with companies like **Bici-Burro** (page 61) or **Rancho del Sol Dorado** (page 60).

STAY OUT LATE

In San Miguel, most businesses stay open into the evening—often until 7pm or 8pm. Often shops and galleries are quieter in the evening, making it a nice time to drop in.

baby Jesus figurine in the rosca de reyes on El Día de los Reyes Magos. While La Candelaria is a Catholic tradition, the tamales and atole may have derived from a pre-Hispanic tradition in honor of the rain god Tlaloc.

In addition to the family gatherings throughout town, San Miguel de Allende celebrates La Candelaria with the opening of the annual plant and flower sale at Parque Juárez. This lovely and aromatic market fills the winding walkways of the already verdant park with an impressive array of plants, flowers, hanging vines, trees, fresh herbs, cacti, and succulents. Vendors come from as far away as Veracruz and Puebla, and many set up tents to camp in the park during the 10 market days. If you are on an extended sojourn in San Miguel de Allende, La Candelaria is an excellent occasion to buy well-priced plants and flowers, or to just stop by the park to see the many exotic plants and cacti on sale.

San Miguel Writers Conference

Feb.; www.sanmiguelwritersconference.org; tickets for individual events $5-35, packages US$350-1,250

Just as it has attracted many visual artists, San Miguel de Allende is home to writers of every stripe, from memoirists to poets. Organized by the English-language writers' group the San Miguel Literary Sala, the annual San Miguel Writers Conference is a high-quality, well-organized five-day event that invites dozens of editors, publishers, literary agents, and published authors to give talks and workshops to conference participants. The long weekend has a full schedule of panel discussions, readings, classes, and parties, including keynote presentations by internationally famous writers, for which you can purchase individual tickets or a package, which includes several events or the full weekend program. Events include readings, panel discussions, practical advice on getting published, and fiction- and memoir-writing workshops. Past speakers include Wally Lamb, Rita Dove, Emma Donoghue, Barbara Kingsolver, Laura Esquivel, Alice Walker, Tom Robbins, and Molly Ringwald. Packages include meals.

March-April
First Day of Spring
Mar. 20 or 21

For the ultimate cute fix, don't miss the parade on March 20 or 21 heralding the first day of spring. Just as San Miguel's many jacaranda trees begin to bloom, all the town's children dress up as flowers, bumblebees, butterflies, and bunnies, then process through the streets of downtown as their proud parents snap photos. At **El Charco del Ingenio,** the spring equinox is celebrated annually with live musical concerts or theater performances within the adjoining canyon, an incredibly unique backdrop for this unique and well-attended annual event.

Semana Santa
Mar.-Apr.

San Miguel de Allende is well known throughout Mexico for its beautiful and solemn Semana Santa (Easter week) celebrations. There is amazing color and pageantry throughout the week, with major events drawing thousands of spectators. Semana Santa technically begins on Palm Sunday, but in San Miguel the festivities begin earlier.

Most Mexican schools have a break in the weeks preceding and following Easter Sunday, bringing a flood of domestic tourists to town. If you are planning a visit during this time, make hotel reservations in advance and be prepared for a more bustling version of the city. Once you touch down, be sure to pick up a copy of *Atención San Miguel,* which publishes a detailed list of Semana Santa events. Alternatively, you can look over the week's schedule on the municipal message boards in the town square.

One of the first major events related to Holy Week takes place two weeks before Easter. On the fifth Sunday of Lent, a massive pilgrimage departs from the Santuario de Jesús Nazareno, and the sacred figure of **El Señor de la Columna** is carried, along with La Virgen de Dolores and the Señor de San Juan, from Atotonilco to San Miguel de Allende. The journey is made slowly and in silence, with a mass held at the midpoint. Just before daybreak, the procession passes through San Miguel de Allende via the Avenida Independencia, where families have lined the streets with palm leaves, balloons, and flowers. With much fanfare, the figure of El Señor de la Columna is carried to the church of San Juan de Dios, where it will stay until Easter Sunday.

A lovely local tradition, **Viernes de Dolores** is celebrated on the final Friday of Lent, two days before Palm Sunday. This holiday is dedicated to La Virgen de Dolores (Our Lady of Sorrows), who is remembered with special masses in the town's churches, fresh flowers in the city fountains, and the distribution of aguas de fruta in the local community. At the workplace, employers will often provide aguas or ice cream to their employees, and some will also give out miniature popsicles to clients and passersby. The aguas are said to be symbolic of the virgin's tears.

The same evening, Our Lady of Sorrows is honored with hundreds of small home-built altars, erected in the windows and doorways of family homes throughout San Miguel de Allende. These altars are traditionally adorned with a statue or image of the virgin, chamomile, purple flowers, and little parcels of green wheat sprouts. All the town's lovely altars are open to the public, so there is quite a buzz on the street. As children go from house to house visiting with their neighbors, they are served hibiscus juice, ice cream, and popsicles.

Two days later, **Domingo de Ramos** (Palm Sunday) officially begins the Holy Week festivities. All day long, beautifully woven palm crosses and other palm adornments are sold outside every church in San Miguel. Local families buy their palms and take them to the church for blessings. There are also several religious processions on Palm Sunday, commemorating Jesus's arrival in Jerusalem.

Viernes Santo (Good Friday) is the single most important day during Semana Santa. In fact, it is more likely that a shop or restaurant will close to business on Good Friday than on Easter Sunday. Good Friday is not a day of celebration so much as a day of mourning, with solemn processions throughout the town. The jardín is the locus of activity, with huge crowds gathered there from morning until evening.

The events of Viernes Santo begin when the cross from Atotonilco is carried to the parroquia, followed shortly thereafter by the statue of El Señor de la Columna. The revered statue will spend the weekend in the parroquia before being returned to Atotonilco on the following Wednesday. Around midday, there is a live and unflinching reenactment of the Stations of the Cross, which concludes with Jesus's trial by Pontius Pilate in the esplanade of the parroquia. In preparation, a slow and serious procession weaves through town, carrying statues of Jesus and the saints aloft. The men are dressed in dark suits, and the women, or mujeres dolientes, are clothed in mourning attire. Among them, young girls in white dresses with bright purple sashes drop chamomile along the path to the parroquia. As evening falls, another mournful parade, the **Procesión del Silencio,** weaves through town toward the parroquia. For this beautiful and solemn event, capped men and women dressed in black proceed slowly and silently to the jardín, holding flickering candles.

In the days before Easter Sunday, or **Domingo de Pascua,** colorful papier-mâché Judas figures are hung over the plaza principal, between the Presidencia Municipal and the jardín. Just after Easter mass, a crowd gathers to burn the Judases, which have been rigged with explosives. One at a time, these paper giants spin in circles until they burst into flame, to the delight and applause of onlookers. Today many of the Judas figures are fashioned to look like politicians or other famous (but controversial) figures. Other than this colorful event, Easter Sunday is generally a quieter day, spent with family and attending mass.

May-June
Fiesta de la Santa Cruz
May, dates vary

During May, four historic neighborhoods in San Miguel de Allende hold their annual celebrations. The most raucous of these celebrations, the Fiesta de la Santa Cruz, is held in the Valle del Maíz. This major block party has roots dating back to the 16th century and includes live music, pageantry, and plenty of libations.

San Antonio de Padua:
Fiesta de Los Locos
First Sunday after June 13

Saint Anthony is one of San Miguel's most popular saints, as well as the namesake for one of the city's biggest neighborhoods. On the Sunday after Saint Anthony's feast day (June 13), San Miguel has a very particular way of feting this favored figure. On this auspicious day—also dubbed **Los Locos**—thousands of San Miguel residents march through the streets in silly and sometimes provocative costumes, from political masks to gorilla suits. Ogle all you want, but remember that onlookers are routinely pegged (and with gusto!) by handfuls of hard candy from the marchers. After the parade ends, the party continues well into the evening. From morning through afternoon to the wee hours of the night, wigged and costumed revelers dance ceaselessly, until they finally run out of steam the following morning.

July-August
Festival Internacional de Cine de Guanajuato
July; www.giff.mx

What began as a small, shorts-only festival is now one of Mexico's largest film events. Held annually at the end of July, El Festival Internacional de Cine de Guanajuato, or the Guanajuato International Film Festival, shows hundreds of films selected from thousands of international entries. Screenings are all free and open to the pubic, and they take place in venues across host city San Miguel de Allende, as well as in theaters, parks, and cultural centers across the state, including in León and Irapuato. The venues themselves are part of the fun, from the breathtaking (the jardín principal in San Miguel de Allende) to the unusual (the municipal graveyard as part of GIFF's traditional "Cine entre los Muertos" event). While the festival is still largely dedicated to shorts, there are numerous feature-length films included in the program, some of which make their debut at the festival. Many films are in Spanish; in most cases, international selections are subtitled in Spanish or English (language is indicated in the program).

Festival Internacional de Música San Miguel de Allende
International Music Festival of San Miguel de Allende, Hernández Macías 75; tel. 415/154-5141; www. festivalsanmiguel.com

Every summer, the Festival Internacional de Música San Miguel de Allende, formerly the **San Miguel Chamber Music Festival,** invites renowned quartets, soloists, and other classical ensembles from around the world to play in a series of concerts in San Miguel de Allende. Often excellent and sometimes avant-garde, concerts take place in a variety of venues and vary in price, though there are always several free events included in the program. Proceeds from this not-for-profit festival benefit the music education programs, also run by the organization, through which promising young musicians from across Mexico are invited to San Miguel to work directly with acclaimed international musicians. Shut down entirely during the Coronavirus pandemic, the festival has been working to reestablish its preeminence in the years that followed.

Vendimia
July 15-Oct. 15

San Miguel de Allende's wineries come to life with harvest-related events throughout the late summer and early fall, when grapes are ripe and ready to be made into wine. Vendimia events vary widely between wineries, but most put on upscale ticketed parties with star chefs, special wine pairings, and live performers. At Cuna de Tierra, the 2023 harvest was celebrated with a wine tasting and sushi pairing event with live bands and a design market, Viñedos Los Arcángeles led a wine-making workshop, and family-friendly Dos Búhos hosted a full-day event with live music, grape stomping, hay rides, and winery tours. Note that the harvest typically takes place in July-August in central Mexico, several weeks or months earlier than the harvest farther north.

September
Independence Celebrations and El Grito
Sept. 15-16

The birthplace of many of Mexico's independence heroes and an important meeting ground for Mexican pro-independence conspirators in the 19th century, San Miguel de Allende is often described as "the cradle of independence." Today this party-loving town

is a major destination for the national Día de la Independencia de México (Independence Day) celebrations. In the weeks leading up to the festivities, public spaces are festooned with tricolor decorations, local families hang Mexican flags outside their windows, and vendors appear in the streets with every manner of patriotic kitsch. Festivities technically begin on the night of September 15 with the traditional cry "¡Viva Mexico!" delivered in the jardín by the town's mayor. After the crowd is riled up, fireworks explode over the parroquia while special, semi-precarious pyrotechnic towers constructed for the event burst into multicolored flames. Seriously, you must watch out that your hair does not catch on fire.

During the independence celebrations, the town is flooded with national tourism, including the inevitable and noisy crowd of youngsters who've come to party in San Miguel's nightclubs. After the pyrotechnics, Independence Day is a big night out. Bars and clubs are packed and riotous until daybreak. While September 15 is the biggest party, the anniversary of the independence movement is actually September 16, a national holiday, with banks and most business closed. Needless to say, the parties continue.

Día de San Miguel Arcángel
First weekend following Sept. 29
The gorgeous festivals in honor of San Miguel's patron saint begin almost immediately after the Independence Day parties end. **Saint Michael's feast day** is technically September 29. However, if the 29th falls on a weekday, the festivities are pushed to the following weekend, culminating with the largest and most well-attended fiestas on Sunday.

The festivities in honor of San Miguel actually begin with a novena, nine days of prayer and celebration leading up to the saint's feast day. During each of these nine days, one of

the city's neighborhoods, along with various civil and religious groups, organizes processions around the city. The sounds of drums or marching bands echo through the narrow streets as those in the procession dance through town, eventually arriving at the Parroquia de San Miguel Arcángel, where the festivities often continue.

On Friday afternoon (two days before the official feast day celebrations), a procession departs from the Aurora neighborhood, accompanied by the Aguascalientes Brothers band. They arrive at the parroquia at dusk, just as vendors are setting up hot punch and taco stands in preparation for the night ahead. At this point, marching bands, dancers, and devotees of Saint Michael have begun to arrive from across Mexico—some coming from as far as the United States. At 4am on Saturday, the festivities officially begin with **La Alborada,** an astonishing hour-long fireworks display over the jardín. During this endless spray of pyrotechnics, the town square is filled with smoke, and the sound of explosions is almost deafening. The party continues until 6am, when the revelers sing "Las Mañanitas" (Mexico's birthday song) to San Miguel and then attend mass.

The weekend continues with dances, masses, and celebration. On Saturday afternoon, a long and beautiful procession of dancers and Indigenous groups heads up Canal Street to the parroquia. When they arrive, they decorate the parroquia with flowers and banners. The beautiful **Voladores de Papantla** from Veracruz perform their unique treetop ceremony as the dancing continues, and inevitably, there are more fireworks. The party continues through Sunday, with another procession of dancers up Zacateros street to the jardín. The fireworks and dancing don't stop until late Sunday night.

October-November
Día de Muertos
Nov. 1-2
Día de Muertos (Day of the Dead) is one of Mexico's most well-known holidays.

The name is a bit of a misnomer, as the holiday is actually celebrated during two days, November 1 and November 2, with November 2 recognized as a national holiday. In San Miguel de Allende, like everywhere in Mexico, regional traditions distinguish local Day of the Dead festivities. During the final week of October, San Miguel families and prominent organizations build traditional altars in the town square using sugar skulls, pan de muerto, gourds and jicama, colored sand, and cempasúchil (marigolds), the flower of the dead. You may notice that traditional altar design in this region tends to be neater and more geometrical than in other parts of Mexico.

Throughout the two-day holiday, the municipal cemetery (behind the Real de Minas hotel on the Salida a Celaya) is packed with families who have come to leave flowers and treats on the graves of loved ones. Many families spend the entire day there, cleaning the gravesite, laying flowers, offering food and drink to their ancestors, or eating a picnic lunch together. By the evening, the crowds are so dense that it can take several hours to get into the cemetery.

December

Mexico's long holiday season stretches from the day of the Virgin of Guadalupe, on December 12, to Three Kings' Day, on January 6. In most of the country, it's a relaxed, celebratory time, often spent with family. Cities are quieter and businesses run with reduced hours. In San Miguel, however, it is a bustling, busy season, when many domestic and international visitors flood the city.

Posadas and the Christmas Holidays
Dec. 12-25

Preparations for Christmas begin in November, but the season really kicks off on December 12, the day of **La Virgen de Guadalupe.** From December 12 onward, families gather for posadas, parties that occur during the nine days leading up to Christmas. On the night of a posada, guests gather at a neighbor's house with candles and costumes, asking the host family for shelter (and thereby reenacting Mary and Joseph's search for shelter on the night that Jesus was born). Once inside, the families say a rosary and sing Christmas songs. Then children may break a piñata while adults sip on punch. Posadas conclude on December 24, the most important night of the season. Traditionally, Mexican families gather for a late dinner, attending midnight mass afterward. December 25 is a quiet day, usually spent relaxing with family.

New Year's Celebration
Dec. 31-Jan. 1

In San Miguel de Allende, New Year's Eve is celebrated with lots of parties, people, and bubbly. There are often live music performances in the town square and, at midnight, a large fireworks display over the Parroquia de San Miguel Arcángel (a perfect chance for that postcard-perfect photo). If you want to follow Mexican tradition, eat 12 grapes for good luck when the clock strikes midnight—one grape for each month of the year. But be aware that the price of grapes in the market is always much higher on December 31! The season officially ends with **El Día de los Reyes Magos** (Three Kings' Day), on January 6.

Shopping

With a slew of unique stores and many creative minds at work, San Miguel de Allende is a wonderful place to shop. Although there are a few chain supermarkets and large department stores in San Miguel's outskirts, the centro histórico is still largely populated by mom-and-pop bakeries, corner stores, specialty boutiques, and artist-owned galleries. Here local proprietors usually tend their own shops, and many are on a first-name basis with their clients.

San Miguel excels in everything related to art, design, craft, and interiors, and among shops there is quite a bit of diversity for a town of its size, as a few hours of window-shopping will quickly reveal. From small gifts and contemporary art to a unique piece of jewelry or even a new couch for your living room, San Miguel's creative climate is reflected in the many unique and local products it sells.

TRADITIONAL CRAFTS
Centro Histórico
Casa de Cultura Banamex - Casa del Mayorazgo de la Canal

Canal 4; tel. 415/152-7584; 11am-6pm Tues.-Sat., 11am-2pm Sun.

The giftshop and bookstore inside the Casa Del Mayorazgo de la Canal is run by the Citibanamex cultural foundation, which also runs the galleries inside the space. The top-quality selection of traditional craftwork on sale here was created as part of the foundation's Grandes Maestros del Arte Popular (Great Masters of Popular Art) program, which helps to fund talented traditional artisans working across Mexico. The work here is of a very fine quality, including delicately painted gourds, glossy ceramic pineapples, elaborately hand-sculpted and painted árboles de la vida, and more. There is also a selection of art books published by the foundation, including some beautiful tomes documenting

Mexican folk art

Shopping for Artesanía

Shopping for traditional craftwork, or artesanía, is one of the great pleasures of a trip to Mexico. It's also an important way to support the country's historic artistic traditions. San Miguel de Allende is a wonderful place to shop for traditional craftwork, with a range of styles and techniques represented in its many well-stocked shops, most run by knowledgeable buyers.

CERAMICS

Santa María Atzompa, Oaxaca, produces distinctive **forest-green glazed pottery and cookware.** Another distinctive tradition is the elaborate **ceramic pineapples** from the towns of Patamban and San José de Gracia in Michoacán, where potters produce their wares without the use of a potter's wheel. Since the 16th century, the states of Puebla and Guanajuato have been major producers of tin-glazed **majolica-style ceramics,** with the finest and most expensive ceramics, known as Talavera, produced in Puebla.

Unglazed burnished clay pottery, known as **barro bruñido,** is polished with pyrite and prolifically produced in several colorful and distinctive styles in Tonalá and Tlaquepaque, Jalisco. Another type of **burnished clay pottery** is native to Michoacán, specifically the town of Capula. The most recognizable Capula pottery is painted with hundreds of white dots. Also look for the shiny **glazed platters, plates, and pots** from Huancito and the typical **green and black pottery** from Tzintzuntzan, among other Michoacán pueblos. **Burnished black-clay pottery** from San Bartolo Coyotepec, Oaxaca, is also distinctive and well known, available in some shops in San Miguel.

Where to Buy It

- **Artes de Mexico** carries a range of ceramic work (page 78).

- There are high-end ceramic pieces, like the famous pineapples from Michoacán, at the shop inside the **Casa del Mayorazgo de la Canal** (page 75).

- **Hilo Negro** in the Fábrica La Aurora sells contemporary polished-clay pieces (page 82).

TEXTILES AND CLOTHING

Manta, a light cotton muslin, was mass-produced throughout Mexico and has long been the base for traditional Mexican clothing. Throughout town, you can find beautiful embroidered manta tunics and huipiles from the state of Oaxaca, as well as the geometrically stitched Magdalena huipiles from Chiapas. In addition to manta, Oaxaca is a major producer of beautiful textiles and clothing, the best of which are hand-loomed and embroidered.

Chales, rebozos, and **mantillas** are different types of wraps and shawls produced throughout Mexico. The famous silk rebozos of Santa María del Río are so finely woven that, despite their large size, they can pass through a woman's ring.

Shopping tips: The best (and priciest) shawls are made with natural fibers, usually silk or cotton. Mexican-made textiles and clothing using natural dyes are the most sought-after and priciest.

Where to Buy It

- **Juana Cata** has a stunning selection of textiles from the state of Oaxaca, handmade and colored with natural dye (page 78).

- Boutique **Mixta** has an eclectic selection of contemporary and traditional Mexican clothing (page 78).

HOJALATERÍA AND GLASS BOXES

Hojalatería (tin products) are a specialty in the San Miguel region, most often used in stamped-tin lamps and candelabras, wastepaper baskets, mirrors, and picture frames. San Miguel has also long been known for its delicate **blown-glass lanterns and boxes,** fused with iron.

Where to Buy It

- A number of vendors in the **Mercado de Artesanía** sell stamped tin ornaments, mirrors, and boxes (page 78).

WOOD FIGURINES

Whittled wooden toys and figurines, as well as wooden spoons and cutting boards, are produced locally and sold in many of the older craft shops in San Miguel de Allende. **Alebrijes,** delicately carved and brightly painted animals and figurines, are principally produced in San Antonio Arrazola, Oaxaca.

Where to Buy It

- **Mercado de Artesanía** is a good place to find wood utensils (page 78).

- **Ono,** on the central square, carries many brightly colored crafts, including some substantial alebrijes (page 78).

LACQUERWARE

Gorgeously detailed **lacquered wood trays, boxes, chests, and platters,** as well as decorative gourds, are produced in the states of Michoacán and Guerrero.

Shopping tip: The most famous lacquerware artisans often sign their work, and many have won prizes for their talent; award-winning pieces are the most expensive.

Where to Buy It

- The shop at the **Casa del Mayorazgo de la Canal** often stocks lacquered trays and gourds from Michoacán (page 75).

- **La Calaca** maintains a lovely selection of vintage hand-painted platters and wood figurines (page 84).

CEREMONIAL MASKS

Wooden masks are often used in traditional ceremonies, principally in the states of Oaxaca, Michoacán, and Guerrero. The original designs can range from the head of a jaguar to a garish devil.

Shopping tip: Masks are very individualized artisanal products, and they carry more significance (and a higher price) if they have already been used in a ceremony.

Where to Buy It

- **La Calaca** almost always has a selection of ceremonial masks, some antique and very rare (page 84).

the craftwork created through the Grandes Maestros program.

Mercado de Artesanía

Andador Lucas Balderas s/n; 10am-7pm daily, hours vary by shop daily

There is a large selection of inexpensive and predominantly regional handicrafts at the Mercado de Artesanía, an outdoor artisan market located in a descending alleyway between the Mercado Ignacio Ramírez and Calle Loreto. Here you'll find milagritos (painted tin ornaments) and other metalwork, as well as beautiful handmade mesquite bowls and utensils, ceramics, beaded jewelry, papier-mâché, and textiles. A few shops specialize in art and crafts from Oaxaca and Michoacán, as well as clay miniatures. There is some good work here, but it takes a sharp eye to find the best pieces amid the jumble of storefronts. Along the exit of the mercado on Calle Loreto are many more small shops selling craftwork from across Mexico.

Ono

Plaza Principal 20; tel. 415/152-1366; 9am-8pm daily

Right on the main plaza, this colorful shop carries a range of lovely craft and textiles from traditional Mexican artisans, including lots of wearable items like leather bags and satchels, embroidered manta blouses, silver jewelry, and beautiful hand-loomed shawls and other textiles. They also have a nice selection of alebrijes, painted wood figurines from Oaxaca, and wooden toys, among other small items that can make nice gifts for someone back home. The store represents artisans from central and southern Mexico, and the staff can answer questions about the range of work on display.

Guadalupe and Aurora
Artes de Mexico

Calzada de la Aurora 47; tel. 415/152-0764; https:// artesdemexicosanmiguel.com; 10am-8pm daily

Near the Fábrica La Aurora art and design center, the well-stocked shop Artes de Mexico has a diverse, well-priced, and well-selected

stock of furniture, lamps, blown glass, stamped-tin-frame mirrors, lacquerware trays from Michoacán, papier-mâché, place mats, and other crafts. They also sell a range of equipales: large chairs, couches, and round tables made of lightweight natural wood and pigskin. Based on pre-Hispanic designs, equipales are pieces of comfortable and inexpensive traditional furniture from Jalisco

CLOTHING AND ACCESSORIES
Centro Histórico
Juana Cata

Recreo 5A; tel. 415/152-6417; 11am-8pm Mon.-Sat.

Owned by a family of well-known Oaxacan craft experts, Juana Cata sells gorgeous handmade clothing and textiles from the state of Oaxaca. Take your time perusing the stacks of expertly woven shawls, thick hand-dyed cotton fabrics, and lovely velvet huipiles, lavishly embroidered with colorful flowers in the Isthmus of Tehuantepec. Here every piece is painstakingly created and expertly selected. For those interested in Mexican textiles and weaving traditions, this shop is essential. In addition to textiles, Juana Cata has a nice collection of Oaxacan silver jewelry, known for its delicate filigree details.

Mixta

Pila Seca 3; tel. 415/152-7343; www.mixtasanmiguel. com; 11am-7pm Mon.-Sat., noon-5pm Sun.

Spend some time browsing the beautifully selected mix of crafts, collectibles, art, and clothes at Mixta, an excellent and eclectic design-centric boutique on Calle Pila Seca. Set in the romantic old salons of an 18th-century mansion, the always-changing collection here includes bangles, shawls, beaded necklaces, greeting cards, unique home furnishings, original art, scarves, totes, tunics, oilcloth wallets, votive candles, throw pillows, furniture, and photographs, culled from a range of Mexican and international designers. The shop's warm Australian owner is often behind the register; she selects all the work for the shop, looking far and wide for unusual items you won't find elsewhere in San Miguel.

Abrazos
Zacateros 24; tel. 415/154-8580; www. sanmigueldesigns.com; 10am-7pm Mon.-Sat., 10am-4pm Sun.

The blast of color at Abrazos comes from the lighthearted, Mexican-themed cotton fabrics that form the base of the store's product line. A great place to pick up a gift for yourself or someone at home, Abrazos has a range of cute and colorful aprons, dish towels, handbags, kimonos, eye masks, pajamas, and men's ties as well as funky jewelry, buttons, and notebooks. All the shop's products are handmade in San Miguel de Allende by a cooperative of local seamstresses.

Recreo
Recreo 26; tel. 415/154-4820; http://recreosanmiguel. com; 10am-6pm Mon.-Sat., noon-5pm Sun.

Inspired by traditional Mexican design, the luxe line of ponchos, wraps, shawls, and dresses created at Recreo has garnered a loyal clientele over the boutique's many years in San Miguel. If you are looking for a high-quality and elegant piece to take home from Mexico, this is the place to go. Though focused on women's accessories, it also has a small line of men's clothing. Prices are high, but the designs are original and the quality is excellent. The spacious stone-floored boutique has a swanky ambience, with gleaming chandeliers, polished clay floors, and clothing hung neatly on the racks, and the staff is friendly and generous with their time.

Joyería David
Zacateros 53; tel. 415/152-0056; 10am-5pm Mon.-Sat.

This traditional family-run silver shop has been in business for decades, and over that time it has developed a loyal clientele for its price and quality. From earrings to pendants to chokers, David produces silver pieces in a range of styles—some traditional and some more unusual—and there are hundreds of pieces on display in the shop's glass cases.

Prices are accessible, and much of the work can be adjusted on-site by the team of artisans.

HOME AND FURNITURE
Centro Histórico
Casamidy
Pila Seca 3; tel. 415/152-0403; casamidy@casamidy. com; open by appointment

Opened in 1998 by RISD-trained designers Jorge Almada and Anne-Marie Midy, Casamidy is one of San Miguel de Allende's vanguard home design shops, and a precursor to the many concept boutiques and interiors firms that operate in the city today. Casamidy's constantly evolving line of furniture and accent pieces draws on the Mexican and French backgrounds of the lead designers, but the contemporary simplicity of their designs makes them staples for any home. Though Casamidy isn't usually open to the public, you can make an appointment to visit the showroom via email.

Namuh
Cuna de Allende 15; tel. 415/154-8080; 11am-7pm Mon.-Fri., 11am-8pm Sat., 11am-6pm Sun

Namuh is an interior design shop and importer that showcases a range of beautiful furnishings and home accessories, with an emphasis on Asian-inspired designs and products from countries such as Thailand, China, and Indonesia. The work on sale is high quality, yet the aesthetic is earthy and appealing, with merchandise ranging from leather armchairs and hanging lamps to weathered chests and clay urns, in addition to a proprietary line of furniture. Though the main warehouse (Camino a Alcocer, Km 2.2; tel. 415/154-8080; www.namuhmex.com; 9am-6pm Mon.-Fri., 10am-6pm Sat., 11am-4pm Sun.) is located on a country road west of town, you can get a sampling of Namuh's furnishings, antiques, and textiles at their charming little downtown shop in the Cuna Quince plaza.

Tao Studio Gallery
Sollano 28; tel. 415/154-9790; https://taostudio.net; 11am-7pm daily

A Day in Dolores Hidalgo

Parroquia de Nuestra Señora de los Dolores

The small city of Dolores Hidalgo, about 32 km (20 mi) northeast of San Miguel de Allende, is a worthwhile day trip from San Miguel de Allende. In addition to its important role during the Mexican War of Independence, this small city is well known for its lovely ceramic artisan work, pretty central square, and nearby wineries.

SIGHTS

Dolores Hidalgo's walkable centro histórico boasts some beautiful colonial-era architecture and interesting historical sights, particularly its famous parish church.

- **Parroquia de Nuestra Señora de los Dolores** (Parish Church of Our Lady of Sorrows, Plaza Principal s/n; generally 8am-8pm daily) is one of the most famous churches in all of Mexico and the jewel of Dolores Hidalgo's central square. This impressive sandstone church has an elaborate churrigueresque facade, topped by two soaring bell towers. It was from the steps of the parish that Father Miguel Hidalgo famously summoned the Mexican army to begin the War of Independence.

- **The Plaza Principal,** Dolores Hidalgo's pretty central square, is at the heart of town. For most visitors, the main attraction is the famous **ice cream vendors,** which occupy the four corners of the square. With a vast selection of nieves, or ice cream, on offer, you'll find classics, like chocolate or vanilla, as well as more wacky flavors, like shrimp, tequila, cheese, beer, pork rind, and avocado. Most flavors, even the most bizarre, are surprisingly sweet and appealing.

- **Museo de Sitio Casa de Hidalgo** (Morelos 1; tel. 418/182-0171; 9am-5:45pm Wed.-Sun.; US$4, Sun. free), also known as the Casa de Diezmo, is the former home of Mexico's most famous pastor, Miguel Hidalgo. This large colonial building has been outfitted with period furnishings and didactic texts about the life of the parish priest. There is also a small collection of artifacts from the War of Independence.

WHERE TO EAT

- **El Fruty** (Hidalgo 2; tel. 418/182-3679; 8:30am-10:30pm daily), a tree-shaded patio restaurant just off the main plaza, is a perfect place for breakfast, with a menu that covers traditional dishes like huevos rancheros, as well as fruit-topped house-made organic yogurt and espresso drinks. The prices are economical, the setting is relaxed, and there is always a crowd of locals dining here.

- **Carnitas Vicente** (Av. Norte Mariano Balleza 65; tel. 418/112-7245; 8am-4pm Tues.-Sun.; US$5) is an inexpensive and casual place for a filling almuerzo or lunch. Specializing in carnitas, this excellent little eatery serves delicious braised pork, either by the kilo or wrapped in individual tacos. The maciza is richly flavored yet not greasy, well complemented by the pico de gallo and other salsas laid out on the tables.

CERAMICS

For many tourists, the main reason to visit Dolores is to shop for low-cost and high-quality Talavera-style ceramics, with several large workshops located within easy walking distance of the central square.

- **J M B** (Puebla 60; tel. 418/182-0749; https://jmbtalavera.com.mx; 10am-6pm Mon.-Fri., 10am-4pm Sat., 11am-3pm Sun.): Anything you've ever dreamed of owning in brightly colored Talavera can be found at J M B, a huge shop near the city center. This cavernous factory store contains room after room of hand-painted ceramic goods. There is also a pretty line of lead-free products.

- **Azulejos y Loza Talavera Vázquez** (Puebla 58; tel. 418/182-2914; https://vazquezpottery.com; 9:30am-4pm Mon.-Sat., 10:30am-3pm Sun.): You'll find lots of oversize products, like large ceramic urns and flowerpots, as well as decorative wall pieces and tile sets. The quality of the work is high, and prices are excellent.

WINERIES

A number of wineries are located in the countryside near Dolores Hidalgo, along highway 51 to San Miguel de Allende, and along the highway east of Dolores toward San Luis de la Paz.

- **Cuna de Tierra** (Carretera Dolores Hidalgo-San Luis de la Paz, Km 11, Rancho el Rosillo; tel. 415/152-6060; http://cunadetierra.com.mx; 10am-8pm Tues.-Sat.; $20): Family-owned winery Cuna de Tierra was the first commercial winery in the state of Guanajuato. They have been growing grapes since the 1980s, and today the winery produces red, white, and rosé. They offer guided tours of the vineyard, olive orchards, and wine-making facilities ($16, not including wine), as well as wine tastings (by appointment Tues.-Sun.; $20). Reserve your spot via their website. You can also enjoy the vineyard ambience with wine, pizzas, small plates, and charcuterie at Cuna de Tierra's on-site restaurant (11am-5pm Tues.-Fri. and Sun., 11am-6:30pm Sat.; $16).

- **Viñedos Los Árcangeles** (Carretera Dolores Hidalgo-San Diego de la Union Km 13; tel. 418/134-7118; www.vinedolosarcangeles.com; $30): This young vineyard produces the boutique Canto de Sirenas label wines, which will appeal to those looking for more low-intervention bottles and sustainable practices in agriculture. Tastings and vineyard tours ($30) include three pours and last about an hour, but you can linger with a meal at the winery restaurant, Itaca (noon-8pm Thurs.-Fri., 10am-8:30pm Sat., 10am-6pm Sun.; $12).

GETTING THERE AND AROUND

To get to Dolores, take Highway 110 from San Miguel for about 48 km (30 mi), then follow the Centro signs for Dolores Hidalgo's downtown. After passing through Dolores, you can continue on Highway 110 to Guanajuato. From here, the highway becomes incredibly scenic, climbing into the Sierra de Guanajuato and passing through the small town of Santa Rosa.

Though most of Dolores's attractions are easy to access on foot, there are inexpensive taxis throughout Dolores Hidalgo's city center.

Operated by Flecha Amarilla (tel. 477/710-0060), second-class buses depart for Dolores Hidalgo from the main bus terminal in San Miguel de Allende every 30 minutes or so; the ride takes about 45 minutes to an hour, depending on stops.

Filling the ground floor of a historic mansion on Sollano street, this impressive home design shop has a varied line of originally designed furnishings, from coffee tables to armoires, and elegant accents for the home. Incorporating metal, wood, fiber, and stone, the pieces here are innovative and contemporary, but stand out with their simple, elegant lines. Prices are upscale, but the unique pieces here can anchor the design of a room. The collection includes one-of-a-kind objects and sculpture by the gallery's lead designer, which complement the aesthetics of the home goods collection.

Guadalupe and Aurora
Hilo Negro
Local 3D, Fábrica La Aurora, Calzada de la Aurora; tel. 415/152-4835; www.hilo-negro.com; 10am-6pm Mon.-Sat., 11am-4pm Sun.

A small and stylish shop in the Fábrica La Aurora, Hilo Negro features decorative pieces for the home, designed by the shop's owner, Ricardo Garcia, and created with the help of traditional artisans. The result is an appealing proprietary line of wall hangings, hand-painted platters, and ceramic planters, among other home goods. Garcia's interest in classic Mexican games, like loteria and pissota, often

inspires his work, which is playful yet handsome, and elaborated with a mix of materials like wood, burnished clay, and antique coins. Though inspired by artesanía, Garcia's pieces are more akin to fine art, with the prices to match. In addition, the store has a fine collection of hand-painted majolica platters.

La Bottega di Casa
Local 17A, Fábrica La Aurora, Calzada de la Aurora s/n, Local; tel. 415/152-8636; www.labottegadicasa.com; 10am-6pm Mon.-Sat., 11am-3pm Sun.

In the Fábrica La Aurora, the lovely homegoods store La Bottega di Casa is best known for its proprietary collections of bed linens, table dressings, and other textiles made with European fabrics. The shop also sells unique home goods, like Merino vases and 19th-century lithographs, culled from the Italian owner's travels around the world, particularly Europe, plus a proprietary line Mexican-made blown-glass pitchers, drinking glasses, and white-glazed ceramic table settings, elegantly produced and presented. The owner and her partner, designer Ricardo Garcia, also run the charming home decor and accessories shop **Le Spezie** (Fábrica La Aurora Local 4D; tel. 415/152-1806; http://lespezie.com; 10am-6pm Mon.-Sat.,

Namuh

Respect the Siesta

Though it prevalence is slowly fading in big cities across Mexico, the siesta—or midday rest—remains an important part of family life in smaller towns, including San Miguel de Allende. Throughout Mexico, the midday meal, known as the comida, is the biggest and most important meal of the day. Traditionally eaten around 2pm, the comida is a time that families spend together, just after children come home from school. It's not uncommon to take a short nap after lunch; hence, the entire midday break is often referred to as the siesta.

Notice the operating hours at many small businesses, like pottery shops, galleries, or even real estate offices. They often **close 2-4pm,** a time during which the shop's proprietors will go home for lunch and relaxation. For tourists, the siesta can be a bit of a nuisance, since few expect to find a gift shop or clothing boutique closed during the bright light of day. Most, however, learn to do like the locals and enjoy a long and leisurely lunch with time for shopping in the afternoon. In fact, many businesses stay open later to accommodate a midday rest.

Like the siesta, Sundays are an important family day in Mexico, often undisturbed by the necessity of running a business. It can be very surprising to learn that many shops—and even restaurants—are closed or have **very reduced hours on Sunday,** when tourists flock to San Miguel from nearby towns like Celaya and Querétaro. Yet personal time, family, and tradition are still a priority here.

11am-4pm Sun.), which is worth seeking out for its wonderful and eclectic seletion of candlesticks, jewelry, art, clothing, unique lamps, and light fixtures, both original designs and imported.

GALLERIES AND ARTIST STUDIOS
Centro Histórico
Galeria Casa Diana

Recreo 48; tel. 415/152-0885; www.galeriacasadiana. com; 11am-7pm Mon.-Tues. and Fri.-Sat., 11am-6pm Wed. Born in Florence, Italy, but raised in Mexico, surrealist artist and architect Pedro Friedeberg is one of the most well-known 20th-century artists in Mexico. When Friedeberg moved to San Miguel de Allende, he redecorated the colonial interior of Casa Diana, which now houses an art gallery in the downstairs living spaces. The gallery holds the biggest collection of Friedeberg's work in the country, and seeing his iconic hand-shaped chairs and surrealist prints and paintings is the reason to visit, though the gallery also represents several other interesting artists. During operating hours, ring the bell to be let inside.

Galeria Noel Cayetano

Hernández Macías 68; tel. 415/121-1227; 10am-8pm daily
The Oaxacan gallery owner Noel Cayetano opened a branch of his eponymous gallery Noel Cayetano Arte Contemporáneo in San Miguel de Allende in 2014, just across the street from Bellas Artes. Featuring work by well-known Oaxacan names like Ruben Leyba, Ixrael Montes, Guillermo Olguin, and Sergio Hernandez, this well-curated, white-walled space mostly features large-format oil paintings, though it also boasts a small outdoor sculpture garden. It's a good place to get a primer on the Oaxacan tradition in fine art or shop for a unique piece.

Galeria Nudo

Recreo 10B and Recreo 36; tel. 415/154-7179; www. galerianudo.com; 10am-6pm Mon.-Sat., 10am-3pm Sun.
It's worth stopping into Galeria Nudo, an interesting space that shows a range of painting, sculpture, and work on paper by artists from across Mexico, representing many well-known names, like José Luis Cuevas and Manuel Felguerez, in addition to up-and-coming artists. There's usually a diverse selection of work on display, so you're likely

to find something that catches your eye. If you'd like to know more about a piece's provenance, the knowledgeable staff can answer your questions.

San Antonio
Yam Gallery

Instituto Allende, Ancha de San Antonio 20; Int. 1; tel. 415/150-6052; www.yamgallery.com; 11am-5pm Mon.-Sat.

Yam is one of the city's best art spaces, representing contemporary Mexican, South American, and European artists, including Taka Fernández, Cisco Jiménez, and some talented San Miguel locals. Located on the southeast corner of the Instituto Allende, Yam frequently opens new and interesting exhibits in its two-story space, and it is always represented at a booth at the annual Zona Maco in Mexico City, the country's most prestigious art fair. Even when the Instituto Allende is closed for a special event or wedding, you can visit Yam via the exterior doorway. Look out for new exhibition openings, which are always well-attended events. Just beside Yam's main gallery, the small boutique **Yam Gallery Silver** (11am-6pm Mon.-Sat., 11am-3pm Sun.) is dedicated entirely to silver design, showcasing Spratling's iconic work, jewelry from the Spratling workshop, and other unique pieces by several high-quality contemporary local designers.

Galería Pérgola/B'nai Or Art Gallery

Jesús 19 and Instituto Allende; tel. 415/566-4718; https://bnaiorartgallery.com; 11am-5pm Mon.-Sat.

The B'nai Or artist collective runs two locations of Galería Pérgola in San Miguel de Allende. The smaller, on the street Jesús, focuses on printmaking and works on paper. It's a charming space, well worth seeking out for its diverse collection of well-priced work by Mexican and international artists. The spacious second branch is located on the beautiful back patio of the Instituto Allende, a spectacular location for the large-scale paintings and sculpture on display.

ANTIQUES

The opulence of 17th- and 18th-century San Miguel left behind its share of spoils. Today the former finery from old haciendas and colonial mansions often turns up in dusty antiques shops around town. While the number of antiques is beginning to dwindle, those interested in vintage wares will still find good places to buy them in town. In addition to antique popular art and pottery.

Centro Histórico
La Calaca

Mesones 93; tel. 415/152-3954; www.lacalaca.com; 11am-2pm and 4pm-5:30pm Mon.-Sat.

It is easy to walk right past the little storefront, so keep an eye out for La Calaca, which specializes in antique popular and ceremonial art from around Mexico. The store's owner, Evita, has been trading artesanías for more than 25 years, and her experience has helped compile a lovely collection of masks, platters, ceramics, textiles, and other special objects that wear their age with dignity. A cozy little spot on a bustling street, this tiny store is a good place to find a special piece for your home and to hear a little bit about its history from Evita.

Guadalupe and Aurora
La Buhardilla

Local 4A, Fábrica La Aurora, Calzada de la Aurora s/n; tel. 415/154-9911; www.arteyantiguedades.mx; 10am-6pm Mon.-Sat., 11am-2pm Sun.

Stepping through the door of La Buhardilla is almost like stepping into another world. Inside this vast and artful shop in the Fábrica La Aurora, the walls are covered with antique masks and old oil paintings, vintage lamps swing from the ceiling, and worn but beautiful carpets cover the floors. Owned by experienced antiques dealers and restoration experts from Monterrey, Mexico, La Buhardilla is one of the best places to browse fine Mexican antiques in town.

Classes and Volunteering

San Miguel de Allende is a friendly and livable town, making it an excellent place to spend a few weeks, a few months, or even a few years studying language and arts or pursuing new hobbies. Attending a lecture or an art opening is a quintessential San Miguel experience and the best way to get a taste of the local social scene.

SPANISH LANGUAGE STUDY
Centro Histórico
Academia Hispano Americana

Mesones 4; tel. 415/152-0349; www.ahaspeakspanish. com; 8:30am-4:30pm Mon.-Fri.; US$170-265 for 1 week, $570-800 for 4-week session

For serious students, Academia Hispano Americana is the oldest Spanish school in San Miguel de Allende and one of the best, originally established in 1959. Throughout the year, AHA offers intensive and semi-intensive Spanish curricula, which include grammar, pronunciation, and Spanish-language lectures on Mexican culture, 3 to 6 hours of instruction every day, with native Spanish teachers. New sessions begin each month, and class size is capped at 12. The school will also arrange for students to stay in the homes of local families, where they can eat, sleep, and keep practicing their Spanish. Additionally, the school offers a diploma program in Spanish as a second language, an intensive 6-month course of study that includes 720 hours of class work, 20 hours of one-on-one instruction, 100 hours in an internship, and volunteer work, for $3,310.

Guadalupe and Aurora
Instituto Habla Hispana

Calzada de la Luz 25; tel. 415/152-0713; www. mexicospanish.com; US$130 per week

A family-run language school, Instituto Habla Hispana offers 12 4-week Spanish language sessions throughout the year, though students may join a session after the start date as long as space is available. Typically, programs include 10 hours of classroom instruction per week with additional cultural activities, like walking tours, in the afternoon. Class size is capped at 8 students. While studying at Habla Hispana, students may choose to stay in the simple, reasonably priced accommodations on the school's campus (US$35/night single), or the school can arrange for students to stay with a local family. Most of the year, Habla Hispana's students are principally adults and seniors; in the summer months, however, the school enrolls a range of ages.

Northeast of the Centro
Warren Hardy Spanish School

Aba 6, Col. Santa Julia; tel. 415/125-0022; info@ warrenhardy.com, www.warrenhardy.com; US$295 per session

A popular and effective language school with a proprietary system of Spanish instruction aimed at adult learners, Warren Hardy Spanish School offers a series of intensive, half-day courses that span two and a half weeks per session. Classes run continuously throughout the year and are very popular with American and Canadian expatriates; the full schedule is listed on their website, where you can register for in-person learning or take an online course. This school is not only a great place to brush up your español, it is also a great spot to make new friends in San Miguel.

ART
Centro Histórico
Centro Cultural Ignacio Ramírez "El Nigromante"

Hernández Macías 75; tel. 415/152-0289; http:// elnigromante.inba.gob.mx; from US$30/month

The historic art school at the Centro Cultural Ignacio Ramírez "El Nigromante" offers a rotating lineup of courses in painting, collage, ceramics, photography, singing, and guitar, among other disciplines, as well as workshops for children. The tiny classrooms were once nuns' cloisters, and the quirky atmosphere adds to the charm. Run by the Mexican government's Instituto Nacional de Bellas Artes (National Fine Arts Institute), tuition is incredibly reasonable, though there is often a waiting list for popular courses.

El Sindicato Centro Cultural Comunitario

Recreo 4; tel. 415/152-0131; $8-10/class, with discounted monthly rates

An active multipurpose community and cultural center, El Sindicato offers a variety of dance, music, art, and fitness classes at reasonable prices, as well as cultural workshops, performances, talks, and theater, much of it designed for children and teens. Follow El Sindicato on social media to see upcoming offerings, which may include ballet, son jarocho, traditional Mexican dance, and art therapy for children. For most classes, instruction is in Spanish. In addition, El Sindicato hosts frequent talks and music events, and runs an inexpensive on-site café with a daily vegetarian lunch special, which includes a drink and dessert, for about $4.

Guadalupe and Aurora
Nelly Lorenzo Arte Textile

Local 2A-1, Fábrica La Aurora; tel. 415/105-8358; https://fabricalaaurora.com/en/kora_portfolio/nelly-lorenzo-2; US$40/hour including materials

If you're inspired by all the colorful rugs and textiles produced in Mexico, you may want to channel that feeling into an off-loom weaving or macramé workshop with Nelly Lorenzo at her studio and gallery at the Fábrica La Aurora. Lorenzo is a warm teacher and talented weaver; she offers classes appropriate for both beginners and more experienced weavers. Appointments are scheduled 11am-4pm weekdays year-round, and class size is capped at four students.

Sterling Quest

Guty Cardenas 3, Col. Guadalupe; tel. 415/119-4381; www.sterlingquestschool.com; US$380 for 36 hours

For serious instruction in jewelry creation and design, Sterling Quest offers ongoing group workshops with class size capped at six people. Spirited instructor Billy King has been teaching silverwork for more than 20 years, and he is a talented jeweler himself. His exacting style receives high praise from former students, many of whom later became professional jewelers themselves. Class costs do not include the cost of silver or stones, though vendors come to offer these products during class time each week.

San Antonio
Instituto Allende Escuela de Arte y Español

Ancha de San Antonio 22; tel. 415/152-4538; http://instituto-allende.edu.mx; US$225/week or $440-515/4 weeks

The Instituto Allende is one of the country's oldest art academies, and many of San Miguel's artists have taken (or taught) a class or two there. Though it discontinued its master's program for foreign students, the school still offers an undergraduate fine arts program for Mexican nationals, as well as continuing education courses in disciplines such as jewelry-making, sculpture, weaving, drawing, and painting. The institute also offers a series of adult continuing education classes in history, science, art, classical music, and other disciplines, some taught in English and some bilingual. Courses are designed to run for four weeks, but students can sign up for fewer weeks as needed.

COOKING
Guadalupe and Aurora
Pura Vida Kitchen

www.puravidakitchen.com; starting at US$75 pp

Learning to cook with high-quality, local ingredients is the focus of classes at Pura Vida Kitchen, a collective of chefs who teach out of a lovely professional kitchen in the Guadalupe neighborhood. With a range of backgrounds and experience, PVK's teachers can offer a class that matches your interests: Chef Mario can teach you to make a traditional mole from scratch, while Chef Esmeralda teaches a class on the use of desert ingredients native to Mexico. Doña Maria Luisa focuses her classes on corn masa, made from native corn she cultivates at her ranch. PVK's workshops generally run about 2-2.5 hours and can be combined with a market tour (US$17).

San Antonio
Marilau Traditional Mexican Cooking School
Calle de la Luz 12, Col. San Antonio; tel. 415/152-4376; http://mexican-cooking-school.com; from US$115 pp

Marilau Traditional Mexican Cooking School offers Mexican cooking classes to groups of up to 9 people, all taught by the knowledgeable Marilau herself. Prospective students can select the dishes they'd like to cook from a list of classics, like sopa verde and chicken in pipián (green pumpkin-seed sauce), or choose one of Marilau's classic three-course menus. She also offers detailed multiday workshops on salsas, tamales, and moles.

San Miguel de Allende Countryside
Gaby Green
tel. 415/119-2195; www.chefgabygreen.com; gaby@chefgabygreen.com; from US$150 pp

Gaby Green is a talented chef with a deep knowledge of Mexican culinary traditions. She offers cooking classes and market tours, which can be tailored to a student's interest—whether that's making tortillas by hand or creating elaborate Mexican sauces and salsas. She gives classes in her beautiful home kitchen in La Mesa de Malanquín, to topnotch reviews from participants, in addition to organizing market and winery tours that introduce visitors to regional produce and flavors. Workshop costs include all ingredients and transportation to and from the kitchen, which is located west of San Miguel de Allende.

WRITING
San Miguel Literary Sala
tel. 415/185-2225; http://sanmiguelliterarysala.org

Many published and aspiring English-language writers live in San Miguel de Allende. The well-organized San Miguel Literary Sala, the organization behind February's blockbuster San Miguel Writers Conference, offers literary readings, book discussion groups, and writing workshops throughout the year. Following the pandemic shutdown, many of their workshops moved online and continue to be offered remotely. They also run a free poetry and prose café at Murmullo Café in the Instituto Allende; check their website or Facebook page for dates and lineup of artists.

VOLUNTEERING

Numerous nonprofit organizations and an active expatriate community make San Miguel de Allende an excellent place to get involved. Foreigners routinely volunteer for these organizations (or host benefits to support them); here's a short list of the many opportunities for big-hearted visitors and residents.

Centro Histórico
Sociedad Protectora de Animales
Los Pinos 7, Col. Lindavista; tel. 415/152-6124; www.spasanmiguel.org; volunteer hours 11am-2pm Mon.-Sat.

The Sociedad Protectora de Animales operates a no-kill shelter for strays as well as an animal clinic with low-cost veterinary care, sterilizations, and vaccinations. Most visibly, SPA has a very active animal adoption program, placing hundreds of stray dogs and cats in family homes each year. Walking through the town square, you often see SPA members showing off the newest dogs available for adoption. SPA is always looking for animal-loving volunteers to help with fundraising, animal training, dog walking, or simply socializing with resident dogs and cats. Prospective volunteers should contact info@spasanmiguel.org; interviews are required. You can also help SPA by adopting a pet, which SPA will help you get the paperwork to take home; the animals seeking homes are listed on their website.

Biblioteca de San Miguel de Allende

Insurgentes 25; tel. 415/152-0293; http://bibliotecasma.com; 10am-7pm Mon.-Fri., 10am-2pm Sat.

Founded in 1958, the nonprofit Biblioteca de San Miguel de Allende uses volunteers to help with their numerous education and literacy programs that serve San Miguel youth and families. Positions could range from a newsletter author to an English tutor to fundraising support.

Northeast of the Centro
CASA

Santa Julia 15, Col. Santa Julia; tel. 415/154-6090, U.S. tel. 212/234-7940; https://casa.org.mx

Centro Para Adolecentes de San Miguel de Allende, or CASA, is a multifaceted nonprofit organization that provides health services, social services, and health education to rural families. In 1994 CASA also opened a maternity hospital, where thousands of babies have been delivered. Two years later,

this unique organization officially opened the first accredited school of midwifery in Mexico, which has since trained midwives from dozens of Mexican states and foreign countries. CASA generally looks for volunteers with a background in psychology or health.

Atascadero
Patronato Pro Niños

Av. Reforma 75C, Fracc. Ignacio Ramírez; tel. 415/152-7796; www.patronatoproninos.org; 9am-4pm Mon.-Fri.

Patronato Pro Niños is a nonprofit organization that provides free or very low-cost medical care to children in San Miguel de Allende and environs, in addition to free or very low-cost dental care in their four mobile dental vans, which visit small towns throughout the area. This highly respected and long-running organization is always looking for volunteers who can work in the office, support caregivers in the field, and lead walking tours of the centro histórico (a part of their fundraising programs), as well as experienced doctors and dentists to work in the field.

Food

Eating out is a big part of life in San Miguel de Allende. There is a constant buzz about new restaurants opening (or old ones closing) and a spirited debate about the best bites in town. Satisfying all manner of tastes and appetites, San Miguel's streets are peppered with fruit stands, ice cream carts, traditional bakeries, casual eateries, charming bistros, relaxed cafés, and upscale restaurants.

San Miguel has many beautiful sit-down restaurants serving food from all over the world. However, some of the best and most authentic Mexican fare can be found in the little market stalls and taco stands across town. If you are new to Mexico, open-air taco joints can be tougher on the stomach than sit-down restaurants. That said, most of San Miguel de Allende's eateries—even the

most casual—are hygienic and clean, and adventurous eaters will be well rewarded with memorable meals.

CENTRO HISTÓRICO
Tacos and Quick Bites
★ La Colmena

Relox 21; tel. 415/152-1422; 6am-2pm and 3pm-9pm Mon.-Sat., 6am-9pm Sun.; US$1

In operation since 1901, La Colmena is a traditional Mexican bakery just off the main square, known to many as the "blue door bakery." Every day, La Colmena's ovens turn out an astounding variety of traditional pan dulce (sweet bread) as well as empanadas, cookies, cinnamon rolls, and whole-wheat breads. If you haven't tried Mexican breads, conchas (sweet rolls topped with a sugary crust) are

Best Restaurants

the elegant courtyard dining room at The Restaurant

★ **La Colmena:** Pick up a sweet roll, pastry, or cookie at this traditional Mexican bakery, which has been in operation in San Miguel de Allende for more than 100 years (page 88).

★ **Don Taco Tequila:** This cantina-esque restaurant's appealing menu is entirely vegan, with delicious tacos and a list of inventive cocktails, Mexican spirits, and craft beer (page 90).

★ **Tostévere:** Tostadas get the star treatment at this cozy spot, an ideal place to kick off an evening out with creative small plates and craft cocktails (page 91).

★ **Lavanda:** There is often a wait for breakfast at this beloved café, which serves fresh, creative, and beautifully prepared breakfasts, along with outstanding coffee (page 92).

★ **The Restaurant:** With more than a decade in operation, San Miguel's most popular chef-driven restaurant is still one of the best places to eat in town (page 93).

★ **Bocaciega:** Innovative and refreshing Mediterranean flavors make this Greek-inspired restaurant stand out within the San Miguel food scene (page 93).

★ **Raíces:** Delicious traditional Mexican food, prepared and served with creative flair, makes this casual spot one of the best places to eat in San Miguel (page 98).

★ **Dos Búhos:** For a glass of local wine in the shade of old mesquite trees, this low-key, family-friendly winery is the perfect Sunday afternoon destination (page 100).

a classic introduction. When buying bread, pick up a metal tray and a pair of tongs, then pick out breads you want; the bevy of shop assistants will bag and total your purchase at the end. This place is always filled with a crowd of locals and residents, plus (not surprisingly,

with a name that means The Beehive) some sugar-loving bees.

Carnitas Apolo XI

Mesones 42A; tel. 415/154-6252; 12:30pm-8pm Mon.-Sat., 2:30pm-7pm Sun.; US$4

Braised pork tacos, or carnitas, are one of Mexico's most popular dishes, usually eaten for breakfast or lunch. You can try some very tasty carnitas in downtown San Miguel at Carnitas Apolo XI. If you order your tacos surtido, they will be prepared with mixed meat, including everything from snout to ear. If you order maciza instead, your tacos will be made principally with shoulder. For two people, a quarter or half kilo of carnitas is a good amount to share, and the meat is served with warm tortillas, salsa, and garnishes. There are casual tables on the roof of Apolo XI (which overlooks the parroquia), but the place is pretty self-service. Order downstairs before you sit down, then grab a beer from the fridge.

Nieves Las Monjas

esq. Canal y Hernandez Macías; no tel.; 11am-8pm Wed.-Mon.; $2

There are delicious ice cream carts all over town, and one of the best and most popular is on the corner of Hernández Macías and Canal, just down the street from the entrance to Bellas Artes. Here a family of ice cream vendors scoops heaping cones in exotic flavors like rose petal, cheese, guava, mango, walnut, and peppermint. A single serving includes two flavors, favorable to the indecisive. You can order them in a cup, but the handmade sugar cones are almost as sweet and delicious as the ice cream that fills them.

Mexican
Chocolate y Churros San Agustín

San Francisco 21; tel. 415/154-9102; 8am-11pm daily; US$10

The perennially popular Chocolate y Churros San Agustín is well known for its eponymous hot chocolate and fresh churros. From morning until night, this bustling little eatery is filled with folks getting a serious sugar fix, and on busy weekends there is often a wait for a table. In the spirit of pure excess, every hot chocolate includes an order of three sugarcoated churros, made fresh on the premises and still warm when they arrive at your table. On the savory side, the restaurant is also a nice place for breakfast, with a tasty menu of egg dishes, spicy chilaquiles, and sandwiches, plus espresso drinks, beer, wine, and spirits. During San Miguel's chilly winters, this café is a good destination for its cozy atmosphere.

★ Don Taco Tequila

Hernández Macías 83; tel. 415/154-9608; 2pm-9:30pm daily; US$6

You don't have to be a vegetarian to enjoy the flavorful vegan tacos and bar snacks at cozy cantina-esque Don Taco Tequila. Get one stuffed with tempura cauliflower (a perfect stand-in for Baja-style fish taco), soy chorizo, or slow-cooked mushrooms, among other interesting options, and accompany your meal with one of their excellent creative cocktails, like the margarita made with spicy chile and hibiscus. They also have a nice selection of craft beer and Mexican spirits, including unusual liquors like sotol, from the state of Chihuahua. The tiny dining room is unpretentious and comfortable, with affable service and low prices making it a perfect spot for an evening out—though there can be a wait for a table on busy evenings.

La Posadita

Cuna de Allende 13; tel. 415/154-8862; noon-9pm Mon.-Tues. and Thurs., noon-10pm Fri.-Sat., noon-8pm Sun.; US$20

San Miguel de Allende can spoil you with beautiful views, and La Posadita has one of the nicest views in town. From La Posadita's open-air rooftop dining room, you can have lunch beneath the spires of the parroquia, overlooking the sweeping river valley beyond San Miguel. The menu is diverse, with Mexican classics like guacamole and enchiladas as well as more unusual plates like mixiotes (steamed meat in banana leaves) and cochinita pibil (spiced pulled pork). Food is generally decent, if not excessively seasoned (add their delicious salsas if you want some kick), and the kitchen can occasionally get backed up—though you're unlikely to be in a hurry here. The margaritas, including the tasty version made with tamarind, are the best choice on the cocktail menu, although they also have a nice wine selection, including Mexican bottles.

La Doña

San Francisco 32; tel. 415/688-3131; 1pm-10pm Mon.-Wed., 1pm-11pm Thurs.-Sat., 1pm-9pm Sun.; $22

This upscale Mexican restaurant hits the right notes for a special occasion: a memorable setting, gracious service, and a fancy cocktail menu to kick off your meal. Creative Mexican plates make up most of the menu, like flautas stuffed with hibiscus flowers and duck slow-cooked in maguey leaf. Roast cauliflower and chicken in mole negro are two of the restaurant's signature dishes, both nicely prepared. During the daytime, La Doña principally operates in a tranquil open-air dining room on the ground floor of the Hotel Nena; once the sun goes down, the rooftop terrace is the place to go, with views of the parroquía and the surrounding city from every table. On national holidays or long weekends, the restaurant often hosts live DJs or special menus, in addition to providing a fine view of the fireworks over the parroquía. Drop by or check their social media for details on upcoming events.

Tío Lucas Restaurant and Bar

Mesones 103; tel. 415/152-4996; www.restaurantetiolucas.com.mx; noon-midnight daily; US$12

Tío Lucas Restaurant and Bar is a lively Mexican steak house right across the street from the historic Ángela Peralta theater. Starters and salads are good here, but Tío Lucas is best for enthusiastic carnivores. Try one of the Mexican cuts of beef, like arrachera, puntas de filete, or norteña, which are served with beans, rice, and guacamole. Cocktails are also a specialty, and the bar serves powerful margaritas with your choice of tequila. The atmosphere is among the best in town, with a jazz band every night (music starts around 8:30pm), constant crowds, and

Mexican pottery and stamped metal decorations adorning the walls of the open-air dining room.

★ Tostévere

Codo 4; 1pm 9pm Mon.-Wed., 2pm-10pm Thurs.-Sat., 1pm-7pm Sun.; small plates $6-11

It would be easy to walk right past the unassuming entrance to tiny Tostévere—except that every San Miguel local points you straight to it. This small bar and restaurant is everyone's favorite spot for a casual meal and cocktails, and the ideal place to start—or conclude—a night out in San Miguel. The heart of the menu is creative takes on a classic Mexican dish: the tostada. Here these crunchy flatbreads are given star treatment, piled high with ingredients like seared tuna or roasted cauliflower with herbs. Appealing small plates like spring rolls and sweet potato fries round out the menu, with plenty of vegetarian and pescatarian options to choose from. The drinks menu is short but spot-on, featuring craft beer, wine, and takes on classic cocktails in the basil sour, margarita, and aperol spritz; the smoky mezcal is a favorite. The little dining area is charmingly decorated, with exposed rock walls, colorful tile floors, and a big wood bar, but note that seating is limited; reservations are recommended for weekend dinner.

Breakfast and Lunch
La Cabra Iluminada

Hidalgo 13; no tel.; 9am-4pm daily; $9

For a full meal or an afternoon respite, this peaceful vegan bistro should be on your list. With plenty of nice tables within the clean, minimalist café and adjoining outdoor patio, it's a lovely place to pass an hour or two with a book, a perfectly prepared almond-milk latte, and a vegan chocolate babka. But don't overlook the surprisingly ample menu, which includes creative plant-based versions of Mexican classics, like tamales and chilaquiles, as well as café options, like avocado toast, beet salad, and blueberry pancakes with vegan butter. Vegan or not, you'll find it's one of the best breakfast spots in town.

Garambullo Fonda

Animas 48; tel. 415/152-3388; 9am-3:30pm Thurs.-Mon.; $10

With its soaring ceilings, stone floors, and sweet in-house cat asleep on the windowsill, the rustic patio and dining room at Garambullo Fonda is one of those dreamy, romantic spaces that make San Miguel visitors want to stay in town indefinitely. Come to spend the morning with a book or a friend, enjoying the relaxed atmosphere with a coffee and lovely, healthy-feeling meal. Fresh, local ingredients are the base of dishes like avocado toast, poached eggs on polenta, and chilaquiles topped with goat cheese and eggs, and there are plenty of vegetarian and gluten-free options available. Service is kind and unhurried.

★ Lavanda

Loreto 48A; tel. 415/152-1610; http://lavandacafe.com; 8:30am-3pm Mon.-Fri., 8:30am-2:30pm Sat.; US$9

For fresh, lovingly prepared breakfasts and brunches, Lavanda is the perfect place to start the day. Try the clay pot with shaved potatoes, cheese, razor-thin slices of bacon, and a baked egg. Or see how the restaurant's unique egg-poaching technique—which somehow renders the eggs perfectly cooked into little basket-shaped pockets—puts a new twist on classic Mexican dishes like spicy huevos rancheros. The coffee bar is quite possibly the best in town, with expertly prepared espresso drinks and pour-overs; they also serve lavender lemonade, high-quality loose-leaf teas, a delicious "green juice," and unusual fruit-sweetened cold drinks made with the shell of the cacao seed. There can be a hefty wait for breakfast at this local favorite, but once you're seated in the serene multistory space, the experience is unhurried.

Posada Corazón

Aldama 9; tel. 415/152-0182; 8am-noon daily, by reservation only; $15

There's an enchanted feeling to the atmosphere at Posada Corazón. Hidden behind an old rust-colored facade on Aldama street, an expansive tree-shaded garden leads to this lovely mornings-only restaurant and guest house, where wood tables are set for diners in the library and living areas of a rambling 1960s-era home. All breakfasts are set price and include a main plate (fried eggs, tofu scramble, enfrijoladas, among other options), sliced fruit or juice, and coffee, tea, or hot chocolate, as well as access to the buffet table, set daily with local cheese, olives, dried fruits, and bread. There are ample vegan and vegetarian options on the brunch menu, and the food is clean, generously served, and locally sourced—some from right inside Posada Corazón itself. (Peek over the back deck to see the garden and laying hens who likely contributed to your meal!) There is often music during weekend brunch.

Italian and Pizza
Bennu

Jesús 20; https://bennu.mx; 1pm-9:30pm Wed.-Sat., noon-8:30pm Sun.; $16

Since its 2021 opening, Bennu has established a reputation for serving the best artisanal pizza in town. Here all pies are made fresh on organic sourdough crust, and come out of the oven bubbled and crisp. Topped with largely locally sourced ingredients, the short but interesting menu includes options like "las cabras," a pizza topped with butternut squash, pear, balsamic, and fresh and aged goat cheese—though Bennu also serves a mean margarita for pizza purists. There's a petit list of vegetable sides and salads that pair well with pies, and—as pizza of high caliber demands—a well-selected list of local and imported wines and craft beer. Thoroughly romantic, the tiny dining area is tucked into the quiet patio of a historic home, with marble-topped tables and wood chairs surrounded by crumbling walls, swinging birdcages, and leafy plants.

International and Fine Dining
★ The Restaurant

Sollano 16; tel. 415/154-7862; www.
therestaurantsanmiguel.com; noon-11pm Tues.-Sun.;
US$18

When it opened in 2008, the Restaurant had a huge influence on San Miguel de Allende, heralding a new era of gourmet dining in town. Even today, it remains one of the nicest places to eat in town, housed in a gorgeously restored colonial-era mansion with neoclassical and Moorish details. The courtyard seating plays perfect accompaniment to the seasonal, chef-driven menu, which incorporates both Asian and Mexican influences. For a town with generally uninspired wine lists, The Restaurant does well for itself, offering an excellent assortment of Mexican and Latin American glasses and bottles as well as a full bar and specialty cocktails. On Thursday evenings, The Restaurant hosts the Mo-Betta Burger Night, popular with locals looking for a juicy cheeseburger (or salmon burger or veggie burger) and some good company.

Mediterranean
★ Bocaciega

Quebrada 18A; tel. 415/177-7175; 1pm-10pm Mon.-Sat.,
1pm-9pm Sun.; $25

Inspired by Mediterranean flavors, this gem of a restaurant takes dishes that sound familiar and transforms them into something both original and delicious. Here the Greek salad is spiked with grapefruit and basil, hummus is served with a small stack of roast potatoes, lebneh is streaked with a roasted beet puree, and kibbeh is complemented with pistachios and greens. Warm pita, baked in-house, accompanies every meal, along with drinks from the attractive wine and cocktail list, all as carefully considered as the food. Service is attentive and the atmosphere is lovely. With its wood floors, woven textiles, and oversize tasseled lamps, Bocaciega's dining room feels sophisticated, cozy, and peaceful, worlds away from the chugging buses and traffic on busy Quebrada street outside.

Fátima

Hotel Casa Blanca, Juárez 7; tel. 415/688-1438,
415/118-0945; http://casablanca7.com; 8am-11pm daily;
US$16

Located on the second floor of the boutique hotel Casa Blanca 7, this gorgeous terrace restaurant has views of the churrigueresque sandstone facade and towering cupolas of the Iglesia de San Francisco. The setting alone would make a meal at Fátima special, but the Mediterranean-inspired food matches up to its lovely surroundings. Vegetable-forward starters include Mediterranean staples like hummus with fresh-baked pita, green salads, and roast eggplant, which complement more robust mains like grilled octopus and pork shank. Signature cocktails, a nice wine list, live music events, and an often-buzzing evening atmosphere makes Fátima a recommended spot for a special dinner.

French
Cumpanio

Correo 29; tel. 415/152-2327; www.cumpanio.com;
8am-9pm Mon.-Sat., 8am-8pm Sun.; US$16

On the busy corner of Correo and Recreo, Cumpanio is a stylish bakery, bistro, and bar. It's a good choice for breakfast, when you can accompany your goat-cheese omelet or eggs in salsa verde with a cinnamon roll, made in the on-site bakery, and top-notch cappuccino. (If you need convincing, peek into the kitchen from large windows on Recreo to see the bakers at work.) At lunch or dinner, the appealing pan-European menu includes potato-leek soup, asparagus salad, grilled salmon, and a selection of pizzas. Cumpanio is also an excellent choice if you're looking for a more low-key spot for a cocktail, with a signature drink menu that includes a sake spritz and an Italian take on the classic Mexican margarita.

Salvajes Brasserie

Hidalgo 92; tel. 55/4177-2709; https://salvajesbrasserie.
com; 1pm-10pm Tues.-Sat., 10am-7pm Sun.; $18

A charming French bistro with a decidedly Mexican sense of hospitality, Salvajes Brasserie serves lovely takes on classics, like

onion soup, coq au vin, and ratatouille, offset by a few more unusual options, notably the much beloved French toast with buttered lobster. If you're dropping in for lunch during the week, ask about the prix fixe special (Tues.-Fri. 1pm-4pm; US$20, US$23 with wine pairing), which includes a soup or appetizer, main course, and dessert, and always includes a vegetarian option. House cocktails, though delicious, lean less French, with mezcal and tequila taking center stage in many of the restaurant's concoctions—though of course there are red and white wines, local and imported, for a more thoroughly European-style meal. At press time, chef Jorge Avendaño was reopening his beloved country restaurant Bastardos, previously in Atotonilco, in a space near Salvajes; foodies, stay tuned.

Coffee Shops and Bakeries
Ki'bok
Diez de Sollano 25; no tel.; 8am-6pm daily; US$3
Like the Tulum original, Ki'bok San Miguel is a stylish, laid-back spot for top-notch coffee and a bohemian-chic ambience. Take a seat on a wood bench in the eclectically decorated downstairs café, or head up to the rooftop terrace on a sunny day to sip a pour-over coffee or a perfectly pulled espresso, made with organic beans from Chiapas. Drinks are beautifully served on natural wood boards and with fabric napkins beside them. Though many come just for drinks and Wi-Fi, Ki'bok also has a small menu with quinoa bowls, fruit, breads, and cakes to accompany your drink.

Petit Four
Jesús 2-B; tel. 415/154-4010; www.elpetitfour.com; 10am-6pm Tues.-Sun.; US$5
Petit Four is one of the best places to satisfy a sweet tooth in San Miguel de Allende. This lovely French-style bakery has a glass display case that features a mouthwatering daily selection of perfectly prepared confections,

like delicate vanilla-fig cake, tangy lemon meringue pie, chocolate-covered fruit, assorted truffles, decadent brownies, crisp biscotti, and individual fruit tarts. They also serve espresso drinks as well as savory baguette sandwiches, croissants, and danishes. From the tiny dining room, a large glass window lets you peek into the goings-on in Petit Four's kitchen, where white-clad pastry chefs prepare cakes and truffles right before your eyes.

Markets and Specialty Foods
The Bajío is a major agricultural region, producing a bounty of fruits and vegetables, meats, and dairy. Here farmers markets brim with an abundance of beautiful produce year-round. In addition, the organic and local food movement has taken hold in San Miguel, and numerous specialty shops are now selling handmade and local products, from organic milk to sourdough bread. San Miguel's discerning consumers have also created a large market for specialty products, like sushi rice and Greek olives. You can find everything you need for a fancy dinner party or healthy lunch in San Miguel's lovely food shops.

Bonanza
Mesones 43; tel. 415/152-1260; 8am-7pm Mon.-Sat., 8am-5pm Sun.
If you are planning to do a little cooking during your stay, centrally located Bonanza is a small but well-stocked grocery store, where you can stock up on kitchen basics. This little grocery sells a range of dry goods, like rice, beans, pasta, nuts, raisins, bread, and crackers, as well as milk, yogurt, and cheeses. They also carry a selection of pricey luxury items, like jars of pesto, oyster sauce, dried sea vegetables, canned salmon, coconut milk, and tahini.

Mercado Ignacio Ramírez
Colegio s/n; 8am-7pm daily; vendor hours vary
Behind the Iglesia de Nuestra Señora de la Salud and the Plaza Cívica, the Mercado Ignacio Ramírez is a small covered market selling an abundance of fresh fruits,

---

1: fresh produce, tortillas, and cheese in the Mercado Ignacio Ramírez 2: Garambullo Fonda 3: Cumpanio, a stylish bistro and bakery right off San Miguel's main square 4: Deli Q

vegetables, meat, chicken, and fresh flowers, as well as dry goods like chile peppers, rice, and beans. There is plenty of nice produce at this pretty urban market, and some of the vendors will offer samples to convince you of their fruit's quality. Behind the fruit and flower sellers are several food counters, where you can get a torta, a fresh juice, or a full meal for just a few dollars. Just behind the market (at the entrance to the Mercado de Artesanía), there are more casual stands selling handmade tortillas, farm-style cheese, roasted corn, steamed fresh garbanzos, and prickly pear.

Cava Sautto

Codo 36; tel. 415/178-2627; www.cavasautto.com; 10am-8pm Mon.-Thurs., 10am-9pm Fri.-Sat., 11am-5pm Sun.

It's an exciting moment in the Mexican wine industry, as production and accolades are steadily growing for winemakers in the states of Guanajuato, Querétaro, Aguascalientes, Coahuila, and Baja California Norte. Even so, it can be hard to find Mexican bottles in restaurants or wine shops, beyond the most famous names. That's why it's such a delight to browse the excellent selection of bottles at Cava Sautto, which includes Mexican labels from across the country, including many bottles from winemakers like Cuna de Tierra near San Miguel de Allende. In addition to wine, Cava Sautto stocks spirits from across the world, with a fine selection of tequila and mezcal, as well as ultra high-end liquors.

GUADALUPE AND AURORA
Breakfast and Lunch
Deli Q

Margarito Ledesma 6A, Col. Guadalupe; tel. 415/180-8053; $8

This cheerful worker-owned deli and sandwich shop in the Guadalupe neighborhood is the place to go if you need provisions for a country picnic—or, like many locals, you want to pick up a quick and delicious meal, either to eat in or take home. The menu

emphasizes nutritious and locally sourced ingredients, featuring made-to-order sandwiches, burritos, and a changing selection of salads and sides in the deli case, like peanut-kale salad, falafel, German potato salad, and Asian chicken salad. Veggie burgers, quiche, and carrot cake are some of the standouts, though you really can't go wrong here. Deli Q also sells cookies to go, jarred salsas and nuts, and a wide variety of delicious frozen dishes—like lasagna, soup, and curries—to reheat at home. The sweet and colorfully painted space is amiably attended by the deli's associates.

Mexican
Hierba Santa

Calzada de la Aurora 48A, Col. Guadalupe; tel. 415/104-8361; 9am-5:30pm Mon., Tues.-Sat., 10am-2:30pm Sun.; $10

This tucked-away restaurant is set in a tree-shaded patio in the Colonia Guadalupe, at the end of a narrow alley, not far from the Fábrica La Aurora. Open for breakfast and lunch, it's a small but heartfelt operation, with a menu inspired by the flavors of Mexico's southern states, like Yucatán, Oaxaca, Puebla, and Guerrero. On the well-priced menu, you'll find a range of breakfast and lunch options, like enfrijoladas, a pork-belly tamal with green mole, and panuchos (round corn flatbread topped with achiote-seasoned slow-cooked pork). The popular pescadillas, a deep-fried cheese-and-fish quesadilla, is typical to Acapulco, Guerrero, where the chef-owners are from. Everything is made to order and the service is unhurried, so come here to enjoy a relaxing meal in a lovely, unpretentious atmosphere.

NORTHEAST OF THE CENTRO
Mexican
Tacos Don Felix

Fray Juan de San Miguel 15; tel. 415/154-0505; 1pm-9pm Fri.-Sat., 9am-1pm Sun.; $8

This weekends-only eatery started out as a small taco stand on the Avenida Independencia in 2007. Its friendly service and delicious bites quickly drew crowds from across San Miguel, enough to propel Don Felix into a much larger space around the corner, where the family now operates a full Mexican restaurant in a lovely homelike setting. The ample menu includes traditional dishes like crema de frijol (black bean soup), enchiladas, cuts of meat, and grilled chicken, though you can still get Felix's tacos here, including a sampler platter that combines the restaurant's most popular options, including shrimp, chicken, and huitlacoche (corn fungus). There is beer, wine, aguas frescas, and a full bar too. While the atmosphere is far more formal than it was years ago, Felix's family still offers the great service—and the big smiles—that made their taco stand so popular.

PARQUE JUÁREZ
South American
La Parada

Recreo 94; tel. 415/152-0473; www.laparadasma.com; 1pm-10pm Fri.-Sat.; US$15

A nice spot for lunch on a warm afternoon, the modern open-air dining room at La Parada is something of a surprise, tucked behind the doorway of an old colonial home on the quiet end of Recreo. Settle in the shade beneath a big turquoise umbrella to sample the restaurant's interesting Peruvian menu, which features tasty, fresh ceviche served in a wide variety of creative styles (fish with corn and sweet potato, for example). If you want something more stick-to-your-ribs, there are also South American-style sandwiches, rice plates, and appetizers, many featuring ají, a popular Peruvian chile pepper with a tingly spice. Pair anything with one of La Parada's delicious pisco sours in flavors like cucumber-mint, pineapple-ginger, and orange, made in-house with fresh fruit.

SAN ANTONIO
Tacos and Quick Bites
Tortitlán

Ancha de San Antonio 43; tel. 415/152-8931; 9am-6pm Mon., Wed.-Sat., 10am-6pm Sun.; and Salida a Celaya 18A; tel. 415/152-3376; 10am-6pm daily; US$5

Tortas are warm sandwiches served on a soft roll called a telera, and Tortitlán makes some of the best (and biggest) in town. The surprisingly extensive menu includes a chicken torta with cheese and poblano peppers as well as a vegetarian sandwich with avocado and fresh cheese. Juice and a variety of aguas frescas are made fresh with your order. Many people get their tortas delivered (you'll see Tortitlán's motorcycles whizzing across town midday), though you can also eat in. Both downtown branches of this popular tortería are casual, though the Tortitlán on the Ancha de San Antonio is perhaps a bit nicer for a sit-down meal, with a small dining area where you can watch dozens of tortas being assembled at breakneck speed.

Coffee Shops and Bakeries
Panina

Stirling Dickinson 3; WhatsApp 415/107-6825; www. panina.mx; 8:30am-2:30pm Tues.-Sun.; US$5

Fresh-baked bread made with masa madre (sourdough) is the heart and soul of this excellent bakery and coffee shop, which stocks its shelves with a range of delicious loaves every day, in addition to offering a small menu of breakfast items throughout the week. Breakfasters will be happily sated with a latte and a house-baked berry scone, but there are more robust options on the short but appealing menu, including fresh-baked bagels topped with avocado and a fried egg or a hefty grilled-cheese sandwich with cheddar and apples. It's a low-key yet attractive spot, with a big wooden coffee bar and a few dining tables inside the airy, modern space, and a few more café tables on the patio. For coffee and loaves to go, there's a takeaway window around the side of the kitchen.

Mexican
Cha Cha Cha

28 de Abril 37, Col. San Antonio; 11am-7pm Wed.-Sat.; $8

Amid the spate of pandemic-era closings in San Miguel de Allende, it was a lovely surprise when Mexican restaurant Cha Cha Cha reopened in the summer of 2023, more than a decade after it shuttered. Tucked inside a family home in the residential San Antonio neighborhood, Cha Cha Cha's outdoor dining room is filled with plants and brightly colored tablecloths. The short, reasonably priced menu features homestyle versions of beloved dishes like chicken flautas, chicken in mole negro, and chiles rellenos (cheese-stuffed poblano peppers) served with a side of rice and beans. Accompany your meal with an agua de tamarindo (tamarind water) and finish it off with a big slab of flan, and you'll certainly leave sated, with a feeling akin to having lunched in a friend's home.

★ Raíces

Salida a Celaya s/n (across the street from Mobil gas station); tel. 415/121-8532; 9am-5pm Mon. and Wed.-Sat., 9am-3pm Sun.; $8

You can tell that the food is prepared with love at Raíces, a wonderful breakfast-and-lunch spot right on the busy Salida a Celaya, a short walk (and even shorter taxi ride) from the centro histórico. There's often a crowd in the low-key outdoor dining room, where chef Vanessa Romero gives a creative twist to classic Mexican dishes—like arrachera (flank steak) served with enchiladas in chile morita (a smoked dried chile) or scrambled eggs with Sinaloan chorizo—without straying too far from the authentic flavors that inspire her food. Handmade tortillas and delicious drinks, like agua de aguacate (avocado water) and iced café de olla, complete the experience. Prices are reasonable, plates are generously served, and service is unwaveringly amiable. For an unpretentious but delicious meal, this is a top spot for Mexican food in town.

American
Pork Belly

Stirling Dickinson 10; tel. 415/100-6132; https://porkbellysma.com; noon-8pm Tues.-Sun.; $14

One reason to visit this casually cool restaurant is the eponymous pork belly, which you can order in tacos, in a sandwich, or aside a serving of guacamole. But you might, with good reason, be drawn to the bone marrow appetizer. You might go for smoked octopus or brisket tacos. Or maybe you're in the mood for burgers made with sirloin or lamb, accompanied by a pile of shoestring fries. No matter what you choose, nicely prepared, stick-to-your-ribs meals have made Pork Belly a favorite in San Miguel. Considering the chef's obvious affinity and skill with meat, Pork Belly makes a valiant effort to include vegetarians, with some comforting options like mac-and-cheese and creamed spinach on offer. Mixed drinks and craft beer (including excellent beers produced under Pork Belly's own label) hit the spot. Food is plated on metal trays or on cast-iron pans, a no-fuss presentation that matches the restaurant's relaxed urban vibe.

SOUTH OF THE CENTRO
Breakfast and Lunch
Rústica

Salida a Celaya 34; tel. 415/121-1406; 8am-5pm daily; US$6

A pleasant ambience in a plant-filled outdoor patio, genuinely friendly service, accessible prices, and an appealing menu featuring fresh ingredients make Rústica one of the nicest brunch spots in town, and it's deservedly popular with tourists and locals. Come for the tacos filled with fried eggs and mushrooms, fluffy lemon-ricotta pancakes, vegetable-packed vegan breakfast burritos, or chilaquiles verdes, all beautifully served on rustic wood plates. Accompany your food with an espresso drink, herbal tea, a smoothie, or even a glass of wine. At lunch, the vegetable-and fish-centric menu features a ceviche made with mushrooms, a tostada with seared tuna, and beet salad. There's often a wait at breakfast.

Luna de Queso

Josefina Orozco 10; tel. 415/140-2508; café 8am-4pm Mon.-Sat., shop 9am-7pm Mon.-Sat.; $8

This lovely all-day café is one of San Miguel's best. Whether you're stopping in for breakfast, for lunch, or for coffee and a snack, the menu will deliver with a mix of international bistro fare and Mexican staples, from chilaquiles and avocado toast to ciabatta sandwiches and smoked-trout salad. Mix and match it all with coffee, espresso, fresh juices, smoothies, matcha, beer, and local wine, and don't overlook the outstanding cakes, cookies, and breads. In addition to the café, Luna de Queso operates a deli in the same space, which has one of the nicest selections of high-quality cheeses in town, many local, as well as a wonderful takeaway cake shop. In the fall of 2023, Luna de Queso's owner expanded service with the opening of **Celia** (6pm-10:30pm Wed.-Sat.; $10), a creative Mexican cenaduria (dinner restaurant) in the same space, serving dishes like tostada de patitas (pigs' feet) and short-rib flautas. Day or night, the atmosphere is ace, with tables scattered throughout the big-windowed dining rooms and plant-filled patio of a contemporary architect-designed space.

Mexican
Mario's Mariscos Estilo Mazatlán
Salida a Celaya 81; no tel.; 11:30am-7pm daily; $10-15, cash only

In both food and ambience, Mario's Mariscos is inspired by the beach town of Mazatlán, Sinaloa, a place known throughout Mexico for its distinctively delicious approach to fresh seafood. You'll see the Sinaloan influence in signature dishes like aguachile (raw lime-cured shrimp in a spicy green sauce), ceviche, and seafood cocktails, a perfect choice for warm summer days in San Miguel. The raw bar and ceviches are complemented by offerings like octopus in garlic sauce, grilled fish, and quesadillas with marlin. Beer, mezcal, and margaritas round out the short but appropriate bar menu. Located at the far end of the busy Salida a Celaya, the funky open-air dining room has a colorful, beachy vibe.

EAST OF THE CENTRO
Mexican
La Burger
Carretera San Miguel Allende-Dolores Hidalgo, Km 7.3; tel. 415/185-2247; 1pm-7pm daily; US$12

A giant mesquite-fired grill is the centerpiece of the casual country dining room at La Burger, located on the highway to Dolores Hidalgo. Simple tables surround this aromatic pyre, which feels worlds away from the bustle of downtown San Miguel. If you can take your eyes off the kitchen's near-constant activity, there are spacious views of the mesquite-studded grasslands behind the restaurant. The namesake hamburgers are made of very finely ground beef and served very rare, with a side of shoestring potatoes. The restaurant also serves salads, empanadas and other appetizers, and generous juicy steaks (US$20-45) served on simple wooden cutting boards. La Burger is on the highway to Dolores Hidalgo, about 10 minutes west of San Miguel de Allende, and best reached in Uber or taxi.

El Pato Barbacoa y Mixiotes
Calzada de la Estación s/n; tel. 415/148-6393; 8am-2pm Wed.-Sun.; $6

A popular dish in central Mexico and the Bajío, barbacoa is slow-cooked lamb, prepared over a wood fire in an earthen pit, which is then covered with maguey leaves. The result of this unique preparation is a soft, moist, and nicely flavored meat. Small but mighty El Pato, located west of San Miguel de Allende, has developed a fiercely loyal following for their version of this ultra-savory dish, served in tacos and tortas. They also offer mixiotes (steamed lamb in spicy salsa) and deep-fried quesadillas with sesos (brain). The tortillas are handmade, the salsa is spicy, and there's homemade flan for dessert. Located just beside the main bus terminal, the alfresco dining room is extremely casual, with gravel floors and a tin roof, and it is cheerfully attended by El Pato's friendly proprietors.

SAN MIGUEL DE ALLENDE COUNTRYSIDE

For both visitors and locals, it's lovely to spend a few hours over a leisurely meal in the countryside, surrounded by mesquite trees and nopales. There are several lovely places to eat north of San Miguel de Allende, in and around the community of Atotonilco, that are popular with both visitors and locals.

Italian
Mama Mía Campestre

Carretera Santuario Atotonilco, Km 2.1; tel. 415 688 2331; https://campestre.mamamia.com.mx; noon-8pm Thurs.-Sat., 9am-8pm Sun.; $17

Set in a sprawling grove of mesquite trees, this gorgeous country restaurant is an offshoot of San Miguel classic Mama Mía, owned and operated by the same family. Like the original, it's a genial place with Italian-style food, with something on offer for every member of your party: a treehouse and fish pond for the kids to explore, housemade craft beer for the adults, wood-fired meats and sausages for the foodies, and a more adult-feeling bar area for those who didn't come with kids. Sunday brunch is a highlight, with a buffet of Mexican-style dishes on offer, but overall the setting trumps food here. Just down the road, Mama Mía's 40-hectare (100-acre) orchard and farm, **Huerto Rancho Luna** (https://huerto.rancholuna.mx), is where the restaurant grows some of the organic vegetables it serves, and visitors can arrange for a tour of the farm on foot or horseback. You can ask for more info at the restaurant's gift shop, which also sells some of the farm's fresh herbs and produce, as well as crafts, T-shirts, and other gifts. Located in the municipality of Atotonilco, Mama Mía Campestre is about 15-20 minutes north of downtown San Miguel by taxi.

★ Dos Búhos

Carretera San Miguel-Querétaro, Km 6; WhatsApp 415/124-7583; www.dosbuhos.com; 11am-5pm Wed.-Thurs., 11am-6pm Fri.-Sat., 11am-6pm Sun.; US$20

The beautiful family-run winery and vineyards at Dos Búhos feel delightfully relaxed and unpretentious—yet this small producer makes some of the best wine in the region, from tempranillo and cabernet sauvignon to more contemporary options like orange wine and a delicious pet-nat moscato. Dos Búhos sources grapes from their own vineyards, and tastings include four pours and a winery tour (US$30 pp)—and, unlike many other local wineries, children are welcome to join their parents for US$6. You can also try their wines at the lovely on-site restaurant, where wood-fired pizzas and local cheese-and-charcuterie plates are served under old mesquite trees. The winery also hosts an artist residency program, frequent live music, and other special events throughout the year, so follow them on

outdoor dining at Dos Búhos

social to get the scoop on what's coming up. To reach Dos Búhos, look for the sign about 3 km (1.8 mi) east of San Miguel and (carefully) turn left off the highway. Reservations are recommended via the winery's website; use WhatsApp for same-day appointments or reservations.

Markets
Mercado de Martes
Plaza Municipal; no tel.; 8am-5pm Tues.

A weekly open-air market, casually referred to as the Mercado de Martes (Tuesday Market), descends upon San Miguel's upper municipal plaza once a week. You can find almost anything you're looking for at this huge marketplace, whether it's blender parts, new Converse sneakers, drill bits, or a birdcage. For food shopping, this is the best deal in town. Fruits and vegetables in season often come at rock-bottom prices. There are also plenty of little places where you can grab a bite to eat, though strong stomachs are best for those who want to dig into the delicious green chorizo tacos or deep-fried fish plates. Come prepared for dust and bustle, and bring a shopping bag if you plan to buy. Located on the plains above town, the market is too far to reach comfortably by foot from downtown, but a taxi will get you there in five minutes.

Bars and Nightlife

For most visitors and residents, evenings are best enjoyed in the company of friends, kicking back with a book, or lingering over a good meal. During the week, nightlife is usually limited to hotel bars and a few old standbys, where locals convene for drinks and conversation. Weekends are much livelier, when large crowds of tourists or day-trippers arrive from Mexico City, Querétaro, Monterrey, and beyond. On Friday and Saturday nights, San Miguel's bars extend their hours, and a good party can be found throughout the centro histórico. Though not a major city, San Miguel offers just enough style to feel cosmopolitan and just enough folklore to feel like Mexico.

CENTRO HISTÓRICO
Cantinas
El Manantial
Barranca 78; tel. 415/110-0007; 1pm-midnight Tues.-Sat., noon-midnight Sun.; drinks from $5, no cover

El Manantial is one of San Miguel de Allende's oldest cantinas and among the most pleasant places in town to tip back a drink in a low-key, historic setting. The lovely old building has swinging doors, thick walls, and high wood-beamed ceilings, a distinctly old-fashioned Mexican aesthetic that makes a perfect backdrop to a shot of mezcal or a margarita. Visitors and locals flock here for inexpensive drinks, jovial company, live DJs, and the delicious menu of fish tacos, tostadas, and other seafood-centric small plates. Just a block from San Miguel's central square, **La Hija del Manantial** (Correo 14; tel. 415/688-5022; 1pm-midnight Mon.-Sat., 1pm-8pm Sun.) is another atmospheric cantina by the same team. With its hanging lamps and mirrored bar, it has a more contemporary feel, but also specializes in seafood small plates to accompany your drinks. There's often live music at La Hija on the weekends.

El Gato Negro
Mesones 12; no tel.; 1pm-11pm Wed.-Sat., 2pm-9pm Sun.-Tues.; drinks from US$2, no cover

For a different cantina experience, El Gato Negro is an old multistory watering hole with some of the cheapest drinks downtown. Push through the swinging wooden doors and into the small bar, where locals have been gathering for decades. Those in the know take their beers up to the teensy rooftop terrace, where a few plastic chairs overlook the historic sandstone towers of San Miguel de Allende. Don't expect much in amenities, but it's a top-dollar view at a discount price.

La Cucaracha

Zacateros 22; tel. 415/152-0196; 8pm-2am daily; cover $0-2, drinks from $2

Of all the cantinas in San Miguel de Allende, La Cucaracha is the granddaddy of them all, the most fabled spot for a budget drink in town. This incredibly cheap and often rowdy dive bar is a favorite of students, youthful expatriates, old-timers, riffraff, and young ranchers from the towns surrounding San Miguel. Opened in the 1940s, this historic bar was once located in the Casa del Mayorazgo de la Canal on San Miguel's main square—today, a Citibanamex branch. At the current site on Zacateros, the walls are decorated with original artwork from local artists (in the true spirit of San Miguel, La Cucaracha will occasionally host an art exhibition). Bathrooms leave something to be desired (and may house a few of the bar's namesake critters), but beers are among the cheapest in town, and the laid-back vibe will appeal to dive-bar aficionados. Late at night, the atmosphere can be jovial or aggressive. Use your judgment if you stay into the wee hours.

Bars and Lounges

La Azotea

Umarán 6; tel. 415/688-1405; 1pm-midnight daily; cocktails from $8

Right beneath the spires of the parroquia and overlooking the dome of Las Monjas, La Azotea has one of the most attractive views in San Miguel. This chic rooftop is a good choice for a drink in the early evening as the sun sinks behind the distant mountains, bathing the town in a rosy glow. Here you can lounge on a couch, order some small plates (jicama-shrimp tacos are a favorite), and watch as flocks of birds glide across the sky. For more excitement, hang around a little longer. As it gets later, the crowd swells and the music gets louder. On Friday and Saturday nights, La Azotea draws a trendy crowd of locals and weekenders, and there is often a live DJ. You may not see La Azotea from the street; to get there, enter through the Pueblo Viejo restaurant (once you're inside, the host will direct you to the bar) and take the stairs or elevator to the top floor.

The Bar at the R

Sollano 15; tel. 415/154-7862; https:// therestaurantsanmiguel.com; Thurs.-Sat. 6pm-11pm; cover US$0-20, drinks from US$10, food US$6-20

Tucked inside The Restaurant—one of San Miguel's best (you guessed it) restaurants—this vinyl bar has a stylish look and a fancy sound system. As you'd expect from the team behind The Restaurant, the mixed drinks and the Japanese-inspired dinner menu are top notch, with offerings like spicy tuna rolls, tempura green beans, and teriyaki chicken rice bowls. Live DJs are often excellent, and depending on who's spinning, there may or may not be a cover. Likewise, reservations (available at The Restaurant's website or the bar's Instagram) are recommended when special events or popular artists are booked.

Bekeb

Mesones 14; tel. 415/688-1355; www.bekebsma.com; cocktails $15-20

Rooftop cocktails and a view of the sunset are a San Miguel tradition. Bekeb takes this beloved combo to the next level with a cocktail menu that's unlike anything you've seen before. Here drinks are artisanal, innovative, and made with high-quality and largely local ingredients. Notably, the menu draws on traditional Mexican and pre-Hispanic flavors in drinks like the Pólen, which includes gin, bee pollen, and fermented honey, or the Tepache, created with fermented pineapple and racilla, an agave spirit from western Jalisco. Even the glassware is unique. To get there, enter through the boutique hotel Casa Hoyos; stairs to the rooftop are to the left of the reception desk.

Berlin

Umarán 19; tel. 415/154-9432; 4pm-11pm Mon.-Sat.; drinks from $5, no cover

Top Spots for Sunset

sunset from El Mirador

During the winter and early spring, the sky turns vibrant pink as the sun sets over the Sierra de Guanajuato. A rosy glow blankets the city as the church bells clang and birds streak home against a darkening sky. It's a romantic, moving spectacle from any spot in the city, but if you want to truly experience a San Miguel de Allende sunset, here are the best views in town.

THE SWEEPING VIEW

Everyone's favorite spot for sundown, the Rosewood hotel's open-air rooftop lounge, **Luna Rooftop Tapas Bar,** has a spectacular panoramic view of the city. This spot gets extra points for being one of the only rooftops in San Miguel de Allende that has an elevator and is fully wheelchair-accessible (page 105).

TO THE DOMES OF LAS MONJAS

The bar tables along the balcony at **La Azotea** have a prime view of the dome of Las Monjas, which is illuminated with amber floodlights at sundown. Once the stars come out, though, the party gets started at this popular nightspot (page 102).

THE LOCAL FAVORITE

With lovely views of the parroquia and the many rooftops of San Miguel, **La Posadita** is a relaxed spot for dinner and drinks (page 90).

SIMPLE PLEASURES

No tamarind margaritas or tapas plates here, but locals know there are lovely views from the rooftop of old-time, no-nonsense cantina **El Gato Negro** (page 101).

JUST THE VIEW, PLEASE

Take a taxi or huff up the steep but ultra-charming alleyway Bajada del Chorro to get to **El Mirador,** an outlook on the Salida a Querétaro with a perfect view of downtown San Miguel (page 52).

Just a block from the main plaza, Berlin is a small bar and restaurant that serves well-prepared German and continental food, like grilled chicken and savory crepes, as well as oft-praised hamburgers (dinner is served till closing). While the restaurant has loyal patrons, the bar is the true locus of this convivial joint. Any evening at Berlin, you're likely to find a crowd of graying expatriates nursing inexpensive cocktails and chatting with the waitstaff. You can do like the locals and order dinner or appetizers at the bar while eavesdropping on the night's voluble conversations—if you can snag one of the coveted bar stools.

Xoler

Insurgentes 60; 1pm-midnight Tues.-Sat.; small plates $12, drinks $12

With its flourishing dining and wine scene, San Miguel needs a bar with a thoughtful and locally focused drinks menu. Enter Xoler, a small yet stylish spot, right across the street from the Biblioteca Pública, where the wine list includes a good selection of local labels and natural wines, in addition to craft beer and signature cocktails. If you come with an appetite, there are tapas and other wine-friendly plates (olives, charcuterie, burrata, pasta, steak frites) to accompany your drink. With its exposed rock walls and cozy wood tables, Xoler has a relaxed yet mature feel—a place to sip, not party—even though the space often fills to standing-room-only in the evenings. On that note, make a reservation if you want a table on the weekends.

Pulquerías
Pulquería La Otomí

Antonio Villanueva 10A, Colonia San Rafael; tel. 415/151-0584; no cover, drinks from US$3

Just outside the centro in the residential San Rafael neighborhood, this funky locals' favorite is the place to go when you want to share a drink with friends—and maybe make some new ones. It's the type of convivial joint that was once more common in San Miguel de Allende, and longtime locals appreciate its unpretentious ambience, good vibes, and fresh pulque. A specialty of central Mexico, pulque is a lightly fizzy drink with pre-Columbian origins, made from the fermented sap of the maguey cactus; it is traditionally served natural or in fruit-spiked curados. Pulque is the house

Pulquería La Otomí

drink, but La Otomí also serves beer and mezcal, as well as inexpensive bar snacks like tacos and tlayudas (Oaxacan-style corn flatbreads). There's often live music or DJs in the evening.

Tasting Experiences
Obsidian Bar by Casa Dragones
Recreo 16; https://casadragones.com.mx; by reservation only, US$100-175 per person

In 2023 premium tequila brand Casa Dragones opened the Obsidian Bar inside La Casa Dragones, a 17th-century mansion owned by the company on the street Recreo. The historic house, which was lavishly renovated in a contemporary style, features a beautiful bar made of polished obsidian collected from the earth at the brand's agave farms. The bar opens for small group tequila tasting experiences, by reservation only, each led by a brand educator who can talk about the different processes and flavor profiles in the tequilas that Casa Dragones produces. It's a unique, memorable experience in a one-of-a-kind setting. Advance reservations, which can be made on the Casa Dragones website, are required.

The Room
Hernández Macías 76; tel. 415/180-6725; www.theroomsma.com; 9pm-midnight Tues., 8pm-1am Wed.-Sat.; US$10, tasting flights from US$50

The beautiful blue barroom might first attract you to this tiny mezcalería, but the reason to stay is the excellent selection of mezcal, which The Room sources directly from small-batch producers across Mexico. Come here to learn more about this native Mexican spirit and its varieties with a tasting flight of four or five pours, led by the knowledgeable bar staff, who will also discuss the history and methods of producing mezcal. You can also drop in for a drink; the bar's specialty is classic cocktails made with mezcal, like the "mezhatten," a take on the Manhattan with mezcal in addition to whisky. Advance reservations recommended for tasting experiences.

San Mezcal
Recreo 88; WhatsApp 415/121-1422; 1pm-10pm Mon., Wed., 1pm-11pm Thurs.-Sun.; no cover, food US$10, drinks US$10

Mezcal is the patron saint of this happening bar, where the namesake spirit is exuberantly represented in an array of bottles that goes far beyond the basics, from solid economical choices to hard-to-find producers. There are many ways to enjoy mezcal here: in a shot, in a tasting flight, or in one of the bar's signature cocktails, like the beloved mezcal mule. Or you can take the opportunity to try a lesser-known Mexican spirit, like raicilla or sotol, which the bar also stocks. If you need some direction, the bartenders and waitstaff can help you choose a drink. Despite the emphasis on Mexican spirits on the drinks menu, food is a fusion of Asian and European flavors, served in small plates; the fried chicken sandwich and the tofu with kimchi are go-tos. Located on the quiet end of the street Recreo, San Mezcal is often surprisingly lively in the evenings, with loud tunes and an upbeat vibe.

Luna Rooftop Tapas Bar
Nemesio Diez 11; tel. 415/152-9700; www.rosewoodhotels.com; Mon.-Thurs. 2pm-11pm, Fri.-Sun. 1pm-11pm

For dining, drinking, and taking dozens and dozens of photos, Luna Rooftop Tapas Bar, an upscale lounge on the top floor of the massive Rosewood Hotel, attracts both tourists and locals with an international style that wasn't common in San Miguel until recently. The decor is minimal, but given the spectacular views of San Miguel—beautiful anytime, but especially dramatic at sunset, when the town is often bathed in a rosy light—the food and drinks off the chef-driven menu are far better than they need to be. Try the refreshing cucumber-and-mezcal cocktail rimmed with chile salt and a flavorful plate of tuna-ceviche tostadas.

Accommodations

There is a wide range of accommodations in San Miguel de Allende, with something to fit every style and budget. Hotels in every price range encourage you to enjoy the town's laid-back atmosphere with lovely gardens and comfortable common spaces. Some of San Miguel's beautiful boutique hotels are a destination in and of themselves.

Every bed-and-breakfast, posada, or hotel has its own individual character. For romantic travelers, San Miguel has its share of dark and creaky ex-haciendas, while modernists can sleep in sleek accommodations with smartphone docks and flat-screen TVs. Some hotels are decorated with original art and traditional artesanía, while others are decked out with vintage furnishings and hand-painted tile.

San Miguel attracts tourists throughout the year, with the largest number of foreign visitors coming to town between December and April, the traditional high season in central Mexico. National visitors flock to San Miguel year-round but especially on weekends and during Holy Week, Independence Day, and the Christmas holidays, as well as Mexican holidays and three-day weekends. In some cases, hotels may raise their rates 10-15 percent on the weekends (especially Saturdays) and during peak holidays, though many maintain the same rates all year. The prices listed are for a double room during San Miguel's high season, though note that rates fluctuate.

CENTRO HISTÓRICO
Under US$50

In the blocks surrounding the town square are numerous casual hotels that cater to budget travelers. For a low price, you can find a clean and centrally located crash pad, sometimes just a block or two from the jardín. While budget accommodations may not be the most luxurious, some are surprisingly pleasant, boasting roof decks or common courtyards. In almost every budget hotel, some bedrooms are nicer, lighter, or quieter than others. When you check in, ask to see a few different options.

US$50-100
★ Hotel Posada de las Monjas

Canal 37; tel. 415/152-0171; www.delasmonjas.com; US$85

Housed in a former cloister, the historic Hotel Posada de las Monjas is a central and simple place, which is among the town's best values. This sprawling ex-convent sits on lower Canal, ideally located just a block and a half from the main plaza. Guest rooms are minimally decorated—they were once the residence of nuns, after all—but they are comfortable and clean, and the building itself has a wonderful historic ambience. When you arrive, ask to see a few available rooms: some have beautiful views and semiprivate balconies. The nightly price includes a basic breakfast and, for those with wheels, parking.

Casa Luna

Quebrada 117; tel. 415/152-1117, U.S. tel. 210/200-8758; US$80-120

The quirky-creative style at Casa Luna is quintessential San Miguel. Behind the unassuming door of this brick-red house, there is a charming maze of 14 individually decorated guest rooms, each equipped with a private bath and a chimney for cool winter nights. Many rooms also open onto small private balconies. Though this isn't a full-on luxury establishment, the decor is thoughtful and eclectic, with lots of traditional Mexican touches, like embroidered textiles and hand-painted wooden chests. With its central location, unique ambience, and accessible prices, this is a good value spot.

Best Accommodations

★ **Hotel Posada de las Monjas:** The best option for budget travelers, this sprawling stone building was once a convent. Today the nuns' quarters are simple but lovely bedrooms (page 106).

★ **Casa de Los Olivos:** A comfortable, perfectly central, and time-tested boutique hotel option, right in the center of town (page 108).

★ **Casa No Name:** A gorgeously restored colonial-era mansion is the backdrop for this central six-room boutique hotel, which distinguishes itself with its lovely design and warm service (page 108).

★ **Hotel El Palomar:** You will find some of the most beautiful views in San Miguel de Allende from the spacious suites at this boutique hotel, a good pick for small groups or families (page 110).

★ **Hacienda El Santuario:** The romantic atmosphere in this 30-room hotel is classic San Miguel de Allende, with warm service to complement the style (page 110).

★ **Mesón Hidalgo:** Eclectic and creative interior design distinguishes this tiny guest house hotel on central Hidalgo street (page 110).

★ **Casa Carly:** This comfortable and reasonably priced inn, just a few steps away from the Fábrica La Aurora art and design center, has numerous spacious guest houses for rent (page 110).

★ **Hotel Matilda:** An award-winning luxury establishment that brings a contemporary spin to a San Miguel de Allende vacation (page 111).

US$100-200
Casa Calderoni
Callejón del Pueblito 4A; tel. 415/154-6005, U.S. tel. 713/955-6091; www.casacalderoni.com; US$120-155

The paradigm of a successful bed-and-breakfast, Casa Calderoni is a cute, centrally located, and reasonably priced place to stay, with comfortable rooms, friendly proprietors, and delicious made-to-order breakfasts. At Casa Calderoni, each bedroom is named after a famous artist, and the decor subtly reflects its namesake. The Diego Rivera room, for example, is gussied up with colorful textiles and serapes and decorated with several Rivera posters on the wall. No matter which artist you call home, the cozy rooms are all brightly painted and have large beds with fluffy comforters, cute tiled bathrooms with brass sinks, cable TV, and special touches like painted desk lamps and skylights. The hotel's gregarious owners are meticulous about keeping the lodging clean and up-to-date, and the service is friendly and attentive.

Casa de la Cuesta
Cuesta de San José 32; tel. 415/154-4324; www.casadelacuesta.com; US$180

Staying in a bed-and-breakfast becomes an experience itself at Casa de la Cuesta, located on a bustling residential street above the Mercado Ignacio Ramírez. Throughout this colonial home, the owners' passion for traditional Mexican crafts is amply reflected in the decor—clay figurines, ceremonial masks, and ceramic urns artfully complement the cozy atmosphere. Rooms are decorated with traditional crafts and textiles, painted in bright colors, and equipped with king-size beds.

There are views of downtown from many of the shared spaces and some of the guest rooms. A lovely **Mexican mask museum** (www.maskmuseumsma.com; by appointment only; US$6) on-site, which showcases the owners' collection of ceremonial masks, draws visitors who aren't staying at the hotel.

Casa de la Noche

Organos 19; tel. 415/152-0732; U.S. tel. 831/373-8888; www.casadelanoche.com; US$150-180

Charming Casa de la Noche was once a bordello; today it is a guesthouse with sunny rooms of varying size and amenities. Working with the unusual structure of the original house and its many nooks and crannies, the proprietor redesigned all the guest rooms with a delightfully colorful touch. For those on a tighter budget, there are four cute rooms (from US$150) in the main house that can accommodate one person for a very reasonable price. All other rooms are suites, many quite spacious, with lovely tiled kitchens, comfortable sitting areas, and often small patios and pretty views. All rooms are impeccably clean and sunny with private bathrooms.

Over US$200

San Miguel de Allende's luxury hotels are much more than a place to lay your head. Decorated with love and attention, thoughtfully attended, and incredibly comfortable, these places can become destinations themselves.

★ Casa de los Olivos

Correo 30; tel. 415/152-0309; www.casadelosolivos.com; US$250

Situated in a beautifully restored colonial home, Casa de los Olivos is a sweet five-room bed-and-breakfast that unites cushy comforts with the atmosphere of old San Miguel. Spacious and clean bedrooms open onto the shared courtyard, and each is equipped with a white canopy bed with Italian linens, terracotta tile floors, rustic wooden furnishings, and a big bathroom with a whirlpool tub.

Even with all the modern comforts, the high-beamed ceilings, thick walls, and architectural details retain a distinctly old-fashioned Mexican aesthetic. Upstairs, the hotel's tiny bar serves hotel guests in the afternoon and evening; they can take their drinks out to the terrace and relax amid the historic domes and bell towers of San Miguel. Service is friendly, and the location is ideal, just a block and a half from the town square.

★ Casa No Name

Hernández Macías 52; tel. 415/152-1768; http://casanoname.com.mx; US$295-350

When the owners of Casa No Name were restoring the colonial-era mansion in which the hotel is housed, they uncovered a stunning 18th-century religious mural that had been painted in the home's main courtyard. The mural, as well as the historic Moorish arches that surround the patio, has been restored and is among the first of many beautiful details you'll notice at this top-notch boutique hotel. Each of the six guest rooms is romantic yet comfortable, with high ceilings, wood furnishings, and warm decor, including original artwork and antiques specially selected for the room. Upstairs, there is an open-air bar on the roof, with lounge chairs and a cactus garden. Downstairs, the garden in back is an enchanting place to read with a cup of coffee.

Casa 1810

Hidalgo 8; tel. 415/121-3501 or 415/121-3502; www.casa1810.com; US$265

One of the best features of Casa 1810 Hotel Boutique is its location, just a half block from the jardín, on the pedestrian stretch of Hidalgo. Set back from the bustle of the street, the guest rooms, which surround a central atrium, have clay floors, iron lamps, and Mexican-inspired wood furnishings, giving them a luxe but traditional feeling. Unlike many hotels in San Miguel, 1810 is equipped with an elevator for guests on higher floors,

---

1: Hotel Posada de las Monjas **2:** Hotel Matilda has an impressive art collection.

and upscale restaurant Trazo 1810 is on the rooftop terrace, with pretty views of the surrounding city. On the opposite side of the jardín, the same team owns **Casa 1810 Parque** (Codo 3; tel. 415/688-6873; US$200), which has a similar aesthetic to the original location, but a bit more space in the guest rooms.

★ Hotel El Palomar

San Francisco 57; tel. 415/152-0656 or 415/152-0339; http://hotelelpalomar.com.mx; US$300

Perched just above the centro histórico, Hotel El Palomar has 10 remarkably spacious, modern guest rooms, each done up in soft grays and neutral tones, decorated with artwork, and comfortably stocked with bathrobes, air-conditioning, and Wi-Fi. Depending on which suite you book, you might have a fireplace in the sitting room, a private balcony, or, best yet, gorgeous views of San Miguel's rooftops and church spires. For bigger families, there are two enormous and well-appointed double suites, which have two bedrooms and two full baths in each. Even if you aren't staying at the hotel, you can enjoy the spectacular views from the rooftop restaurant, Antonia Bistro.

★ Hacienda El Santuario

Aldama 41; tel. 415/152-1042; www. haciendaelsantuario.com; US$175-450

The old-fashioned Mexican ambience at Hacienda El Santuario is the perfect backdrop to a visit to San Miguel de Allende, and it's ideally located on a quiet stretch of Aldama, the city's most iconic street. No two rooms are alike in this 30-room establishment, but they share a common aesthetic, with tin lamps, woven textiles, traditional crafts, and other well-chosen accents giving each a distinctly Mexican feel. There's a lovely patio umbrella-shaded restaurant, popular for breakfast with the local crowd, and a small brightly painted cantina inhouse, perfect for sipping tequila. From the restaurant to the reservation desk, service here is genuinely kind and helpful.

★ Mesón Hidalgo

Hidalgo 19; tel. 415/196-0536; https://mesonhidalgo. com; US$325-375

Artful, distinctive, and creative interiors distinguish this tiny guest house on Hidalgo. Tucked into an 18th-century manor house, the hotel's three spacious rooms have king-size beds, writing desks, and tubs with rain showers, but otherwise they are unique, decorated with a blend of antique and modern furnishings, art on the walls, and one-of-a-kind accents, like painted wood chests, tin-framed mirrors, and floor lamps. Designer Laura Kirar, who owns the hotel and created the rooms, also operates a boutique on the first floor, where you can get a glimpse of her aesthetic and find a special piece to bring home. Despite the tiny size, Mesón Hidalgo competes with larger hotels for its personalized service.

GUADALUPE AND AURORA
US$50-100
★ Casa Carly

Calzada de la Aurora 48; tel. 415/152-8900; U.S. tel. 202/391-0004; www.casacarlysanmiguel.com; US$80

At Casa Carly, proprietor Carly Cross designed her bed-and-breakfast to feel like the places she likes to stay in when she travels, at the prices she wants to pay. The result is spacious and comfortable guest rooms at surprisingly good rates. Seven large suites (or casitas) surround a pretty courtyard with a stone fountain, leafy trees, and a fishpond. Large, comfortable, and cheerfully decorated, suites are all illuminated by ample windows and fully equipped with comfy beds and a small kitchen. The location on the Calzada de la Aurora is a few steps farther from the town square but right across the street from the Fábrica La Aurora art and design center.

PARQUE JUÁREZ
US$100-200
Casa de Liza

Bajada del Chorro 7; tel. 415/152-0352; www.fhb.com. mx/hotel-casa-liza.html; US$85-150

There may be no more peaceful place in San Miguel than the cascading gardens of the Casa de Liza. Located along the lush Bajada del Chorro, Casa Liza's sloping grounds are filled with giant maguey, flowering fruit trees, winding stone walkways, and the happy motion of attending butterflies. Scattered across the property, each room at this unusual bed-and-breakfast feels like its own private cabin, with sloping wood-beamed ceilings and big comfortable beds. Some are more spacious than others, though each is individually decorated with Mexican crafts, original art, unique furniture, and tile floors. Your best bet is to choose a room with a private patio.

Over US$200
Santa Mónica
Fray José Guadalupe Mojica 22; tel. 415/152-0451; http://santamonica.mx; US$200-385
Few hotels can boast the sheer history of Santa Mónica. Housed in an enchanting 17th-century mansion bordering the Parque Juárez, guest rooms at this beautiful hotel are entirely comfortable yet retain the original charms of the historic setting. Furnishings lean toward the romantic, with white canopy beds, tile floors, and antique accessories. In the courtyard, the hotel's restaurant serves breakfast and lunch. Lush gardens are filled with lime, jacaranda, and palm trees with well-tended lawns and a very small but pretty swimming pool. Suites are more expensive than standard doubles but are incredibly spacious, with sitting areas and in some cases private terraces.

★ Hotel Matilda
Aldama 53; tel. 415/152-1015; www.hotelmatilda.com; US$350-500
In a town where crimson facades and crumbling fountains are the norm, Hotel Matilda is an anomaly. From the moment you enter, the multicolored art installation glowing behind the reception desks affirms this boutique hotel's commitment to the contemporary. Bedrooms are modern, comfortable, and chic; overstuffed furniture and king-size beds play nice accompaniment to modern art

and accessories. Private baths are comfortably minimalist, with marble tubs, big mirrors, luxury toiletries, and stacks of fresh towels. The hotel's popular bar draws a local and tourist crowd, while the ground-floor restaurant Moxi is a fine-dining destination. Since its opening, Matilda has been consistently ranked among the best hotels in Mexico by readers of *Condé Nast Traveler* and *Travel & Leisure*.

ATASCADERO
US$100-200
Rancho Hotel Atascadero
Prol. Santo Domingo s/n; tel. 415/152-0206 or toll-free Mex. tel. 800/466-0000; www.hotelelatascadero.com; US$95-205
On the eastern edge of San Miguel de Allende, the historic Rancho Hotel Atascadero was built on the grounds of a sprawling ex-hacienda originally constructed in the 1880s. The property has changed hands many times, belonging once to a famous bullfighter, Pepe Ortiz, and later to Peruvian scholar (and founder of the Instituto Allende) Felipe Cossío del Pomar. As a hotel, the Rancho Atascadero has been in business for more than 60 years, and it retains the distinct feeling of a mid-20th-century family-style resort. Rooms are simple affairs, with old, oversize colonial furniture, red tile floors, woven Mexican bedspreads, and working chimneys—and a log fire is included in the price during chilly winters. Amid the stone fountains and pomegranate trees of the hotel's extensive gardens, there are a swimming pool, tennis courts, and racquetball for guests.

VACATION RENTALS
For those planning to spend a week or two in San Miguel de Allende, renting a private home can be a nice way to visit the town and have a bit more space and independence than a hotel offers. From simple apartments to lavish mansions, there are literally hundreds of private homes available for short-term rental in San Miguel. Although a private home does not offer all the services of a hotel, many have

cleaning and kitchen staff, gardens or outdoor spaces, and parking.

Unless you will have a set of wheels, look for rentals in central neighborhoods, like the centro histórico, Guadalupe, Aurora, San Antonio, La Aldea, and Guadiana, all of which are walking distance from the city center. Many locals love living in the quiet residential neighborhood of Los Frailes near the Allende reservoir. You may be able to find a good value vacation rental here, but be aware that you'll need a car or taxi to take you to and from the centro.

Airbnb (www.airbnb.mx) arrived in San Miguel de Allende a little later than other online vacation-rental agents, but once it did, it swept the market. Today it seems like most San Miguel homeowners rent out their home when they are out of town, while many others offer shared apartments, private rooms, and dorm-style beds for rent. The cost of renting via Airbnb is higher in San Miguel than in other parts of Mexico—it can be cheaper to stay in a hotel, in some cases, unlike in other tourist destinations. **VRBO** (www.vrbo.com) also lists many San Miguel properties and has been operating here longer than Airbnb. Though you're less likely to find bargain prices on VRBO, there are some really lovely listings.

Though Airbnb and other online home rental services are now major players in San Miguel, many wonderful vacation rentals are still principally available through agents. For every type of rental property, from simple apartments to lavish multi-bedroom haciendas, **Premier San Miguel** (tel. 415/154-9460; www.premiersanmiguel.com) can help you book a place to stay for short- or long-term excursions to San Miguel. The very friendly staff will answer your questions about rental properties, which are listed (along with pictures) on their website, and they can help arrange airport pickup and other tourist services for your stay in San Miguel de Allende.

Information and Services

TOURIST INFORMATION
Tourist Office
Plaza Principal 10; tel. 415/152-0900, U.S. tel. 646/536-7634; https://visitsanmiguel.com; 9am-8pm Mon.-Sat., 10am-5pm Sun.

San Miguel's tourist office, on the main square, can offer you an annotated map of the town and arrange for accommodations or a tour of the city. For those new to the city, there are various flyers in the office advertising tour guides, hotels, restaurants, and other tourist attractions.

Media
The Spanish-language newspaper *El Sol del Bajío* (www.elsoldelbajio.com.mx) is published in Celaya and occasionally covers news and events in San Miguel de Allende. If you can read Spanish, it is a good place to get regional news. The newspaper *am* (www.am.com.mx) is based in the state capital, León, and also covers regional news in Spanish.

For decades, San Miguel locals relied on the weekly publication *Atención San Miguel,* published by La Biblioteca Pública de San Miguel, for information about upcoming art and cultural events, volunteer opportunities, and more. Since the newspaper stopped publishing following the pandemic, the best place to get information on upcoming events in town is on websites like **Local Guide San Miguel** (https://localguide.mx).

The glossy, luxury-centric *Avenue San Miguel* (https://this.com.mx) covers upscale dining, hotels, shops, and real estate, and you can read previous issues online. Online, **Mexico News Daily** (https://mexiconewsdaily.com) is based in San Miguel de Allende.

Travel Agents

Viajes Vertiz

Insurgentes 63A; tel. 415/152-1856; www.viajesvertiz. com; 10am-3pm Mon.-Fri., 10am-2pm Sat.

The only travel agent left standing, Viajes Vertiz can book plane tickets, cruises, and travel packages, with an emphasis on all-inclusive national tours. Viajes Vertiz is also an American Express representative.

Visas and Officialdom

U.S. Consular Agency

Plaza La Luciérnaga, Libramiento José Manuel Zavala No. 165, Locales 4 y 5, Colonia La Luciernaga; toll-free Mex. tel. 800/681-9374, toll-free U.S. tel. 844/528-6611; conagencysanmiguel@state.gov; https:// mx.usembassy.gov; 9am-1pm Mon.-Thurs.

Thanks to the large American expatriate population, there is a U.S. Consular Agency in San Miguel de Allende, which can process passport renewals (including reports of lost or stolen passports) and provide notary services, among other consular functions.

Instituto Nacional de Migración Delegación Guanajuato

Mexican Immigration Services Guanajuato Branch, Calzada de la Estación de FFCC s/n; tel. 415/152-8991; 9am-1pm Mon.-Fri.

To report a missing tourist card, complete paperwork for a resident visa, or perform any other immigration-related paperwork, go to the Instituto Nacional de Migración Delegación Guanajuato, just outside the center of town and almost to the railroad station. With so many foreigners in such a small town, Migración can get a bit backed up. Lines often form before the offices even open, so set aside several hours to account for long wait times, and arrive with a lot of patience.

SERVICES

Internet Access

In San Miguel de Allende, even 17th-century mansions are wired. In most hotels, there is free wireless or a personal computer that guests can share. There are also plenty of places to hop online throughout town, from coffee shops to restaurants. If you didn't bring a web-enabled device, **La Conexión** (Aldama 3; tel. 415/152-1599; www.laconexionsma.com; 9am-5pm Mon.-Sat., 10am-2pm Sun.) has computers in their main office as well as a fax machine, a scanner, and a wireless printer.

Laundry

With decades in business, cheerful **Limpiecito** (Quebrada 63; 8am-10pm) will wash, dry, and fold your clothes for US$1 per kilo of laundry. **Franco Lavanderia** (Cinco de Mayo 29A; tel. 415/154-4495; 9am-7pm Mon.-Fri, 9am-4pm Sat.) offers inexpensive laundry service, with pickup and delivery service available to your home or hotel on weekdays. They will launder your clothes for about US$1.60 per kilo.

Medical and Emergency Services

Dial **911** from any telephone to reach the government-operated emergency response system. Unlike other Red Cross operations worldwide, the amazing, volunteer-run Cruz Roja Mexicana not only participates in disaster relief work and humanitarian aid but also plays an essential role in emergency response throughout the republic. The San Miguel chapter of the **Cruz Roja Mexicana** (Libramiento Manuel Zavala 117; office tel. 415/152-4225; https://cruzrojasma.org.mx) responds to medical emergencies, traffic accidents, and other life-threatening situations. They can be reached at tel. 415/152-1616 in an emergency, though they are also summoned via 911. The Cruz Roja also offers low-cost COVID tests.

For all types of ailments from stomach flu to altitude sickness, many expatriates turn to **Dra. Silvia Azcarate** (Codo 9A; tel. 415/152-1944), a general medicine doctor who speaks Spanish, English, and French. Another good English-speaking general practice doctor, **Dr. Ricardo Gordillo** (Hidalgo 28; tel. 415/154-9976) runs a clinic with labs and a pharmacy just a block from the main square.

The general hospital, **Hospital General Dr. Felipe Dobarganes** (Primero de Mayo 7, Fracc. Ignacio Ramírez; tel. 415/120-4746 or 415/120-4799), has a 24-hour emergency room. Many foreigners prefer to use the larger private hospitals in Querétaro, a 45-minute drive from San Miguel de Allende.

Money

In most cases, the easiest and most efficient way to **change money** is to use ATMs at Mexican banks, which are located throughout the centro histórico. There are teller services with currency exchange and 24-hour ATMs at **Banorte** (San Francisco 17; tel. 415/152-0019; 8:30am-4pm Mon.-Fri., 9am-2pm Sat.). There are **Citibanamex** ATMs on the corner of the **jardín** (Canal 4; toll-free Mex. tel. 800/021-2345; 24 hours daily) and a **Santander** branch (Calle Portal de Guadalupe 4; tel. 415/152-2334; branch 9am-4pm Mon.-Fri.,

ATMs 24 hours) with ATMs on the other side of the plaza.

If you do bring cash, you can change dollars to pesos only at registered exchange houses, like **Intercam** (San Francisco 4, and Plaza La Luciérnaga, Local 53; tel. 415/154-6660; www.intercam.com.mx; 9am-4pm Mon.-Fri., 9am-2pm Sat.). In addition to changing American dollars, Canadian dollars, and euros, Intercam will change travelers checks. For clients in San Miguel de Allende, Intercam can also change American checks to pesos, though you must be registered as an Intercam client to use this service.

Postal Services

The Mexican **post office** is at Correo 16, on the corner of Correo and Corregidora. Inside, MexPost provides certified and expedited mail services through the regular postal system.

Transportation

GETTING THERE
Air

If you are visiting San Miguel from outside Mexico, the two airports closest to San Miguel de Allende are the Del Bajío International Airport (BJX) just outside the city of Silao, Guanajuato, and Querétaro International Airport (QRO), outside the capital city of Querétaro. There are few direct international flights to BJX and QRO. As a result, many travelers find it is just as easy to fly to Mexico City (MEX) then take ground transportation to San Miguel. Many hotels can help arrange transport to San Miguel from any airport, including the capital.

Del Bajío International Airport (BJX)

Carretera Silao-León, Km 5.5, Col. Nuevo México, Silao, Guanajuato

The most popular choice for visitors to San Miguel de Allende, the Del Bajío International

Airport has daily direct flights to and from U.S. cities, including Houston and Oakland, as well as flights to and from Mexico City, Cancún, Tijuana, and Monterrey, among other national destinations. The airport is in Silao, Guanajuato, just outside the city of León, about a 90-minute drive from San Miguel de Allende. From the airport, most people hire a shuttle or car service to drive them to San Miguel de Allende.

Querétaro International Airport (QRO)

Carretera Estatal 200, Querétaro-Tequisquiapan 22500; tel. 442/192-5500; www.aiq.com.mx

Querétaro International Airport, northeast of the city of Querétaro, is about a 90-minute drive from San Miguel de Allende. This airport is much newer, smaller, and less trafficked than its counterpart in León. Routes and rates change frequently, though there are direct flights from Houston, plus connecting service to other international destinations through Mexico City. You can schedule a shuttle pickup from Querétaro or hire a taxi to take you to San Miguel.

Mexico City International Airport (MEX)

Capitan Carlos León s/n, Peñón de Los Baños Venustiano Carranza, Distrito Federal; www.aicm. com.mx

The country's busiest airport is Mexico City International Airport, officially named the Aeropuerto Internacional Benito Juárez, in the capital. There are direct flights from Mexico City to more than 100 cities around the world. Flights to Mexico City can often be considerably less expensive than those to León or Querétaro, both much smaller airports.

From the airport in Mexico City, travelers must arrange for ground transportation to San Miguel de Allende, usually by bus or through one of San Miguel de Allende's transport companies, which can meet you at the airport. **Primera Plus** (toll-free Mex. tel. 477/710-0060; www.primeraplus.com.mx) offers direct bus service every 30-60 minutes from both Terminal 1 and Terminal 2 in the Mexico City airport to Querétaro's main bus station, for about $28; from there, you can take a second-class bus to San Miguel de Allende, or hire a taxi in the bus station to drive you the last 45-minute leg for a flat rate of about US$45.

Alternately, you can take a taxi from the airport to Mexico City's **Terminal Central del Norte** (Eje Central Lázaro Cárdenas 4907, Gustavo A Madero, Magdalena de Las Salinas, Mexico D.F.) and take a direct bus to San Miguel de Allende from there (see below for more information on bus lines and routes). The trip from the Mexico City to San Miguel by bus takes about four to five hours, depending on road conditions and the infamous Mexico City traffic.

Shuttle Service

Many hotels and home rental agents will help you arrange shuttle service from the airport in León or Querétaro to San Miguel de Allende.

BajíoGo

Jesús 11; tel. 415/185-8665; U.S. tel. 202/609-9905; www.bajiogoshuttle.com; US$30 pp

If you are making your own arrangements, highly professional BajíoGo is the go-to private transport service to or from León and Querétaro. They offer comfortable shared shuttles (which seat around nine) for US$30 per person and to or from Mexico City for US$100 per person.

Viajes San Miguel

tel. 415/152-2537; https://viajessanmiguel.com; from US$90

Another long-running shuttle company, Viajes San Miguel also offers private shuttles to and from the airports in Querétaro and León for US$90 for 1-2 passengers, in addition to offering private transport services around the Bajío region.

Bus

A network of comfortable and reasonably priced bus lines connects all of Mexico. There is ample first- and second-class bus service between San Miguel de Allende and Mexico City, as well as direct service to all major cities in the Bajío and Guadalajara. Both first-class and second-class buses are comfortable; the major difference is that second-class buses tend to stop along the roadways to pick up and drop off passengers; therefore, travel on a second-class bus can be slower and more tiring, though also a bit cheaper. First-class buses also have a bathroom onboard, which is convenient on longer trips.

Direct buses operated by ETN and Primera Plus (see below) leave from Mexico City's **Terminal Central del Norte** (Eje Central Lázaro Cárdenas 4907, Gustavo A Madero, Magdalena de Las Salinas, Mexico D.F.) several times a day. The trip from Mexico City to San Miguel de Allende takes about four to five hours. Travelers should also prepare for heavy traffic in the capital, which can affect travel time.

Primera Plus

tel. 477/710-0060; www.primeraplus.com.mx; from US$28

A first-class bus company covering central to northern Mexico, comfortable and efficient Primera Plus offers direct service between the Terminal Central del Norte in Mexico City and the Central de Autobuses in San Miguel de Allende (US$24). Primera Plus also operates direct routes from San Miguel de Allende to Morelia, Guadalajara, Guanajuato, León, and Lagos de Moreno, with connecting service to more distant cities, like Puerto Vallarta and Manzanillo. Comfortable buses include bathrooms, snack packets, and reclining seats, plus televisions projecting noisy Hollywood movies—usually dubbed into Spanish.

If you are arriving on a flight to Mexico City International Airport, Primera Plus also offers direct service from both airport terminals to Querétaro's main bus station (about US$28). From the bus station, you can hop a second-class bus for the remaining 80 km (50 mi) to San Miguel de Allende. Alternatively, Querétaro's city taxis will drive you all the way to San Miguel de Allende from the bus terminal for about US$45. Before you go outside to grab a taxi, you must buy a ticket from the registered taxi stand inside the bus terminal and let them know you are going to San Miguel.

ETN

tel. 415/152-6407, toll-free Mex. tel. 800/800-0386; www.etn.com.mx; from US$36

The poshest bus line in central Mexico, ETN also provides comfy first-class bus service between the capital and San Miguel de Allende (about US$36), with five departures daily. These stylish two-story coaches have reclining seats, bathrooms, snacks, and coffee service. ETN's routes are a bit more limited than Primera Plus, but the company also offers direct service to Guadalajara, León,

Guanajuato, and Querétaro, with connecting service elsewhere.

Servicios Coordinados Flecha Amarilla

tel. 477/710-0060; from US$4

For shorter trips or a more spontaneous agenda, it can be easiest to use second-class bus service, especially when traveling between San Miguel de Allende and Querétaro (about US$5) or San Miguel de Allende and Dolores Hidalgo (about US$4), which leaves almost every half hour. Second-class bus Flecha Amarilla, which is run by the same company that operates Primera Plus, offers service from San Miguel de Allende to cities across the Bajío region. No need to book ahead; it's easiest to simply arrive at the bus terminal and get on the next departing bus. The ticket sellers loudly announce each departure. **Pegaso/Herradura de Plata** (tel. 415/152-0725) is another bus company operating out of San Miguel, with hourly departures to both Querétaro (US$5) and Dolores Hidalgo (US$4) as well.

Car
From the United States

From the southernmost tip of Texas, San Miguel de Allende is just one (very long) day's drive from the U.S.-Mexico border. For decades, many Texan families drove down to Mexico's high plains to escape the summer heat in the Lone Star State. Unfortunately, driving to San Miguel de Allende from the United States has become less safe due to the widespread drug-related violence along Mexico's border and on Highway 57 near San Luis Potosí. If you plan to drive to San Miguel de Allende from the United States, use precaution by traveling **during daylight hours** and **using toll roads,** which tend to be in better condition and less dangerous than free highways.

Most drivers coming to San Miguel de Allende cross the border at the well-trafficked **Laredo/Nuevo Laredo crossing;** this remains the best choice, as opposed to the more southerly crossing at Brownsville/Matamoros. From there, head south toward Monterrey then on toward Matehuala. From Matehuala, take the toll highway south toward San Luis Potosí, passing outside the city, and continue on Highway 57 toward Querétaro. Turn off at the Dr. Mora/San Miguel de Allende exit (just past San Luis de la Paz), heading west until you arrive in San Miguel de Allende. The drive from the border should take about **10-12 hours,** but getting lost in the outskirts of a major city can make the trip much longer. If you are going to do the drive, make sure your phone's GPS will be activated.

From Mexico City

San Miguel de Allende is about 255 km (160 mi) northwest of Mexico City. The drive takes **3-4 hours** on fairly well-maintained toll highways. From Mexico City, exit the city via the Periférico Norte and head north toward Tepotzotlán. After passing through the caseta (tollbooth), continue on Highway 57 north toward Querétaro. Just past San Juan del Río (but before arriving in Querétaro), turn off at San Luis Potosí/San Miguel de Allende Via Corta. You will pass another tollbooth and then cross Highway 57 again; continue straight on the overpass and follow the

winding two-lane road for another 30 minutes until you arrive in San Miguel de Allende.

If you miss the turnoff for the Via Corta, you can continue straight on Highway 57 all the way to Querétaro. Once you pass the city, keep an eye out for the turnoff to San Miguel de Allende on the right-hand side. Cross the overpass and follow the two-lane highway all the way to San Miguel de Allende. This is also the route you take to and from the downtown districts in Querétaro.

GETTING AROUND

If you come to San Miguel, you should be prepared to use your legs. This hilly little town is best for walking, and it will give you quite a workout! When you're worn out, there are several other ways to get around.

Car

With everything just a stone's throw away (and parking somewhat infuriating), it isn't necessary to have a car in downtown San Miguel de Allende. However, a car can make it easier to visit the hot springs or the botanical gardens or to eat at some of the nice restaurants out in the countryside. Generally, drivers are courteous in San Miguel, even if streets feel a bit narrow for those used to suburbs and highways.

Motorcycles can be a nice way to get around town and avoid San Miguel's traffic.

You can rent a car for the day or for the week at **BajíoGo** (Jesús 11; tel. 415/185-8665, U.S. tel. 202/609-9905; www.bajiogoshuttle.com). All you need is a valid driver's license and a credit card. Rates start at US$65 a day and US$400 per week.

The most difficult part about driving in San Miguel is finding a place to park downtown. Fortunately there are several low-cost parking garages, if you get fed up with circling. There are covered spots at **Estacionamiento Hidalgo** (Hidalgo 57) between Callejón del Pueblito and Insurgentes for about US$2/hour. There is also a large lot on Tenerías, right where the small street Jesús dead-ends, which will run you about US$3/hour.

Taxi

Taxicabs constantly circle San Miguel, providing the most convenient and inexpensive way to move around town. Anywhere within the town limits, a taxi ride costs about US$3. Longer trips to outlying neighborhoods, or up the hill to El Charco del Ingenio, will cost a buck or two more, and you can expect to spend US$10-15 to visit a winery or country restaurant outside of town, depending on its distance. Taxis will also take you out to the hot springs for around US$10, and if you ask, most will be happy to return to pick you up at an appointed time. You can also call **Taxis San Miguelito** (tel. 415/152-0124; https://taxisanmiguelito.com) to pick you up.

Ride-Hailing Services

Uber operates in San Miguel de Allende, though the low cost and general abundance of taxis have kept demand for ride-hailing low.

Bus

Inexpensive **city buses** crisscross the city of San Miguel, improbably turning around tight corners, barreling down narrow colonial streets, and filling the air with the sweet aroma of exhaust fumes. For around 50 cents, the city buses will get you anywhere you need to go, though finding a direct route can be a bit of a challenge.

Generally speaking, it is much easier to find your way into the downtown district than to get out to a distant neighborhood. Buses head to the centro histórico from every corner of the city, and they will almost always have a sign in the front window that reads Centro.

Downtown, a major **bus stop** is located on Insurgentes and Pepe Llanos, across the street from the Oratorio San Felipe Neri. Here you can catch a bus to the Independencia, San Rafael, and San Antonio neighborhoods, among others. If you are going to the Tianguis Municipal, you can get a bus on Calle Colegio, to the east of the Plaza Cívica. Buses depart from the Mercado San Juan de Dios for the La Cieneguita neighborhood. Most buses have their destination posted in the front window, and in many cases, the driver's assistant will shout out the bus's destination to the crowd at the bus stop. When in doubt, ask the driver where the bus is going.

Guanajuato

Unique and almost mythical in its beauty,
Guanajuato is a city to stroll in, to observe from courtyard cafés, or to experience from a shady bench in the Jardín de la Unión. The city is best explored on foot; it is a pleasure to get lost in the twisted maze of picturesque streets, where people walk largely uninhibited by traffic—in a pedestrian-friendly innovation, many roads in the centro histórico occupy a circuit of tunnels belowground. Even with fewer automobiles, the streets of Guanajuato are surprisingly busy, crowded with tourists, families, musicians, candy sellers, and fruit stands. The atmosphere is decidedly bustling, bordering on frenetic on the weekends and especially during festivals or religious holidays.

Home to a prestigious public university, Guanajuato is a place of

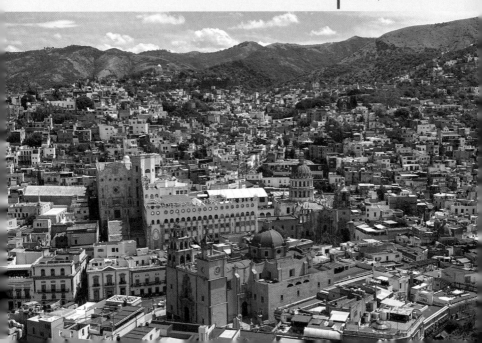

Highlights

Look for ★ to find recommended sights, activities, dining, and lodging.

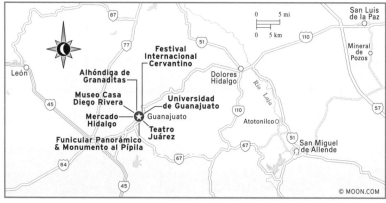

★ **Funicular Panorámico and Monumento al Pípila:** Take a ride on the funicular to visit the monument to independence hero El Pípila and snap some impressive scenic photos of the city below (page 125).

★ **Teatro Juárez:** Marvel at this majestic turn-of-the-20th-century theater, one of Guanajuato's principal performance venues and worth visiting even if you aren't seeing a show (page 127).

★ **Universidad de Guanajuato:** Guanajuato's university campus makes an enormous cultural contribution to the city, architecturally and culturally (page 129).

★ **Museo Casa Diego Rivera:** Learn more about the great Mexican muralist and painter Diego Rivera by visiting his childhood home, now a museum showcasing some of the artist's early work (page 133).

★ **Mercado Hidalgo:** Shop for fresh produce, pick up some traditional Mexican sweets, or grab a snack at this one-of-a-kind municipal market (page 134).

★ **Alhóndiga de Granaditas:** Delve into Guanajuato's history at this wonderful regional museum, housed in a historic public granary that holds a famously grisly place in Mexican history (page 135).

★ **Festival Internacional Cervantino:** Celebrate the arts during Mexico's largest and most prestigious cultural festival, when a massive program of music, theater, and dance performances is presented in Guanajuato's theaters, public plazas, and churches (page 145).

intellectuals and the arts. The university influences local culture in many ways, most noticeably in its youthful spirit, as well as its dusty bookstores, cheap eats, and cool outdoor cafés. For foreign exchange students and backpackers, Guanajuato is an appealing and inexpensive place to spend a few days (or a few months).

Despite the youthful atmosphere, Guanajuato offers a good measure of cultural sophistication, including unique architectural sights and a smattering of international and gourmet restaurants, while the fantastic Festival Internacional Cervantino brings an array of world-class artists to town every year. Like much of the surrounding region, Guanajuato is a town with a tremendous role in Mexican history. A prominent silver-mining settlement in the 17th century, it was the site of one of the most famous battles of the Mexican War of Independence. Guanajuato's many historic sites bring the visitor close to history, yet the vibe is never stuffy or old-fashioned. Here art exhibitions take place in 17th-century cloisters while medieval troubadours play songs for Mexico City weekenders. The mix is appealing, unusual, and refreshing.

PLANNING YOUR TIME

Guanajuato is a popular destination, welcoming national and international tourists, visiting artists, and exchange students throughout the year. Even so, the city doesn't overtly cater to its many visitors. There are a few sporadically staffed tourist information booths, and local police officers stationed around the centro can offer directions or advice. However, visitors to Guanajuato should not expect to find a well-oiled tourist machine at work here. In this low-key city, planning a worthwhile visit is largely up to you.

Most of Guanajuato's interesting museums and architectural sights are located within a few blocks in the centro histórico. If you are visiting Guanajuato on a day trip from San Miguel de Allende, plan to focus on the centro histórico: choose two or three sites to visit, wandering between plazas and coffee shops as you go. Those spending more than **a day or two** in Guanajuato don't need to plan their time too carefully. It is easy to see the major sights downtown in just a few days of exploring. In fact, you'll bump into most of them without even trying!

Especially for those on a budget, Guanajuato can make an excellent **home base** for a longer trip to the region, as it is affordable, authentic, and friendly. Many foreigners come here to study Spanish, while others simply practice their language skills during a longer sojourn. Anyone staying **a week or more** should consider a jaunt outside the centro histórico to see the Templo de San Cayetano in La Valenciana and the Presa de la Olla neighborhood, among other worthwhile destinations.

No matter how long you stay, a good way to experience Guanajuato is through the many cultural offerings and performances (both formal and impromptu) throughout town. There are weekly concerts at the city's theaters, street performers, and callejoneadas (an evening tour through the centro histórico led by a band of medieval-style troubadours), among other options for arts and entertainment. Check the Universidad de Guanajuato's website to see what cultural events are going on around town, or pass by the box office at the Teatro Juárez when you arrive. More informally, many of Guanajuato's bars and restaurants have live music, especially on the weekends. Look for announcements and flyers around town.

ORIENTATION

Navigating Guanajuato's unusual topography can be a challenge for newcomers—and even for sophisticated GPS systems, which are often unable to chart the correct path from

Guanajuato City

To Santa Rosa and
Dolores Hidalgo

CARRETERA A DOLORES HIDALGO

110

Presa de la
Esperanza

Presa
de la
Soledad

CAMINO ANTIGUO
A SANTA ANA

CAMINO ANTIGUO
A SANTA ANA

CAMINO MINERO

LA VALENCIANA

SEE
"LA VALENCIANA"
DETAIL

BARBEROS

PANORÁMICA LA VALENCIANA

SAN
LUISITO

SAN CLEMENTE

TRAMO

PANORÁMICA

SEE
"CENTRO HISTÓRICO"
MAP

UNIVERSIDAD
DE GUANAJUATO

MUSEO CASA
DIEGO RIVERA

TEATRO
JUÁREZ

ALHÓNDIGA
DE GRANADITAS

AV. JUÁREZ

MERCADO
HIDALGO

FUNICULAR
PANORÁMICO &
MONUMENTO AL PÍPILA

Cerro
del Gallo

PANORÁMICA

PIPILA

SAN
JAVIER

PIPILA

CASA MERCEDES
RESTAURANT

CALLE
DE ARRIBA

ALHÓNDIGA

INSURGENCIA

INSURGENCIA
DEL
CANTADOR

PASEO
Parque
Porfirio
Díaz

Porfirio
Díaz

PUERTA ALTA

TEPETAPA

CERRO TROZADO

MUSEO DE
LAS MOMIAS

PLAZA
DE RANAS

TRANSV. DEL
PANTEÓN

M. HIDALGO

BAN

LA VALENCIANA

BOCAMINA
SAN
RAMÓN

SAN JOSÉ DE
VALENCIANA

TEMPLO DE
SAN CAYETANO

Plazuela de
Valenciana

BARBEROS

CJÓN JALISCO

110

CAMINO ANTIGUO A SANTA ANA

CAMINO
A MINA
VALENCIA

ERIZO

CAMINO
ANTIGUO
A SANTA ANA

CAMINO

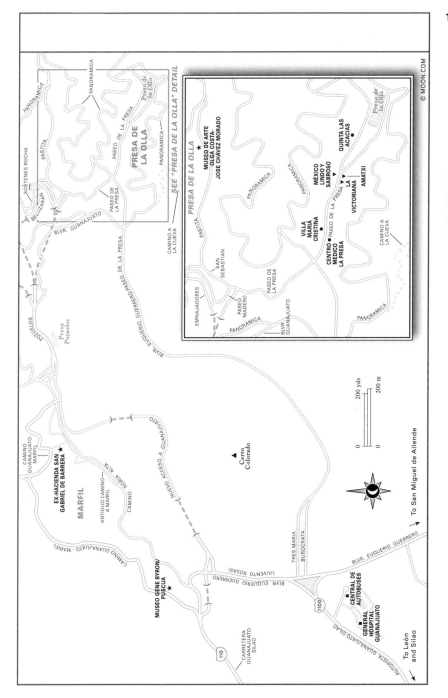

© MOON.COM

SEE "PRESA DE LA OLLA" DETAIL

PRESA DE LA OLLA

PANORAMICA

PASTITA

MUSEO DE ARTE OLGA COSTA-JOSE CHAVEZ MORADO

QUINTA LAS ACACIAS

MÉXICO LINDO Y SABROSO

LA VICTORIANA

AMATXI

CENTRO MEDICO LA PRESA

PASEO DE LA PRESA

VILLA MARIA CRISTINA

SAN SEBASTIAN

PASEO DE LA PRESA

CAMINO A LA CUEVA

PASEO MADERO

EMBAJADORES

PANORAMICA

BLVR. GUANAJUATO

PANORAMICA

Presa de la Olla

PRESA DE LA OLLA

PANORAMICA

PANORAMICA

SOSTENES ROCHA

PASTITA

BELIZARAN

PASEO DE LA PRESA

PASEO DE LA PRESA

CAMINO A LA CUEVA

BLVR. GUANAJUATO

BLVR. EUQUERIO GUERRERO

PASEO DE LA PRESA

POZUELOS

Presa Pozuelos

CAMINO GUANAJUATO-MARFIL

EX-HACIENDA SAN GABRIEL DE BARRERA

MARFIL

NORIA ALTA

ANTIGUO CAMINO A MARFIL

CAMINO

NUEVO ACCESO A GUANAJUATO

Cerro Colorado

CAMINO GUANAJUATO - MARIEL

MUSEO GENE BYRON/PUSCUA

CARRETERA GUANAJUATO-SILAO

110

TRES MARIA

BUROCRATA

BLVR. EUQUERIO GUERRERO
(JUVENTO ROSAS)

BLVR. EUQUERIO GUERRERO

110D

CENTRAL DE AUTOBUSES

GENERAL HOSPITAL GUANAJUATO

AUTOPISTA GUANAJUATO-SILAO

To San Miguel de Allende

To León and Silao

200 yds

200 m

point A to point B. The urban city center is built along the walls of a canyon, dotted by public plazas, and ribboned with tiny pedestrian alleyways. It has no grid pattern to follow, no numbered streets, and few accurate maps. Alleys often zigzag in unexpected directions and can lead to a serious cardiac workout if you follow them in their steep ascent up the ravine. It may take a few hours—or even a few days—to get acquainted with the topsy-turvy street map. During the adjustment period, a sense of adventure is your greatest ally. Even as you find yourself lost in the tangle of small streets, there is always a sense of pleasant curiosity about what lies around the next corner.

Unlike most Mexican cities, Guanajuato's downtown was not designed around a big central square, or zócalo. The **Jardín de la Unión** is generally considered the city center, culturally if not geographically. Therefore, it can be easiest to start your tour of the city there. From the Jardín de la Unión, several pedestrian streets run roughly from the northwest to the southeast across the downtown, making a few unexpected dips and turns. From the Teatro Juárez, follow Luis González Obregón northwest toward the Plaza de la Paz, where you will see the Basílica de Nuestra Señora de Guanajuato and the state government buildings. From there, take Juárez past the Plaza San Fernando and the Plaza de los Ángeles until you arrive at the Mercado Hidalgo, just below the Alhóndiga. Heading southeast from Jardín de la Unión, Sopeña is a pedestrian street lined with shops and restaurants. One block to the east (just behind the Jardín de la Unión), Calle Cantarranas runs loosely parallel to Sopeña, though it is open to auto traffic.

Centro Histórico

Guanajuato's charming centro histórico is a compact labyrinth of narrow streets and cobblestone plazas, crammed with old churches, theaters, and former mansions. While the elaborate churches and civic buildings are the city's most celebrated architectural

sights, the entire downtown district is filled with colonial buildings that are historic and beautiful. As you walk, look up to see the crumbling facades, old stone niches, and wrought-iron balconies of former mansions and government buildings. They are beautifully preserved and largely intact, so it is easy to imagine this city center as it was 200 years ago.

La Valenciana

With sweeping views of the city center, La Valenciana is a residential neighborhood home to the **Templo de San Cayetano** and **Bocamina San Ramón.** Here, on the rocky bluffs, the mining industry continues to play a big role in Guanajuato's economy and identity. You can get to La Valenciana in a taxi or Uber, or by taking a bus marked "Valenciana" from the bus stop below the Alhóndiga de Granaditas.

San Javier

San Javier is a residential neighborhood about 4 km (2.5 mi) north of the city center, where you'll find the family-run restaurant **Casa Mercedes.**

West of the Centro

The primary attraction in the area a steep 2.5 km (1.5 mi) west of the centro is the famous **Museo de las Momias** (Mummy Museum), one of Guanajuato's most bizarre and enduringly popular places.

Marfil

The Marfil neighborhood to the southwest of the city center was once a small village, quite separate from downtown Guanajuato. Originally set up as a protective settlement to guard the nearby mines, it eventually became the center of Guanajuato's metal refineries during the colonial era. Many of these refineries were later converted to haciendas, some of which are now museums and restaurants. Though it's too far to walk, it only takes about 10 minutes in a taxi to get to Marfil from the centro histórico, or you can take a bus from the Juárez tunnel (look for the buses marked "Marfil").

Presa de la Olla

Here you'll find the Presa de la Olla, the oldest city reservoir. The neighborhood around the Presa de la Olla is a pleasant 30-minute walk from the centro. Nearby, the quiet, tree-filled **Pastita** neighborhood is a largely residential area to the east of the centro histórico.

Sights

Throughout the narrow streets and curving alleyways of Guanajuato's centro histórico, there is a veritable album of photo opportunities. The city boasts some of the finest 18th-century baroque architecture in the country, as well as a few lovely structures dating back to the 17th century. Adding to the unique mix of architectural styles, Guanajuato also has some spectacular civil buildings from the 19th century, often characterized by neo-classical design. After its induction into the UNESCO World Heritage Program in 1988, Guanajuato's churches, chapels, and civil buildings were beautifully restored, yet they haven't lost the crumbling majesty of their age and history. In addition, there are many small but interesting museums as well as several public galleries. When touring the city, it's worth a stop in one of the museums that catch your eye.

Several restaurants, hotels, and sights are outside the city center, specifically in the **Marfil, San Javier, de la Presa,** and **La Valenciana** neighborhoods. These neighborhoods are easily accessible by taxi or bus. These outlying neighborhoods may not look very distant on a map, yet steep, winding hills can make them quite a trek on foot! Plan to drive, take a taxi, or ride the bus.

CENTRO HISTÓRICO
Iglesia de San Francisco

San Francisco Church, Manuel Doblado 15; tel. 473/732-0377; generally 7am-8:30pm daily; free
Just beside the Quixote museum, the lovely Iglesia de San Francisco is a church and former convent, originally constructed in the 18th century by Franciscan friars as accompaniment to their school and orphanage. Situated along a pedestrian stretch of Manuel Doblado, this small church has a stunning pink sandstone churrigueresque entryway. Inside is a neoclassical altar and a nice collection of colonial-era oil paintings, including a particularly fine piece from the 18th century depicting San Francisco and Santa Clara.

Museo Iconográfico del Quijote

Manuel Doblado 2; tel. 473/732-6721; www.museoiconografico.guanajuato.gob.mx; 9am-7pm Tues.-Sat., noon-5pm Sun. and holidays; US$2, free on Tues.
Guanajuato is the proud bearer of the Cervantes tradition, and the figure of Don Quixote is a big part of the city's cultural identity. Statues of Cervantes's mythical hero are scattered throughout the city center, and the name Quixote is forever on the tip of your tongue, thanks to the dozens of namesake restaurants, hotels, and shops. At this small but well-stocked museum, you can see hundreds of representations of Don Quixote and his sidekick, Sancho Panza, from highly abstract to highly figurative pieces in a variety of media. The predominantly Mexican collection includes numerous local artists as well as some famous names, like Zacatecan artist Pedro Coronel. Taking advantage of its courtyard, the museum occasionally hosts cultural events as well as weekly live music concerts.

★ Funicular Panorámico and Monumento al Pípila

Constancia s/n; 8am-8:45pm Mon.-Fri., 9am-8:45pm Sat., 10am-8:45pm Sun.; US$2.50

Centro Histórico

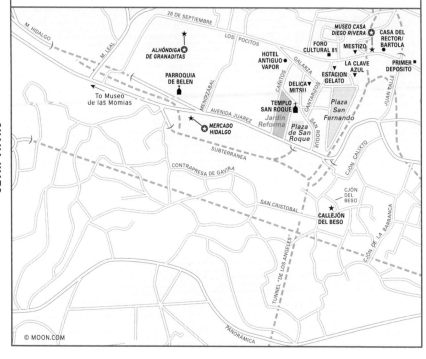

Above the city center, a giant rose-colored statue of the famous War of Independence hero Juan José de los Reyes Martínez Amaro, or El Pípila, towers above the ravine, where it presides over a large public esplanade with spectacular views of the city below. From just behind the Teatro Juárez, you can take a short but fun ride up the hillside to the plaza in the glass-walled Funicular Panorámico. You can also ascend via staircase to a claustrophobic glass box at the very top of the statue (US$0.50), though it's worth it for the novelty rather than the view.

To get your blood pumping, skip the funicular and follow the maze of alleys up to the top of the hill. One way to get there on foot is via the alley Constancia, just behind the Templo de San Diego and above the public parking lot; follow the signs from there. Though it's

less than half a kilometer, the climb will take you anywhere from 15 to 25 minutes, depending on your pace and how many pictures you stop to take. Once you get to the top, the attraction is the view of the city—from this vantage point, you get a real sense of Guanajuato's unique urban landscape. The plaza offers a pleasant buzz of craft vendors, some snack shacks, and lots of other tourists snapping the ultimate Guanajuato photo.

You can return to the centro via funicular, but it's even more fun to walk, if you are able to comfortably descend uneven surfaces and staircases. Narrow alleyways depart from either side of the plaza, weaving steeply through the picturesque residential neighborhoods of Guanajuato toward the centro histórico. If you feel a little lost on the descent, just keep heading down to reach the city center.

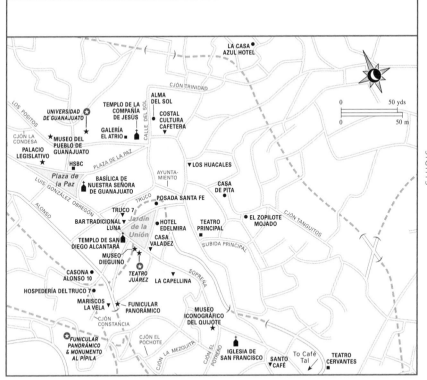

★ Teatro Juárez

Sopeña s/n; tel. 473/732-0183 or 473/732-2529; 9am-1pm and 4pm-6pm daily; US$2.50 for entry; ticket prices vary

Teatro Juárez is a jewel on the crown of Guanajuato's beautiful centro histórico. The building's opulent eclectic facade is emblematic of the Porfiriato, the long 19th-century rule of President Porfirio Díaz, which ended with the Mexican Revolution of 1910. Designed by Antonio Rivas Mercado, Teatro Juárez was inaugurated in 1903 with a performance of Giuseppe Verdi's *Aida*. Porfirio Díaz was in attendance at the opening event. After Díaz's presidency was toppled in the Revolution of 1910, the theater was leased for cinema and, eventually, fell into disrepair. Efforts to restore the building began in the 1950s, receiving an additional boost from the founding of the Festival Internacional Cervantino in 1973. Since then, Teatro Juárez has been a prominent performing arts venue, continually hosting high-caliber theater, concerts, and dance performances.

Towering over the Jardín de la Unión, Teatro Juárez has a striking exterior, with 12 Doric columns supporting a cornice topped by a row of black stone muses. There is often a crowd of locals chatting on the staircase below the portico. Inside, the ceiling and floors of the main auditorium, the Gran Salón Auditorio, are spectacularly decorated with hand-cut wood-and-stucco relief, painted in a brilliant multicolor array of deep red, blue, and gold. Heavily influenced by Moorish design, the Gran Salón is elaborate and dazzling. From the Gran Salón, you can follow the creaky wooden staircases to the foyer upstairs, an art nouveau salon complemented by even more neoclassical marble sculptures.

Even the bathrooms have gilded moldings. At press time, the theater had just reopened following a multiyear renovation of the space.

Jardín de la Unión

between Sopeña, Obregón, and Allende; 24 hours

Built along the banks of a river, Guanajuato's winding downtown district is composed of small plazas linked by narrow streets. The most bustling of these many plazas, the Jardín de la Unión is the heart of the city. Once the atrium of a large San Diegan convent in the city center, it was converted to a public space during the post-independence Reformation of the early 19th century. Today the Jardín de la Unión is always buzzing with activity. From morning to night, its wrought-iron benches are packed with crowds of tourists and locals. By early afternoon, mariachis and norteño trios arrive to play songs on request. The party continues through the evening, as the garden's cafés fill with people dining alfresco. For any first-time visitors to Guanajuato, the Jardín de la Unión is a great place to put your finger on the pulse of downtown Guanajuato.

Museo Dieguino

Jardín de la Unión; tel. 473/732-5296; 10am-6pm daily; US$3, children free

Since the days of its founding, the downtown district of Guanajuato was repeatedly flooded by the river that ran through the city center. After a devastating flood in the late 1700s, the entire city center was raised several meters, including the buildings of the San Diegan convent. On the temple's north side, a small staircase leads down to the Museo Dieguino, where the ruins of the original 17th-century temple have been excavated. The space is very small but interesting, revealing the old crumbling walls and archways (now reinforced with wood supports) of the original cloister. Often the museum exhibits contemporary art or photography within this historic space, adding a tasteful and interesting juxtaposition between the past and the present.

Templo de San Diego Alcantará

Calle de Sopeña s/n; generally 8am-8pm daily; free

The Templo de San Diego Alcantará was originally constructed as a part of the large San Diegan convent that occupied the city center, including the current site of Teatro Juárez and the Jardín de la Unión. Of the entire complex, only this small chapel is left standing today. One of the older buildings in Guanajuato, the Templo de San Diego has a beautiful rococo

The Funicular Panorámico goes up to the monument to El Pípila.

Place of Frogs

The name Guanajuato comes the language of the Purépecha, native people who currently reside in southern Guanajuato and Michoacán. The name is generally believed to derive from the term "Quanaxhuato" ("place of the monstrous frogs," or "place of many hills").

It seems a strange nickname for a semiarid town in the crevice of the Cordillera de Guanajuato, and there are varying theories about its origin, though most historians believe the name refers to the rock formations near the city center, some of which resemble giant frogs.

Whatever the reason, the city has embraced its amphibious identity, mysterious though it is. In shops across town, frog souvenirs are popular merchandise, and a major thoroughfare is named Cantarranas (Singing Frogs). From the city's southwest entrance from León, you are welcomed to town by the **Plaza de Ranas** (Plaza of Frogs), where a host of sandstone frogs form an informal gateway to the city.

exterior, replete with life-size saints surrounded by decorative hand-carved stone embellishments. Inside, the church has a lovely collection of large-format oil paintings from the viceroyalty through the 19th century. Two small temples adjoin the nave on either side of the neoclassical altar; the chapel to the south of the altar is smaller but has another impressive collection of 18th-century oil paintings depicting the life of San Diego de Alcántra.

Basílica de Nuestra Señora de Guanajuato

Plaza de la Paz s/n; tel. 473/732-0314; generally 8am-9pm daily; free

The striking yellow Basílica de Nuestra Señora de Guanajuato was the city's first parish church. In 1957 the church was upgraded from parroquia (parish church) to the elevated title of basilica. Constructed in the 17th century with funds from the mines, the building's brightly painted facade is largely original, though its churrigueresque bell tower was added in the 19th century. Each of the church's three entryways is surrounded by a lovely hand-carved sandstone facade.

In contrast to its bold exterior, the basilica's interior is a wash of subtle pastels, marble floors, and shiny crystal. The walls are painted with delicate frescoes in pink, aqua, and white. The church's original baroque altarpieces were lost in the 19th century and have since been replaced by a large

neoclassical altar in the front and in the two side chapels. The centerpiece is the *Virgen de Guanajuato*, a carved wooden sculpture of the Virgin Mary and son from the 16th or 17th century, displayed atop a baroque silver pedestal. When you go inside, be respectful of masses and worshippers. Even today, the church's congregation is very active.

★ Universidad de Guanajuato

University of Guanajuato, Lascuráin de Retana 5; tel. 473/732-0006; www.ugto.mx

The Universidad de Guanajuato, a large and prestigious public university, has a major influence on the city of Guanajuato culturally and architecturally. The school dates back to the early 18th century, when Jesuits founded the Colegio de la Santísima Trinidad in Guanajuato. This same school became a college in 1744. After the War of Independence, the school was designated a state college and the curriculum was reformed under the first state governor, Carlo Montes de Oca. In 1945 the college was elevated to the status of university, offering undergraduate, master's, and doctoral programs. Today the Universidad de Guanajuato is one of Mexico's most prominent and well-respected institutions. There are around 30,000 students, and their jubilant and youthful attitude flavors the downtown district of Guanajuato.

The central campus is the school's most iconic structure, an unusual neoclassical

City of Silver

The settlement of Santa Fe and Real de Minas de Guanajuato was established around 1548, when Spanish settlers discovered silver veins in the surrounding sierra. Initially a modest contributor to New Spain's wealth, the city flourished with the opening of the productive La Cata mine in the 1720s. A large San Diegan convent was constructed along the banks of the Guanajuato River, churches and mansions cropped up around the city center, and the first Jesuit school (a precursor to the modern-day Universidad de Guanajuato) was established. Water systems were built, and the first dam, La Presa de la Olla, was constructed to curb flooding downtown. The Spanish government officially recognized the city in 1741; by then, 50,000 people were living there.

In 1769 Antonio de Obregón y Alcocer and Pedro Luciano de Otero discovered a silver vein at La Valenciana, north of central Guanajuato. The massive wealth from La Valenciana made Obregón a rich man and the city of Guanajuato a jewel on the crown of New Spain. With renewed vigor, mansions, churches, temples, and haciendas were built across town. When a great flood sank the San Diegan convent in 1780, the city had plenty of funds to replace it. By that time, Guanajuato was the world's single biggest silver city, producing between a fifth and a quarter of all New Spain's silver.

Guanajuato's prosperity was interrupted by the War of Independence. When Guanajuato's governors refused to surrender, the Mexican army invaded the city on September 28, 1810, and the Alhóndiga de Granaditas, the public granary, was the site of one of the most important battles in the War of Independence.

While other Bajío cities went into decline, Guanajuato's silver mines continued to produce throughout the 19th century. During his multi-decade rule of Mexico, President Porfirio Díaz commissioned more monuments in Guanajuato, including the Teatro Juárez and Mercado Hidalgo, adding to the unusual mix of spectacular architecture in Guanajuato's city center.

building constructed in the 1940s. Soaring skyward above the narrow street of Lascuráin de Retana, the giant white facade dominates the cityscape to the east, peeking above the government buildings and chapels from the Plaza de la Paz below. Its long ascending stairway, cut of green sandstone, rises from the street to auditoriums and classrooms above. If you don't mind a brisk workout, you can climb the many stairs for a nice view of the city.

Templo de la Compañía de Jesús

Lascuráin de Retana s/n; generally 8am-8pm daily; free
Also known as the Oratorio San Felipe Neri, the Templo de la Compañía de Jesús is an exquisite pink sandstone church that was constructed from 1747 to 1765 by Jesuit priests. Another boon of the silver trade, the large neoclassical cupola behind the main facade was added to the building during the 19th century, commissioned by the Jesuit brother of a mining magnate. Today the church's lovely churrigueresque exterior and single

bell tower are well preserved, yet enchantingly aged. After Guanajuato's inauguration into the World Heritage Program in 1988, this church was the first structure to be totally restored.

Inside, the soaring nave is impressively high, with a vaulted dome where even pigeons drift comfortably from one sandstone perch to the next. Note the elaborately wrought sandstone columns that line the main corridor. Hand-carved altars adorn the walls, where there are several beautiful wooden statues, a fine hand-painted pulpit, and a collection of 18th-century oil paintings, including some by master artist Miguel Cabrera.

Plaza de la Paz

Between Ponciano Aguilar and Luis González Obregón
Just below the Basílica de Nuestra Señora de Guanajuato, the Plaza de la Paz is a lovely

1: Teatro Juárez 2: Jardín de la Unión 3: Basílica de Nuestra Señora de Guanajuato, originally built in the late 17th century 4: Universidad de Guanajuato's main campus

Best Views

lookout near the El Pípila monument

Thanks to Guanajuato's hilly topography, there are spectacular views from alleyways and rooftops across the city.

Take the Funicular Panorámico to **Monumento al Pípila** (page 125), where the outlook boasts a sweeping view of downtown. Or see the city from a different angle with a glass of wine at rooftop lounge **Bartola** (page 158) as the sun goes down.

triangle-shaped esplanade, originally considered Guanajuato's main square until the establishment of the Jardín de la Unión in the early 19th century. In the center of the plaza, well-manicured gardens and metal benches surround the *Monumento de la Paz,* dedicated to the city by President Porfirio Díaz in 1903. (The original fountain that stood in the center of the Plaza de la Paz was relocated to the Plaza Baratillo to accommodate the new sculpture.) On the north side of Plaza de la Paz (just to the north of the basilica), the **Palacio Legislativo** is a noted neoclassical construction from the 19th century, now home to state government offices.

Museo del Pueblo de Guanajuato

Positos 7; tel. 473/732-2990; 10am-7pm Tues.-Sat., 10am-3pm Sun.; US$2

The beautiful old building that houses the Museo del Pueblo de Guanajuato contains three stories of small galleries exhibiting the museum's permanent collection, as well as rotating exhibitions of artwork by Mexican and international artists. Downstairs, the Sala Teresa Pomar has a nice collection of traditional Mexican miniatures, including ceramics, masks, alebrijes, and corn-husk dolls.

Depending on when you visit, you may see work by young artists or great Mexican masters; recent exhibitions have included work by Pedro Reyes and a retrospective of work by Gabriel Macotela.

At the Museo del Pueblo, the lovely building itself is part of the attraction, housed in the former mansion of the wealthy Sardeneta family. Of particular note is the small 18th-century baroque chapel, which was later decorated with a mural by artist José Chávez Morado.

★ Museo Casa Diego Rivera

Positos 47; tel. 473/732-1197; 10am-6:30pm Tues.-Sat., 10am-3pm Sun.; US$1.50

The famous early-20th-century artist Diego Rivera was born in the city of Guanajuato. Today his childhood home has been refashioned as a small museum, the Museo Casa Diego Rivera. Although the artist only lived in this house for the first few years of his life before relocating with his family to Mexico City, he is nonetheless one of Guanajuato's favorite sons.

On the first floor of the museum, the family's living quarters have been decorated with period furnishings, re-creating the atmosphere typical to a wealthy family at the time of Rivera's birth. The three rather topsy-turvy floors above (the structure is sinking and slanted, which gives it a bit of a funhouse feeling) are filled with small, nicely designed galleries of Rivera's work, including some of his earliest oil paintings, drawings, watercolors, and lithographs. Several rooms display work from Rivera's contemporaries, many of whom were exploring the same themes in Mexican identity and culture. For fans of the artist, this museum is an essential stop, as it offers enormous insight into his artistic development. The museum also presents rotating exhibitions in a few gallery spaces, and there are often movies, artistic talks, and other cultural programs on-site.

Plaza San Fernando

between Cantaritos and Independencia; 24 hours; free

One of the prettiest public squares in central Guanajuato, tree-filled Plaza San Fernando is ringed by shops and restaurants and always bustling with activity. Once part of a large hacienda, it is now a nice place for an afternoon coffee break, with a stone fountain at its center.

Templo de San Roque

Plaza de San Roque s/n; no tel.; hours vary

An old and endearing 18th-century chapel, the Templo de San Roque overlooks a small plaza of the same name. Originally constructed in 1726 by Father Don Juan José de Sopeño y Cevera, the building served as a santa escuela (Jesuit school) from 1746 to 1794. The pink sandstone exterior is enchanting in its simplicity; there are few embellishments here, just a simple stone entryway and three stone saints, embedded into a wall of thick-cut sandstone bricks. Inside the church, the crumbling frescoes and incredibly weathered wooden doors reflect the building's age and many years of use. The series of paintings depicting the Stations of the Cross were done in the 18th and 19th centuries by Lorenzo Romero.

Plaza de San Roque

north of Av. Benito Juárez; 24 hours; free

Right in front of the Templo de San Roque, the small Plaza de San Roque also has historical importance to the city of Guanajuato. Since the mid-20th century, the plaza has been the site of Guanajuato's famous *Entremeses Cervantinos. Entremeses,* the series of short comedies by Cervantes, are performed weekly in this square. Over the years, these performances became so popular that they eventually formed the cornerstone of Guanajuato's annual Festival Internacional Cervantino. On the south side of the church is a bronze statue of Enrique Ruelas, the Universidad de Guanajuato professor who founded the festival.

Jardín Reforma

north of Av. Benito Juárez; 24 hours; free

Just to the west of the Plaza de San Roque, Jardín Reforma is a peaceful public square, home to the architecture department at the Universidad de Guanajuato. The grounds were once a part of the Templo de Belen and were expropriated to make a public space in the mid-19th century. Quieter than neighboring Plaza San Fernando, this plaza is shaded by trees and filled with quiet spots to rest.

Callejón del Beso

Callejón del Beso, entrance via the Plaza de los Angeles; 24 hours; balcony access US$6

Only 70 centimeters (28 inches) separates one house from another on the tiny Callejón del Beso (Alley of the Kiss). Located just above the Plaza de los Ángeles, this little alley is typical of those in Guanajuato, with a staircase cutting through a narrow passage between residences. However, the Callejón del Beso has become a bit of a tourist attraction, thanks to the local legend of two lovers who lived in houses on opposite sides of the alley. According to this Romeo and Juliet-esque story, the young lovers were from different social classes and their families opposed the romance. Doña Carmen was a rich young woman with a jealous father, while her lover, Don Carlos, was a poor miner. At night, when Carmen was locked into her bedroom by her father, they would lean over their adjoining balconies for evening kisses.

As characters in these legends often do, the lovers on the Callejón del Beso met a tragic end, when Doña Carmen's father discovered their affair and plunged a knife into his daughter's heart. Today you can reenact the lovers' secret romance by climbing up to the balconies and leaning over it for a photo opportunity; admission is about US$6. Note that there is often a wait on busy weekends. Many tourists simply choose to exchange a kiss on the staircase below, which supposedly brings good luck to your relationship—even though it didn't bring much luck to Doña Carmen and Don Carlos!

★ Mercado Hidalgo

Av. Juárez s/n, esq. Mendizábal; no tel.; 8:30am-9pm daily; hours vary by shop

One of the nicest examples of turn-of-the-20th-century architecture in Guanajuato is the beautiful Mercado Hidalgo, inaugurated on September 16, 1910, by President Porfirio Díaz. It was a gift to the city in commemoration of the 100th anniversary of the Mexican War of Independence. Little did Díaz know that his own long presidency would come to a violent end just a few months later, with the outbreak of the Mexican Revolution of 1910.

Housed in an unusual structure that, according to local history, was originally designed as a train depot, this covered market holds a jumble of fruit stands, taco joints, juice bars, and stands selling dulces típicos (traditional Mexican candies). The second floor is dedicated to crafts and souvenirs, though most vendors sell inexpensive trinkets like key chains and bottle openers rather than high-quality artisan work. Nonetheless, it's worth taking a walk around the second-floor

Mercado Hidalgo

promenade to snap some photos of the market below.

Parroquia de Belen

Av. Juárez s/n; tel. 473/732-2283; https://parroquiabelen.jimdofree.com; 7am-9pm daily; free

Just across the street from the Mercado Hidalgo, the Parroquia de Belen, also known as the Parroquia del Inmaculado Corazón de María, is a lovely parish church with a baroque facade. Constructed by Bethlemite nuns in the 18th century, the original complex included a school, gardens, and a cemetery; today only the church is left standing. The spacious interior contains lovely mosaic walls and a nice collection of retablos and oil paintings.

★ Alhóndiga de Granaditas

Mendizábal 6; tel. 473/732-1180; 10am-6pm Mon.-Sat., 10am-3pm Sun.; US$4

The colonial-era Alhóndiga de Granaditas is home to a fascinating regional museum; it was originally designed, however, to store wheat, corn, and other staple grains for the Guanajuato populace. Completed in 1809, the building's usefulness was short-lived: the Alhóndiga became one of the major battle sites early in the War of Independence in September 1810, after which it was cleared out and served as a military barracks and warehouse. During the 19th century, the Alhóndiga was the city jail; if you look closely, you can find names and dates carved into many of the building's stone walls and columns by former prisoners.

Designed in a spare neoclassical style, the Alhóndiga resembles a fortress from the outside. Inside, the granary is surprisingly lovely, with a spacious patio framed by green sandstone columns. Adding to the charm, the walls of the building's staircases are painted with dramatic murals by celebrated early-20th-century artist José Chávez Morado.

Today the Alhóndiga is a two-story museum, officially named the **Museo Regional de Guanajuato,** which illustrates the city's 500-year history with artifacts, texts, and photographs. On the second floor are several rooms displaying a small but interesting collection of pre-Columbian art, much of which was donated to the museum by artists José Chávez Morado and Olga Costa. The lovely collection of pre-Columbian stamps from across Mexico is one of the museum's highlights. From there, the visitor can follow the city's history from the colonial era through the turn-of-the-20th century through mining artifacts and reproductions of weapons and furniture from baroque Spain. The final salons contain vintage photographs of Guanajuato in the early 1900s, as well as local craftwork.

LA VALENCIANA

Departing the city center to the north, the state highway ascends a beautiful, curving route toward the Sierra de Guanajuato and the hamlet of Santa Rosa. Following this road to the outskirts of the city of Guanajuato, La Valenciana is a beautiful neighborhood that has held one of the most important roles in the history of the city's development.

History

In 1769 a silver vein larger than any other in Mexico was discovered at La Valenciana in Guanajuato. In the early years, the mine's owners did not have the funds they needed to properly exploit their bounty; to compensate, they introduced an unusual labor system that granted mine workers a small share of the profits instead of a salary. The workers had to provide their own tools. The mine produced prolifically for centuries. At peak production, La Valenciana was New Spain's largest silver producer, as well as an important source of other minerals, like gold, quartz, and amethyst.

Miners from La Valenciana were among the men who took arms against the Spanish at the Alhóndiga de Granaditas during Mexico's War of Independence. Even after the fighting ended, La Valenciana continued to yield rock, metal, and mineral. The entire mine was under the direction of a workers cooperative

El Pípila and the Storming of La Alhóndiga

The Alhóndiga de Granaditas was a famous battle site in the Mexican War of Independence; today it is a historical museum.

Mexico's War of Independence began on the night of September 15, 1810, in the rural town of Dolores. Under the command of pastor and insurgent leader Miguel Hidalgo y Costilla, the Mexican army rode through the Bajío region, taking first San Miguel el Grande (today San Miguel de Allende) and next the city of Celaya. From Celaya, Hidalgo called for Guanajuato to surrender, but the royalist governors refused. On September 28, Hidalgo's army of 20,000 soldiers descended upon the city.

As the army entered town, Guanajuato's wealthy criollo (Spaniards born in the colonies) and Spanish families took refuge in the fortresslike **Alhóndiga de Granaditas,** the city's public granary, under the direction of Spanish intendent Juan Antonio Riaño, while awaiting Spanish reinforcements from the capital. La Alhóndiga was a difficult target for Hidalgo's ill-equipped army; despite their aggressive efforts, the perimeter was difficult to penetrate.

Juan José de los Reyes Martínez, popularly known as **El Pípila,** was an Indigenous silver miner known for his enormous strength. El Pípila tied a heavy stone to his back as a shield and, carrying a torch in one hand, struggled beneath a shower of bullets and set fire to the granary's wooden doors. As the doors burned, the rebel army swarmed inside and massacred the aristocratic families within.

A year after the storming of La Alhóndiga, Spanish forces took their revenge. In March 1811 prominent insurgents, including Allende and Hidalgo, were ambushed and arrested by royalist forces. A few months later, Ignacio Allende, Juan Aldama, and Mariano Jiménez were executed by firing squad in Chihuahua, followed by Miguel Hidalgo a few days later. Their bodies were decapitated, and the heads of the insurgent leaders were paraded around the country as a warning to other conspirators. The heads were then carried to Guanajuato, where they were hung in cages from the four corners of La Alhóndiga on October 14, 1811.

According to local history, the heads swung from the corners of the granary for more than a decade until they were transported to the monument of the Ángel de Independencia in Mexico City. Today there are plaques of each leader's name on the corners of the building, posted beside the giant iron hook that once held his head.

until the mid-2000s, when it was finally closed to production.

Getting There

You can get to La Valenciana in a taxi or Uber, or by taking a bus marked "Valenciana" from the bus stop below the Alhóndiga de Granaditas.

Bocamina San Ramón

Callejón de San Ramón 10, Col. La Valenciana; tel. 473/732-3551; 10am-7pm daily; US$2

In its heyday, the mine at La Valenciana expanded to astonishing proportions, comprising a vast underground network of connected tunnels that stretched for kilometers below the surface of the earth. Just behind the Templo de San Cayetano, the Bocamina San Ramón was one of the principal entrances to the mine, first excavated during the 16th century. Though long left in ruins, the hacienda surrounding the mine shaft has been restored and refashioned as a museum and event center, which showcases a bit of the history behind Guanajuato's most prosperous silver vein.

Independent, Spanish-speaking tour guides are on-site and can provide some historical context. Working for tips, they can guide you around the site, which includes some tools and artifacts preserved from the colonial-era mine. The main attraction, however, is the mine shaft itself; it descends 48 m (158 ft) via a slippery stone staircase, where you can get a small taste of the dampness, darkness, and stale air that the miners endured during grueling shifts underground. To accompany the relief of returning to the earth's surface, there are beautiful views of the surrounding mountains and countryside.

Templo de San Cayetano

Plazuela de la Valenciana, Carretera Guanajuato-Dolores Hidalgo, km 1.5; tel. 473/732-3596; generally 6:30am-6pm Tues.-Sun.

Antonio de Obregón, the Spanish co-owner of La Valenciana silver mine, became incredibly wealthy during his lifetime. To thank God for his great fortune, he constructed the spectacular Templo de San Cayetano. Built between 1765 and 1788, this mountaintop church is one of the finest examples of Mexican baroque architecture in the country, presiding over the city of Guanajuato and drawing daily busloads of tourists.

The church's highly elaborate sandstone facade is lavishly carved with saints, angels, and decorative adornment. Inside, the church is a direct testament to the riches of the adjoining mines, a splendor of hand-carved wood altarpieces washed in gold leaf. Wonderful multicolored wooden saints are embedded within the many niches, all beautifully restored. Also note the delicately carved and painted wooden pulpit.

Obregón's former estate across the street from the church is the subject of many tales of wealth and splendor. Among other legends, it is said that when his daughter was married in the Templo de San Cayetano, the count presented her with a rug of silver and gold coins, which led from her doorstep to the church. Today Obregón's home is known as the Casa del Conde (Obregón later gained the title of conde, or count, of La Valenciana), with a fine-dining restaurant inside.

WEST OF THE CENTRO
Museo de las Momias

Explanada del Panteón Municipal s/n; tel. 473/732-0639; www.momiasdeguanajuato.gob.mx; 9am-6pm Mon.-Thurs., 9am-6:30pm Fri.-Sun.; US$3

This museum's backstory begins in the early 19th century, when several mummified corpses were dug up in the Santa Paula cemetery. The mummification occurred naturally due to the unusual mineral content in the soil, which preserved the corpses in a state of horrific recognizability. Thereafter, more corpses were dug up, with similar results. This curiosity has now become the concept behind a macabre museum, where the bodies of more than 100 disinterred and mummified corpses are on display for visitors behind glass cases. It's not recommended for the squeamish nor for the claustrophobic: there are children and

Mummies in the Movies

With so many other things to recommend a trip to the city, it's a bit curious that Guanajuato's **Mummy Museum** has become such a vitally important part of the town's public image. Whatever the reason behind their popularity, the mummies of Guanajuato have become almost as famous as the Alhóndiga de Granaditas.

In 1972 Guanajuato's mummies were immortalized in the Mexican film *Las Momias de Guanajuato* (The Mummies of Guanajuato). This campy semi-action flick stars wrestling hero El Blue Demon, who is called upon to save the city of Guanajuato from the attack of a mobile band of mummies who had made a pact with the devil. As the mummies wreak havoc downtown, El Blue Demon and his companion, Mil Máscaras, must protect the city from these bald and oddly slow-moving villains (a wildly adored wrestling hero, El Santo, also makes a cameo toward the end of the film). In the final sequence, a gang of masked wrestlers attacks a legion of strong but stiff-jointed mummies (dressed in suits!) in Guanajuato's municipal graveyard.

In addition to the gripping story line, *Las Momias de Guanajuato* depicts the city of Guanajuato in amusing detail. As the movie begins, a group of tourists visits Guanajuato's Mummy Museum, where they are told the story of the evil mummies. Later a key scene includes the Estudiantina troubadours playing for a band of tourists on the stairs of the university. Thanks to the film's popularity, *Las Momias de Guanajuato* was followed by several other mummy movies, including a lower-budget flick the following year, *El Castillo de las Momias de Guanajuato*. This film stars the wrestlers Superzan, Blue Angel, and Tinieblas and was shot in Guatemala, not Guanajuato.

Though not a classic of Mexican cinema, this film is emblematic of Mexico's popular lucha libre movies of the 1950s, 1960s, and 1970s. Studios no longer make these flicks, but films starring El Blue Demon, and especially El Santo, continue to garner a loyal cult following for their comic-book-style story lines, theatrical violence, and hammy acting.

babies among the mummified bodies, and the narrow hallways are perpetually packed elbow-to-elbow with museum visitors.

If you don't plan to visit the unintentionally calcified remains of former Guanajuato residents, you can celebrate this oddity in other ways—like with a mummy gummy candy, sold at sweet shop **Dulceria Galereña.**

Getting There

On foot, it's a steep 2.5-km (1.5-mi), 20-minute walk uphill to the Mummy Museum, making taxi or Uber is the easiest way to come and go from this macabre sight, which is located in an outlying neighborhood near the municipal graveyard, or panteón. Buses marked "Panteón Municipal" or "Momias" depart from the stop near the Plaza de la Paz and Mercado Hidalgo in the centro.

MARFIL
Ex-Hacienda San Gabriel de Barrera

Carretera Guanajuato-Marfil, Km 2.5, Col. Marfil; tel. 473/732-0619; 8:30am-6pm daily; US$2

The Ex-Hacienda San Gabriel de Barrera is a green and pleasing respite from downtown Guanajuato's inexhaustible bustle. Located in the Marfil neighborhood, the extensive grounds of this former hacienda were originally designed as a metal refinery. It was among numerous refineries owned and operated by a wealthy businessman, Gabriel de la Barrera, in the 17th century. With several acres of space, the hacienda's crumbling courtyards are home to a series of beautifully designed and well-tended gardens. Wander through the neat English garden with its tall, shady trees and a Mexican garden featuring a lovely collection of cacti. You can linger beside gurgling fountains on one of the many crumbling stone benches or have a drink at the small coffee shop near the hacienda's entrance. Unfortunately, the hacienda is right next to the highway into Guanajuato, so you never fully lose touch with the 21st century.

Admission to the hacienda includes entrance to the **museum** within the complex's former living quarters. Family rooms have been redecorated with period furniture, which displays the strong Spanish influence popular with the wealthy during the colonial era.

To get to the Ex-Hacienda San Gabriel de Barrera, you can hail a taxi from the centro histórico or take a bus marked "Marfil" from the tunnel of Hidalgo (beneath Av. Juárez), getting off at the Hotel Misión de Guanajuato (the hacienda is just below the hotel).

Museo Gene Byron

Guanajuato-Marfil 10; tel. 473/733-1029; http:// museogenebyron.org; 10am-3pm Mon.-Sat.; US$2, children under 12 free

In the 1960s, Canadian artist and designer Gene Byron purchased a splendid 18th-century ex-hacienda de Santa Ana. Today the building is home to the interesting Museo Gene Byron, where rooms are filled with Byron's work, as well as her wonderful collection of antiques, Mexican furnishings, original art, and traditional crafts. It's worth visiting for the hacienda itself, which wears its age handsomely, with vines and trees sprouting out of the old stone walls. An active cultural organization, the museum often hosts music concerts on Sundays, and there are guided tours (free) in both English and Spanish. While you're there, have brunch: The on-site restaurant, **Puscua** (tel. 473/733-5018; 8:30am-2pm Tues.-Sun.; US$9), is among the nicest in Guanajuato. Most visitors take a taxi to the museum (US$4), which is about a 15-minute drive from the city center. Alternately, you can take a bus marked "Marfil" from the stop just west of the Alhóndiga; ask the driver to let you know when you've arrived at the museum, which is located along the bus route, on the main road through the Marfil neighborhood.

PRESA DE LA OLLA
Presa de la Olla

Barrio de la Presa s/n; 24 hours; free

Constructed between 1741 and 1749, the Presa de la Olla is Guanajuato's oldest reservoir and the centerpiece of a tranquil neighborhood that bears its name. Wandering around the water's edge can provide a respite from the commotion of downtown Guanajuato, with views of the surrounding hillsides, including the famous peak known as the Cerro de La Bufa. On the west side of the reservoir, there is a small park with footpaths that are nice for strolling. On the east side is a small dock where you can rent rowboats.

Getting There

It's a pleasant half-hour walk from the city center to the Presa de la Olla neighborhood. Head south along Sostenes Rocha (past Café Tal) to the Jardín Embajadores, then head south again along the street San Sebastián, which will become the Paseo de la Presa. The Paseo de la Presa leads directly into the heart of the neighborhood and to the reservoir. Alternately, you can navigate the underground circuit of tunnels in car or taxi (US$4) to arrive in about 15 minutes, or take a bus marked "Presa de la Olla" from the center of town.

PASTITA
Museo de Arte Olga Costa-José Chávez Morado

Pastita 158; Col. Pastita, tel. 473/731-0977; 10am-4pm Tues.-Sat., 9:30am-3pm Sun.; US$2

The Pastita neighborhood was once the home of Olga Costa and José Chávez Morado, two notable early-20th-century Mexican artists who settled in Guanajuato after meeting and marrying as young artists in Mexico City. Costa and Chávez Morado first came to Guanajuato when Chávez Morado began work on the murals inside the Alhóndiga de Granaditas.

At the artists' behest, their home is now a small museum featuring some more of the artists' collection of pre-Columbian artifacts

and rare decorative objects, as well as artwork by their contemporaries. There is also a selection of Costa and Chávez Morado's work on display. Note, however, that the museum's permanent collection is periodically swapped out for itinerant art and cultural exhibits of

varying (sometimes poor) quality; it's worth calling ahead if you want to see work by these two artists. No matter what's on show, it's a pleasant glimpse of Costa and Chávez Morado's lovely home and this quiet corner of Guanajuato.

Sports and Recreation

SPAS
Presa de la Olla
Villa María Cristina

Paseo de la Presa 76; tel. 473/731-2182, toll-free Mex. tel. 800/702-7007; www.villamariacristina.com; 9am-5pm daily; from US$100 for 60-minute treatment

The luxury boutique hotel Villa María Cristina operates a lovely little spa on the first floor of the hotel property, located in the pretty, quiet neighborhood near the Presa de la Olla. Spa facilities include a dry sauna, Swiss showers, a gym, and a whirlpool, which are open to hotel guests or to those who book a treatment. Day passes for those not staying at the hotel are also available; they include tea, snacks, and access to all spa facilities for up to three hours for about US$45.

GUIDED HIKES
Cacomixtle

cell tel. 473/738-5246 or 473/122-5033; www. cacomixtle.com; US$55-115 per person

If you'd like to take a guided hike or explore regions farther off the beaten path, Cacomixtle offers ecotours in the countryside around Guanajuato, as well as cultural tours of the city, the mines, and several small towns in the region. Some hiking and bird-watching trips head to the craggy peaks of Sierra de Santa Rosa; though just outside the city, this small mountain range offers a chance to visit a largely untouched wilderness and small rural communities.

Entertainment and Events

In this city of the Cervantes tradition, there is a citywide passion for the arts, cinema, and performance, with frequent events in the city's churches, theaters, or public plazas. The university is a major cultural influence, hosting concerts, art exhibitions, and festivals throughout the year. Numerous municipal events and holidays also often draw crowds from throughout the city and beyond. There is often music in the streets, and the bustling city center is constantly flooded with people and events.

LIVE MUSIC AND THEATER

Guanajuato is a theatrical town, deep in the throes of a love affair with Cervantes and surprisingly inclined toward medieval-style pageantry. If you're not in town for the spectacular **Festival Internacional Cervantino,** a three-week-long arts bonanza, which takes place every October, you can still enjoy the city's penchant for performance. Every Friday, the university orchestra plays at the **Teatro Principal,** often featuring soloists and special guests. Smaller spots, like **Foro Cultural 81,** also host frequent musical performances and open-mic nights. Or just

1: Museo Gene Byron, located in an old hacienda
2: paddle boats for rent at the Presa de la Olla

Callejoneadas

Groups of troubadours in Renaissance-style garb process through the streets of Guanajuato every night, playing mandolins and other stringed instruments as a crowd of revelers gathers behind them, passing canteens of wine between them as they wind down narrow alleyways. This is a callejoneada, a uniquely Guanajuato occurrence.

For first-time visitors to the city, callejoneadas are a quintessential Guanajuato experience, led by the Estudiantina, medieval-style troubadours dressed in capes and pantaloons. After nightfall, groups of Estudiantina jubilantly stroll through town, playing stringed instruments and singing in unison. Behind them, a band of tourists and revelers follows, often passing flasks of wine or spirits between them. For new visitors to the city, these evening jaunts can provide a sort of nocturnal tour of Guanajuato, as the Estudiantina often stops at the Callejón del Beso, the Plaza de San Roque, and other famous locales.

Estudiantina on a callejoneadas

HOW TO JOIN

Callejoneadas usually depart the **Jardín de la Unión** 8pm-9pm, though you can also join a group as they make on their way around town. Estudiantina performers sell tickets (US$10) to the callejoneadas in the Jardín de la Unión during the day, though you do not need to buy tickets in advance. It's best to simply purchase a ticket from a member of the group when you join the tour.

---

catch a clown performing for the crowd gathered on the steps of **Teatro Juárez.**

Teatro Principal

Hidalgo s/n, esq. Cantarranas; tel. 473/732-1523; www.cultura.ugto.mx; tickets US$5-30

Under the directorship of the Universidad de Guanajuato, the Teatro Principal presents a small public program of dance, live music, and theater throughout the year, including performances by the university's Ballet Folklórico (traditional Mexican dance) and student musical ensembles, as well as hosting important university events like conferences and graduations. Notably, the Teatro Principal is a venue for major artists during the Cervantino festival in October. The first of Guanajuato's city theaters, the original building was constructed in 1788, but was abandoned during the Mexican War of Independence, reopening

again in 1826. The ill-fated building was destroyed by a fire in 1921, and replaced by the current neoclassical building several decades later, reopening in 1955.

Teatro Juárez

Sopeña s/n; tel. 473/732-0183 or 473/732-2521; box office 10am-8pm Mon.-Sat., 10am-6pm Sun.; tickets $8-50

Teatro Juárez has been Guanajuato's most important performance venue since its inauguration more than a century ago. It is one of the most important venues during the Festival Internacional Cervantino, when many big names take the stage, though events are held intermittently throughout the year, including film festival screenings. Note that the theater's box office, a small window on the southeast side of the building, handles sales for Cervantino events across venues.

Teatro Cervantes
Plaza Allende s/n; tel. 473/732-1169 or 473/732-0289; tickets $8-30
A boxy stone theater overlooking the Plaza Allende, the Teatro Cervantes is a small venue that sporadically opens for concerts, films, dance, and opera throughout the year. Given its namesake, it is not surprising that the theater is a major venue during the Cervantino festival. Inaugurated in 1979 and overseen by the State Cultural Institute, the theater is occasionally used for government functions or talks. Tickets can be purchased at the box office at Teatro Juárez.

Foro Cultural 81
Positos 81; tel. 477/690-3709; www.forocultural81.com; 10am-2pm and 4pm-8pm Tues.-Fri., 10am-5pm Sat.-Sun.; tickets free or starting at $8
Occupying a lovely, high-ceilinged colonial-era building on art-centric Positos Street, the Foro Cultural 81 is a multidisciplinary art and cultural center that hosts a series of ongoing musical performances, classes and workshops, speakers, culinary events, and visual art exhibitions; most are offered for free or at a low cost. Uniting a variety of disciplines and eras, offerings might include a jarocho concert, an open mic for writers, a show of new artwork by students at the University of Guanajuato, or a talk by a historian.

GALLERIES AND MUSEUMS
Centro Histórico
Corredor Artístico Tomas Chávez Morado
C. Pedro Lascurain de Retana 5; tel. 473/735-3700, ext. 2731; www.cultura.ugto.mx; 10am-2:30pm and 3pm-6pm Mon.-Fri.; free
The Universidad de Guanajuato has several well-managed gallery spaces overseen by the university art department. These galleries feature rotating exhibitions with a focus on contemporary art, and they are free and open to the public. Located just beside the university's famous sandstone staircase, the small but beautiful Corredor Artístico Tomas Chávez Morado is dedicated to interdisciplinary visual art, with pieces, often by local artists, designed to fit the space. The gallery itself is unusual, with an arched entryway leading into a cave-like salon with thick stone walls and a bi-level exhibition space—a surprising backdrop for the experimental pieces on exhibit. Sometimes the entire space is dedicated to a single piece of work.

Galería Hermenegildo Bustos
C. Pedro Lascurain de Retana 3; tel. 473/735-3700, ext. 2731; www.cultura.ugto.mx; 10am-2:30pm and 3pm-6pm Mon.-Fri.; free
Just inside the main university entrance, the Galería Hermenegildo Bustos is a free exhibition space often featuring work by student artists, both Mexican and international. Just beside it, **Galería Polivalente** (tel. 473/735-3700, ext. 2731; www.cultura.ugto.mx; 10am-2:30pm and 3pm-6pm Mon.-Fri.; free) is a large gallery with high ceilings, clean white walls, and exposed piping. The atmosphere feels contemporary, as do the artists who show here, most of whom are students from Guanajuato and beyond. With two large rooms, plus several smaller spaces ideal for installation, this gallery can accommodate large-format pieces and extensive collective exhibitions.

Galería El Atrio
Plazuela de la Compañía s/n; www.cultura.ugto.mx; 10am-2pm and 3pm-6pm daily; free
Just a block from the main university campus, Galería El Atrio is an unusual art gallery, fitted into a long and thin salon that runs along the base of the Templo de la Compañía de Jesús. Since there isn't enough room to really step back from the work, this gallery tends to show smaller-format pieces, ranging from painting to photography. The gallery has a rotating schedule of exhibitions, showing contemporary work by local artists in group or individual exhibitions.

Primer Deposito

Positos 25; tel. 473/732-1125; primerdepositogto@
gmail.com; 10am-6pm Tues.-Sat., 10am-5pm Sun.; US$1

Beloved Guanajuato ceramics artist Capelo owns the contemporary gallery and museum Primer Deposito. Housed in a beautiful old mansion on art-centric Positos Street, the building includes several downstairs galleries, plus one accessible via a narrow spiral staircase. Here you'll have a chance to see work by Capelo, including his signature ceramics and oil paintings, in addition to work by other Mexican contemporary artists. There are also plates, platters, pitchers, urns, mugs, and other creative flatware hand-painted with flowers, fruits, animals, and other traditional designs for sale in an accompanying shop.

FESTIVALS AND EVENTS

In the party-loving town of Guanajuato, there are constant cultural events, religious festivals, and live music in the centro histórico. If you choose to visit Guanajuato during a well-known festival or holiday, you will likely find an increase in national tourism, fewer hotel rooms available, and a lot of activity throughout the public plazas and performance venues. Of particular note, the Cervantino festival in October is a huge event, during which the city is very full and rather expensive. You can get more information about Guanajuato's cultural events at the **Dirección Municipal de Cultura y Educación de Guanajuato** (Av. 5 de Mayo 1; tel. 473/732-7491).

Semana Santa

Holy Week; Mar.-Apr.

Generally considered the most important religious holiday of the year, Semana Santa is colorfully celebrated in the city of Guanajuato. If you plan to visit during Holy Week, book your hotel reservations in advance. Most of Mexico's schools and businesses take their spring break during Semana Santa, so there is a lot of national tourism, especially in popular destinations like Guanajuato.

Viernes de Dolores

Sixth Friday of Lent

Though Semana Santa runs from Palm Sunday to Easter Sunday, the festivities in Guanajuato begin earlier, with beautiful celebrations in honor of Viernes de Dolores, observed on the sixth Friday of Lent. For this popular festival, the Jardín de la Unión is a locus of activity, filled with people and decorated with papel picado and lavish bouquets of flowers. Politicians and local government officials weave through the crowds, handing out flowers and ice cream to passersby. It is also traditional for young men to give flowers to young women, in the spirit of love or friendship, and then walk with them through the Jardín de la Unión. Throughout the city's homes, offices, businesses, mines, markets, and plazas, small altars are built in the Virgin's honor, traditionally decorated with Easter candles, chamomile, dill, gold-painted oranges, wheat, and flowers as well as an image of the Virgin. Visitors to the altars are given aguas de fruta, usually limeade. In the Valenciana neighborhood, the mines also traditionally host large celebrations and are often open to the public.

Domingo de Ramos

Palm Sunday

On Palm Sunday, you'll see beautifully woven palm crosses and other palm adornments sold outside churches across the city, which families bring to the church for blessing.

Viernes Santo and Domingo de Gloria

Good Friday

The city expresses a more solemn portrait on Viernes Santo, generally considered the most important day of Holy Week. At midday, the Passion of the Christ is reenacted in the city center with townspeople playing the roles of Romans and Hebrews. In the evening, the Procesión del Silencio (Silent Procession) commemorates Christ's suffering and death in a moving parade, during which hundreds of mourners march in chilling silence through the twisting alleys of downtown Guanajuato. The procession continues for hours, often concluding late in the night.

Easter Sunday itself, usually called Domingo de Gloria, is a quieter day in Guanajuato, when most families spend time together and possibly attend mass.

Apertura de la Presa de la Olla and the Fiestas de San Juan

Opening of the Dam; July

The Presa de la Olla, a small reservoir to the east of the city center, was originally built in the 18th century to help prevent the frequent flooding that plagued Guanajuato's city center. Today the reservoir is surrounded by a lovely colonial neighborhood and flanked on its west side by the Florencio Antillón Park. The reservoir can be a relaxing place to visit for an afternoon stroll, and it is also the site of an annual festival, the Apertura de la Presa. The festival is believed to date back to the mid-18th century, when locals gathered together to drain and clean the river to prevent backups and flooding. Though originally organized for utilitarian purposes, the cleaning and opening of the dam have also become a merry municipal party.

The ritual cleaning continues on the first Monday of July, with the city's mayor arriving to command the opening of the dam's floodgates at 1pm. The rushing water creates a rather pleasant breeze through the neighborhood. Thereafter, the party continues with swimming competitions and a big local party in Florencio Antillón Park. There are dozens of food stands and live music from the state band. The festival is generally associated with St. John the Baptist, whose feast day is June 24 and whose association with water is reflected in the opening of the dam.

Día de la Independencia

Sept. 16

The capital of a state known for its large role in the independence movement (not to mention, the site of one of the most famous battles

in the War of Independence), Guanajuato is a fitting place to spend the **fiestas patrias,** the patriotic festivals commemorating the anniversary of Mexico's independence from Spain. Like most Mexican cities, Guanajuato gets dressed up in patriotic attire during the month of September, decked out with tricolor flags, lights, and banners that read ¡Viva México! At 11pm on September 15, the town's mayor holds a brief ceremony in the Palacio Municipal (in the Plaza de la Paz), calling out "¡Viva México!" to the crowd. Fireworks and general merriment follow. The big thing to do, however, is hit the bars and party until dawn. The following day, September 16, is a national holiday, commemorating the day Mexico declared independence from Spain, launching the War of Independence.

Día de la Toma de la Alhóndiga

Anniversary of the Taking of the Alhóndiga; Sept. 28

If you didn't get your fix of independence events, on September 28 the city of Guanajuato celebrates the first major battle of the War of Independence, the Día de la Toma de la Alhóndiga with a municipal parade.

★ Festival Internacional Cervantino

Various venues; Oct.; advanced tickets recommended

One of the biggest and most prestigious cultural events in Latin America, the extraordinary Festival Internacional Cervantino (FIC) is held every October in Guanajuato. At this three-week-long festival, the emphasis is on the performing arts, including dance, theater, opera, and live music events, which are held throughout the city's theaters, churches, and plazas. Every year, more than 2,000 ensembles, soloists, dance troupes, bands, orchestras, and singers are invited to Guanajuato to perform, with shows running morning to night. Additionally, the visual arts have taken on an increasingly robust presence, with galleries and museums throughout town showing special exhibits to coincide with the festival.

Like performing events, many of these are included in the program on the festival's website; however, visual arts venues generally don't require advance tickets to visit.

Although Mexican artists are well represented in the program, the event is distinctly international, with several foreign countries elected as honorary guests each year. Several Mexican states are also specially invited, with each setting up a showroom dedicated to their crafts, food, and culture.

History

In 1952 Universidad de Guanajuato professor Enrique Ruelas began directing short plays, or entremeses, by Spanish writer Miguel de Cervantes Saaevedra, the author of *Don Quixote*, in the Plaza San Roque in Guanajuato. The entremeses became increasingly popular over the years, eventually garnering attention from well-known artists and politicians. The performances gained public support in the 1970s and the variety of performances rapidly expanded, growing tremendously in prestige and scope throughout the 1980s. Since 2013 acclaimed Mexican writer Jorge Volpi has been the festival's director. The festival celebrated its 50th anniversary in 2022.

Tickets

- The full FIC festival program is announced to the public every year in **July,** and tickets go on sale online the following day. Search the program and find ticket booth locations at https://festivalcervantino.gob.mx.

- You need to **buy tickets in advance** for major acts. While **same-day tickets** may be available for some of the smaller events at lesser-known venues, tickets for the most **well-known performers will sell out within a week**—or even days—of going on sale.

- Ticket prices vary widely, from US$8 to US$50. Students and teachers with a valid ID can get reduced-price tickets to most events. In addition to ticketed events, many

free performances are held in parks and civic plazas during the festival. You cannot reserve advance tickets for free events, so it's best to arrive early to the venue if there's something you want to see.

Venues

In addition to seeing wonderful music and art, attending the Festival Internacional Cervantino is an opportunity to take an informal tour of Guanajuato's many theaters and performing arts venues, as well as the public plazas and parks where many shows take place. In recent years, performances have been held in such diverse venues as the **Ex-Hacienda San Gabriel de Barrera,** the beautiful churrigueresque **Templo de la Compañía de Jesús,** and the interior patio of the **Alhóndiga de Granaditas.** It is particularly special to see a show within the splendid Moorish-style interior of **Teatro Juárez.**

Accommodations

Budget and midrange hotels can cost two or even three times the usual price during the festival. Many locals also rent out rooms or houses during the festival via Airbnb and other services. If you want to visit Guanajuato during the FIC, it's best to book **at least three months in advance** and as far out as six months for the best range of options. If you can't find reasonable accommodations, consider staying in San Miguel de Allende, just two hours away, and driving to Guanajuato for events.

Transportation

If you are arriving in Guanajuato by **intercity bus,** book tickets well in advance for both your arrival and departure. Bus tickets sell out in advance of the events. If you are **driving** to Guanajuato, avoid the traffic in the centro by parking your car outside the city center (there are places to park near the bus terminal), then take a cab or city bus into the center of town. **Plan to walk almost everywhere** you're going. Traffic is heavy throughout the festival and taxis can be difficult to find. If you are booking tickets for two events on the same day, make sure you have enough time to get from one venue to another.

The Cervantino Ambience

Among the reasons to attend the Cervantino is to enjoy the unique atmosphere, being among the huge crowds of international artists and revelers that flood the town during the festival. During the festivities, the streets are constantly filled, restaurants and cafés are hopping, and amateurs take advantage of the crowds to show off their talents (expect plenty of young street musicians, clowns, or living statues performing in coffee shops and open spaces). In addition, there are special events and **visual arts exhibitions** in the city's museums, galleries, and shops, as well as special shows in the university's art galleries. It is also a great time to visit for those who love a party. In addition to festival events, there are **electronic dance parties** and other special events specially aimed at attracting Guanajuato's student residents.

Festival Internacional de Órgano Antiguo de Guanajuato "Guillermo Pinto Reyes"

International Antique Organ Festival; usually Nov.; free

Guanajuato's churches contain some of Mexico's most beautiful and historic organs. Every year, these beautiful instruments are put to use at the annual Festival Internacional de Órgano Antiguo de Guanajuato "Guillermo Pinto Reyes." For this unique event, artists from across Mexico are invited to perform in the city's chapels and churches, including the Oratorio San Felipe Neri and the Templo de San Cayetano in the Valenciana neighborhood. Events are free and open to the public. The festival dates are usually published in newspapers and in flyers around town in advance of the event.

Shopping

Although Guanajuato is not a shopping destination like nearby San Miguel de Allende, the town offers plenty of places to pick up a nice gift or do some casual browsing. In the centro histórico, several traditional craft shops sell clothing and ceramics, and several famous artisans work in the city.

CENTRO HISTÓRICO
Traditional Crafts
Rincón Artesanal

De Sopeña 5; no tel.; 10:30am-6pm daily

For regional craftwork, Rincón Artesanal sells the distinctive ceramics produced in a community called La Purísima in Tarandacuao, Guanajuato. Unlike the majolica-style pottery that is most commonly sold in the Bajío region, this hand-wheeled ceramic is painstakingly painted with delicate geometric patterns, applied in an ultra-high-temperature glaze. Rincón Artesanal presents work from several Tarandacuao artists, each producing a slightly different version of this traditional craft with a different palette of colors. Small espresso cups and saucers are sweetly sophisticated and sold by the set, while the large ceramic platters are impressively detailed. With decades in business, the store's senior owners will be happy to tell you about the work.

Artlalli

C. de la Galarza 94; tel. 473/732-1096; www.artlalli. com; 10am-8pm daily

Pick up a small gift to take home from Artlalli, which sells a colorful, reasonably priced selection of trinkets and crafts from across Mexico, including blown glass from Jalisco, milagritos (small tin ornaments), alebrijes (painted wood figurines) from Oaxaca, printed artwork, Frida Kahlo wallets, Huichol beaded animals, and enamel cookware, all stuffed into a tiny storefront on Positos. The staff can provide the background on a piece's provenance, technique, and significance.

La Casa del Quijote

De Sopeña 17; tel. 473/732-8226; www.lacasadelquijote. com; 11am-9pm daily

Next door to the Museo Iconográfico del Quijote, La Casa del Quijote is a large craft and jewelry shop in a grand old building. The airy showrooms are not particularly complemented by the sleek electronic music playing on the sound system, but they are well stocked with textiles and pottery from across Mexico. In addition to some nice ceramic work by artisans from the state of Guanajuato, the store has a large supply of Mata Ortiz pottery from Chihuahua and Oaxacan textiles. There is also a wide selection of silver jewelry showcased in the shop's two large front rooms.

Galleries and Artist Studios
El Pinche Grabador

Positos 77; tel. 473/732-3394; www.elpinchegrabador. com; 9am-8pm Mon.-Fri., 10am-6pm Sat-Sun.

El Pinche Grabador is a gallery and print shop that sells a delightful collection of handmade prints with fun, distinctly Mexican themes—wrestling heroes, skeletons in love, cactus and flowers—created by artist Luís Carlos Rodriguez, the pinche grabador (damn printer) himself. Made in a variety of printmaking techniques, the pieces are often small (and easy to fit into a suitcase), and everything is sold at very accessible prices. It's a wonderful place to browse or pick up a unique souvenir from your visit to Guanajuato.

Corazón Parlante Galería & Café

De Sopena 13B; no tel.; 10am-6pm Sun.-Mon., 11am-6pm Thurs., 11am-9:30pm Fri.-Sat.

A printmaking studio, gallery, and café on heart-of-it-all Sopeña, Corazón Parlante sells a selection of original books, handcraft, and artwork, much of it created on-site. Sold at reasonable prices and created by young local artist, the print work is largely linocut (using a linoleum plate), a popular medium for graphic work in Mexico, with themes that have a distinctive Mexican feel. Work is generally reasonably priced. The studio hosts special events, like artists talks or workshops, but you can just stop in for a coffee and a concha to enjoy the atmosphere.

La Catrina, a massive candy shop

Gourmet Goodies
Mercado Hidalgo
Juárez s/n, esq. Mendizábal; no tel.; 8:30am-9pm daily; individual shop hours vary

Sweets are produced throughout the state of Guanajuato, and dulces típicos (traditional sweets) from the region are sold at the stands inside the main entrance to the Mercado Hidalgo. In addition to sweets, the market is also a good place to pick up dried chiles, dried beans, cheese, tortillas, fresh fruit and vegetables, and other staples.

Dulceria Galereña
Juárez 188; tel. 473/732-5934; 9am-8pm daily

This old-fashioned candy shop opened in 1955. Here, you'll find jars of cajeta (goat-milk caramel), ates (fruit pastes), house-made candied fruit and nuts, marmalades made from Mexican fruits, and the strange confection known as queso de tuna (a thick sweetened paste made of the prickly pear fruit), all presented in no-nonsense piles on the shelves. You can also find a few amusing treats amid the traditional stock, like gummy mummies commemorating Guanajuato's oddest sight.

La Catrina
Sopeña 4; tel. 473/732-6089; www.dulcerialacatrina.com.mx; 9am-9pm daily

The delightfully sugary La Catrina is a massive, colorful Mexican sweets shop, right across the street from Teatro Juárez. Within this shiny two-story shop are some wonderful and unusual candies, like fig and walnut paste, shredded coconut bars, and palenquetas (honey-covered discs of nuts, pumpkin seeds, or amaranth). Regional treats include cajeta, which is largely produced in nearby Celaya, as well as xoconostle jam, made from the fruit of a sour prickly pear that is popular in the region. The store's employees will be happy to give you a basket to collect your goodies, as well as free samples of some of the more unusual candies.

Classes

TOP EXPERIENCE

For many foreigners, Guanajuato is an ideal place to spend several weeks on the cheap, hanging out with other travelers, sipping coffee in inexpensive eateries, studying Spanish, or reveling in rowdy nightlife. Fortunately, there are plenty of excellent and popular language schools in this little town. Even if you don't sign up for a formal language program, check out the university's art and cultural offerings, which often include lectures and workshops open to the public.

SPANISH LANGUAGE
Centro Histórico
Escuela Falcon
Callejón de Gallitos 6; tel. 473/732-6531; www.escuelafalcon.com; US$59-443/week

At Escuela Falcon, one of Guanajuato's most popular language schools, students can sign up for Spanish language classes, and they have the opportunity to take classes on Mexican art and culture, dance, history, and politics. There are special programs for children with guiding themes like art, dance, or cinema. The school has several apartment rentals available to students at the school, which you can book even if you aren't studying with them. They can also arrange for homestays with locals.

Escuela Mexicana
Potrero 12; tel. 473/732-2944; www.escuelamexicana.com; $200-300/week, or $889 for 12-week program

Founded in the early 1990s, the affordable Escuela Mexicana is located in a cheerful colonial building in Guanajuato's centro histórico. This school's diverse Spanish programs let you tailor coursework to your needs, with the option of taking private classes by the week or signing up for a 12-week session with a mix of group and individual instruction. This school donates a percentage of its proceeds to charitable causes in the region. Depending on your desires, Escuela Mexicana will help students arrange a homestay with a local family ($30/night, including two meals), or students can rent private rooms on the campus (from $40/night). They also offer day trips, extracurricular activities like cooking lessons, and airport pickup for students.

Southeast of the Centro
Colegio de Lenguas Adelita
Callejón Agua Fuerte 56; tel. 473/732-0826; www.learnspanishadelita.com; from US$8

Offering basic-, beginner-, and intermediate-level classes, Colegio de Lenguas Adelita has experienced teachers who hold degrees in Spanish. Both private classes and group classes are surprisingly well priced (a single group class costs US$8 for an hour, and US$39 for a week of one-hour classes), with further discounts for students who choose to study longer (US$100 a month for daily group classes).

In addition to grammar and conversation, students can sign up for history and culture classes, as well as guided tours of the city.

ART
Centro Histórico
Piramidal Grafica Studio
Piletas 6 Masaguas; tel. 473/733-5423; https://piramidalgraficastudio.com; classes with accommodations and breakfast US$160/day

Professional artist and Guanajuato native Hugo Anaya offers printmaking workshops in a variety of techniques in his gorgeous top-floor printmaking studio, right in the center of the city. Appropriate for beginners as well as more advanced printmakers, classes can also be combined with a stay at the lovely bed-and-breakfast Alma del Sol, which occupies the first two floors of the building (US$160 single or US$220 for two people, including accommodations, breakfast, coursework, and materials). In addition to his warm and enthusiastic teaching style, Hugo is a true Guanajuato insider, and he can offer excellent tips on where to eat, drink, and visit around town.

Food

Plenty of tourist-friendly restaurant options fill the Plaza San Fernando, the Jardín de la Unión, and other picturesque locales across town; these eateries can be a great pick for a cold beer, a plate of guacamole, and an amazing atmosphere (not a bad combination by any standard). Generally speaking, however, the most visible restaurants may not be the best place for a satisfying or authentic Mexican meal in Guanajuato. Catering to a transient tourist crowd, the service can be slow and the food unmemorable.

That said, Guanajuato's restaurant scene has made some considerable leaps forward. Not traditionally renowned for its cuisine, the city now offers some wonderful places to eat, a handful of cool cafés for sipping coffee, and a smattering of nice international options,

adding a measure of welcome sophistication to this student-centric city.

CENTRO HISTÓRICO
Quick Bites
Throughout Guanajuato, there are casual **food stands** on almost every corner, many selling gorditas (stuffed and griddled corn cakes), tamales, sweets, fruit, potato chips, snacks, and juices. For a quick meal, you'll find the most variety on the first floor of the **Mercado Hidalgo,** where there are a host of tacos, tortas, gorditas, seafood and shrimp cocktails, fruit juices, cakes, and sweets at a variety of informal food stands. Carnitas (braised pork) is a specialty here, and you can order it in tacos or a torta, served sandwich-style inside a white roll.

Best Restaurants

Mexican restaurant Puscua

★ **Truco 7:** A classic stop for students, backpackers, and families, this casual all-day eatery serves simple, inexpensive Mexican fare in a funky, upbeat environment (page 152).

★ **Mestizo:** At this lovely Mexican restaurant, traditional dishes, like pollo con mole and sopa de tortilla, are served with a chef-driven flair (page 152).

★ **Delica Mitsu:** For a fresh, inexpensive, healthy, and veggie-friendly lunch, stop into this bohemian Japanese joint on Campanero (page 154).

★ **Café Tal:** Everyone's favorite Guanajuato coffee shop serves up strong brew and cool vibes, as well as a killer hot chocolate (page 154).

★ **Casa Mercedes Restaurante:** Here heirloom Mexican recipes are lovingly prepared and served in the cozy dining room of a family home overlooking the city center (page 155).

★ **Puscua:** In a romantic stone-walled dining room at the Casa Museo Gene Byron, this innovative Mexican restaurant is one of Guanajuato's best, presenting fresh local flavors with artistry and imagination (page 156).

Mariscos La Vela

Constancia 3; tel. 473/164-9037; noon-8pm Tues.-Sun.; US$5

Feeding the Mexican national obsession with shrimp cocktail, Mariscos La Vela is a small seafood counter behind the Teatro Juárez. Choose from a range of cocktails and tostadas with shrimp, oyster, and octopus; ceviche; seafood empanadas; and fried fish fillets, all made fresh in the moment and served with a plate of limes and some hot sauce. With two locations in Guanajuato, La Vela's seafood is brought in continuously from the coast, meaning the catch is fresher than what you might expect to find in the Mexican highlands (stick to fully cooked food if you're concerned about the distance from the ocean). This is an inexpensive, easygoing place for a good bite.

Mexican

Casa Valadez

Jardín de la Unión 3; tel. 473/732-0311; www. casavaladez.com; 8am-11pm daily; US$7

An atmospheric restaurant on the Jardín de la Unión, Casa Valadez gets double points for ambience. Located on the east end of the Jardín de la Unión, the old-fashioned dining room is decorated with gray-and-gold columns, brass chandeliers, and patterned wallpaper. Bathrooms are particularly fancy. Always packed with tourists and families dining alfresco or lounging indoors in one of the restaurant's big booths, there is often a wait for a table on the weekends. The menu covers a full spectrum, including soups, salads, burgers, sandwiches, enchiladas, and meat dishes; plates run from economical to pricey.

Los Huacales

Súbida de San José 15; tel. 473/734-2359; https://los-huacales.negocio.site; 9am-9pm Tues.-Sat.; US$4-8

The cozy dining room at Los Huacales often fills up at breakfast, lunch, and dinner, and for good reason: the extensive menu is an appealing mix of classic Mexican dishes, plates are generously served, and the prices are surprisingly economical for a restaurant smack dab in the middle of downtown. Here you can get a big plate of enchiladas, flautas, chicken with mole poblano, or a huarache (large corn flatbread) topped with chiles, chicken, or potato, among other offerings. The ceiling of the dining room is decorated with a collection of the restaurant's namesake huacales (wood crates traditionally used in markets); other than that simple adornment, it's a no-fuss atmosphere for a filling, delicious meal. Note that no alcohol is served.

★ Truco 7

Truco 7; tel. 473/732-8374; 8:30am-11pm daily; US$6

On a small alley just a block from the Jardín de la Unión, Truco 7 is a popular and inexpensive café that serves a range of tasty Mexican staples as well as a daily comida corrida, an economical three-course set-price lunch. This casual restaurant has the cozy and convivial atmosphere of a cool college hangout, with exposed brick walls, comfy wooden furniture, low lamps, and eclectic art on the walls. The restaurant is open from early in the morning until late at night, and the menu is classic Mexican, featuring enchiladas, sopa azteca, sopes (thick corn tortillas topped with beans and chicken), and several mole dishes. With decades in operation, it's a Guanajuato classic.

★ Mestizo

Positos 69; tel. 473/732-0612; 1pm-10pm Tues.-Thurs., 9am-10pm Fri.-Sat., 9am-6pm Sun.; $US10-16

Owned and operated by the chef Javier Cruz Hernández Vallejo, son of beloved local ceramic artist Capelo, Mestizo is a wonderful contemporary Mexican restaurant, perfect for a special meal or date night. Located in what was once Capelo's downtown showroom, Mestizo's dining room preserves the gallery feel with wooden dining tables tucked between shelves of pretty hand-painted platters, flatware, and urns. Food relies on local ingredients to create innovative flavors, to good effect. Risotto with huitlacoche, pork in red berry sauce, and steak with chile ancho and roast tomatoes are some recent menu offerings. For the quality of the food, the surprisingly accessible prices, and the beauty of its presentations, Mestizo has become a favorite with locals, and it is certainly one of the most satisfying places to eat in town.

Fusion

Costal Cultura Cafetera

San José 4; tel. 473/163-4001; www.costalrestaurante. com; 2pm-10pm Mon.-Sat. 2pm-9pm Sun.; US$9-20

This sweet afternoon café and supper spot occupies a creaky wood-floored dining room on the second floor of an old mansion, just off the Plaza Baratillo. Serving comida (the midday meal) and dinner, the menu is a mashup of Mexican and European dishes, from lettuce wraps to roast tomato soup to pork in

---

1: Mariscos La Vela **2:** bridge-top coffee shop Santo Café

tamarind sauce with sauerkraut. Service is friendly and food is beautifully plated, but the main reason to visit is the romantic atmosphere, whether you're having a leisurely supper or just dropping in for an afternoon coffee break with a slice of Basque cheesecake. The Estudiantina passes right below the restaurant every night, so choose a balcony seat at dinnertime.

La Capellina

Sopeña 3; tel. 473/732-7224; 1:30pm-midnight daily; US$10

A Mexican-European fusion restaurant and pizza place with years in business in downtown Guanajuato, La Capellina is set in a spacious modern dining room with high ceilings and art on the walls, with a couple of nice tables overlooking bustling Sopeña street. The menu runs the gamut in cuisine (and quality), with offerings like chipotle-shrimp tacos, beet carpaccio, and four-cheese fettucine on offer. Most diners come for the thin-crust pizzas, which are among the best options on the menu. A great spot for a night out, the kitchen is open late and there are often live musicians playing jazz, Latin rhythms, or classical guitar during dinnertime.

Japanese
★ Delica Mitsu

Campanero 5; tel. 473/116-6491; noon-9pm daily; US$6-14

A longtime Guanajuato favorite, Delica Mitsu started out as a hole-in-the-wall Japanese deli, tucked into a narrow alley behind the Plaza Fernando. Today the operation has expanded to a funky sit-down café off Campanero where, for surprisingly low prices, you can order a lovely plate of sushi rolls or teriyaki chicken with sides from the deli case, or pick up a made-to-order bento box with the day's offerings (note that popular sides in the deli often run out by early afternoon). While the lineup changes daily, Delica Mitsu always offers wonderful salads and noodle dishes, as

well as more unusual options like cabbage cakes and teriyaki potatoes, plus miso soup, tempura, Japanese green teas, Japanese beers, and sake.

Coffee Shops and Dessert
Santo Café

Puente de Campanero, Campanero 4; tel. 473/122-2320; www.santocafegto.com; 10am-midnight Mon.-Sat., noon-midnight Sun.

With outdoor seating on a tiny footbridge over the pedestrian street Campanero, Santo Café might have the city's most appealing location. It can be a trick to snag one of the best tables, though, as you'll always find a small crowd here, chatting, reading, or relaxing away the afternoon in a ray of golden sunlight. The café sells beer, wine, and coffee as well as sandwiches, flautas, and salads. The food is good, and the setting makes it even better. There is also wireless Internet.

★ Café Tal

Callejón Temezcuitate 4; tel. 473/732-6212; 7am-10pm Mon.-Fri, 8am-10pm Sat.-Sun.; US $2

Everyone's favorite Guanajuato coffee shop, Café Tal is the type of place that takes coffee seriously. Here all beans are dark roasted in-house and expertly brewed to be strong and full-bodied. Open from early in the morning until late at night, the café's two rooms of shaky granite tables are continuously populated with hipsters on laptops, while waiters in black T-shirts serve brew and breads. There's another branch with a sunny rooftop terrace near the Presa de la Olla (Paseo de la Presa 130; tel. 473/192-1074; 7am-10pm Mon.-Fri., 8am-10pm Sat.-Sun.).

Estación Gelato

Callejón de Cantaritos 29; tel. 473/732-801; www.estaciongelato.com; noon-9pm Mon.-Fri., 11am-9pm Sat.-Sun.; US $2

A little café and ice cream parlor tucked into a narrow pedestrian alley, Estación Gelato is a sweet spot to stop for an afternoon

Queso de Tuna and Other Desert Desserts

The state of Guanajuato has a serious sweet tooth. **Dulces típicos** (traditional sweets) are produced in various cities across the state and consumed by the populace with appetite and pleasure. In the city of Guanajuato, there are wonderful sweets stands in the market and numerous traditional sweets shops boasting enormous selections and unique regional candies. Here are some to try.

CAJETA AND DULCE DE LECHE

Among the most popular flavors in Mexico, cajeta (slowly simmered caramelized goat milk) is produced in the states of Guanajuato and Jalisco, most famously in the nearby city of Celaya. Popular throughout Mexico, cajeta is sold in jars as a caramel syrup or is incorporated into sweets. A popular treat is cajeta spread between two obleas, thin wafers made with the same process as the communion wafers served in Catholic churches, yet not blessed by a priest. Dulces de leche (chewy cow's-milk caramels) are also produced in the Bajío region and can be bought by the piece.

Sweets made with cajeta and dulce de leche can be purchased in sweet shops like **La Catrina** (page 149), markets, and corner stores throughout the region.

ATE AND CRYSTALLIZED FRUIT

You'll find ate (sweetened fruit paste) produced in Guanajuato. Quince, guava, and mango are among the most popular flavors for ate, though it can be made of many different fruits. Ate is traditionally served with cheese as a dessert. Crystallized fruits, tubers, and cactus are also popular desserts, commonly made from orange, fig, sweet potato, or lime stuffed with shredded coconut.

In the desert environment, confectioners also make use of the abundance of cactus and succulents, such as **xoconostle** (sour prickly pear fruit). Note that crystallized **biznaga** or **acitrón,** sweets made from the barrel cactus, should be avoided; in 2005 Secretariat of Environment and Natural Resources federally protected the endangered barrel cactus, banning its culinary uses without special permit.

QUESO DE TUNA

For the adventurous, the strongly flavored queso de tuna (prickly pear cheese) is one of the more unusual sweets of the semidesert. While it's difficult to get your hands on this old-fashioned Mexican dessert, it is more widely available in the city of Guanajuato. This thick and heavy candy is made from ground prickly pear fruit mixed with unrefined sugar, which is slowly cooked until it forms a thick, dark paste. The paste is then cooled in giant molds and cut into blocks. The resulting sweet is unusually dense and chewy, with a rich and concentrated flavor quite unlike anything else.

Look for it in the shops and stands surrounding the **Mercado Hidalgo** (page 134) and at the **Dulceria Galereña** (page 149).

pick-me-up. There's a full coffee bar with beans from Chiapas, tea, brownies, homemade ice pops, and a range of gelato in flavors like bittersweet chocolate, passionfruit, and hazelnut, including sugar-free and keto options. Grab one of the round café tables downstairs—the nicest is placed in a window overlooking the alley below—or on a sunny day, head up to the roof deck, where you can sit amid the rooftops of Guanajuato. If you'd like your sweets to go, there's an Estación Gelato storefront on the alley Truco (Truco 8; 11am-9pm Mon.-Fri., 11:30am-9pm Sat., 11:30am-9:30pm Sun.), just around the corner from the Jardín de la Unión.

SAN JAVIER
★ Casa Mercedes Restaurante
Calle de Arriba 6, Fracc. San Javier; tel. 473/733-9059, reservations WhatsApp 473/171-8866; www.

casamercedes.com.mx; 2pm-10pm Tues.-Sat., 2pm-6pm Sun.; US$25

It is well worth a trip to the San Javier neighborhood to dine at the lovely family-run Casa Mercedes. Offering a constantly changing menu of heirloom Mexican recipes, Casa Mercedes presents traditional flavors with creative flair. From memorable starters like a bean-stuffed tamal in guava-and-marigold mole to entrées like poblano chile stuffed with Veracruz-style crab, it is tempting to try everything on the menu. Whatever you choose, you'll enjoy flavorful, unique, and perfectly prepared food that is both elegant and pleasingly homemade. The restaurant maintains a nice selection of Mexican wines as well as margaritas, spirits, beer, and a mezcal-xoconostle cocktail made with the fruit of a sour prickly pear. Despite its off-the-beaten track location, this place has gotten enough buzz to attract a nightly seating of tourists and locals. Reservations are necessary; come with an appetite. The restaurant is located in a residential neighborhood about 4 km (3 mi) north of the city center; a taxi will get you there in 15 minutes.

MARFIL
★ Puscua, Cocina de Herencia
Museo Gene Byron, Camino Real de Marfil Ex-Hacienda de Santa Ana s/n; tel. 473/733-5018; 8:30am-5pm Tues.-Sun.; US$6-9

The rustic stone dining room at Puscua, located within the hacienda at the Museo Gene Byron, is one of the nicest places to eat in Guanajuato. At this half-day breakfast-and-lunch spot, you can start your morning with a creative and beautifully plated dish, like panela cheese served with roast tomatoes and poblano chiles, an omelet with salsa verde and purslane, or tongue birria (stew) served with nopales. Between the enchanting setting and the wonderful food, eating here feels like a special occasion, though prices are very reasonable. The restaurant does not serve alcohol, though they do have a daily agua (fruit drink),

coffee, tea, and limonadas, as well as a petit bakery selection, which includes carrot cake and conchas. Reservations recommended.

PRESA DE LA OLLA
Mexico Lindo y Sabroso
Paseo de la Presa 154; tel. 473/731-0529; 9am-9pm Tues.-Sun.; US$5-14

Away from the bustle of the centro histórico, Mexico Lindo y Sabroso is a nice place to linger over an afternoon meal. The airy dining room has a pleasingly Mexican atmosphere, with red-lacquer furniture, crafts on the walls, and ranchera music overhead. In front, the lovely covered patio overlooks the Paseo de la Presa, with big, comfortable seats and large tables. Service is attentive, and the waitstaff adds to the Mexican atmosphere with spiffy tricolor bow ties and white collared shirts. The extensive menu is entirely Mexican, offering a range of inexpensive and generously served dishes like enchiladas, enmoladas, and sopa azteca as well as some more unusual yet tasty Yucatec dishes, like papadzules (egg-filled tortillas topped with pumpkin-seed sauce and more hard-boiled egg) and cochinita pibil (pulled pork with achiote and spices). Everything tastes freshly prepared and is nicely seasoned; chips and salsa at the table make a nice start.

Amatxi
Paseo de la Presa 109; tel. 473/731-0692; https://amatxi.negocio.site; 2:30pm-9:30pm Wed.-Mon.; US$15-30

This upscale pan-European restaurant feels worlds away from the student-friendly bustle of downtown Guanajuato. Located in a contemporary top-floor dining room in the Presa de la Olla neighborhood, the atmosphere and menu have a decidedly adult feeling, with food that leans heavily on Spanish-, French-, and Italian-style classics, like baked brie and ratatouille, though Mexican options, like tacos, also make an appearance. Meats are a specialty of the kitchen, including dishes like smoked pork ribs, arrachera (a Mexican cut that is similar to skirt steak), and a filet guanajuatense served with a lightly sweetened dried chile sauce. Top-notch drinks and a nice wine list that includes Mexican labels make Amatxi a good choice for a memorable date night. Reservations recommended for weekend dinner.

La Victoriana

Paseo de la Presa 109; tel. 473/731-1406; noon-10pm Tues.-Fri., 9am-7pm Sat., 9am-5pm Sun.; US$5

There are several businesses operating inside a historic art nouveau building known as the **Casa de la Presa,** including this highly atmospheric café, an ideal place to land after a walk around the Presa de la Olla neighborhood. Come in the morning for French toast, pastries, and a drink from the espresso bar, or stop in at lunchtime for a sandwich and a glass of wine, which you can enjoy on the outdoor terrace or the marvelous indoor dining rooms, which are replete with carved moldings, soaring ceilings, stained-glass windows, and chandeliers. Reservations recommended on the weekends.

Bars and Nightlife

Guanajuato is a bustling, noisy, and occasionally rowdy city, filled with students, backpackers, and tourists looking to have a good time. In the evening, there is always a crowd pushing through the Jardín de la Unión, while groups of friends chat on the steps of Teatro Juárez. In sidewalk cafés, musicians mill through the crowd as bars and cantinas turn up the volume on their sound systems. While life can be more subdued during the week, Guanajuato feels like a citywide party on the weekends. Throughout the centro histórico, bars, cafés, and nightclubs cater to a late-night crowd. Most don't start pumping until after midnight, and some stay open until the break of dawn. Even if you don't indulge, you may hear the pumping beats of reggaeton from your hotel room!

Centro Histórico
Bar Tradicional Luna

Jardín de la Unión 10; tel. 473/734-1864; 12:30pm-midnight Mon.-Sat., 12:30pm-11pm Sun.; drinks $3-10

In the Jardín de la Unión, Bar Tradicional Luna is a wonderful place to tip back a tequila. As the name indicates, Luna is a traditional cantina—often full, noisy, and packed with tourists and locals enjoying a view of the plaza and a friendly Mexican atmosphere. On the weekends, it can be difficult to snag a seat on the patio. At any hour, traditional Mexican tunes play loudly on the jukebox as mariachis and trios gather around tables offering their services for a live song (on a Saturday night, they'll find plenty of takers among the tipsy crowds). During the day, polite waiters serve drinks along with complimentary botanas (appetizers), like shrimp soup or pork skin tostadas. There's a fine list of tequila.

La Clave Azul

2a de Cantaritos 31; tel. 473/732-1561; 1:30pm-9pm Mon.-Wed., 1:30pm-11:30pm Fri.-Sat., food service 1pm-6pm; US$6

Located on a tiny alley at the very back of the Plaza San Fernando, La Clave Azul is a lovely old cantina, perfect for a low-key afternoon of eating and drinking. Like many classic cantinas, La Clave Azul serves a small plate of food, or botana, along with each drink you order. Although the menu changes daily, the lechón (suckling pig) is one of the specialties. Supposedly designed in homage to Luis Buñuel's set designer, Juan Yanes, this spot has a tavern-like atmosphere with exposed rock walls and dim lighting. To get here, walk to the very back of the Plaza San Fernando. A teensy alleyway ascends from the plaza; La Clave Azul is just a few yards beyond the mouth of the alley.

Bartola

*Positos 33; tel. 473/732-9200; www.casadelrector.com;
2pm-11pm Mon.-Sat., 1pm-10pm Sun.; drinks US$4-11*

Beside the petite rooftop pool at boutique hotel Casa del Rector, Bartola is a lovely open-air cocktail lounge with gorgeous bird's-eye views of the city and the surrounding sierra. It is a particularly spectacular spot for a sunset, and they light heat lamps on cool Guanajuato evenings after the sun goes down. The cocktail list is creative, and, not surprisingly, a bit more expensive than those at the student-friendly spots downtown. Despite its million-dollar view, this welcoming lounge isn't pretentious; even families show up in the afternoon to enjoy the atmosphere.

La Casa de los Espiritus

Galarza 76; tel. 473/740-7831; 3pm-1am Mon., 2pm-1am Tues.-Sat., noon-1am Sun.; cover US$0-3, drinks US$2-5

There is almost always something going down at this artsy, youth-friendly bar. Here you can drop in for live music, DJs, movie screenings, clothing swaps, drinks specials, and even on-site art workshops, like drawing classes and printmaking sessions. If you aren't, head out to the terrace, which has beautiful views of the city, including the Alhóndiga de Granaditas. The well-priced menu includes mixed drinks, pulque and curados (flavored pulque), and beer, offered in both regular bottles or super-size caguamas.

Accommodations

Guanajuato is a big national and international tourist destination, drawing crowds of visitors year-round. While winter is technically the high season in Mexico, Guanajuato's tourist season is a bit more inconsistent. In fact, hotel rates tend to fluctuate substantially in Guanajuato, depending on demand. Most notably, the city's many cultural events, especially the annual Festival Internacional Cervantino in October, draw large crowds and can have a huge effect on hotel prices. Most hotels double or even triple their rates during this period, even if they aren't at capacity.

If you'd like to visit during Semana Santa, Christmas holidays, or, especially, the Festival Internacional Cervantino, it is necessary to reserve a hotel room in advance. At any other time of year, hotels rarely fill up. It is usually possible to snag a room on short notice. However, to spare yourself trekking around steep alleyways, it's best to have a hotel destination in mind before you arrive.

Perhaps because demand is high and fairly continuous, very few of Guanajuato's hotels offer really great value. Many of the hotels in the centro histórico are unapologetically basic, offering little more than a spring bed and a small bathroom—not even a poster on the wall. Nicer hotels may add a bit of charm, but most tend to be fairly pared down. Boutique properties, where design and comfort are prioritized, are becoming more common, but they are notably pricier.

CENTRO HISTÓRICO
Under US$50
Casa de Pita

Callejón Cabecita 26; tel. 473/732-1532; http://casadepita.com; US$40-60

The laid-back and quirky Casa de Pita is a great find in the budget category. Tucked into an enchanting alleyway behind the Plaza Mexiamora and only a few blocks from the Jardín de la Unión, the location could not be better. Some larger rooms have cute little kitchenettes that can be used to whip up a snack, and most are eclectically decorated with tiles and lamps. While these aren't luxury accommodations, the rooms are comfortable, and the style is fun and colorful. Pita herself is a friendly host who enjoys chatting with her guests over breakfast.

Best Accommodations

★ **El Zopilote Mojado:** At this well-priced guest-house, clean and cheerful bedrooms are located in buildings that surround a quiet plaza, right in the center of town (page 160).

★ **Alma del Sol:** At this small, quirky, and perfectly located bed-and-breakfast, the extravagant morning meals on the rooftop patio are an ace way to start the day (page 160).

★ **Hotel Antiguo Vapor:** The nicest rooms at this traditional Mexican inn have big windows overlooking the city center (page 161).

★ **Hotel Edelmira:** Posh yet comfortable and friendly, this stylish hotel has a center-of-it-all location, with some rooms overlooking the Jardín de la Unión (page 161).

boutique property Hotel Edelmira

★ **Casa del Rector:** This luxury boutique hotel in a gorgeous historic building has sweeping views of the city from the rooftop pool and cocktail bar (page 161).

La Casa Azul Hotel

Carcamanes 57; tel. 473/731-2288; www. casaazulguanajuato.com; US$45-55

It is a steep walk up a narrow alley, but the aerobic workout is just another benefit of staying at the friendly, family-run La Casa Azul Hotel. Perched high above the Plaza Baratillo, this six-room inn feels like the home of your abuela (grandmother), with the quirky details and comfort to match. The rooms vary in size and decor, but each is full of creaky old wooden furniture, crooked lamps, and thick Mexican bedspreads. Comfortably appointed, all rooms are equipped with a private bath and cable television, and some have sitting areas. There is a beautiful terrace on the roof; from here, you can enjoy the views you earned after the walk up the hill. The inn is owned by a Guanajuato family, and service is friendly and personable.

US$50-100
Hospedería del Truco 7

Constancia 15; tel. 473/732-6513; US$75

Hospedería del Truco 7 is owned by the same folks who run the popular Truco 7 restaurant. The guesthouse, unlike the restaurant, is not at the address Truco 7, as the name implies, but perched on a hillside just behind the Teatro Juárez and the Templo de San Diego. The seven rooms are simple and cozy, with comfortable Mexican-style furniture, oversize headboards, and cotton bedspreads. Every room has low wood-beamed ceilings, a TV, and a small, tiled bath with hand-painted sinks and showers. The nicest rooms in the front of the house have small balconies that open onto the alley below, offering a wonderful view of downtown Guanajuato. There's not much by way of sitting areas or shared facilities, but all of Guanajuato is at your doorstep.

★ **El Zopilote Mojado**

Plaza Mexiamora 51; tel. 473/732-5311; www.
elzopilotemojado.com; US$80

El Zopilote Mojado is a cute and tidy hotel, scattered across several small houses on the pretty Plaza Mexiamora. Located above a coffee shop of the same name, there are just three guest rooms in the main building, plus several more rooms in another building on the same plaza. The guest rooms are decorated with cheerful Mexican-style furnishings and comfortably outfitted with fans, electric blankets, closets, clock radios, bathrobes, and plenty of lighting. Some also have small balconies or terraces. At night, guests let themselves in via coded lock on the door. Management can feel a bit absent on Sundays when the café is closed, but this hotel is one of the nicer establishments in its price range. For those who like a little more space, El Zopilote also rents small apartments with kitchenettes.

US$100-150

★ **Alma del Sol**

Calle del Sol 3; tel. 472/733-5423; www.almadelsol.
com; US$100-115

An intimate bed-and-breakfast in an old colonial-era mansion, Alma del Sol is tucked behind huge mesquite-wood doors in the alley that runs alongside the Templo de la Compañía de Jesús, right in the center of town. This is a quirky place, with five second-floor rooms with towering ceilings and creaky wooden doors, decorated with traditional Mexican furniture and an impressive collection of traditional and antique textiles from India and Indonesia. Two double street-facing rooms have fabulous private balconies with views of the surrounding churches and mansions, though they can be a bit noisy in the evening. The nightly price includes what may be the best breakfast in town—served on the gorgeous roof deck, where you can chat with Alma del Sol's friendly proprietor, Hugo, a Guanajuato native who can give you a full rundown of things to do, see, eat, and experience while you're in town.

Posada Santa Fe

Jardín de la Unión 12; tel. 473/732-0084, toll-free
Mex. tel. 800/112-4773; www.posadasantafe.mx;
US$100-150

First opened in 1862, Posada Santa Fe has a long history of welcoming visitors to Guanajuato, in addition to an enviable location smack-dab in the middle of the Jardín de la Unión. The lobby of this old colonial mansion is beautiful, with hand-painted tiles on the

El Zopilote Mojado

walls and big chandeliers overhead. Rooms are decidedly less fancy, but a recent renovation has left them clean and comfortable, though still boasting, in many cases, old colonial-style furnishings. Some rooms are brighter than others, some are quieter; the prettiest have French windows that open onto the plaza below (though note that rooms with views on the plaza cost about US$50 more per night). The restaurant downstairs, with seating right in the Jardín de la Unión, is a great place to unwind with a drink at the end of the day.

US$150-200
★ Hotel Antiguo Vapor
Galarza 5; tel. 473/732-3211; www.hotelavapor.com; US$150-175

Atmospheric Hotel Antiguo Vapor is perched on a hill just above the city center, providing excellent views of the Mercado Hidalgo, the monument to El Pípila, and the surrounding cityscape. Guest rooms are small, simple, and comfortable, decorated in a warm, traditionally Mexican style, with Saltillo tile floors and colorful woven bedspreads adjoined by a pretty private bath with hand-painted tiles and showers. Some rooms have vaulted ceilings and stone walls; perhaps the nicest are those on the south side, with wee balconies and beautiful views overlooking the ravine below. The location is ideal—close to everything, yet just a bit removed from the noisy nightlife of downtown.

Casona Alonso 10
Alonso 10; tel. 473/732-7657; https://casonaalonso10.com; US$180-300

Perhaps it's the remarkably affable service that makes boutique hotel Casona Alonso 10 feel like a discreet, tucked-away place to stay, despite its center-of-it-all location in a three-story colonial-era mansion. The guest rooms, all named after Mexican artists, are tastefully decorated, letting the building's original architecture stand out, notably the incredibly high ceilings on the second floor. Each room is different: Some have interior windows opening into the hotel's atrium, others have pretty Juliet balconies opening onto the street, and top-floor rooms have private terraces overlooking Calle Alonso and the many cupolas of the city. Ask to see what's available when you check in, or ask for your preference beforehand. Breakfast is served in the highly rated on-site restaurant, **Comedor Tradicional.**

★ Hotel Edelmira
Allende 7, Jardín de la Unión; tel. 473/732-3743; www.edelmirahotel.com; US$180

Achieving a perfect balance of romantic and posh, Hotel Edelmira is a beautiful boutique hotel right on Guanajuato's Jardín de la Unión. The 27 guestrooms are tastefully decorated with wooden furnishings, glass lamps, wool rugs, and rough stone walls; the best suites have balconies that open directly onto the Jardín de la Unión. There's a small, turquoise-tiled indoor pool and whirlpool for hotel guests, as well as a downstairs restaurant that offers room service. In a city filled with pretty roof decks, Edelmira's is one of the nicest, with spectacular views of Guanajuato's domes, churches, and pastel-shaded houses rising all around. As with many Guanajuato hotels, prices fluctuate year-round and you can sometimes snag excellent deals with a last-minute booking here.

Over US$200
★ Casa del Rector
Positos 33; tel. 473/690-1512 or 473/732-9200; www.casadelrector.com; US$240-400

Located in one of the oldest buildings in Guanajuato, Casa del Rector is a spectacularly pretty boutique hotel, right in the center of town. Though all the guest rooms share a luxe decor, high ceilings, and warm lighting, it's worth spending a little extra on the master suites on the upper floors, which have windows opening onto the outdoor patio and restaurant, rather than the stuffier interior atrium. The small rooftop swimming pool is a true luxury, surrounded by lounge chairs and a sweeping view of downtown Guanajuato, and you can stop into the adjacent bar for a cocktail after taking a dip.

PRESA DE LA OLLA

US$100-200

Quinta Las Acacias

Paseo de la Presa 168; tel. 473/731-1517; www. quintalasacacias.com.mx; US$160

On the lovely Paseo de la Presa, just a few blocks from the reservoir, Quinta Las Acacias has a creaky old-world feeling. Housed in a converted 19th-century mansion, the common areas and restaurant feel like an old-fashioned parlor, with crystal chandeliers, heavy curtains, and floral wallpaper. In the bedrooms, furnishings are designed in an antique style, complementing the mansion's high ceilings and old wooden floors. Everything looks aged and full of character, yet doesn't feel worn or shabby. In fact, there are plenty of comforts in each guest room, including safes, televisions, and bathrobes. Rooms in the front of the house have windows overlooking a leafy park, which is a particularly nice way to greet the day. For those who want something a bit more "new world," there are also eight Mexican-themed suites located in the back part of the house.

Over $200

Villa María Cristina

Paseo de la Presa 76; tel. 473/731-2182, toll-free Mex. tel. 800/702-7007; www.villamariacristina.net; US$275

Guanajuato's most luxurious establishment, the Villa María Cristina is a petite boutique property in the quiet residential neighborhood near the reservoir. In this lovely renovated mansion, guest rooms are arranged around tiled terraces, overlooking the pointed peak of the Cerro de la Bufa and the green hills below. Sparkling with brass and marble, rooms have high ceilings and French furniture, and they are decked out with every luxury, like heaters in the bathrooms, French toiletries, iPod docks, and Dutch-made sound systems. The hotel's gorgeous restaurant has its own small wine cellar, and guests can order drinks on any of the hotel's sun-drenched verandas. Guests can also use spa facilities, including the sauna and Swiss showers. Service is impeccably attentive. Note that prices drop significantly during the weekdays, making this hotel a good value if your dates are flexible.

Information and Services

TOURIST INFORMATION

The **Oficina de Convenciones y Visitantes** (Jardín de la Unión; 10am-5pm daily) operates a small tourist information kiosk in the Jardín de la Unión. They will provide you with a map of Guanajuato's centro histórico, which points out the city's most important sights. The office offers walking tours of the city center as well as package tours of the city's more distant sights, like the mines.

Media

The daily Spanish-language newspaper *El Correo* (www.periodicocorreo.com.mx) is published in Guanajuato. *El Correo* covers regional, national, and international news, with sections dedicated to the cities of León, Irapuato, Salamanca, and Guanajuato. There is a weekly cultural supplement on Saturdays. It is the best place to read up on what's going on in Guanajuato; all text is in Spanish.

If you want to see what's happening around town, the Universidad de Guanajuato's cultural department lists upcoming arts events and movie screenings via their website at www.cultura.ugto.mx. An eclectic university radio station, **Radio Universidad** (www. radiouniversidad.ugto.mx) will keep Spanish-speaking listeners up to date with the city's news and cultural events. It also broadcasts an excellent international news program from the Latin American correspondent of Radio

Francía Internacional each morning at 9am. Even if you don't speak Spanish, it can still be great fun to tune in to the music programs on this arts-and-letters radio station. Depending on the DJ, you will hear a rather eclectic range of music, from jazz to classical to the Beatles. You can tune in at 970 AM or 100 FM in Guanajuato. From San Miguel de Allende, Radio Universidad is at 91.3 FM.

SERVICES
Medical and Emergency Services

For police and other emergency services, dial **911** from any ground line to reach the city emergency services.

Centro Medico La Presa

Paseo de la Presa 85; tel. 473/102-3100; www. centromedicolapresa.mx; 24 hours

The well-regarded Centro Medico La Presa is a full-service medical clinic with general medicine doctors, specialists, and surgeons. In the case of emergency, there are doctors in the clinic 24 hours a day.

General Hospital Guanajuato

Carretera a Silao, Km 6; tel. 473/733-1573 or 473/733-1576; https://salud.guanajuato.gob.mx

The government-run General Hospital Guanajuato is to the southwest, outside the city center on the toll highway toward Silao and also receives emergencies.

Cruz Roja

Red Cross; Av. Juárez 131; tel. 065 or 473/732-0487; www.cruzrojamexicana.org.mx

For medical emergencies, the Cruz Roja offers emergency response, medical services, and ambulances.

Money

There are banks and ATMs throughout Guanajuato's central districts, including an **HSBC** (Plaza de la Paz 59; tel. 473/732-0018; 8:30am-4:30pm Mon.-Fri.) on the Plaza de la Paz and a **Citibanamex** (Plaza de los Ángeles s/n; 800/021-2345; 9am-4pm Mon.-Fri., 9am-2pm Sat.) on the Plaza de Los Ángeles. You'll find a number of other ATMs and banks along Benito Juárez, near the Mercado Hidalgo.

Transportation

GETTING THERE
Air
Del Bajío International Airport (BJX)

Carretera Silao-León, Km 5.5, Col. Nuevo México, Silao; tel. 472/748-2120

Guanajuato is about 40 km (25 mi) from the Del Bajío International Airport, on the highway to León, just beyond the auto plants in Silao. From BJX, there are daily direct flights to and from Dallas, Houston, and Los Angeles, as well as several flights to and from Mexico City and Monterrey.

From the airport, you can take a registered taxi to Guanajuato for about US$30. The drive to downtown takes about 30 minutes. There are taxis available at the airport to meet arriving flights, even late at night. Buy a ticket

for your taxi at the ticket booth inside the airport terminal and then meet the cabs curbside. Alternately, you can rent a car at the airport and drive it to Guanajuato. There are several rental car companies with offices in the airport, most of which are open from early morning to late night.

Mexico City International Airport (MEX)

Capitan Carlos León s/n, Peñón de Los Baños Venustiano Carranza, Distrito Federal; tel. 55/2482-2400; www.aicm.com.mx

It can be less expensive and, in some cases, more convenient for international visitors to fly to Mexico City International Airport in the capital. From the airport in Mexico City, travelers must arrange for ground transportation to Guanajuato, usually by bus.

Bus

Direct buses operated by ETN and Primera Plus (see below) leave from Mexico City's **Terminal Central del Norte** (Eje Central Lázaro Cárdenas 4907, Gustavo A Madero, Magdalena de Las Salinas, Mexico D.F.) several times a day. The trip from Mexico City to Guanajuato takes about five hours; some buses stop in Irapuato en route. Travelers should also prepare for heavy traffic leaving the capital, which can affect travel time.

Central de Autobuses

Carretera de Cuota Guanajuato-Silao, km 7
Guanajuato's Central de Autobuses is about 8 km (5 mi) outside the city center on the highway toward Silao. Once you arrive at the terminal, you can take a city bus downtown for about US$1; they are marked "Centro" in the front windshield and depart from right in front of the station every 15 minutes or so. Buses often stop in the underground tunnels below the centro histórico, so if you have never been to Guanajuato before, ask the driver to notify you when to get off. For quicker service, you can take a city taxi from the bus station to the centro histórico for about US$6.

Primera Plus

Carretera de Cuota Guanajuato-Silao, km 7, Central de Autobuses; tel. 477/710-0060; call center open 7am-midnight daily; www.primeraplus.com.mx
From Mexico City, San Miguel de Allende, and other points in the Bajío, there is ample first-class bus service to and from Guanajuato, as well as connecting service to cities all over the country. Primera Plus operates several direct first-class buses between the Terminal Central del Norte in Mexico City and the Central de Autobuses in Guanajuato every day (US$45). Primera Plus also operates direct routes to and from San Miguel de Allende, León, Celaya, and Guanajuato. Buses are comfortable, air-conditioned, and equipped with bathrooms; Primera Plus even provides its clients with

a small snack and soft drink for the ride. During big events like the Cervantino festival or nationwide holidays like Semana Santa, Primera Plus will often extend its daily service to include two or three extra departures.

Servicios Coordinados Flecha Amarilla

Carretera a Silao, km 8; tel. 477/710-0060; call center open 7am-midnight daily; www.primeraplus.com.mx
For local travel, Servicios Coordinados Flecha Amarilla, operated by the same company as Primera Plus, offers second-class bus service from nearby towns, including Dolores Hidalgo (US$5, roughly 10 departures 7am-9pm). You don't need to book your ticket ahead of time; just arrive at the station and buy a ticket for the next departing bus.

ETN

Carretera de Cuota Guanajuato-Silao, km 7, Central de Autobuses; toll-free Mex. tel. 800/800-0386; www.etn.com.mx
Another swanky first-class bus line serving central and northern Mexico, ETN has five first-class buses between Mexico City and Guanajuato (US$50) each day. As on Primera Plus, you'll get bathrooms, snacks, and a movie, though ETN's seats are even bigger and more comfortable (and tickets are correspondingly a little bit costlier). ETN also offers service from Guanajuato to Guadalajara, San Miguel de Allende, and León, with connecting service to the beach or to other major cities.

Group Estrella Blanca

Carretera Guanajuato-Silao, km 6, Central de Autobuses Guanajuato; toll-free Mex. tel. 800/507-5500; www.estrellablanca.com.mx
Group Estrella Blanca offers first-class bus service between Guanajuato and cities Bajío, but not San Miguel de Allende, on their luxury line Futura Plus and their first-class line Futura. It also offers second-class bus service on its economy line, Estrella Blanca, which services most towns and cities in the Bajío and central Mexico.

GETTING AROUND

The easiest and most efficient way to get around Guanajuato's city center is on foot. In fact, many of Guanajuato's sights and restaurants cannot be accessed any other way, since roads run underground in many parts of the centro. However, if you are planning to spend some time outside the downtown district, you may need to arrange other transportation.

Car

Driving in Guanajuato is another challenge altogether. With all the underground tunnels and one-way streets, navigation devices often fail to mark the correct route or lose signal while traveling underground. Throughout the city center, the former riverbed has been converted to an underground system of tunneled roads, marked with rather unspecific signage. **Calle Belaunzarán** is the only major thoroughfare that goes through the city center (it later becomes Calle Miguel Hidalgo, which runs underground).

Don't lose your calm when driving through the centro histórico. Very few underground roads will lead you far from the downtown district before they come up for air. When in doubt, ask for directions. In almost every case, it is easiest to park your car and walk when exploring the centro histórico.

You can park along the underground tunnels (look for signs that indicate where parking is permitted); one multilevel public parking lot is located at Constancia 11, just behind the Teatro Juárez. If you are staying overnight in Guanajuato, ask your hotel about parking options.

Like walking, driving in Guanajuato can be a bit of a challenge. Maps tend to be confusing, thanks to the bilevel structure of the city, and satellite-connected GPS systems, like Google Maps, are impossible to use, as they are frequently confused by Guanajuato's many alleys, tunnels, and one-way streets. However, there are road signs at every fork and turn. In most cases, if you follow these signs, you will eventually get to your destination (though probably not without a few wrong turns!). The most important thing is to keep an eye out for one-way signs before making a turn and to be careful of the many pedestrians and frequently stopping buses.

Car Rental

If you plan to do some driving while in Guanajuato, the easiest place to rent a car is

one of Guanajuato's underground tunnels

at the airport, where you will find desks for several major car rental companies. **Avis** (León-Bajío International Airport, Carretera Silao-León, km 5.5, Silao; tel. 472/748-2054, toll-free Mex. tel. 800/288-8888; www.avis.mx; 6am-11pm daily) rents compact cars and regular-size sedans at low daily rates. **Budget** (León-Bajío International Airport, Carretera Silao-León, km 5.5, Silao; tel. 472/748-2001; www.budget.com.mx; 5am-midnight daily) also operates out of the airport.

Taxi

There are inexpensive taxis circling throughout Guanajuato's downtown district as well as around the bus station. Most charge a flat rate for service anywhere in the downtown area, usually about US$3. For service to neighborhoods outside the centro histórico, like La Valenciana or the bus station, the rate may go up to US$4. You can also call a taxi from **Taxi Express Linea Dorada** (tel. 473/732-6142) for service within the city of Guanajuato, or for service from Guanajuato to the BJX/León airport (about US$28 one way).

While cabs are inexpensive, they aren't omnipresent. Many of Guanajuato's alleys and plazas are not accessible by taxi. Most cabs will get you as close to your destination as they can, but door-to-door service isn't always possible.

Bus

Inexpensive city buses can take you to all of Guanajuato's major neighborhoods from the city center. Most buses run from morning until night, roughly 7am-10pm. Bus routes are not numbered; however, each bus lists its destination in the windshield. While the system may seem a bit disorganized, it is actually fairly simple to master. There are very few major thoroughfares in Guanajuato's city center and likewise few bus routes.

Buses to the Marfil neighborhood depart from bus stops in the centro histórico via the largest underground thoroughfare, Hidalgo, and run via the Marfil-Guanajuato Camino Real. You can catch the city bus up toward the Valenciana neighborhood on Avenida Juárez, right near the Alhóndiga, which then travels northward via the Guanajuato-Dolores Hidalgo highway. When in doubt, ask the driver where the bus is going.

Querétaro

The handsome city of Santiago de Querétaro—

generally referred to as just Querétaro—was one of the first settlements in New Spain.

Almost 500 years later, it is a sprawling, safe, and modern city, with a large industrial sector and a population of over two million. Passing through the city on traffic-choked Highway 57, which runs to Mexico City, it is easy to imagine that there is nothing but chugging big rigs and massive factories from one end of Querétaro to the other. The reality is quite the contrary: Querétaro's stately centro histórico is quiet, clean, and pedestrian-friendly, filled with sun-drenched plazas and ornate Mexican baroque architecture. Remarkably well preserved, it is

Highlights

Look for ★ to find recommended sights, activities, dining, and lodging.

★ **Plaza de Armas:** Wander under the arcades of colonial-era mansions surrounding this lovely 18th-century plaza, the historic heart of Querétaro (page 171).

★ **Templo y Ex-Convento de Santa Rosa de Viterbo:** The gorgeous Santa Rosa de Viterbo stands out among Querétaro's many impressive colonial-era churches, and its adjoining cloister is home to CEART, an interesting art and cultural center (page 174).

★ **Museo de Arte de Querétaro:** See a contemporary art exhibition at this excellent museum, housed in a spectacular former Augustinian convent (page 174).

★ **Mercado de la Cruz:** Shop for food, explore regional specialties, and take photos at this big, colorful, and bustling urban market (page 177).

★ **Cerro de Sangremal and Templo de la Santa Cruz:** Visit the historic colonial-era church and convent on the hill of Querétaro's founding, then stop into the adjoining Museo de Arte Contemporáneo de Querétaro to see what's on show (page 179).

★ **Peña de Bernal:** Enjoy the views from one of the world's largest monoliths while on the wine and cheese route through the Querétaro countryside (page 207).

considered one of the finest surviving examples of architecture and city planning during the Spanish viceroyalty.

Querétaro has played an important role in Mexican history since the early colonial era, as its many interesting sights attest. But history is only part of what recommends a trip to the city. A rapidly growing metropolis, Querétaro has attracted many Mexico City natives looking to relocate to the relative peace and safety of this medium-size city, bringing with them a taste for the arts, culture, and coolness. In Querétaro today, you'll find a growing arts scene, music and film festivals, local craft beer and wine, and first-rate restaurants.

Home to a major public university, the Universidad Autónoma de Querétaro, the city also has a notable youth culture, which supports a multitude of quick eats, cheap bars, artsy movie screenings, and other student-friendly diversions. Despite its increasing modernity, Querétaro has remained delightfully old-fashioned, too. Travelers of any stripe will appreciate the classic Mexican atmosphere in the city's many public plazas, where children play and seniors gather on shady benches. And it's equally worth a visit to one of Querétaro's enduring, old-timey cafés and fondas, some of which have been in business for two or three generations.

The capital of the small state of Querétaro, the city is a well-located jumping-off point for trips to the countryside. Warm, traditionally Mexican towns like Tequisquiapan and San Sebastián Bernal, both located within an hour of Querétaro, are popular destinations with the local crowd as well as with weekenders from Mexico City. Surrounded by ranchland, these small towns have also become known as the locus of a modest wine-tasting route within the state, which provides a good excuse to do some driving on Querétaro's clean, sometimes scenic, and well-maintained state highways.

Despite its impressive architecture, proximity to the capital, agreeable climate, and important place in history, Querétaro has remained relatively undiscovered by international tourists. Visitors here will be happy to find a surprisingly cosmopolitan and largely authentic city, where restaurants, museums, and other attractions are pleasingly aimed at a local crowd. That said, the local government has taken steps to improve the city's reputation as a tourist destination, to good effect. There are ample guided tours and visitor services, the tourist office is outgoing and helpful, and there are plenty of well-marked and interesting sights throughout the city center. All in all, Querétaro is a wonderful place to visit, either for a day, a weekend, or an extended trip.

PLANNING YOUR TIME

Querétaro's major tourist sights are located in the **centro histórico,** and they are all within easy walking distance of one another. While Querétaro has plenty of restaurants and shopping in its suburban neighborhoods, most tourists will have little reason to travel outside the downtown districts.

If you are coming to Querétaro on a day trip from San Miguel de Allende, **one (well-planned) day** will give you sufficient time to visit a museum or two, see some of the nicest churches and plazas, and enjoy a good meal in one of the city's restaurants. Two or three days, however, will give you more time to really explore the major sights and get a taste of life in this pleasant metropolis.

With more than a **couple of days** in Querétaro, day trips to the surrounding countryside are worthwhile and not too difficult to plan. **Tequisquiapan** and **San Sebastián Bernal** are both popular day trips from the capital, with historic churches, a few places to eat and drink, and a small-town ambience. There is also a burgeoning **wine industry** in the state, and it can be fun to rent a car and

---

Querétaro State

© MOON.COM

HIDALGO

GUANAJUATO

5 mi

5 km

San Pablo

100

100

120

120

126

Rio San Juan River

San Sebastián Bernal

CAVAS DE FREIXENET

BODEGAS DE COTE

VIÑEDOS LA REDONDA

PEÑA DE BERNAL

Ezequiel Montes

120

540

Presa Centenario

CAVA BOCANEGRA

Tequisquiapan

San Juan del Rio

120

To Mexico City

110

111

Colón

El Saucillo

QUESOS VAI

200

Presa El Divino Redentor

Presa Constitución de 1917

57

45D

400

Atongo

El Lobo

QUERÉTARO INTERNATIONAL AIRPORT

100

433

Ajuchitlancito

Santa Cruz

500

500

57D

420

Cerro El Aguila

415

Huimilpan

420

SEE "CENTRO HISTÓRICO" MAP

QUERÉTARO AQUEDUCT

PLAZA DE ARMAS

TEMPLO Y EX-CONVENTO DE SANTA ROSA DE VITERBO

MUSEO DE ARTE DE QUERÉTARO

MERCADO DE LA CRUZ

CERRO DE SANGREMAL AND TEMPLO DE LA SANTA CRUZ

QUERÉTARO

411

413

57

57

To San Miguel de Allende

111

Presa Santa Catarina

Santa Rosa Jauregui

Juriquilla

Mopani

ZONA ARQUEOLÓGICA EL CERRITO

El Pueblito

45D

45

510

HIGHWAY WITH TOLL

CHEESE AND WINE ROUTE INDICATOR

spend the day driving along Querétaro's pretty and well-maintained country roads, visiting vineyards and tasting the local product.

ORIENTATION

When the city of Querétaro was founded in the 16th century, distinct Indigenous and Spanish neighborhoods were constructed side by side. While the Spanish town was laid out in a neat grid pattern, the Indigenous neighborhood was planned in the native style, with narrow and sinuous streets winding along the hillside. Today Querétaro's central district retains the original street plans from these two neighboring districts. In the eastern end of the **centro histórico,** wide avenues and large esplanades are flanked by Mexican baroque churches and mansions. On the eastern end (near the hill of Sangremal), the streets are more winding and circuitous, with small alleyways and low colonial homes.

Centro Histórico

Querétaro's centro histórico is bordered to the west by the Universidad Autónoma de Querétaro, the city's large public university, and to the south by Avenida Zaragoza and the Alameda Hidalgo, a flat, tree-filled urban park. The convent of Santa Cruz borders the centro histórico to the east, and it is from that same hilltop that the city's impressive aqueduct stretches north.

North of the Centro

In a pretty residential area of the northern edge of the centro histórico, you'll find Querétaro's former rail depot, the **Antigua Estación de Ferrocarril.** Now a small museum and event space, it's a worthy detour.

East of the Centro

Most of Querétaro's major sights and museums are clustered around the Jardín Zenea and the Plaza de Armas, but don't neglect to visit the eastern side of the centro, especially the lively street **Cinco de Mayo,** where many of Querétaro's bars, restaurants, shops, and galleries are located.

Southwest of the Centro

El Pueblito, just 20 minutes from the centro, is home to the urban archeological site surrounding a pre-Columbian stepped pyramid. The **Zona Arqueológica El Cerrito** features a museum and artifacts from the ceremonial center, which flourished in the 6th century BC.

Sights

Since the early years of New Spain, Querétaro has been one of Mexico's most prominent cities. Centuries of history left their mark on the metropolis, which shows vestiges of its colonial past, the French occupation, and the modern day in its impressive centro histórico. You can easily see the difference between the two distinct sections of the centro: gridlike on the west and twisting on the east.

CENTRO HISTÓRICO
★ Plaza de Armas
esq. 5 de Mayo y Av. Louis Pasteur Sur, Centro Histórico; 24 hours

The Plaza de Armas is a good place to begin your tour of Querétaro. This picturesque 18th-century plaza was constructed in the Spanish style, with arcades and mansions surrounding a neat public square and a stately stone fountain. Pick up a map at the tourist office (located at Pasteur 4, just across the street from the plaza), then plan your day on a public bench between perfectly manicured trees and shoe-shine stands. On Sundays, the Plaza de Armas is a nice place for people-watching or to enjoy a drink in one of the many cafés or eateries along the square.

Centro Histórico

To Panteón de los Queretanos Ilustres

To Jardin de Cerveza Hércules

250 yds

250 m

LA SELVA TAURINA LA CRUZ

CONVENTO DE LA SANTA CRUZ

CERRO DE SANGREMAL AND TEMPLO DE LA SANTA CRUZ

20 DE NOVIEMBRE

MANUEL ACUÑA

DAMIAN CORONA

FELIPE LUNA

INDEPENDENCIA

MERCADO DE LA CRUZ

Plaza de los Fundadores

PANICO COMEDOR

MUSEO DE ARTE CONTEMPORÁNEO DE QUERÉTARO

DE LAS ARTES

MANUEL GUTIERREZ NAJERA

LA CENADURIA DOÑA URRACA

DOS PATIOS

SAYIL CENTRO

CASA DE CULTURA DR. IGNACIO MENA ROSALES

PANICO

REFORMA

LUIS PASTEUR

16 DE SEPTIEMBRE

5 DE MAYO

VENUSTIANO CARRANZA

Alameda Hidalgo

IGNACIO MANUEL ALTAMIRANO

HOTEL CRIOL

MARIA Y SU BICI

RIO DE LA LOZA

ALQUIMIA

TEATRO LA CARCAJADA

INDEPENDENCIA

DE NOVIEMBRE

LUIS PASTEUR

PROSPERO C VEGA

CENTRO DE ARTE BERNARDO QUINTANA

TOURIST OFFICE

EL MESON SANTA ROSA

GAD

CANTINA

BRETON

EL MESÓN DE CHUCHO EL ROTO

VERGARA

15 DE MAYO

A. PERALTA

TEATRO DE LA REPUBLICA

CASA DEL CORREGIDORA

5 DE MAYO

PLAZA DE ARMAS

GALÍA

LIBERTAD

LIBERTAD

Queretaro

Rio

LUIS PASTEUR

LONCHERIA LAS TORTUGAS

Jardin Zenea

NEVERIA GALY

Plaza de la Constitucion

CORREGIDORA

TEMPLO DE SAN FRANCISCO & MUSEO REGIONAL

LA CASA DE LA MARQUESA

BENITO JUAREZ

CENTRO QUERETANO DE LA IMAGEN

BENITO JUAREZ

LA CASA DEL NARANJO

HOTEL QUINTA ALLENDE

16 DE SEPTIEMBRE

LA CASA DEL ATRIO

BISQUETS QUERÉTARO

JOSE MA ARTEAGA

AVENIDA UNIVERSIDAD

AVENIDA UNIVERSIDAD

15 DE MAYO

IGNACIO ALLENDE

TEATRO DE LA CIUDAD

TEMPLO DE SANTA CLARA

CASA DEL ARTESANO

MUSEO DE ARTE DE QUERÉTARO

HOTEL VILLA DEL VILLAR

SUPER TAMALES Y ATOLES LOS ARCOS

VICENTE GUERRERO

AVENIDA IGNACIO ZARAGOZA

MARIANO ESCOBEDO

CINETECA ROSALÍO SOLANO

JOSE MA PINO SUAREZ

MELCHOR OCAMPO

CENTRO DE LOS ARTES QUERÉTARO

To Cerro de las Campanas

MUSEO DE LA CIUDAD

MUSEO DE LA REPUBLICA

LA RESTORACION DE LA REPUBLICA

MADERO

ZAPOTECO

ECO.

To The Antigua Estación del Ferrocarril

JOSE MARIA MORELOS

LA DULCE COMPAÑIA

AVENIDA MIGUEL HIDALGO

ANDRES BALVANERA

CATEDRAL DE QUERÉTARO

FOGÓN

TEMPLO Y EX-CONVENTO DE SANTA ROSA DE VITERBO

CALZ. EZEQUIEL MONTES

AVENIDA IGNACIO ZARAGOZA

NICOLAS CAMPA

© MOON.COM

On the north side of the square, the historic **Casa de la Corregidora** is an 18th-century mansion and the current seat of the state government offices. Once the home of Querétaro's mayor, this aristocratic house was written into history during the War of Independence. Here Josefa Ortiz de Domínguez alerted the revolutionary hero Ignacio Pérez that the independence conspiracy had been discovered by Spanish royalists, prompting the start of the Mexican War of Independence. Today you can walk into the covered courtyard of the Casa de Corregimiento, where there is a statue of Ortiz de Domínguez in the foyer.

Museo de la Restauración de la República

Museum of the Restoration of the Republic, Vicente Guerrero 23 Sur; tel. 442/224-3004; 10:30am-6:30pm Tues.-Sun.; free

During the post-independence turmoil of the mid-19th century, the French monarchy took control of Mexico with the backing of the French government and a group of prominent monarchists in Mexico. Led by Benito Juárez, Mexico's liberals resisted French rule, eventually forcing the monarchy into its final stronghold in the city of Querétaro. Emperor Maximilian I of Habsburg spent his last days in a Querétaro jail; he, along with other monarchist leaders, was executed by firing squad at the Cerro de las Campanas in Querétaro.

The Museo de la Restauración de la República is dedicated to this unusual era in Querétaro's history. Most fit for history buffs, this small but beautiful space exhibits documents, maps, and artifacts from 19th-century Querétaro. Most of the collection chronicles the history of the French rule through photos, texts, and mock-ups, though there are also some nice 19th-century costumes and antique weapons. The six small rooms were once a part of an 18th-century Capuchin convent, and the space itself is just as interesting as its contents. It was in this very building that Emperor Maximilian spent the last night before his execution.

Catedral de Querétaro

Av. Francisco I. Madero y Melchor Ocampo; tel. 442/212-1974; generally 9am-7pm daily

The church that is today the seat of Querétaro's diocese isn't the largest in town, but it's worth noting this historic building's beautiful baroque facade, elaborately carved in sandstone, which stands in dramatic relief to the red tezontle (red volcanic rock) wall behind it. Originally commissioned by the order of San Felipe Neri, it was built between 1786 and 1800, and was consecrated by none other than independence hero Miguel Hidalgo. It was officially recognized as a cathedral by the Vatican in 1931.

Templo de Santa Clara

Jardín Guerrero; tel. 442/212-1777; generally 9am-6pm daily

The beautiful Templo de Santa Clara is a convent and church originally commissioned by Don Diego de Tapia, the son of one of Querétaro's founders, Fernando de Tapia, also known by his Indigenous name, Conín. Begun in 1606 and completed in 1668, this chapel and its adjoining convent were considered one of the most beautiful architectural achievements in the country during the colonial era. Today just the chapel and a small annex remain; large parts of the church and convent were destroyed during the Reformation. Nonetheless, Santa Clara is still recognized among the country's finest baroque buildings, particularly noted for its elaborate interiors. Step inside to marvel at the beautifully carved baroque altars, washed in gold leaf and accompanied by painted saints. Few churches rival Santa Clara, filled with the unique handwork of master craftsmen.

In the lovely plaza outside the Templo de Santa Clara, be sure to note the neoclassical **Fuente de Neptuno** (Neptune Fountain), right on the corner of Madero and Allende. Originally constructed in 1797, the fountain's pink sandstone arch frames a statue of the Roman god Neptune. One of the city's most noted landmarks, this opulent fountain was originally built as a part of the Convent of San

Antonio, which was located in what is today the Jardín de la Corregidora. When the government decided to build a monument to the independence movement in 1908, the entire fountain was picked up and moved to its current location.

★ Templo y Ex-Convento de Santa Rosa de Viterbo

Jose María Arteaga at Ezequiel Montes; tel. 442/214-1691; generally 9am-6pm daily

The magnificent Templo y Ex-Convento de Santa Rosa de Viterbo is one of the finest baroque structures in the city. This former convent and its adjoining church were originally designed and built by architect Ignacio Mariano de las Casas in 1754. Quite distinct from other baroque churches in Mexico, Santa Rosa de Viterbo distinguishes itself with an ornately designed exterior, replete with massive flying buttresses, carved stonework, delicate frescoes, and garish gargoyles. It stands over a small stone fountain in Plazuela Mariano de las Casa, and the overall effect is impressive.

Inside, the church is equally spectacular. The principal altar was destroyed in 1849, but in the main nave are six gold-drenched churrigueresque altars from the 18th century, as well as a collection of important colonial-era paintings and retablos. Be sure to note the carved confessional and baroque organ above the nave. Well worth a visit, Santa Rosa de Viterbo is one of the most original structures in the region.

Centro de Los Artes Querétaro

Jose María Arteaga 89; tel. 442/251-9850; 8:30am-9pm Tues.-Sat.; free

The beautifully restored 18th century convent that adjoins the Templo de Santa Rosa de Viterbo is today home to Centro de los Artes Querétaro, or CEART, an active art and cultural center overseen by the city government. The building's soaring open-air arcades, sunny courtyards, and hundreds-of-years-old frescoes make an interesting backdrop for rotating exhibits of contemporary art, often by Querétaro locals. In addition to gallery spaces, CEART hosts an impressive lineup of educational and cultural events on-site, from clay modeling classes for children to mariachi musical performances, as well as artist residencies. Follow CEART on social media or stop by the space to see what's coming up.

★ Museo de Arte de Querétaro

Museum of Art of Querétaro, Exconvento de San Agustín, Allende 14 Sur; tel. 442/212-2357; 10am-6pm Tues.-Sun.; free

The spectacular Museo de Arte de Querétaro—or MAQRO, as it is often nicknamed—is housed within a former Augustinian monastery built between 1731 and 1745. It's among Querétaro's most impressive buildings: the monastery's baroque courtyard is filled with elaborately carved sandstone archways, replete with detailed stone gargoyles, surrounding a central fountain. Formal exhibition spaces are tucked behind the long arcades that surround the courtyard, though the museum makes use of all its beautiful spaces for showing art: the hallways upstairs, the staircase, and the outdoor porticoes all host exhibits on a regular basis. If you want to take pictures of the building, you must pay an extra fee at the ticket booth (art exhibitions are always off-limits to cameras).

Besides the spectacular setting, MAQRO's curatorial staff oversees a well-planned schedule of rotating exhibitions in the museum's many galleries. Often on view in the large exhibition halls downstairs, the museum's permanent collection includes religious paintings from Querétaro from the 17th and 18th centuries. The museum's newest director has made great efforts to plan original shows by contemporary artists from the surrounding region as well as prominent exhibitions by important Mexican masters. MAQRO also hosts intermittent speakers and art courses;

1: Centro de los Artes Querétaro 2: Jardín Zenea
3: Plaza de Armas

opening events are well-attended and engaging, so keep an eye out for what may be coming up on the program.

Jardín Zenea

between Corregidora, Benito Juárez, Madero, and 16 de Septiembre, Centro Histórico; 24 hours

If you follow one of several andadores (pedestrian pathways) west from the Plaza de Armas, you will reach the Jardín Zenea, occupying a full city block between the streets Corregidora and Juárez in the centro histórico. Named after a former Querétaro governor, Benito Santos Zenea, this lovely garden is one of the most popular gathering points in town. Often there are performances in the round kiosk in the middle of the plaza.

Just across the street (on the corner of Corregidora and 16 de Septiembre), the **Plaza de la Corregidora** is a smaller public square surrounding a monument to Josefa Ortiz de Domínguez. A number of little coffee shops and restaurants line the plaza, which can be a pleasant place to relax and watch the crowds. The Plaza de la Corregidora is also the starting point for **Querebus** (page 200) trolley and bus tours of the city.

Templo de San Francisco de Asís

Corregidora s/n, esq. 5 de Mayo; tel. 442/212-0477; generally 9am-5pm daily

Standing above the Jardín Zenea, the Templo de San Francisco de Asís is one of Querétaro's oldest and loveliest buildings. Construction on this church and the adjoining Franciscan convent began as early as the 1540s, though the temple wasn't completed until the middle of the following century. The church's original baroque sandstone entryway is adorned with life-size saints, which stand in relief against the construction's tall, rust-colored facade. Formerly Querétaro's cathedral, the church is still in use today, though its former monastery is now home to the city's regional museum.

Museo Regional de Querétaro

Regional Museum of Querétaro, Corregidora Sur 3; tel. 442/212-2031; 9am-5pm Tues.-Sun.; US$6

The beautiful former convent that adjoins the Templo de San Francisco is home to the Museo Regional de Querétaro, originally opened in 1936. The 11 rooms in this historic space display artifacts from Querétaro city and state, including a nice collection of ceramics and sculpture from the region's

Templo de San Francisco de Asís

Not long after Hernán Cortés's victory over the Mexica in Tenochtitlan, Spanish conquest of the Bajío region began. In 1531 a vicious battle broke out between the native Chichimeca and Spanish forces. According to local history, the battle concluded when a miraculous image of Saint James appeared over the hill of Sangremal and the Chichimeca surrendered.

Shortly after the Spanish victory, evangelicals arrived in Querétaro, followed by Spanish ranchers and farmers. Like San Miguel de Allende, Querétaro was a strategic town on the silver route to Mexico City, known as the Camino Real de Tierra Adentro. Following the discovery of silver in Zacatecas in 1546, wealth from the mines helped fund a multitude of religious and municipal projects in Querétaro, from baroque churches to the impressive 1,200-m (0.75-mi) aqueduct that provided water to the city center.

Like other cities in the region, Querétaro played a prominent role in the Mexican War of Independence. Most famously, the wife of the town's corregidor (mayor), Josefa Ortiz de Domínguez, sent a crucial warning to Ignacio Allende and Miguel Hidalgo when the plot against the crown was uncovered by royalist officials. Today she is celebrated throughout Mexico for her role in the early independence movement.

As the new Mexican state struggled to define itself amid ongoing instability, Querétaro remained prominent. During the Mexican-American War, Querétaro became the country's temporary capital when the United States invaded Mexico City in 1827. Here President Santa Anna, in a move that remains infamous, signed the 1827 Treaty of Guadalupe Hidalgo, which ceded half of Mexico's territory to the United States. Following the French invasion and the Second Mexican Empire, Emperor Maximilian I of Austria was imprisoned and executed in Querétaro in 1867 after a successful uprising by the liberal powers aligned with President Benito Juárez.

Querétaro was not the site of major battles during the Mexican Revolution of 1910, but the city suffered the effects of political unrest. In postrevolutionary upheaval, Querétaro was renamed the capital of Mexico in 1917, and the Mexican Constitution (which is still in use today) was signed and ratified in the Teatro Iturbide, known as the Teatro de la República today.

QUERÉTARO
SIGHTS

pre-Columbian cultures. As you progress through the museum, exhibits address each era in Querétaro's history, with rooms dedicated to the colonial era, the Reformation, the American invasion, the 19th century, and the Mexican Revolution. Texts are in Spanish. In addition, the museum is frequently used as a venue for special events, like culture-related conferences, speakers, and temporary art exhibitions, and it offers art courses for both adults and children.

★ Mercado de la Cruz

Manuel Gutiérrez Nájera s/n; 8am-6pm daily; individual shop hours vary

Querétaro's large covered market, Mercado de la Cruz is a wonderful place to shop for fresh produce, fish, meat, flowers, and crafts. It is also a great place to get a bite to eat, with a wide array of food stalls and fruit

stands throughout the interior. It opened on September 28, 1979. A bustling urban market, Mercado de la Cruz is typical of large Mexican cities, though more picturesque and photogenic than many others. Visitors can shop or simply take in the sights, wandering past fresh whole fish chilling on ice, neatly stacked towers of vegetables, big cauldrons of menudo, and overflowing flower stands. On weekends, the market overflows into the parking lot, with additional food and wares on offer.

Cerro de las Campanas

Centro Universitario; no tel.; 9am-5pm Tues.-Sun.; US$1 museum entrance

This picturesque hilltop park, on the western edge of the centro histórico, has a rather grim claim to fame: It was here in 1867 that Habsburg Emperor Maximilian was killed by

La Corregidora: Heroine of the Independence

One of the few women known to have participated in the early independence movement, **Josefa Ortiz de Domínguez,** or "La Corregidora," was vital to the success of the conspirators who sought Mexico's sovereignty from New Spain. Born to a wealthy family in Valladolid (today Morelia, Michoacán) in 1768, she married lawyer Miguel Domínguez, who was later appointed corregidor (mayor) of Querétaro. As his wife, Josefa Ortiz was known as the corregidora.

According to her biographers, Josefa Ortiz was a critic of the rigid class system in New Spain, and she sympathized with the mestizo and Indigenous people of Mexico, who benefited little from the great wealth of the colonies. A supporter of Mexican independence, Ortiz secretly met with Mexican conspirators across the Bajío, including Ignacio Allende. When the independence plot was uncovered by royalists in Querétaro, Spanish governors conducted a search of the city, locking Josefa into her bedroom. Though confined, she managed to send warning to co-conspirator Ignacio Pérez, who in turn set out for San Miguel on horseback.

Riding through the night, Pérez arrived in San Miguel on the morning of September 15. Unable to find Allende, he rode on to Dolores with Juan Aldama, where he informed Miguel Hidalgo of the situation in Querétaro. The war began that night, September 16, 1810, when Hidalgo gathered the Mexican army before the church in Dolores and set out toward Atotonilco.

The day the war began, both Miguel Domínguez and Josefa Ortiz de Domínguez were imprisoned in Querétaro convents on suspicion of conspiracy. Domínguez, a popular governor, was cleared of charges, but Josefa Ortiz de Domínguez was found guilty and remained imprisoned in the convent, where she was allowed minimal contact with her husband and 14 children. In 1814 she was convicted again and sent to the convent Santa Teresa La Antigua in Mexico City. She was freed in 1817.

Ortiz paid a high price for her participation in the independence movement. Nonetheless, she continued to meet with liberal-minded intellectuals and support the Mexican republic for the remainder of her life. She died in 1829, at the age of 61.

LEARN MORE

- You can visit the famous home of Domínguez and Ortiz, known today as the **Casa de la Corregidora,** on the Plaza de Armas. Its facade is little changed since the day when Ortiz's bravery and ingenuity saved the Mexican independence movement from failure (page 173).

- Her remains, along with the remains of her husband, Miguel Domínguez, are entered at the **Panteón de los Queretanos Ilustres** (page 181).

- Learn more about colonial-era Querétaro and the city's role in the War of Independence at the **Museo Regional de Querétaro** (page 176).

firing squad after symbolically handing over his sword to General Mariano Escobedo and ending the French reign in Mexico. After the execution, three crosses were installed on the Cerro de las Campanas, followed by a small monument, but it was only after diplomatic relations reopened between Mexico and Austria that the Austrian government built a **chapel** on the site of the emperor's execution. In addition to the chapel, there is a small historical **museum;** and the surrounding grounds, a national park since 1967, are lush and beautiful, with plenty of shady spots for resting. At the top of the hill, an impressive sculpture of Benito Juárez (president of Mexico both before and after Habsburg rule) is said to be the largest in the country. Located just beside the Universidad Autónoma de Querétaro's main campus, it's worth a trip if you have a few extra days in the city.

★ Cerro de Sangremal and Templo de la Santa Cruz

C. Damián Carmona 5, Barrio de la Cruz; temple generally 8am-10pm daily, plaza 24 hours; free

On the east end of the centro, the hill of Sangremal is the historic site of the 1531 Spanish victory over the native Chichimeca people of the Bajío, who were fighting to defend their territory against colonization. According to local history, the Spanish forces, helmed by Otomí leader Fernando de Tapia (also known by his Indigenous name, Conín), subdued the Chichimeca warriors after an image of a cross and Saint James on horseback miraculously appeared over the hilltop at Sangremal.

Located on the site of this historic battle, the Templo de la Santa Cruz and its adjoining monastery were built by Franciscan friars who arrived in Querétaro shortly after the Spanish conquest of the region in the 16th century. Inside the main nave of the church, a large sandstone cross hangs above the altar, meant to replicate the cross that appeared above the battle for Querétaro's conquest.

The plaza in front of the church is the site of the annual **Fiesta de la Santa Cruz,** a celebration of Saint James and the city's founding. Across the street, the **Plaza de los Fundadores** honors several of Querétaro's early founders, including Conín and Father Junípero Serra, a missionary and Catholic saint who evangelized throughout the state of Querétaro and New Spain.

Convento de la Santa Cruz

C. Damián Carmona 5, Barrio de la Cruz; 9am-2pm and 4pm-6pm Mon.-Sat., 9am-4pm Sun. by guided tour only; $2

Founded in 1653, this influential convent and theological college trained many generations of Spanish missionaries to carry on the Franciscan tradition throughout the New World. Among the most well-known of its former residents is Father Junípero Serra, the Spanish-born Franciscan priest and Catholic saint who oversaw the construction of missions throughout central Mexico, Baja California, and Alta California (today the state of California, in the United States). Following the 19th century Reformation, the monastery's buildings were taken over by the Mexican government. The buildings were used as military barracks and, later, an elementary school before being abandoned in the 21st century.

Today the complex is again home to a theological college and convent. Student areas are off-limits to visitors, but there are delightful guided tours of the convent's historic spaces (Spanish only), which include a visit to the original kitchen (including a unique colonial-era "refrigerator"), a re-creation of a monk's cell, and a visit to a celebrity tree inside the complex that naturally grows thorns in the shape of crosses. Interestingly, the "hidden" final arch in Querétaro's impressive colonial-era aqueduct is also located within the monastery; water from the aqueduct flowed directly into the convent and was distributed to the rest of the city from there.

Museo de Arte Contemporáneo de Querétaro

Manuel Acuña esq. Reforma s/n, Barrio de la Cruz; https://macq.mx; 10am-6pm Tues.-Sun.; free

In wonderful complement to its historic spaces, a large segment of the Convento de la Santa Cruz is now home to the Museo de Arte Contemporáneo de Querétaro, a contemporary art museum. There are usually multiple art exhibitions on show across the museum's 14 rooms, which were completely restored and renovated to serve as gallery spaces before the museum's 2018 opening; they make an excellent backdrop for art while retaining the quirks and charm of the original convent design. In recent years, the museum's exhibits have included collective shows featuring work from the Jumex collection (Latin America's biggest art collection), installations and video art by international artists, and new work by Mexican artists like Betsabee Romero, Esmeralda Torres, and Pancho Westendarp.

Panteón de los Queretanos Ilustres

Ejército Republicano 4, Barrio de la Santa Cruz; 9:30am-7pm daily

At this monument to Querétaro's most famed citizens, the remains of several important heroes of the independence era—notably Josefa Ortiz de Domínguez, Miguel Domínguez, and Ignacio Pérez, among others—are safeguarded in the Panteón de los Queretanos Ilustres, a small mausoleum and chapel, located on the hill of Sangremal, just behind the Templo de la Santa Cruz, in an area that was once a part of the convent's orchards. On the patio outside the chapel, which boasts beautiful views of the city and the old municipal aqueduct, there are statues of some of the great names buried inside. The chapel, known as the Capilla de la Virgen de Dolores, contains a modest museum honoring their lives.

Querétaro Aqueduct

Calzada de los Arcos, between Ejército Republicano and Avenida Hércules

Cutting east more than 1.2 km (0.75 mi) from the centro histórico, Querétaro's spectacular 74-column aqueduct was built between 1726 and 1735. Today it is considered one of the most important public works in 18th-century Mexico. According to local history, the aqueduct's construction was funded by the wealthy marquis Juan Antonio de Urrutia y Arana at the request of the Capuchin nuns of Querétaro, who lived in the Convento de la Santa Cruz. The aqueduct terminates within the monastery walls, from which water was distributed to the rest of the city via public fountains.

At its highest point, the aqueduct soars 23 m (75 ft) above the ground. It is an astonishing architectural achievement that continues to lend majesty to downtown Querétaro and its surrounding neighborhoods. You can get the best view of it from just a block or two behind the Templo de la Santa Cruz, at the Panteón de los Queretanos Ilustres. From here, the hill of Sangremal makes a dramatic drop, with the aqueduct stretching across the valley below.

NORTH OF THE CENTRO
Antigua Estación del Ferrocarril

Héroe de Nacozari s/n, esq. Cuauhtémoc; tel. 442/340-22780; 11am-8pm Mon.-Sat., 11am-6pm Sun.; free

Located about a kilometer (0.6 mi) north of the Jardín Zenea, Querétaro's former rail depot, which was constructed in the early 20th century, no longer receives passenger trains. Today the Antigua Estación de Ferrocarril has been refashioned as a small museum and event space, located in a pretty residential area of the edge of the centro histórico. Inside, a small gallery chronicles the history of the train station, and upstairs is a scale model (noon-4pm Sun. only) of Querétaro's train station and rail line. There are often events on-site, from karaoke concerts to classical music performances. Though they don't stop, the freight trains that still frequently run along the rails beside the station are also a worthy spectacle. Across the street, **Cao Cao Café** (Héroe de Nacozari 25-B1; tel. 442/629-1251; 8:30am-8pm Mon.-Sat., 9am-2pm Sun.) is a cute spot for a coffee before you make your way back to the heart of the centro.

SOUTHWEST OF THE CENTRO
Zona Arqueológica El Cerrito

Hidalgo s/n, Col. El Pueblito; tel. 442/209-6000; https://lugares.inah.gob.mx/es/zonas-arqueologicas/zonas/1780-el-cerrito.html; 9am-4:30pm Wed.-Sun.; $4

Long before you arrive at the entrance to this urban archeological site, the summit of El Cerrito is visible above the buildings of El Pueblito, a neighborhood about 20 minutes southwest of Querétaro's city center. This pre-Columbian stepped pyramid was once at the heart of a large ceremonial center,

---

1: A segment of the Convento de la Santa Cruz is now home to the Museo de Arte Contemporáneo de Querétaro. 2: chapel at the Cerro de las Campanas 3: Querétaro's aqueduct 4: El Cerrito archeological site which flourished between the years 450 and 600. First rising to prominence as an ally of the great city of Teotihuacán in the Valley of Mexico, the site was occupied by different cultures over many centuries, finally going into decline in the post-Classic period. While not actively inhabited when the Spanish conquest began, there are historical records of native people continuing to visit and leave offerings at the site as late as the 17th century. Though excavation of El Cerrito began in 1932, only a small portion of what was once an expansive city has been uncovered.

You cannot ascend the pyramid, but from the base you can see the remains of a neo-Gothic structure at the summit, constructed in the 19th century, when the archeological site was part of a larger hacienda. Aside from the pyramid, the foundations of several palaces and patios that surrounded have been uncovered. A small on-site museum provides background information (in Spanish) and an exhibit of some artifacts uncovered here.

Getting There

If coming from Querétaro's centro histórico, it is easiest to reach El Cerrito by car, taxi, or Uber (US$5), which takes about 10-15 minutes each way, depending on traffic.

Sports and Recreation

PARKS
Alameda Hidalgo
between Avenida Ignacio Zaragoza and Avenida Constituyentes; 8am-8pm daily

Bordering the centro histórico to the south, the large Alameda Hidalgo is a beautiful, tree-filled urban park, which first opened to the public in 1804. Its flat, shaded paths are great for strolling, chatting, or jogging. The metal fencing that runs along the borders of the park is often hung with photo exhibitions, just like the famous rejas de Chapultepec in the Bosque de Chapultepec in Mexico City.

SPECTATOR SPORTS
Estadio Corregidora
Av. de las Torres s/n, at Calle Estadio, Col. Cimatario; open during events; US$10-30

the entrance to Alameda Hidalgo

Querétaro Fútbol Club, more commonly known as Los Gallos Blancos de Querétaro, is a professional soccer team in the Liga MX, Mexico's first-division league. They play home games at the Estadio Corregidora, a 10,000-seat venue in the Cimatario neighborhood, southeast of the centro histórico. Throughout the 1980s, 1990s, and 2000s, the team bounced between first-division and second-division standing, but today they hold a firm place in the premier league. Despite a rocky record, they have some very loyal fans in the city, and attending a first-division soccer game is always a fun and spirited experience. Tickets are available through www.eticket.mx.

Entertainment and Events

With strong support from the local and state governments, Querétaro has developed a lively art scene, and any visitor is likely to find a performance or exhibition of interest in the city's vibrant centro histórico. Throughout Querétaro, music, cinema, theater, and visual art events are frequent and well attended, often free or low-cost, and refreshingly untouristy.

in 1917, when the Mexican Constitution was signed here after the conclusion of the Mexican Revolution of 1910. Today this historic venue continues to function intermittently as a performance space, participating in film festivals and special events. Its neoclassical, semicircular interior has terraced balconies and plush red seats, creating a rather sophisticated backdrop for any performance.

LIVE MUSIC, THEATER, AND CINEMA

Teatro de la Ciudad
16 de Septiembre 44-e; tel. 442/340-2735; free
This centrally located midsize theater, which first opened in 1946, presents a diverse program of music, drama, dance, and speakers throughout the year, from Pink Floyd tribute evenings to film screenings to performances by the Querétaro Philharmonic. Wonderfully, most events are free, sponsored by the city government, though the venue occasionally hosts ticketed concerts or other performances with well-known artists ($10-45). The theater is an active participant in local film festivals and other special citywide events.

Teatro de la República
Juárez 22 Nte.; generally 9am-2pm Mon.-Sat.; free to visit theater, ticketed events from $20
The lovely neoclassical Teatro de la República was built in 1845, and it was the very first place that the Mexican national anthem was played. It logged another claim to fame

Teatrito la Carcajada
Cinco de Mayo 48; reservations tel. 442/212-9999; www.teatritolacarcajada.com; from US$17
A carcajada is a loud laugh, and Teatrito la Carcajada seeks to elicit exactly that response from its audience. Focusing on upbeat, fun, comic performances and improv shows, this 140-seat venue usually runs shows Wednesday to Saturday—though they often sell out, so reserve in advance. There's an adjoining café for drinks or coffee that opens before and after the show. Programs are all in Spanish.

Casa de Cultura Dr. Ignacio Mena Rosales
Cinco de Mayo 40; tel. 442/214-0262; https:// ccignaciomena.wordpress.com; 9am-2pm and 4pm-7pm Mon.-Fri.; admission generally free
A multipurpose cultural center located in a lovely colonial-era building, the Casa de Cultura Dr. Ignacio Mena Rosales hosts ongoing exhibits of contemporary art, often by local artists, as well as frequent performances, lectures, chamber music, children's programming, and theater, all held in one of

the galleries or in the casa's courtyard, usually without cost. In addition to their cultural programming, the center offers classes at low prices in a range of interesting topics, such as yoga, African dance, digital photography, tango, and theater.

Cineteca Rosalío Solano

16 de Septiembre 44 Poniente; tel. 442/214-2783; showtimes vary; free

Opened in 2000, this publicly owned movie house screens several films every week, showcasing an appealing mix of documentary, classics, foreign films, shorts, children's movies, and other high-quality choices. The theater participates in citywide film and arts festivals, when it is often a venue for live performances, including dance, theater, and music. Follow their social media accounts or drop by the venue to see what's coming up.

GALLERIES AND MUSEUMS

Museo de la Ciudad Santiago de Querétaro

Guerrero 27 Nte.; tel. 442/224-3756; noon-8pm Tues.-Sat.; US$2

The Museo de la Ciudad Santiago de Querétaro has an extraordinary commitment to emerging artists and contemporary art. Located in the Capuchin convent that houses the Museo de la Restauración de la República, the museum's old and crumbling space plays perfect accompaniment to a largely youthful and experimental set of rotating exhibitions, many by local artists. Video art and installation pieces are not uncommon. In addition to art, there is a cinema series, live music, workshops, and other special events held onsite, keeping the museum busy well into the evening.

Centro de Arte Bernardo Quintana

Rio de la Loza 23; tel. 442/192-1200, ext. 3151; www. uaq.mx; 10am-2pm and 4pm-8pm Tues.-Fri., 10am-4pm Sat.; free

The Universidad Autónoma de Querétaro operates the multipurpose Centro de Arte Bernardo Quintana, where there are frequent, high-quality visual arts exhibitions in addition to an ongoing program of workshops, classes, book presentations, and other cultural events. Through the opportunity to exhibit, perform, and learn, the center specifically supports young and emerging artists; for example, they have announced a new biennial for sustainable printmaking, aimed at supporting young local artists.

Galería Libertad

Andador Libertad 56; tel. 442/214-2358; 10am-8pm daily; free

Among the largest of Querétaro's many public exhibition spaces, Galería Libertad is a spacious two-story gallery. Since 1984, this dynamic space has been showing exhibitions of fine art by querétenses, as well as well-known Mexican and international artists. They also hold frequent special events, like lectures and poetry readings; posters announcing upcoming events are often hung on the door or announced on social media. The gallery is just steps from the Plaza de Armas on the pedestrian street Libertad.

Centro Queretano de la Imagen

Juárez 66; tel. 442/212-2947; 10am-6pm Tues.-Sat. during exhibitions; free

Located in an early-20th-century schoolhouse, the Centro Queretano de la Imagen is a public art space dedicated to the preservation, conservation, and exhibition of both still and moving images. In addition to the center's work in research and preservation of historic photographs of the city, it exhibits contemporary and historic photography in its creaky, high-ceilinged galleries. The space is open to the public even if there isn't a show, though the doors are often closed. The center frequently shows films, in addition to offering workshops in film preservation, video and digital editing, and photography.

FESTIVALS AND EVENTS

Fiesta de la Santa Cruz

Sept. 12-15

One of Querétaro's most important religious and cultural events is the annual Fiesta de la Santa Cruz. The festival begins on the night of September 12 with an all-night procession and ceremony by thousands of concheros, or Aztec dancers, who move in unison along the Avenida Los Arcos to the hill at Sangremal in reverence for Saint James, who, according to local history, miraculously appeared here at the moment of Querétaro's founding. The high-energy, rhythmic dancing—based on pre-Columbian dance traditions said to ignite happiness in the heart of the dancer—continues in the plaza in front of the temple all night long. As dawn breaks, the city streets close as food vendors set up and the temple is decorated. The dancing continues until the celebrations conclude with a mass on September 15, just in time for Independence Day celebrations.

Fiestas de la Independencia

Independence Day; Sept. 15-16

Like San Miguel de Allende and Guanajuato, Querétaro played a central role in Mexico's independence movement. Accordingly, the Fiestas de la Independencia are celebrated with enthusiasm here. During September 15 and 16, the city is dressed in lights and decoration for the independence holidays, and you'll find traditional music and dance performances, fireworks, and lots of parties throughout the plazas, bars, and restaurants of the centro histórico. The traditional grito—"¡Viva México!"—is delivered from the Casa de la Corregidora in the Plaza de Armas at 11:45pm on September 15, followed by fireworks.

Teatro de la República

Shopping

TRADITIONAL CRAFTS
Casa del Artesano
Allende 20; tel. 442/169-3445; 10am-7pm Wed.-Mon.

As part of its mission to promote traditional art and handcraft in Mexico's native communities, the Casa del Artesano contains a large open-air market in the back patio. Among dozens of booths, you'll find craftwork typical to a variety of Mexican regions, including Guerrero, Michoacán, and the state of Mexico. Most, however, is produced locally by Indigenous artisans who have relocated to the state of Querétaro—some working right in the Casa del Artesano. Items include molcajetes (mortars for cooking), embroidered blouses, dolls, and other fine work. You'll find the greatest variety on weekends or during civic holidays, when up to 80 booths are open.

Casa Queretana de las Artesanías
Andador Libertad 52; tel. 442/214-1235; https:// casaqueretanaartesanias.gob.mx; 11am-5pm Mon.-Wed., 11am-6pm Thurs.-Fri., 11am-7pm Sat., 11am-4pm Sun.

With support from the state government, this pretty gift shop along the Andador Libertad is dedicated to the promotion of traditional craftwork from local artisans. Here you'll find a variety of techniques typical to the Bajío region, including textiles, hand-tooled leatherwork, ceramics, and kitchen accessories, and dolls. Pieces are high quality and purchases directly support local artisans.

Quinto Real
Andador V. Carranza 10A-B; tel. 442/212-8601; www. quintoreal.com.mx; 10am-2pm and 3pm-7pm Mon.-Sat.

For a very nice selection of traditional crafts, seek out Quinto Real. This lovely little shop is set in the living areas of a colonial-era home, a cozy showroom for the store's collection of arts and crafts. You'll find a little bit of everything from the Querétaro region

and beyond, including tin ornaments, textiles and table runners, wooden masks, handmade jewelry, and a large selection of glassware. Merchandise is artfully designed and displayed, making it easy to imagine one of these colorful accents in your own home.

CLOTHING
Sombrerería La Popular
Independencia 98; tel. 442/212-0474; generally 10am-8pm Mon.-Sat., hours vary

Step into the past at 100-year-old hat shop Sombrería La Popular, which sells a range of classic men's hats from legacy brands from Europe and the United States, like Stetson, as well as Mexican-made Tardan (the shop originally opened as a Tardan branch, though later began representing other hatmakers). Merchandise is laid out in creaky glass display cases, which appear to have been in use since the shop's opening in the early 20th century—though the shop itself relocated to its current site in the 1980s. Although no hats are made on the premises, the shop can clean, iron, and repair high-quality hats in need of some loving care.

ANTIQUES
El Garabato Bazar
Venustiano Carranza 59, Barrio de la Cruz; tel. 442/212-1563; 10:30am-8:30pm daily

There are a number of interesting vintage and antiques shops along Carranza, nearing the Templo de la Santa Cruz, in Querétaro's centro histórico; Garabato is among the most well-stocked and friendly. You'll find vintage iceboxes, baskets, old wooden furniture, lamps, LPs, books, dolls, mirrors, and other unique pieces, from rare and pricey colonial-era antiques to fun collectibles. Prices are a bit high, but vintage hounds may not be able to resist a purchase.

GOURMET GOODIES
Dulzura Mexicana
Juárez Nte. 69; tel. 442/312-1873; noon-8pm Mon., 10am-10pm Tues.-Sun.

Anyone with a sweet tooth will enjoy Dulzura Mexicana, a small but super-stocked traditional candy shop kitty-corner from the Teatro de la República. Here you'll find all the most popular Mexican goodies, like ate (fruit paste), jamoncillo (flavored milk-fudge), and crystallized fruit, as well as more unusual sweets like queso de tuna and gomitas de guanábana (tropical fruit gumdrops). The friendly staff can explain the difference (in Spanish) between different types of sweets as well as provide samples of some items. Pile your pickings into a wicker basket, take them to the register, and get ready for a sugar high.

BOOKSTORES
El Alquimista
José Ma. Morelos 1 B; tel. 442/212-6944; 8:30am-8pm Mon.-Sat., 10am-4pm Sun.

Filling several storefronts along the street Morelos, this old-timey Querétaro bookseller has a wonderful selection used books, as well as a small selection of new titles, at very low prices. Here you'll find everything from vintage comics to 1930s tomes on Mexican politics to novels by Jorge Ibargüengoitia. While books are predominantly in Spanish, there is a smattering of titles in Italian, French, and English. Come with time to browse.

Food

Querétaro is not traditionally known as a culinary destination within Mexico, but the city's food scene has begun to take off. Today modern Mexican restaurants and traditional eateries are abundant in the centro, and there are a few nice international spots adding welcome variety to the dining options. In some of the most historic places in town, the atmosphere is the attraction: Querétaro, unlike most modern cities, has managed to hang on to a number of its old-fashioned cafeterias and fondas, which maintain a loyal clientele within the local crowd. You'll also find plenty of cheap eats and tacos, though street stands aren't as abundant here as in other parts of the country.

TACOS AND QUICK BITES
Mercado de la Cruz
Manuel Gutiérrez Nájera s/n, corner 15 de Mayo; 8am-6pm daily; individual vendor hours vary

For a quick but tasty bite, there are dozens of mouthwatering taco stands and fondas in the extensive Mercado de la Cruz. Gorditas (round corn cakes stuffed with beans, cheese, or other savory fillings), a regional specialty, are abundant, as is barbacoa (slow-cooked lamb), served in tacos and topped with white onion and cilantro. A rule of thumb in any market is to follow the crowds: Popular food stalls tend to be the freshest and tastiest.

Lonchería Las Tortugas
Andador Cinco de Mayo 27A; no tel.; 10:30am-6pm daily; US$3

There are only stools to sit on at Lonchería Las Tortugas, but that's the best way to eat a torta (a Mexican-style sandwich served on a soft roll called a telera). In fact, the old-fashioned atmosphere at this hole-in-the-wall tortería, with its funky bullfighting theme, makes everything taste better—though, after more than half a century in business, it's evident that Las Tortugas knows how to make a good lunch. Order a torta stuffed with carnitas, chorizo, or milanesa (breaded steak) and topped with pickled chiles and the shop's proprietary salsa, accompanied by a fresh horchata.

Best Restaurants

Jardín de Cerveza Hércules

★ **Sayil Centro:** Perfect for a leisurely lunch or a memorable date night, this upscale restaurant serves delicious and authentic food from the state of Yucatán (page 189).

★ **Maria y Su Bici:** Delicious, inexpensive Oaxacan-style eats, craft beer and mezcal cocktails, and a lively setting has made this small spot a local favorite (page 189).

★ **Breton:** At this sweet French bistro, you'll find the best croissants in Querétaro, perfectly made espresso drinks, and an appealing European-style breakfast and lunch menu (page 191).

★ **Jardín de Cerveza Hércules:** The excellent selection of craft beer and the one-of-a-kind setting in a renovated textile factory make this unique beer garden worth the trip outside the centro (page 191).

★ **Pánico:** This itty-bitty bakery sells delicious Mexican- and European-style pastries, baguettes, cookies, and jams, as well as delicious coffee (page 191).

★ **Arrayán:** San Sebastián Bernal's standout restaurant boasts delicious, creative Mexican food and a beautiful setting (page 209).

Nevería Galy

Andador Cinco de Mayo 8; tel. 442/219-6781; 11am-8pm daily; US$2

While there are only a few flavors on the menu, all the ice cream at friendly Nevería Galy is made with all-natural ingredients, a fact they proudly display on many jovial posters tacked along the shop's walls. The delicious and icy lime nieve is the perfect salve to a hot afternoon. Take it to go or enjoy your ice cream at a Formica table inside the authentically retro shop. They also serve lime ice cream topped with a shot of red wine, an unusual yet popular option.

Super Tamales y Atoles Los Arcos

Arteaga 40 Pte.; tel. 442/212-4298; 8am-noon and 6pm-11pm Mon., 7:30am-noon and 5pm-11pm Tues.-Sun.; US$4

Tamales are a classic Mexican breakfast or dinner food, traditionally accompanied by atole, a sweet corn-based drink. In Querétaro there are several small storefronts specializing in tamales and atole along Arteaga, a few blocks east of Santa Rosa de Viterbo. Most are open, as is traditional, in the early morning and late at night. Try Super Tamales y Atoles Los Arcos, where you can order delicious tamales stuffed with chicken, cheese, red salsa, green salsa, chile peppers, or pork. In addition to traditional tamales steamed in corn husks, Super Tamales prepares Oaxacan-style tamales, which are steamed in banana leaves and generally denser and moister. Whether you go in the morning or in the evening, get there well before closing, as many of the options sell out.

MEXICAN
La Cenaduria

Cinco de Mayo 125; tel. WhatsApp 442/848-5277; 8am-11pm daily; $3-5, cash only

La Cenaduria, also known as Cenaduria Blas, has been in operation in Querétaro's centro histórico since 1940. A cenaduria is a traditional dinner-only restaurant, and this old-timey spot is still at its best during suppertime, though they are now open all day. Try a version of local specialty enchiladas queretanas (folded tortillas bathed in a mild chile sauce and topped with potato and cheese), or order a few gorditas de maiz quebrado, chewy corn flatbreads toasted till crispy and stuffed with potato, chorizo, and other fillings. It's a popular spot with families, and the feeling here is homey and casual; plaid tablecloths, soft lighting, and a pleasant bustle make it a relaxing place to wrap up a day.

★ Sayil Centro

Cinco de Mayo 92; reservations WhatsApp 442/342-2091; https://sayil.com.mx; Sun.-Wed. 9am-6pm, 9am-1am Thurs.-Sat.; $15-20

This upscale restaurant specializes in the distinctive cuisine from the southeastern Mexican state of Yucatán. The extensive menu includes beloved dishes like cochinita pibil (achiote-rubbed pulled pork) and sopa de lima (citrus soup), as well as more unusual offerings like queso relleno (a round of gouda cheese stuffed with spiced ground pork, olives, and raisins), all beautifully prepared with a contemporary touch. The setting is lovely, with an elegant indoor dining room and an expansive open-air courtyard to choose from, and there is live music almost every night of the week (check the lineup before you make plans, as offerings vary widely, from jazz to rock). If you're new to Yucatec food, a good option is the brunch buffet on Saturday and Sunday mornings, when a wide range of dishes, many made-to-order, are served. Service is warm and attentive.

★ Maria y Su Bici

Cinco de Mayo 81; tel. 442/214-1403; www.mariaysubici.com; 1pm-midnight Mon.-Sat., 9am-7pm Sun.; US$9

Maria y Su Bici achieves the Mexican gold standard of bueno, bonito, y barrato (good, pretty, and cheap) with delicious Oaxacan-inspired dishes served in a colorful and casual setting. Here you can sample well-made renditions of Oaxacan regional cuisine, including stuffed chile pasilla, quesadillas with yellow mole, and crunchy tlayudas made with or without meat. In addition to beer (national and artisanal) and wine, the restaurant offers a lovely selection of Oaxacan mezcal as well as various mezcal cocktails, which are served in a gourd and garnished with salt and chile powder. Service is friendly and unhurried.

Bisquets Querétaro

Pino Suárez 7; tel. 442/214-1481; 7am-11pm daily; US$4

A Querétaro classic, Bisquets Querétaro is always bustling with a local crowd. Savory chilaquiles with a fried egg or spicy huevos a la cazuela (eggs and salsa cooked in a clay pot) are two of the many delicious options on the breakfast menu. Café con leche (coffee with milk) is served in the traditional style; waitstaff bring hot pitchers of milk and strong coffee to the table, and you indicate how much you'd like of each served in your mug. In the afternoons, enchiladas verdes and enchiladas queretanas are two solid choices, though there is also a daily comida corrida, which is cheap and filling. The atmosphere could not be more casual, with a small courtyard dining room as well as a larger dining room overlooking the street below. Service is efficient and professional, if not particularly verbose.

El Mesón de Chucho el Roto
Pasteur 16, Plaza de Armas; tel. 442/212-4295; www. chuchoelroto.com.mx; 8:30am-11pm daily; US$12
There is nothing nicer than watching the crowd mill through the Plaza de Armas while relaxing in one of the restaurants along the picturesque plaza. A popular choice with visitors to the city, El Mesón de Chucho el Roto serves classic Mexican food in a pleasant garden setting. With a gated patio beneath the trees of the Plaza de Armas, this restaurant is a perfect place for a leisurely meal and excellent people-watching. On Sunday, El Mesón de Chucho el Roto often draws a crowd of chic

locals; expect to share the dining room with ladies in heels and sunglasses or men in sport coats and shiny watches. Food isn't the highlight of the experience, but it's a good place to try popular regional dishes, like gorditas or a (very shareable) molcajete, a volcanic-rock bowl filled with a variety of meats, onion, cactus, cheese, and a chile sauce.

Tikua Sur-Este
Ignacio Allende Sur 13; tel. 442/403-4677 or 442/455-3333; https://tikua.mx; 1pm-11pm Mon.-Fri., 9am-11pm Sat., 9am-8pm Sun.; US$10
It's hard to decide what to order on the expansive menu at Tikua Sur-Este, which is dedicated to food from Mexico's southern states, ranging from Atlantic to Pacific, Oaxaca to Yucatán. As such, it's a good place to sample food you won't typically find in the Bajío. Start with the chapulines (grasshoppers) with cheese, then fill up on a nicely served plate of enchiladas in mole. Don't be turned away by the fact that Tikua promotes its food as being served without spice. While they do keep main dishes mild, one of the best parts about eating here is the array of salsas they bring to the table when you sit down—from a delightful roasted habanero variety to a spicy

Fogón Zapoteco

peanut salsa—some of which have quite a kick. Located in a large colonial-era mansion, there are two pretty indoor dining rooms and an outdoor patio dressed up with big, colorful murals. Friendly, attentive service and a drink menu that includes artisanal beer and mezcal complete the experience.

Fogón Zapoteco

Madero Poniente 86; tel. 442/214-1143; 7am-9pm Tues.-Sat., 9am-7pm Sun.; US$5-7

At this casual restaurant, you'll find Oaxacan-style mole, tamales, and tlayudas on the menu, among other southern Mexican specialties, as well as a nice selection of mezcal. The rich, slightly sweet mole negro, which combines chocolate, chiles, and spices, is made fresh in house. It can be served with eggs for breakfast or with chicken breast or on enmoladas (cheese- or chicken-stuffed tortillas covered in mole sauce) at lunch. The atmosphere here is as casual as they come, with colorful oilcloth-topped tables, and the prices are very reasonable.

FRENCH
★ Breton

Andador Libertad 82; tel. 442/299-6207; 8am-5pm Tues.-Sun.; US$10-15

Everything about Breton recommends it: an adorable location on the quietest block of the Andador Libertad, a stylish yet comfortable atmosphere, and an appealing French breakfast and lunch menu. It's the ideal place to start the day with house-made muesli or savory quiche, accompanied by a beautiful café latte—or just stop in for a surprisingly perfect croissant and a coffee to go. The atmosphere is as charming as the food—whether eating in the bistro-style dining room downstairs or on the roof deck, where French doors open onto the alleyway below.

GASTROPUBS
★ Jardín de Cerveza Hércules

Avenida Hércules Oriente 1; tel. 442/403-6140; 2pm-midnight Tues.-Thurs., 2pm-1am Fri., 10am-1am Sat., 10am-7pm Sun.; US$8

Cervecería Hércules, one of Querétaro's most well-known craft breweries, operates the delightful Jardín de Cerveza Hércules, an expansive beer garden and restaurant located in an early-20th-century textile factory just outside the centro histórico. The old factory facilities have been outfitted with shared picnic tables and hanging lightbulbs, creating a rustic industrial-chic atmosphere, and there are frequent live performances under the stars in the restaurant's main patio. Though you'll see Hércules's beer on menus throughout Mexico, you can sample a much larger selection of their small-batch brews here, from IPAs to porters to pilsners—as well as mezcal and wine, if beer isn't your thing. To make an afternoon of it, accompany your drinks with some of the tasty bar snacks on offer, from pizza and hot dogs to guacamole and tacos. Popular with Querétaro families, it's also a great place to take the kids on the weekends, with old factory rooms and patios to explore, a swing set and table tennis, and even a free craft table and other activities for children.

BAKERIES AND COFFEE
★ Pánico

Reforma Oriente 96; 8am-4pm daily; $5

The selection is short and sweet at Querétaro's best bakery, a tiny shop where you'll find outstanding bolillos (white rolls) and baguettes made with masa madre (sourdough starter), alongside a delicious selection of sweets and sweet breads, which roll out of the oven throughout the morning. Think flaky ham-and-cheese croissants, rich apple strudel, and ginger cookies spiked with clove and topped with sesame seeds. There is only one table inside the space, so get your bread and coffee (also excellent) and take them to a bench in the nearby Plaza de Armas. Come afternoon, **Pánico Comedor** (Manuel Gutiérrez Nájera Sur 46, Barrio de la Cruz; tel. 442/212-5117; 2:30pm-10:30pm daily), the bakery's lunch spot on the Plaza de los Fundadores, serves a selection of Pánico's breads, as well as pizza, prepared toasts, and salads at tables overlooking the square.

La Dulce Compañía

Ocampo Norte 27; tel. 442/461-0099; 7:30am-9pm Mon.-Fri., 8am-4pm Sat.-Sun.; $5

This sweet café is an ideal spot for a light meal or a coffee in a pleasant, youthful atmosphere. Come in the morning for a latte, eggs, and avocado toast, or drop by in the afternoon for a croissant sandwich and cold brew. While there, order a fig roll or a brownie to go. For a bigger dining room and a larger menu, La Dulce Compañía's sister restaurant, **La Compañía Café** (Pino Suárez 57; tel. 442/746-9856; 8:30am-10pm Mon.-Sat., 9am-8:30pm Sun.), has a more robust menu of breakfasts, salads, and, most notably, delicious pizzas.

Bars and Nightlife

As a big city and a university town to boot, Querétaro has plenty of bars and cantinas, with prices, people, and atmosphere of every stripe. There are many inexpensive bars and pubs catering to students, both on the street Cinco de Mayo and near the university, as well as some nice old cantinas that maintain a more traditional atmosphere. Many of the best places are concentrated on or around Cinco de Mayo in the eastern end of the centro histórico, where an evening stroll is likely to conclude in a cocktail.

CENTRO HISTÓRICO

La Selva Taurina La Cruz

Independencia 159; tel. 442/248-3733; 11:30am-3am Mon.-Sat.; $6

An old cantina near the Convento de la Santa Cruz, La Selva Taurina is an excellent place to quench your thirst and fill your stomach. During the day, food is served cantina style: With each drink, they bring you a small plate of food. The meal usually starts with a caldo (broth soup), followed by dishes like pork in green sauce, prickly pear tacos, or chorizo. You don't get to pick the dish, but the quality is across-the-board excellent. A shrine to bullfights, the walls are decorated with the heads of unfortunate bulls and festooned with vintage photos. At night, the place is hopping with a crowd of mixed ages, attended by easygoing bartenders.

Alquimia

Cinco de Mayo 71; tel. 442/212-1791; 6pm-2:30am Tues.-Sat.; drinks US$6-10

Alquimia is a small, attractive, and low-lit cocktail bar in a colonial-era building. There's something of an old-fashioned feeling to the main room, where dozens of glimmering glass bottles are stacked behind the dark-wood bar and leather booths overlook the street. Despite the traditional look, bartenders put together some rather newfangled cocktails—martinis adorned with Oreos or gummy bears—though the no-nonsense crowd can also order a straight shot of mezcal, served with orange wedges. It's a good place to start the evening, as they often have drinks specials in the afternoon.

GAD Cantina

Libertad 51; tel. 442/325-8099; 2pm-10pm Wed., 2pm-3am Thurs.-Sat.; generally no cover, drinks US$3-14, small plates US$2-7

Restaurant with a hip vibe by day, popular bar with good food by night, GAD is a solid choice for a night out in downtown Querétaro. A highlight of the drinks menu is the proprietary line of artisanal Gracias a Dios mezcal, made using traditional methods in the state of Oaxaca. Try it straight, in one of the bar's signature cocktails, or with a craft-beer chaser. Located in an old mansion on the pedestrian street Libertad, this popular spot stays busy through the night, when live DJs spin for a local crowd.

Accommodations

Still off the beaten track for most international tourists, Querétaro doesn't have the same range of hotel options you'd find in San Miguel de Allende, but there are still plenty of excellent choices in the centro histórico including some design-centric boutique properties and well-priced independent hotels.

CENTRO HISTÓRICO
US$50-100
Hotel Villa del Villar
Vincente Guerrero Sur 33; tel. 442/322-7093; www. villadelvillar.com.mx; US$80-110

Once you step inside the peaceful Hotel Villa del Villar, it's hard to remember that you're right in the middle of downtown Querétaro. Perhaps the most romantic of the hotel's 10 rooms, located in a restored colonial-era mansion, are those surrounding the central courtyard, with soaring ceilings and doors opening onto the patio (though the rooms in the back of the hotel are a bit quieter and more private). The decor is traditionally Mexican—wooden furniture, tile floors, and lamps—though bathrooms are fully modern, and guests can relax in the peaceful stone-floored courtyard. The atmosphere is comfortable, and service is down-to-earth and very friendly.

★ La Casa del Naranjo
Hidalgo 21; tel. 442/212-7606; https://lacasadelnaranjo. com; US90-120

La Casa del Naranjo is a small, stylish family-run hotel in the center of Querétaro. Each room is decorated in a comfortably rustic style, with exposed rock walls and soft, fluffy bedspreads. All rooms have flat-screen televisions, bathrobes and slippers, and pretty bathrooms with onyx accessories and shower massagers. Upstairs bedrooms are more luxurious, with sofas and sitting areas or canopy beds, some opening onto the roof garden. However, even the smallest room downstairs gets points for its well-designed atmosphere.

There is a small bar downstairs, and guests can also relax on the hotel's roof deck, which has a whirlpool, chaise longues, and pretty views of the city. The hotel also offers spa services.

★ Hotel Quinta Allende
Allende Norte 20; tel. 442/224-1050; www. hotelquintaallende.mx; US$85

The emphasis isn't on trendy design at well-priced Hotel Quinta Allende, though all the hotel's impeccably clean guest rooms, which are arranged around an open-air courtyard, are tastefully decorated with modern furnishings and plenty of natural light. Instead, what makes this small hotel such a nice place to stay is its comfort, with bedrooms that deliver in all the important areas: hot showers, comfortable beds, privacy, quiet, and cleanliness. Though this isn't a full-service luxury accommodation, the friendly front-desk and cleaning staff make it a welcoming place to come home to after a tour around Querétaro. Plus, the central location makes it a perfect jumping-off point for exploring downtown.

US$100-150
Hotel Criol
Río de La Loza Norte 6; tel. 442/213-7782, toll-free Mex. tel. 800/837-7606; https://hotelcriol.com; US$100

The ultramodern design at stylish Hotel Criol is a surprising contrast to the old-fashioned aesthetic in colonial Querétaro. Perhaps the best part about staying here is getting to enjoy the hotel's lovely shared areas, including a subterranean reading library, a glassed-in sitting area, and an outdoor garden with a small but attractive heated pool, a rarity in Querétaro. Rooms are also designed in a modern, Instagram-friendly style, and each is equipped with a safe, cable TV, and air-conditioning; some also have balconies or outdoor sitting areas, or bunk beds for

Best Accommodations

★ **La Casa del Naranjo:** This lovely, well-priced inn with individually decorated guest rooms, some with outdoor patios, is right in the center of town (page 193).

★ **Hotel Quinta Allende:** Impeccably clean and perfectly located in the center of town, this modern hotel is a very good value (page 193).

★ **Casa Mateo:** Spend a night in the Mexican countryside at this pretty boutique hotel, located in the heart of the small town of San Sebastián Bernal (page 210).

kids. Though the property is clean and quiet throughout, the hotel sometimes sacrifices function for style (glass-doored bathrooms, for example, are not as practical as they are attractive).

Dos Patios

Cinco de Mayo 109; tel. 442/212-2030, toll-free Mex. tel. 800/831-5790; www.curamoria.com; US$115-175
Dos Patios is a quiet and comfortable hotel in a renovated colonial-era mansion that markets itself as the first and only holistic hotel in the city. The on-site spa and holistic center are open daily, with offerings including massage, yoga, harmonization of the chakras, reiki, and other modalities. Occupying a colonial-era building, the hotel's 20 rooms are rather modern in their comforts, with plush beds and cotton bedspreads, televisions, big armoires, and clean bathrooms. The nicest accommodations are those surrounding the back garden, which are set back off the street and feel both quiet and private.

La Casa del Atrio

Allende Sur 15; tel. 442/212-6314; http://lacasadelatrio. com; from US$120
La Casa del Atrio stands out with impressive attention to detail and style. Doubling as a gallery, the old home is filled with antiques, art, artesanía, and collectibles, which give the common areas a particularly nice ambience. The shared courtyards have an abundance of plants and reading nooks, creating a relaxing, escape-within-the-city feeling. Rooms are each distinguished by unique details, from bathrooms with flagstone showers to antique chests or original murals on the walls. The location just across the street from the Museo de Arte de Querétaro is ideal, and the friendly owner makes sure service is invariably excellent. Breakfast is included in the price, though this hotel would be a bargain without it. Note that children under the age of nine are not allowed, but the hotel is pet-friendly.

US$150-200

Casa de la Marquesa

Madero 41; tel. 442/212-0092, toll-free Mex. tel. 800/401-7100; http://lacasadelamarquesa.mx; US$175
Querétaro's most famous hotel is the Casa de la Marquesa, an opulent colonial-era mansion on Calle Madero. This beautiful building is one of Querétaro's most prized; in fact, it is often listed among the city's notable tourist attractions, even though the building is privately owned (for that reason, the hotel often keeps the lobby closed to the public). The interior of the hotel retains many of the old-world charms you'd hope to find in a historic building: tiled walls, Moorish archways, and tons of antique furniture. Guest rooms are divided between the main house, or Casa de la Marquesa, and a neighboring structure, the Casa Azul, so double-check when reserving if you want to stay in the colonial mansion—and

1: Hotel Quinta Allende 2: interior courtyard at boutique property Hotel Criol 3: Casa de la Marquesa

note that they often have promotions, so it may be possible to book a room at a discount.

El Mesón Santa Rosa

Luis Pasteur Sur 17; tel. 442/161-2001; http://hotelmesondesantarosa.com; US$130-165

Ideally located on the southeastern corner of the Plaza de Armas, El Mesón Santa Rosa has a long history of hospitality, first opening its doors as a guesthouse as far back as the 17th century. The hotel changed hands in 2014, and the new management gave the old place a thorough update, replacing the aging carpets and heavy traditional furniture with cozy but stylish decor—white fluffy beds, throw rugs, lamps, and armchairs—that highlights the natural charms of the property. Some rooms have balconies onto the street, while others open onto the central courtyard and restaurant (ask for a room in back if you are a light sleeper). Though one of the more expensive options in central Querétaro, it's a spot with a lot of history and character—and the stylish in-house wine-and-cocktail bar, right on the corner of the Andador Libertad, is worth visiting even if you aren't staying in the hotel.

Over US$200

Doña Urraca Hotel and Spa

Cinco de Mayo 117; tel. 442/238-5400; www.donaurraca.com; US$150-215

Light, modern, and incredibly friendly, Doña Urraca Hotel and Spa is a relaxing place to spend a few days in Querétaro's centro histórico. Built within the remains of a colonial mansion, the hotel's architecture blends old and new; stone archways from the site's original structure are nicely incorporated into the hotel's clean and modern design. Inside the guest rooms, decor is minimalist and comfortable, with big fluffy beds, leather sofas, and spacious baths. White was the decorator's color of choice, complemented by wicker and leather details that give the whole place a rather earthy feeling. All 24 suites overlook the central pool and lawn, cascading with plants and flowers. Service is excellent.

Information and Services

TOURIST INFORMATION

Querétaro is working hard to become a more widely recognized tourist destination, and the result is some excellent visitor services.

Tourist Office

Pasteur 4 Nte.; tel. 442/238-5067, toll-free Mex. tel. 800/715-1742; www.queretaro.travel; 9am-7pm daily

The tourist office is almost directly across from the Casa de la Corregidora in the Plaza de Armas. Representatives can provide you with excellent maps of the city center as well as maps and information packets about visiting other parts of the state. They also have the most up-to-date information on booking cultural tours of the city and can help recommend a guide or company.

Media

An excellent guide for visitors, the free monthly booklet ***Asomarte*** (www.asomarte.com), published by the state's tourism board, lists cultural and arts events throughout the city of Querétaro. In addition to short pieces about local culture and travel, the magazine has a comprehensive agenda of special events and concerts happening in town. *Asomarte* is distributed for free throughout the city. Look for a copy at the front desk of museums or hotels. Note that it's published in Spanish only.

There are several local periodicals published in Querétaro, including the Spanish-language newspaper ***Diario de Querétaro*** (www.diariodequeretaro.com.mx), which covers local and international news as well as arts and culture in town. Every week, the *Diario* publishes weekend itineraries for art and activities in and around the state of Querétaro, as well as a section dedicated to Mexican tourism and travel. The big Mexico City-based newspaper ***El Universal*** (www.eluniversalqueretaro.mx) publishes a daily edition in Querétaro. It covers national news, politics, sports, and the arts while also providing additional coverage of news and politics in Querétaro city and state.

Visas and Officialdom

To extend a tourist card, replace a lost or stolen visa, or perform other immigration-related paperwork, contact the regional delegation of the **Instituto Nacional de Migración** (INM, Mexican Immigration Service, Prolongación Pino Suárez No. 479, Col. Ejido Modelo; tel. 442/214-1538; www.gob.mx; 9am-3pm Mon.-Fri.) in the Ejido Modelo neighborhood. There is also an immigration office at the Querétaro airport, but this branch is only equipped to provide exit and entry permits.

SERVICES
Medical and Emergency Services

Dial **911** from any ground line in Querétaro to reach the emergency response services.

Hospital General de Querétaro

Av. 5 de Febrero 101, Col. Virreyes; tel. 442/101-2900

Opened in 2021 beside the former general hospital facility, the new Hospital General de Querétaro will treat emergencies.

Hospital Ángeles de Querétaro

Bernardino del Razo 21, Col. Ensueño; tel. 442/192-3000 for appointments and emergencies; http://hospitalesangeles.com

A well-recommended private hospital, Hospital Ángeles de Querétaro also takes emergencies, in addition to offering a full staff of doctors available by appointment.

Cruz Roja

Cll Luis Vega y Monroy Esq Estadio; emergencies 442/229-0505 or 442/229-0669; https://queretaro.cruzrojamexicana.org.mx

The volunteer Red Cross will also respond to emergencies.

Querétaro has information kiosks throughout the city center.

Money

There are large national banks throughout the city center in Querétaro, all equipped with ATMs. Most bank branches can also exchange currency, including the Mexican credit union **BanBajío** (Corregidora 153; tel. 442/214-2920; www.bb.com.mx; 9am-4pm Mon.-Fri.) and **Santander** (6 de Septiembre No. 1 y 3 Oriente; tel. 442/214-0569; 9am-4pm Mon.-Fri.) in the centro histórico.

Transportation

GETTING THERE

Air

Querétaro International Airport (QRO)

Carretera Estatal 200, Querétaro-Tequisquiapan 22500; tel. 442/192-5500; www.aiq.com.mx

Transportation to Querétaro has become even more convenient with the opening of Querétaro International Airport, about 32 km (20 mi) outside the city center. There are daily flights to and from various locations in the United States and Mexico, including Houston, Dallas, Cancún, Guadalajara, and Monterrey. Once on the ground, there are registered taxis; most will drop off anywhere in town for a flat rate of about US$30.

Mexico City International Airport (MEX)

Capitan Carlos León s/n, Peñón de Los Baños Venustiano Carranza, Distrito Federal; tel. 55/2482-2400; www.aicm.com.mx

Depending on where you are coming from, visitors to Querétaro may find an easier route or less expensive flight into Mexico through Mexico City International Airport, in the capital. By bus or car, the drive from Mexico City to Querétaro takes about three hours (depending on traffic leaving the city, which can be tremendous on the weekends or during road construction projects). From the airport, **Primera Plus** (toll-free Mex. tel. 800/375-7587; www.primeraplus.com.mx) offers direct bus service from both terminals directly to the bus station in Querétaro.

Bus

From the bus station, a taxi ride to downtown Querétaro takes about 15 minutes from the bus station and costs about US$5. You can also take a taxi all the way to San Miguel de Allende for about US$40.

Central de Autobuses

Prol. Luis Vega y Monroy 800; tel. 442/229-0181

There are dozens of daily buses between Mexico City and Querétaro, as well as dozens more buses linking Querétaro to other cities in the Bajío, Guadalajara, Puerto Vallarta, and beyond. Intercity buses come and go from the Querétaro's Central de Autobuses, near the south end of the city just off Highway 57 (México-Querétaro). There are four major bus stations in Mexico City; generally, buses depart Mexico City's Terminal Central del Norte for Querétaro, with departures every 20-30 minutes. In addition, buses leave directly every hour from Mexico City's airport (Terminals 1 and 2) for Querétaro.

Primera Plus

Central de Autobuses, Prol. Luis Vega y Monroy 800; tel. 477/710-0060; www.primeraplus.com.mx

Primera Plus is one of the biggest bus lines serving Querétaro, with buses between Mexico City and Querétaro departing every 20-30 minutes 6am-midnight daily. During peak hours, buses leave for Querétaro from Mexico City every 15 minutes. Primera Plus also offers direct service between both airport terminals in Mexico City and Querétaro's main bus station, departing every hour 6:30am-midnight.

ETN

Mex. toll free tel. 800/800-0386; https://etn.com.mx
Between San Miguel de Allende and Querétaro, ETN offers first-class bus service, in addition to frequent service between Querétaro and the capital and to cities throughout Mexico.

Servicios Coordinados
Flecha Amarilla

Central de Autobuses, Prol. Luis Vega y Monroy 800; tel. 477/710-0060
Servicios Coordinados Flecha Amarilla offers second-class service to and from Querétaro, with buses running every 20 minutes or so 6am-10pm. You do not need to book ahead; just buy a ticket at the bus station.

Car
From San Miguel de Allende

From San Miguel de Allende, the drive to Querétaro takes about **1 hour.** Follow the Salida a Querétaro southwest out of the city, continuing through the traffic circle and onto the two-lane highway (Mexico 111) for about 40 km (25 mi). After passing through the small town of Buenavista, exit left on Highway 57 (México-Querétaro). Continue south on Highway 57 for about 40 km (25 mi), exiting either via the Boulevard Bernardo Quintana (a large avenue that runs through Querétaro and includes many popular chain stores, like Costco and Home Depot), or Constituyentes, an avenue just before the bus terminal, which leads directly downtown.

From Mexico City

Querétaro is on Highway 57 (México-Querétaro), a major and well-marked federal thoroughfare that runs from Mexico City to the north via San Luis Potosí, ending at the U.S. border in Piedras Negras, Coahuila. From Mexico City, take the Periférico Norte to exit the city, following signs toward Tepotzotlán. After passing through the tollbooth, continue straight on Highway 57. The drive takes **2-3 hours.** Once you arrive in the city, exit at Constituyentes and follow the signs downtown.

GETTING AROUND
Car

Driving in Querétaro can be challenging for those who don't know the city well. In addition, heavy traffic can be a problem during peak hours, since many of Querétaro's residents drive to and from their jobs. Fortunately, Querétaro is much easier to navigate than many other large Mexican cities, with decent signage and generally courteous drivers. For reference, Avenida Zaragoza and Luis Pasteur are both major avenues that lead downtown from the highway.

Car Rental

If you plan to spend time outside of Querétaro's historic downtown or you would like to explore the surrounding countryside, renting a car can be a convenient and fairly inexpensive option. Most of Querétaro's car rental companies operate out of the international airport, though several also have offices in downtown Querétaro. **Hertz** (Carretera Estatal 200, Querétaro; toll-free Mex. tel. 800/709-5000; 24 hours daily) has locations at Querétaro International Airport and downtown (Avenida de las Artes 61; toll-free Mex. tel. 800/709-5000; 8am-midnight daily). Hertz offers low daily rates for cars, SUVs, and minivans.

If you are arriving in Querétaro via bus, an inexpensive rental car company, **EHL Rentacar** (Terminal de Autobuses, Local 113, Prol. Luis Vega y Monroy 800, Local 120; tel. 442/229-0219, Mex. toll free 800/345-5000; http://ehlrentacar.mx) has offices in the main bus terminal. You only need a credit card and a driver's license to get a set of wheels, but do book ahead to avoid delays. All cars have automatic transmission and air-conditioning.

Taxi

Within the downtown district, it is easy to get everywhere on foot. But Querétaro is a large city, with 1,800,000 inhabitants and sprawling residential neighborhoods. Most residents travel by car; public transportation is rather limited. As a visitor, either renting a vehicle or taking taxis is usually the easiest solution when heading outside the downtown district.

Cheap and reliable taxis circle throughout Querétaro, which you can hail directly in the street. Fares start as low as US$2 within the city center and generally run about US$5 from downtown to the bus station and US$25 to the airport. You can also call **Radio Taxi Los Arcos** (Andador 6 1916, Lomas de Casa Blanca; tel. 442/222-8293) or hail an Uber from anywhere in the city if you need a lift.

Bus

Buses continuously run from Querétaro's city center to the outlying suburbs, with many running along Avenida Ignacio Zaragoza and Constituyentes on the southern side of the centro histórico. You can hop on any of these buses to traverse the city center, though it's usually easier to take a taxi; if you need to go to an outlying neighborhood, the bus's destination will be marked in its window. Most rides cost about US$0.50.

Sightseeing and Cultural Tours

Tourist Office

Pasteur 4 Nte.; tel. 442/238-5067, toll-free Mex. tel. 800/715-1742; www.queretaro.travel; 9am-7pm daily

The state tourist office can give you up-to-date information about tour operators in Querétaro city and state. If you've got an idea of what you'd like to do but don't know how to make it happen, this is the place to start.

Querebus

tel. 442/312-2966; one-hour trolley tour US$5, bus tour US$8

Querebus offers guided double-decker bus tours and motorized-trolley tours of Querétaro's centro histórico throughout the year, with several routes taking you past the city's most important monuments, including a route to the impressive aqueduct, and another to the Cerro de las Campanas. You can buy tickets for either the trolley or the bus tours at the tourist information kiosks on the Cinco de Mayo (across the street from the Jardín Zenea), in the Plaza de la Constitución, or at the Monumento a la Corregidora.

Wine and Cheese Route

The state of Querétaro has a long history as an agricultural center, and today it is building on that tradition with a new emphasis on artisanal and locally produced foods. In a nice day trip from the city of Querétaro or San Miguel de Allende, visitors can take a tour of the region's ranches and wineries, stopping to rest or eat in the small towns of **Tequisquiapan** or **San Sebastián Bernal.** You'll pass through some industrial towns on your way, but overall the landscapes are lovely and interesting.

If you are thinking about visiting Querétaro's countryside and happen to be in the capital, stop by the state tourist office in the city, **Secretaría de Turismo de Estado de Querétaro** (Pasteur 4 Nte.; tel. 442/238-5067, toll-free Mex. tel. 888/811-6130; www.queretaro.travel; 9am-8pm daily). The tourist office can provide you with an annotated map of the region, which includes the ranches and wineries open to the public as well as the small towns of Tequisquiapan and Bernal.

CHEESE PRODUCERS BETWEEN QUERÉTARO AND SAN SEBASTIÁN BERNAL

What goes better with wine than cheese? The state of Querétaro has brought this eternal pairing to central Mexico. When driving through Querétaro's countryside, you can stop in at one of the many small cheese factories around the state to sample the local products and, in some cases, take a tour of the ranch. On Sundays, the highways can get quite busy as Querétaro families do a turn around the countryside with their kids.

Quesos VAI

Carretera Querétaro-Tequisquiapan, km 30, Municipio de Colón; tel. 442/190-7618; www.quesosvai.com; 8am-6pm daily

On the highway from Querétaro to Tequisquiapan, Quesos VAI is one of the most well-known cheese factories in the state of Querétaro. Though originally founded by a Spanish cheese-maker, VAI is a Mexican-owned business today. All the cheese is produced from the milk of the hundreds of sheep and cows on VAI's Querétaro ranch, which is open to the public. Their roadside food shop sells VAI products, including provolone- and manchego-style cheeses, as well as other artisan and local products, like homemade cajeta, jams, honey, and local wines.

Tours (10am-5pm daily; US$10) of the cheese-making process and the ranch last an hour or so and include samples of assorted VAI cheeses. Fun for families (though a bit hokey for adults), the best part of the tour is visiting the ranch's live animals, including a large bovine particularly fond of visitors. If you are so inclined, you can buy a bottle of wine and a piece of cheese from VAI's small and nicely stocked shop, then sit amid the sheep and chickens while you eat.

Getting There

Quesos Vai is located on Highway 200 to Tequisquiapan, about 30 km (18 mi) from downtown Querétaro. By car, it is about a half hour from downtown Querétaro and an hour and a half from San Miguel de Allende.

Cava Bocanegra de Quesos Néole

Carr. Est. 200 Tequisquiapan-Qro., km 50 Fuentezuelas; tel. 414/273-3369; www.cavabocanegra.com; 9:30am-4:30pm Mon.-Fri., 9:30am-5:30pm Sat.-Sun.

The attractive Cava Bocanegra is owned by Quesos Néole, a producer of artisanal and aged cheeses, which operates this pretty country store and restaurant above its cheese-making facilities. Visitors can take a tour of the cellars to learn more about how Bocanegra makes their products (US$14) or just pick up provisions from the store. In addition to selling their own products, Cava Bocanegra carries local produce, like honey, wine, fruit preserves, and a wide range of craft brews to drink on-site or take away. The on-site restaurant (noon-6:30pm Mon.-Fri., noon-7pm Sat.-Sun.) has a lovely outdoor terrace with views of the countryside, and a menu that includes pizzas, pastas, and burgers, as well as a nice selection of Querétaro wine, local craft beer, and cocktails.

Getting There

Cava Bocanegra is located on Highway 200 near Tequisquiapan, about 55 km (35 mi) from downtown Querétaro. By car, it is about 45 minutes to reach Cava Bocanegra from Querétaro and two hours from San Miguel de Allende.

TEQUISQUIAPAN

A warm little town in the heart of Querétaro state, Tequisquiapan, founded in 1555, has a pretty colonial-era atmosphere, with narrow streets and stucco houses lining the city center. Considered the heart of Querétaro state's wine and cheese region, it is propitiously located above copious natural springs, some boasting thermal water. As a result, Tequis (as it is called) is greener than many other local cities, with large trees shading the city sidewalks and plenty of swimming pools at local hotels. Though this small city doesn't offer much by way of sights or dining, its attractive downtown and country ambience make it a relaxing place for a respite.

On the weekends, Tequisquiapan is swarmed with tourists, mostly day-trippers from Querétaro and weekenders from Mexico City. It's downright bustling on a Saturday night in the square, where families stroll between shops or rest on a bench with ice cream. Those who prefer utter peace and quiet may choose to visit Tequisquiapan during the week; however, note that many restaurants and shops may be closed or have reduced hours Monday-Wednesday.

Sights
Plaza Miguel Hidalgo
between Independencia and Morelos Nte.; 24 hours
Plaza Miguel Hidalgo is Tequisquiapan's central square and the locus of activity in town, surrounded by gift shops and restaurants. Presiding over the square is the **Templo Santa María de la Asunción,** for which construction began during the 16th century, though it wasn't finished until the end of the 19th century. This church isn't an opulent baroque spectacle, like you'd find in Guanajuato or Querétaro; however, its delicately painted pink facade and large pink cupola have a stately, refined appeal. At the front of the church, the stone entryway surrounds a pretty stained-glass window. Santa María de la Asunción is Tequisquiapan's patron saint, and her feast day, August 15, is merrily celebrated in the town square.

Parque La Pila
Av. Ezequiel Montes s/n; 7am-7pm daily
A sprawling park in the city center, Parque La Pila is filled with large and stately cypress and ash trees as well as expansive lawns. On Sundays, it is a popular place for locals to relax in the shade.

Geographic Center of Mexico
Centenario and 5 de Mayo; 24 hours
The town of Tequisquiapan in Querétaro

state and the monument to El Cristo Rey del Cubilete in Guanajuato state both claim the honor of being Mexico's exact geographical center. It's unclear who really holds the title. But in 1916, President Venustiano Carranza inaugurated a modernist monument in Tequisquiapan, at the spot that allegedly marks the center of the country. The monument is just a block from the Plaza Miguel Hidalgo on Centenario and 5 de Mayo.

Food
Camino a Bremen
Guillermo Prieto 19; tel. 414/273-1134, WhatsApp 414/104-1090; 2pm-10pm Fri.-Sat., 1pm-10pm Sun.; US$10-18
Just around the corner from the main square, Camino a Bremen is a friendly little bakery and restaurant serving delicious homemade pizzas and pastas, as well as a selection of organic breads, pastries, and coffee. Drop in at dinner for a plate of handmade ravioli stuffed with gorgonzola and pistachios, a classic pizza margherita, and a slice of house-baked pie. Though just off the main plaza, it's a quiet yet quality spot, with just a few tables in the simple dining room.

Freixenet World's Wine Bar
Andador 20 de Noviembre s/n; tel. 414/273-3995; www.freixenetmexico.com.mx; noon-8:30pm Mon., Thurs., Sun., noon-11pm Fri.-Sat.; US$10
This lovely little bar is run by sparkling-wine producer Cavas de Freixenet, which operates a vineyard and winery in the state of Querétaro. Here you can order still and sparkling wine by the glass, the half bottle, and the bottle to drink at the bar's pretty rooftop tables, or right on the plaza. For nibbles, there are beautifully plated local cheese and charcuterie platters to accompany your drinks and other wine-appropriate snacks. One of the best options in the center of town, the bar is always very busy on the weekend evenings, but come during the afternoon or on a weekday, and you may be one of only a few people there.

Mercado Guadalupano

Av. Ezequiel Montes s/n; no tel.; generally 7am-7pm
daily; individual vendor hours vary; $2-3

Just beside the main square, the Mercado Guadalupano is the town's very small municipal market. It's one of the cheapest spots to grab a bite in Tequisquiapan. At the front of the market, a number of stands specialize in carnitas, many still preparing the day's meat in huge metal pots as crowds gather on Saturday and Sunday mornings. In the back of the market, several low-key sit-down eateries serve economical breakfasts, lunches, and dinners. A good choice is **Fonda Lulu** (Loc. 54; no tel.; generally 8am-4pm Mon., Wed.-Sun.), a family-run comedor where you can get a generous plate of chilaquiles verdes, topped with an egg, for a couple of bucks.

Festivals and Events
Feria de Queso y Vino

May-June

Tequisquiapan's annual spring festival celebrates the bounty of the Querétaro countryside with a free gastronomy and wine festival, which takes places over several weekends. Purchasing tickets to the event (US$20) allows you to taste wine and cheese from local producers, as well as a selection of booths from a featured country (Spain and Italy were both recent participants). Throughout the weekend, there's live music and dance, cooking demonstrations, and a variety of booths from local artists and artisans exhibiting their work.

Vendimia

July-Aug.

Many Querétaro wineries celebrate the annual grape harvest, or vendimia, with grape stomping, concerts, and other special events at their vineyards. In recent years, Freixenet hosted ticketed concerts (from US$40) with big-name musical acts to celebrate the harvest, while La Redonda held free family-friendly grape-stomping festivals. If you're in Querétaro for harvest, check with the state tourism office to see what's happening. Note that because

of Querétaro's wet, warm summer climate, grapes are typically ready for harvest in July and August, a month or two before the harvest farther north.

Accommodations
La Granja

Morelos 12; tel. 414/273-2004 or 414/273-6378; http://
hotelboutiquelagranja.com; US$165

Pretty boutique hotel La Granja is a nice choice for an overnight trip to Tequisquiapan. On a quiet street just a half-block off the Plaza Miguel Hidalgo, spacious and comfortable bedrooms with modern decor are arranged along the tiled corridors, which surround a pretty, plant-filled courtyard. Each has a spacious bath, some with tubs, and flat-screen TVs. In the back is a big pool for swimming, surrounded by lawn chairs and umbrellas, as well as a whirlpool (limited to an hour a day for each guest).

Information and Services

Though small, Tequisquiapan is a friendly town and well equipped to receive its many weekend visitors. Tequisquiapan's helpful tourist office, **Dirección de Turismo de Tequisquiapan** (Independencia 1; tel. 414/273-0841; www.tequisquiapan.com.mx; 8am-7pm Mon.-Fri., 9am-7pm Sat.-Sun.), is right on the main plaza. The friendly Spanish-speaking representatives can answer questions and provide you with an annotated map and booklet about the town as well as maps of the Querétaro countryside. Although they do not provide walking tours of the city, the tourist office can recommend several tour operators that do.

In the central square, there is a **Bancomer** branch (Independencia 5; 8:30am-4pm Mon.-Fri.) with ATMs open 24 hours, located just next to the tourist office and the Rincón Mexicano restaurant. There is also a **Citibanamex** branch (Niños Heroes 40; tel. 800/021-2345; 9am-4pm Mon.-Fri.) with ATMs right behind the central plaza, near the monument to the geographic center of Mexico.

For emergencies, dial **911**. The volunteer-led Red Cross (tel. 414/273-4560) responds to natural disasters and other emergencies.

Getting There and Around

The easiest and most popular way to get to Tequisquiapan is by car. From the city of Querétaro, it is an easy 45-minute drive to Tequis. From San Miguel de Allende, you can get to Tequisquiapan in about twice that time.

Bus

Although the majority of Tequisquiapan tourists drive into town, you can also catch a bus from Querétaro's bus station to Tequisquiapan with **Transportes Queretanos Flecha Azul** (Plaza Capuchinas 105, Plazas del Sol; tel. 442/229-0102). Buses depart every half hour 6:30am-9pm daily and cost about US$3. From Mexico City, the bus line **ETN** (Central de Autobuses Tequisquiapan, Carretera San Juan del Río-Xilitla s/n; tel. 414/273-3797 or 414/273-3623, toll-free Mex. tel. 800/800-0368; www.etn.com.mx) offers numerous daily buses between the Terminal Central del Norte in Mexico City and the bus station in Tequisquiapan (US$15). The trip takes about three hours.

Car

The most direct way to get to Tequisquiapan is to take Highway México-Querétaro (south from Querétaro or San Miguel, and north from Mexico City), and then exit at the signs for the Sierra Gorda, taking Highway 120 north until you reach the town. The 60-km (37-mi) drive takes about 1 hour from the city of Querétaro and double that from San Miguel de Allende. Alternatively, it takes about the same amount of time to take Highway 200 west from the city of Querétaro to Tequisquiapan. If you are traveling from San Miguel de Allende, you can skip the México-Querétaro highway altogether by following the smaller Highway 500 to 200, traveling through countryside and past the Querétaro airport to Tequis; going this way will add another 15-25 minutes to your drive

time (and a good GPS is a must), though it's an overall more interesting route through the countryside.

WINERIES BETWEEN TEQUISQUIAPAN AND SAN SEBASTIÁN BERNAL

Wine arrived in Mexico along with the Spanish and has been produced throughout the country since the colonial era. Though Mexico has not been traditionally recognized as a wine-producing country, it is now home to a rapidly growing wine industry. In northern Mexico, Baja California's wines have become more internationally renowned. Vineyards in the states of Aguascalientes and Chihuahua also produce some excellent vintages. In the states of Querétaro and Guanajuato, grape-growing and wine-producing are nascent industries, yet they appear poised for expansion.

Bodegas de Cote

Libramiente Norponiente, Km 5+900, Tunas Blancas, Ezequiel Montes; tel. 441/277-5000; www.decote.mx; 11am-6pm daily

A relatively new and well-respected wine-maker, Bodegas de Cote produces the De Cote, Atempo, and Inédito labels, which you will find in restaurants throughout the state of Querétaro and beyond. Their beautiful Querétaro vineyard and tasting rooms, located near Bernal, are among the best in the area. For visitors, there are many ways to experience the De Cote vineyards, from a bicycle tour ($30, including a glass of wine) to a motorized train ride ($32 adults, including a glass of wine, $20 children). Inside the massive white-adobe building, you can tour the cool subterranean cellar where the vinos are aged, or try De Cote's wines alongside a pizza or Wagyu hamburger at Bistró, the winery's more casual eatery. In the main dining room and upstairs terrace, both boasting sweeping views of the vineyards, the on-site restaurant

---

1: Cava Bocanegra **2:** Plaza Miguel Hidalgo **3:** Freixenet World's Wine Bar **4:** shopping in Bernal

serves a daily tasting menu, as well as cheese and charcuterie boards to accompany sipping.

Getting There

Bodegas de Cote is located on Highway 120, north of the town of Ezequiel Montes, about 65 km (40 mi) from Querétaro. The drive takes about an hour from Querétaro and two hours from San Miguel de Allende.

Viñedos La Redonda

Carretera San Juan del Río, Km 33.5, Ezequiel Montes; restaurant reservations WhatsApp 55/8075-8373; http://laredonda.com.mx; 10am-6pm daily

Though it's surrounded by rather unromantic ranchland, you get an authentic wine country feeling once inside Viñedos La Redonda. Turning off the highway near the town of Ezequiel Montes, you suddenly find yourself surrounded by the gentle green leaves of grapevines. La Redonda operates a small country store at the front of the property, where you can buy bottles of the wines (and buy tickets for a tasting). The real action, however, takes place toward the back of the property. Follow the small road to the country-style barn to find a lovely patio, an Italian **restaurant** (noon-6pm daily; for weekends, reservations are required 2-5 days in advance via WhatsApp 55/8075-8373), and a bar where you can do a tasting or order a bottle of red or white (US$7-25) to enjoy on-site. Many of the wines are young, but robust and tasty. In comparison to much of the local market, they are also rather inexpensive. The winery also offers guided tours 10am-6pm daily.

Getting There

Viñedos La Redonda is located on Highway 120, between Ezequiel Montes and Tequisquiapan, about 65 km (40 mi) from Querétaro. The drive takes about an hour from Querétaro and two hours from San Miguel de Allende.

Cavas de Freixenet

Carretera San Juan del Río-Cadereyta, km 40.5, Ezequiel Montes; tel. 441/277-0147, 441/277-5100; www.freixenetmexico.com.mx; 11am-5:30pm daily

A well-known international producer of sparkling wine, Cavas de Freixenet has a long history in Querétaro, operating here much longer than most of the state's vineyards. Freixenet's massive wine cellars draw hordes of tourists, especially on the weekends, who come to taste and tour the cellar (11am, noon, 1pm, 3pm, 4pm Mon.-Fri, and every half hour 11am-5pm Sat.-Sun.; US$12 for tasting and tour) or tip back a bottle of bubbly in the many open-air tables and courtyards. If you're coming with kids, a fun option is to take the Uva Bus, a motorized trolley, for a tasting and tour around the vineyards (11:30am, 1:30pm, 3:30pm, Mon.-Fri, every hour 11:15am-5pm Sat.-Sun.; US$18 adults, US$14 children). You can also just buy a glass or bottle of sparkling to enjoy on the many tables and courtyards. The winery's special events, like the well-attended Paellafest in May, are very popular, with huge crowds in attendance.

Getting There

Freixenet is located on Highway 120, north of the town of Ezequiel Montes, about 30 km (18 mi) from Querétaro. The drive takes about an hour from Querétaro and two hours from San Miguel de Allende.

SAN SEBASTIÁN BERNAL

Tiny San Sebastián Bernal (usually referred to as just Bernal) is a lovely colonial-era town, just below the famous Peña de Bernal, a massive 335-m (1,100-ft) monolith that towers over the city center. Founded in 1642, Bernal is today one of Mexico's Pueblos Mágicos, a national program designed to recognize special or historic cities across the country. Bernal is indeed a magical place, with a small and charming city center and an attractive country location. It can be a wonderful place to stop for lunch or spend the evening while visiting the Querétaro countryside—though

☆ Peña de Bernal

The Peña de Bernal is one of the world's largest monoliths, rising above the semiarid plains of Querétaro state with natural majesty and power. On clear days, you can see the rock's pointed crown for miles. Many believe the peña (rock) has healing energy, and it is a popular pilgrimage site during the spring equinox. It is a stunning sight to behold at any time of year.

Measuring over 335 m (1,100 ft), La Peña de Bernal is one of the tallest and largest rocks in the world. Once at the top of the trail, you can sit on a sloping ledge of the peña and gaze over the valley below. The views are beautiful and sweeping. On the weekends, the peña is illuminated by floodlights at its base, so you can enjoy its dramatic face under a canopy of stars.

GETTING THERE

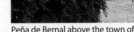

Peña de Bernal above the town of Bernal

For those who'd like to feel Bernal's healing energy for themselves, there is a 1-km (0.6-mi) trail leading to a shoulder of the monolith, which takes about an hour to hike uphill. You'll pass souvenir shops, ice cream stands, and restaurants along the walking path before arriving at the official entrance to the trail (accessible via C. Corregidora; 8am-5pm daily), where you must pay a modest access fee (US$3 per person). From there it is a somewhat vigorous ascent along rocky terrain and steep staircases, so come prepared with sunscreen, sun-protective clothing, and water.

Experienced climbers are permitted to scale the tip of the monolith to its peak, though they must advise the municipal offices in the city center before setting up the climb.

note that the town's inherent charms are often diminished by the massive throngs of tourists on the weekends. The upshot to Bernal's growing popularity as a tourist destination is many restaurants and shops are open during the weekdays, not just on weekends, as in the past. Visiting midweek is an attractive option for a quieter visit to town.

Sights
Parroquia de San Sebastián Mártir
Plaza Principal s/n; generally 9am-7pm daily
Constructed 1700-1725, Bernal's pretty parish church, the Parroquia de San Sebastián Mártir, stands right in the center of the town square. Although the church does not represent any dominant architectural style, it has a small neoclassical facade, set against its striking yellow walls and bold brick-red trim. The work of Indigenous architects is visible in the bell tower.

Museo del Sitio Capilla de Ánimas
Mesón 7; 11am-6pm Tues.-Fri., 11am-7pm Sat.-Sun.; $2
At the foot of the monolith, the Capilla de Ánimas is a small country chapel with yellow stucco walls and brick-red trim. According to local legend, a merchant took refuge from thieves in the spot where the chapel now stands. In appreciation, he began the construction of a church at the site. Built in 1725, the church boasts a small but lovely domed ceiling and the three original church bells, hanging over the entryway. Today the building is a small regional museum that contains antique maps, documents, and other paintings from Bernal's history.

Museo de la Máscara
Independencia 19; tel. 441/296-4605; 11am-7pm Fri.-Sun.; $2
It's worth taking a moment to visit this small but interesting museum, which displays over

300 traditional and decorative masks from Mexico and around the world, from the pre-Columbian era to the present. Traditional Mexican masks make up most of the collection, but the museum also displays pieces from North Africa, Asia, South America, and more. Included among the collection are pieces created by local artisans in Bernal over several decades.

Festivals and Events
Spring Equinox
Peña de Bernal, Mar.

The spring equinox, which takes place on or near March 21, is considered a very powerful day to visit the Peña de Bernal. The event is celebrated annually with pre-Hispanic rituals in town and massive groups of pilgrims heading to the top of the rock, most dressed in white. In the evening, the monolith is lit up and fireworks fill the sky. For those who'd like to experience the healing energy of Bernal, the equinox is an exciting time to visit. At the same time, the town of Bernal is incredibly crowded and bustling during the event, so book your hotel ahead of time or plan to stay in nearby Querétaro or Tequisquiapan.

Fiesta de la Santa Cruz
Peña de Bernal, May

At the beginning of May, the Fiesta de la Santa Cruz (Day of the Holy Cross) is another nice event in the town of Bernal. In commemoration, Bernal locals head to the top of the monolith, where they install a Christian cross, also recognized by Indigenous cultures as an árbol de la vida (tree of life).

Shopping
Artesanías de la Concordia
Hidalgo 6; no tel.; 10am-8pm Sat.-Sun.

Though it's right in the center of town, it's easy to walk past the quiet storefront of Artesanías de la Concordia, which specializes in locally made wool serapes and sweaters, lambskins, cotton shirts, and shawls. While it was once widespread, few artisans in the region continue to produce handmade wool products,

so it's nice to support their work—as well as the work of the dedicated shop owners, who have been in business here for decades. The wool serapes, which are made with undyed local wool, are particularly nice and very well-priced. You'll sometimes find the shop open during the weekdays, but inconsistently; on weekends they're open till evening.

Centro Artesanal la Aurora
Jardín Principal 1; tel. 441/296-4134; 10am-6pm daily

Located right on the main plaza, this family-owned workshop specializes in handmade wool serapes, wall hangings, shawls, rugs, sweaters, pillows, and more. All wool textiles are durable and made by hand on traditional looms, by local artisans, and pieces can be made to order. In operation since the 1970s, the shop is one of Bernal's longest-running businesses.

Dulces Bernal
Calle Hidalgo s/n; tel. 441/296-4148; www.dulcesbernal. com; 10am-7pm daily

Pick up some outstanding cajeta and candied fruits, among other regional sweets, at beloved Dulces Bernal, one of the oldest and most famous candy-makers in Querétaro. You can fill a basket with goodies at the well-stocked shop in the town center, though children (or those with a sweet tooth) may enjoy visiting the shop's bigger location, just on the edge of downtown, which also includes the small but colorful **Museo de Dulces** (Juárez 2; tel. 441/296-4148; 10am-5pm daily, shop 10am-7pm daily; $2), or Candy Museum, which introduces the history and techniques behind traditional Mexican candies.

Food and Drink
El Mezquite
Iturbide 1; tel. 442/367-4239; 9:30am-6:30pm daily; US$8

El Mezquite is one of the most popular restaurants in Bernal, and it is easy to see why. This open-air patio has one of the best views in town, overlooking the peña from its patio dining room. Despite the million-dollar view, El

Mezquite is a casual, inexpensive, and family-oriented restaurant, where big groups of week-enders convene for a leisurely afternoon meal on the colorful patio, shaded by the large tree that is the restaurant's namesake. The menu is standard Mexican fare. Food is tasty enough, and the view is unbeatable. To get to this convivial spot, look for a small colonial plaza on 5 de Mayo, just off the main square. The restaurant is in the patio behind the gift shops (there are signs at the entryway).

★ Arrayán

Ignacio Zaragoza 9; tel. 441/296-4534; 1pm-9pm Wed.-Thurs., 1pm-10:30pm Fri.-Sat., 1pm-9pm Sun.; US$12

Located inside hotel Casa Tsaya, surprisingly chic Arrayán serves creative Mexican-inspired dishes, combining traditional ingredients with contemporary preparations. The menu includes appealing plates like a tlayuda (Oaxacan-style corn flatbread) with hummus and mushrooms, and shrimp in vanilla sauce, alongside options that lean more toward traditional than experimental, such as arrachera with beans and guacamole. A particular delight of dining here is the drink menu, which includes numerous Mexican-made small-batch beers, mezcal, tequila, and Mexican wines. The light-filled main dining room is clean and modern, while the outdoor terrace boasts beautiful views of the monolith.

Folk

Aldama 11; tel. 441/120-5651; 2pm-10pm Thurs.-Sun.; US$6

A low-lit little bar and restaurant right in the center of Bernal, Folk has a fine selection of Mexican wines, many produced locally in the state of Querétaro, as well as mezcal, bottled craft beer from local producers, and excellent cocktails. There's an array of shareable plates, pastas, and pizza on the appealing and well-executed menu, from Greek salad to tuna tartar, though you can also just stop in for a drink and a chat with the friendly waitstaff, who are knowledgeable about the drinks on offer. The bar's owner is often there, too, doling out advice on locally made libations.

Accommodations
Casa Tsaya Hotel Boutique

Ignacio Zaragoza 9; tel. 441/296-4534; www. casatsayahotel.com; US$120-170

Casa Tsaya Hotel Boutique is a lovely property in the center of town, with a low-key rustic-chic feeling. Rooms, though not particularly spacious, are nicely designed and clean, surrounding the in-house restaurant, Arrayán, or the

Arrayán, Bernal's best restaurant

QUERÉTARO
WINE AND CHEESE ROUTE

small grassy courtyard in back. It's a nice good-value spot, with a perfect location, just steps away from Bernal's main plaza. Adults only.

★ Casa Mateo

5 de Mayo s/n, esq. Colón; tel. 441/296-4472; US$100
If you are planning a romantic getaway to the country or a family trip to La Peña de Bernal, Casa Mateo is a well-designed boutique hotel in the very center of Bernal. Guest rooms are comfortable and tastefully furnished, equipped with ceramic floors, fireplaces, down comforters, and modern bathrooms. Though each room is slightly different from the next, decor is pleasingly minimalist throughout the hotel; family-style rooms have a loft bed for the kids. In the center of the hotel, there are nice views of the peña rising above a small swimming pool and lawn. Just a block from the main plaza, this hotel is right in the middle of town but feels secluded and private. Service is friendly and attentive.

Information and Services

Technically a part of the municipality of Ezequiel Montes, Bernal is a small town—even smaller than its neighbor Tequisquiapan. Although Bernal is well accustomed to tourism, there are few services here. Even the tourist office is located in the city of Ezequiel Montes. To make things all the more complicated, many shops and restaurants are closed during the week (Bernal's tourism is principally weekenders). The upshot of visiting Bernal from Monday through Friday is that you will enjoy the tranquility of a sleepy country town.

There are no banks in Bernal, but there is one ATM in the city's central plaza. If you need to visit a bank or change money, the closest banks are in downtown Ezequiel Montes. Right on the main highway passing through Ezequiel Montes, there is a branch of **Banamex** (Av. Constituyentes 114-A; tel. 441/277-1279; 9am-4pm Mon.-Fri.), with ATMs, currency exchange, and other services.

Getting There and Around

To get to Bernal from Querétaro by car, take Highway México-Querétaro and exit at the signs for Sierra Gorda. From there, take Highway 100 for about 40 km (25 mi) until you reach Bernal.

If you are coming from Tequisquiapan, follow the highway toward Cadereyta, passing through the industrial town of Ezequiel Montes. Continue on the highway past Cavas de Freixenet until you reach a fork in the road; signs indicate that Bernal is to the left, or east, along a small two-lane highway. You will be able to see the monolith as you approach the town.

Once you've made it to Bernal, park and explore the city on foot.

Background

The Landscape

GEOGRAPHY

The cities of San Miguel de Allende, Guanajuato, and Querétaro are located in the Mexican states of Guanajuato and Querétaro and are part of a region known as the Bajío, a geographically and culturally linked valley within the Mexican Altiplano, a massive plateau that stretches from the U.S. border to the Trans-Mexican Volcanic Belt near Mexico City. The Bajío region covers the states of Querétaro and Guanajuato as well as segments of southern Jalisco and eastern Michoacán. León and Querétaro are the two largest and most important cities in the

Bajío, though the region also includes the well-known colonial towns of Guanajuato, San Miguel de Allende, and Dolores Hidalgo. Though situated at about 1,800 m (6,000 ft) above sea level, the term "bajío" means something similar to "lowlands." While not technically "low," the Bajío lies below the impressively tall mountains of the Cordillera de Guanajuato and the Sierra Gorda, which run past the plains to the north and east, respectively.

There are several important water sources within the Bajío. The Río Laja basin covers about half the state of Guanajuato and is the principal water source near San Miguel de Allende. The Río Laja is a tributary of the larger Río Lerma. One of the country's longest and most important watersheds, the Lerma passes along the border between the states of Querétaro and Michoacán and then through the state of Guanajuato on its course northward. It empties into Lake Chapala in Jalisco.

CLIMATE

The Bajío's climate is temperate, dry, and semiarid. With very little humidity in the air, the weather can fluctuate significantly over the course of a single day. Throughout the year, evening temperatures are significantly lower than daytime temperatures; travelers should pack accordingly.

It rarely rains in the Bajío during the long dry season, which runs from October to mid-June. During summer's erratic wet season, rain typically falls during brief but furious thunderstorms in the afternoon or early evening. Thunderstorms rarely last more than an hour or two; however, their fierce downpours can cause destruction and flooding. By the end of the rainy season, the dry landscape of the Bajío is totally transformed. September and October can be particularly pleasant months to visit, when the desert blooms with wildflowers. In total, the Bajío receives somewhere around 50-64 cm (20-25 in) of rain each year.

Although the Bajío enjoys a temperate climate year-round, there are distinct seasons. December and January are the coolest months, with average daytime temperatures hovering around 20°C (70°F) and nighttimes dropping to around 0°C (32°F). Evening frosts are not uncommon, with temperatures sinking below freezing on the coldest nights. Though surprisingly chilly, the winter season is very short. Spring begins as early as the end of February, and weather is reliably warm by March. Throughout March and April, the climate is warm and dry, averaging 24-30°C (75-85°F), though the evenings continue to be chilly.

May is typically the warmest month in the Bajío, with temperatures reaching 30-35°C (85-95°F). Few tourists visit the area in May, the one month of the year when the climate is uncomfortably hot. In June the rains begin, tempering the heat. During the rainy months, the climate tends to be warmest in the mornings, cooling off after the afternoon showers. By September and October, the rains have begun to subside, but the climate remains pleasant, hovering around 25°C (77°F).

The climate is similar throughout the Bajío, though there are some regional differences. Located in a mountainous valley, the city of Guanajuato tends to be a few degrees cooler than San Miguel de Allende, whereas Querétaro may be a few degrees warmer. In the town of Santa Rosa de Lima, in the mountains outside Guanajuato, the climate is rather chilly all year long.

ENVIRONMENTAL ISSUES

Although anthropologists have discovered the remains of several pre-Columbian cities in the Bajío region, it was sparsely populated when Spanish settlers arrived in the 15th century. Thereafter, extensive ranching and agriculture in the region changed the quality of the land, which was once far more lush and

---

Previous: El Pípila overlooking Guanajuato.

verdant than it is today. Throughout the Bajío, human settlements and farming have led to massive deforestation, as well as an overall degradation of natural plant and animal ecosystems. Due to the resulting decrease in plant cover, the floodplains of the Río Lerma have suffered from severe erosion, with dramatic flooding causing major problems during the short but intense rainy season. Deforestation has also made it more difficult for the soil to absorb rainwater, depleting the underground water table.

Human activities have polluted freshwater sources in most of Mexico, including the Bajío region. The Río Laja and especially the Río Lerma have been polluted by untreated sewage from surrounding towns and cities.

The heavy agricultural, ranching, leather, paper, and petrochemical industries around the Bajío have further added to the contamination of drinking water sources. Currently there are few water recycling or treatment programs in the region.

Water has become a particular concern for rural populations, especially around San Miguel de Allende. Here semiarid land supports a relatively large population with a very modest annual rainfall. Rapid urban growth around the city of San Miguel has created a new necessity for sustainable urban planning and resource allocation. However, there are few programs in place to ensure that water will continue to be available for the growing populace.

Plants and Animals

Mexico is one of the world's most biodiverse countries, encompassing a wide range of extremely distinct ecosystems, from arid desert to tropical wetland. Located in the center of Mexico, the Bajío region is covered by several high-altitude semiarid ecosystems, including xeric shrubland, coniferous forest, and dry forests. Today much of the Bajío's original flora and fauna has been affected by human development and agriculture. At the same time, ecological reserves, parks, and botanical gardens continue to protect large swaths of the region's native ecosystems and environments.

TREES AND SHRUBS

Many beautiful trees grow naturally around the Bajío, in addition to several decorative species, which were introduced to the area and are common in cities. In the region's scrubland, the hardy deciduous mesquite tree continues to flourish despite widespread deforestation for agriculture. Mesquite rarely grows taller than 8-9 m (26-30 ft) and can be identified by its dark bark, fringe of narrow green leaves, and thorny branches. This tree is native to Mexico, and its name comes from

the Nahuatl word "mizquitl." Mesquite is particularly well known for its fragrant, hard, and slow-burning wood, which is used for charcoal grilling. Its yellow flowers are frequently used in honey production.

Huizaches (sweet acacias) are another hardy and drought-resistant tree native to central Mexico. Growing naturally around San Miguel de Allende and the Bajío, they have fluffy yellow flowers and slender green leaves and look similar to the mesquite. Both huizaches and mesquites grow in lower-lying scrubland, with grass and underbrush rising beneath them.

Throughout the Bajío, the sprawling branches of the jacaranda tree make pleasant shade throughout the year. In the spring, jacarandas become a particularly stunning aspect of the landscape during their annual bloom in March, when they explode into a canopy of purple blossoms. Though not native to Mexico (they are originally from Brazil), these tropical plants thrive in the Bajío's natural environment. Within the cities of San Miguel de Allende and Guanajuato, it is also common to see guava, orange, pomegranate, lime, and

other fruit trees, which flourish in the sunny climate.

San Miguel de Allende would not be the same without its brightly hued vines of bougainvillea spilling into the alleyways and brimming over gardens. Although not indigenous to Mexico, bougainvillea flourishes here. In some cases, their woody trunks can be as large as trees; their colored leaves come in a variety of hues, from magenta to orange to white. Another popular decorative plant, poinsettia, is native to Mexico. When not trimmed for a Christmas flowerpot, poinsettia will often grow rather large. The red "flower" of a poinsettia is not a flower at all; in fact, the red petals are actually the plant's upper leaves, which have a hue distinct from the lower, green leaves.

CACTI AND SUCCULENTS

A famous native of the New World, the phenomenal, water-saving cactus proliferates blithely in the low-rainfall region of the Bajío. Consumed as food, distilled for drink, candied for desserts, and artfully planted for low-water landscaping, cacti and succulents play myriad roles in the region.

The large nopal (prickly pear or paddle cactus) is perhaps the most common and recognizable cactus in the region. From a central stalk, a prickly pear grows flat oblong paddles, covered in spines. Its fruit, called tuna in Mexico, ripens in the late summer and is very juicy, sweet, and delicious. In addition, the prickly pear paddle is an easy-to-cultivate, flavorful, and highly nutritious food source. They are sold throughout markets in the Bajío, served in stews, or fried up and stuffed into quesadillas.

Also abundant in the region, the maguey has played a central role in traditional Mexican life for centuries. This fleshy cactus is the source of mezcal, tequila, and pulque,

three iconic beverages in Mexican culture, and they were used for myriad purposes by native cultures, such as papermaking. While all maguey have juicy leaves growing in rosettes around their central stalk, there is a wide variety within the genus. All maguey bloom just once and at the end of their life cycle, sprouting a giant stalk and flowers, which can reach up to 9 m (30 ft).

Cacti are also popular for gardens and landscaping. Often used as a form of natural fencing, the beautiful columnar organ cactus grows naturally in the region, and it can be found as far north as the United States.

BIRDS

Bird-watching in the Bajío can be interesting for both the novice and expert, as there are huge populations of migrant and resident birds throughout the region. The Laja River Valley is one of the first major wetlands south of the U.S. border. Therefore, it is an important route for migrating birds, as well as home to a surprisingly abundant supply of shorebirds and waterfowl. You may be surprised to learn that Mexican ducks, gulls, and grebes can be spotted around San Miguel de Allende. In fact, a large and rather noisy flock of egrets lives inside the city itself; they nest at Parque Juárez and in the trees around El Chorro.

Throughout the Bajío, casual observers will notice hummingbirds, wrens, doves, woodpeckers, warblers, towhees, and sparrows. Even those who don't routinely look for birds will undoubtedly spot the gorgeous vermillion flycatcher, a small bird with a black back and a brilliant red chest.

The Bajío is also an important habitat for birds of prey, notably American kestrels, red-tailed hawks, white-tailed kites, crested caracaras, and turkey vultures. In the evenings, it is not uncommon to see large white barn owls soaring over the churches in San Miguel de Allende.

MAMMALS

You are unlikely to spot any large mammals near an urban center, though field mice,

1: Bajío countryside during the summer rainy season 2: banded-backed wren at El Charco del Ingenio garden 3: bougainvillea, a common sight in the Bajío's cities

Birds of the Bajío

- **Belted Kingfisher:** These compact waterbirds have a bluish-black back, a thick beak, and a large crested head on a stocky body. This bird is best known for its impressive diving abilities, splashing headfirst into the water from great heights and emerging with a fish in its beak.

- **Broad-Billed Hummingbird:** This medium-size, nectar-loving hummingbird is a dazzling emerald green, and it often nests in the trees and rooftop gardens around San Miguel de Allende. These wee creatures can consume more than their body weight in a day.

- **Cactus Wren:** A speckled brown-and-white bird with a distinctive white eye-stripe, the lovely cactus wren forages for food in the desert chaparral and is often at home among the spiny branches of the mesquite tree. As its name implies, this large wren may make its nest in the hole of a cactus.

- **Crested Caracara:** These large and striking raptors are found in central Mexico, though a few can be spotted in the southernmost regions of the United States. Sometimes called a Mexican eagle, this impressive bird has a black back, white belly, and a wingspan over 1 m (3 ft).

- **Golden-Fronted Woodpecker:** One of several woodpeckers tapping around the Bajío, the golden-fronted woodpecker has a golden stripe along the back of its neck. In addition to insects, these birds love to eat the fruit of the prickly pear cactus.

- **Great-Tailed Grackle:** The male members of this grackle species can be distinguished by their long tails and shiny jet-black feathers. Their loud squawks can be heard in cities, where many great-tailed grackles live, and they enjoy a wide range of foods, from insects to berries.

- **Inca Dove:** Despite its name, this long-tailed, pigeon-like dove does not live anywhere near Peru. Instead, you might see these light brown or grayish doves flitting around the Bajío.

- **Peregrine Falcon:** One of the world's fastest predators, the compact and beautiful peregrine falcon has gray feathers and a speckled white or rust-colored underbelly. These falcons like to feast on other birds, rather than rodents or insects, and they catch their unlucky prey mid-flight.

- **Roadrunner:** If you are both observant and lucky, you may catch a glimpse of the wonderful roadrunner in the Bajío countryside. A member of the cuckoo family, this large speckled bird has a feathery crest and strong legs. As in the cartoon, they are incredibly fast runners, capable of catching a snake on the ground. They thrive in semiarid ecosystems, which are filled with insects and reptiles—the roadrunner's favorite fare.

- **Snowy Egret:** Few expect to find the elegant, long-legged egret—a classic waterbird—in the Mexican high desert. However, the snowy egret has found a happy nesting spot in the trees around Parque Juárez in San Miguel de Allende as well as along the shores of the city's reservoir.

- **Vermillion Flycatcher:** The small but brilliant vermillion flycatcher makes its home in the southwestern United States and central Mexico. Its plump body with red chest is a welcome sight among the green leaves of a mesquite tree, where it feasts on insects.

- **White-Throated Swift:** Swift as its name implies, this high-speed bird has a black back and wings, though this species can be distinguished from other regional swifts by its white throat feathers. One of the fastest birds, it has bursts of speed that may reach 320 kph (200 mph).

squirrels, and other rodents are abundant. In the evenings, it is not uncommon to see jackrabbits or cottontails running through the grasslands outside the cities. Other nocturnal critters will occasionally wander into the city center, including opossums, skunks, and the elegant ring-tailed cat. Although you are unlikely to catch a glimpse of them, the Bajío is also home to coyotes, gray foxes, and even bobcats.

INSECTS AND ARACHNIDS

Mosquitoes are common throughout the Bajío during the summer and fall. Though they can be a nuisance, most mosquito-borne illnesses have not been reported in the Bajío for many years. In addition, the Bajío makes a cozy home for scorpions, spiders, cockroaches, grasshoppers, praying mantises, crickets, and beetles. While scorpions and spiders are the most universally feared, they are usually reclusive and avoid human contact.

In addition to pests, the Bajío is a good place to spot colorful dragonflies, damselflies, and dozens of butterfly species. Often, in the early spring or late fall, you can spot monarch butterflies traveling over the Bajío on their way to their winter nesting grounds in the state of Michoacán.

History

EARLY HISTORY

Anthropologists believe that the first humans arrived in the Americas about 30,000 years ago, crossing a narrow land bridge over the Bering Strait from Asia. In the Bajío region, little is known about the first human inhabitants; however, archaeologists have discovered marble weapons and tools that date back to 20,000 BC in the state of Guanajuato.

Though they lived on the land for millennia, the original migrants to North America were eventually supplanted by a new wave of immigrants at the beginning of the Stone Age. These people, believed to have likely been of Asian descent, settled the entire continent, reaching all the way into the Andes Mountains of South America. As the planet began to warm, the oceans rose, and the land bridge between Asia and the Americas disappeared. Thereafter, the Americas were physically isolated from Asia and Europe.

MESOAMERICAN CIVILIZATIONS

Between 8000 and 2000 BC, sedentary human settlements began to develop in southern Mexico, Belize, Guatemala, Honduras, El Salvador, and Nicaragua. This swath of culturally linked territory is generally called Mesoamerica. Like all humans during the Stone Age, early Americans were hunter-gatherers. While the first agricultural settlements in Eurasia date back to 6200 BC, studies suggest that farming began around 2500 BC in the western hemisphere. With farming came civilizations of increasing complexity. By the time the Spanish arrived in the New World, Mesoamerica was home to some of the largest, most sophisticated, and most populous civilizations in the world.

The first great Mesoamerican culture, the Olmecs appeared in the lowlands of the modern-day states of Veracruz and Tabasco around 1500 BC. Little is known about the Olmec culture (even their name was given to them by anthropologists), though they left behind both the remains of their urban centers and their signature hand-carved colossal stone heads, many of which had been ritually buried. The Olmecs began to decline after 400 BC, but their culture and city planning laid the groundwork for the Mexican and Mesoamerican cultures to come.

Centuries later, another largely unknown culture built the city of Teotihuacán in the Valley of Mexico, during what anthropologists

BACKGROUND
HISTORY

and historians call the Early Classic period, around 200 BC. With an estimated population reaching 150,000 (and possibly more) at its peak, Teotihuacán's influence reached throughout Mesoamerica. It was overtaken and destroyed around AD 800, though its lofty pyramids (two of the tallest in the world) remain standing today.

Until recently, anthropologists believed that the complex sedentary civilizations of Mesoamerica did not extend farther north than Tula, in the modern-day state of Hidalgo. We now know that there are ruins of pre-Columbian civilizations scattered throughout the states of Guanajuato and Querétaro, though to date the majority have not been studied or opened to tourism. Just 7 km (4.5 mi) outside the center of Querétaro, the archaeological site of El Cerrito was inhabited in two phases, in AD 400-600 and again during AD 650-1050, after which the population dispersed. La Cañada de la Virgen, a small but interesting site near San Miguel de Allende, is believed to have been built somewhere around AD 530. Both those cities, like many others in the region, had been abandoned by the time the Spanish arrived in the Bajío. By then, the region was dominated by nomadic tribes of hunter-gatherers, collectively referred to as the Chichimecas by the Spanish.

As small city-states were being built in northern Mesoamerica, the first Maya civilizations began to flourish around the Yucatán Peninsula, Guatemala, and Belize, ushering in the Classic Period in Mesoamerican history. The Maya were great artists, astronomers, architects, and mathematicians who built massive temple-pyramids at the center of their cities. On the eve of the conquest, the Maya were still a populous people in southern Mexico, as they are today, though their cities had been mysteriously abandoned in the 8th and 9th centuries AD. To the west, the Zapotec civilization began to flourish in the modern-day state of Oaxaca. The great city-state of Monte Albán was founded in 400 BC but reached preeminence during the Classic Period, eventually declining somewhere

around AD 500-700. Like their contemporaries to the east, the Zapotecs were accomplished architects, artists, and scientists. They employed a writing system to record their people's history, which new evidence suggests may have been the first writing system in Mesoamerica.

Power was consolidated again in central Mexico when the massive Toltec empire rose to prominence in AD 800-1000. Ruling from their massive city-state of Tula, in what is today the state of Hidalgo, the Toltecs would eventually disperse about a century before Nahuatl-speaking nomads arrived in the Valley of Mexico, founded a settlement on an island in Lake Texcoco, and eventually came to rule Mesoamerica from the tri-city alliance of Tenochtitlan, Tlacopan, and Texcoco. When the Spanish arrived in the Americas in the 15th century, Tenochtitlan's emperor, Moctezuma, presided over a vast empire that stretched from the Atlantic to the Pacific.

THE CONQUEST

During the 15th century, Nahuatl-speaking people called the Mexica dominated Mesoamerica from the tri-city alliance of Tenochtitlan, Tlacopan, and Texcoco, in what is today Mexico City and the state of Mexico. This alliance was ruled by Moctezuma from Tenochtitlan, a massive metropolis of grand pyramids and large public squares, connected by waterways and teeming with markets and activity. The Mexica were accomplished artists and thinkers, with advanced city planning and agricultural capabilities, a calendar system, and complex religious beliefs. They were also bellicose warriors, hated and feared by the other civilizations in Mesoamerica. During the 15th century, Tenochtitlan was one of the largest cities in the world—more populous than any city in Spain.

Christopher Columbus landed in the Americas in 1492, and Spanish colonization of the Caribbean began swiftly thereafter. In 1519 Hernán Cortés set sail for Mexico from the Spanish colony in Cuba. Having come with the intention to secure the land for

La Gran Chichimeca

When the Spanish arrived in the Americas, power was concentrated in the regions around modern-day Mexico City, where the Nahuatl-speaking Mexica people dominated Mesoamerica from their island city of Tenochtitlan. To the north, the land was more sparsely populated, principally inhabited by semi-nomadic or nomadic tribes that were not under the control of the massive Mexica empire. The Mexica used the term "Chichimeca" to collectively refer to the tribes of this area, which included the **Pame,** the **Zacatecos,** and the **Caxcanes.** As Spanish missionaries and ranchers began to settle the Bajío, they picked up the term and named Mexico's great central plateau La Gran Chichimeca, a territory that covers the modern-day states of Guanajuato, Querétaro, San Luis Potosí, and Aguascalientes, as well as parts of bordering states.

Little is known about the people and cultures who lived in this region at the time of the conquest. Even their numbers are disputed. Based on different evidence, historians have estimated that there were between 150,000 and 625,000 Indigenous people in the area, some of whom were sedentary and practiced modest agriculture, and many who were nomadic or semi-nomadic hunter-gatherers. One thing we do know is that the Spanish settlers, like the Mexica, were frightened of them. Bellicose rival tribes of the Chichimeca were often at war with each other, and their battle tactics were psychologically terrifying; warriors would strip down and cover themselves in full body paint, screaming as they ran in for attack. When victorious, they often tortured prisoners of war.

Nonetheless, the obsessive pursuit of silver and gold pushed the Spanish deep into Chichimeca territory. Hoping to settle the region, the Spanish royalty doled out many land grants during the 1540s, sending migrants and farmers to the Bajío and beyond. In addition to gold seekers, Franciscan friars were among the first to make inroads into this vast territory, setting up schools and churches in remote Chichimeca outposts. In so doing, Spanish settlers encroached on Chichimeca land. They let their horses and donkeys graze on native cornfields. Cattle ranches changed the quality of the land and its soil; in Zacatecas, large grasslands were eventually rendered semiarid due to extensive livestock grazing.

In defense of their lands and way of life, Chichimecas began to raid the Spanish settlements, stealing cattle, robbing stores, and attacking donkey trains headed for Mexico City along the silver route. In the 1550s, the tribes of La Gran Chichimeca began to launch more serious attacks on the Spanish settlers, who retaliated in kind. This period of violent clashes is often called the Chichimeca War. Spanish silver barons largely financed this war against the native people; surprisingly, they had more expendable funds than the Spanish crown. Many Chichimeca prisoners of war were enslaved after their capture. Those who lived peacefully on the land were also enslaved to work in the mines or on ranches.

It wasn't until the beginning of the 1600s that the Spanish were able to fully dominate the lands along silver route to Mexico City. Some Chichimeca pueblos were established, but even these were eventually reduced and finally disappeared. Of the many tribes that were once considered part of El Gran Chichimeca, very few survived. Today the Pames of San Luis Potosí and Chichimeca-Jonaz people, who live in Guanajuato and San Luis Potosí state, are contemporary descendants of the Chichimeca tribes.

Spain (and against the express command of the Cuban governor, to whom he was a subordinate), Cortés and his soldiers initially made peaceful contact with the rulers of Tenochtitlan and were welcomed into the city by Moctezuma. Tensions brewed, and after a poorly executed Spanish attack on Mexica nobles, made in Cortés's absence, the Spanish attempted to escape under the cover of darkness and in possession of as much stolen gold and jewelry as they could carry. The Spanish lost hundreds of soldiers to angry Mexica attackers while trying to flee the city in a massacre remembered as the Noche Triste (Night of Sorrows).

Over the following months, the Spanish

regrouped their forces and returned to launch an offensive on the city. Though the fight between the Spanish and Mexica was long and brutal, many tribes near Tenochtitlan assisted the Spanish forces in battling the Mexica, which had terrorized their villages for centuries. The Spanish were further assisted by the smallpox virus, which they had unwittingly introduced to the Americas. Once infected with smallpox, thousands of native people fell sick and died, greatly weakening the Mexica's power. Cuitlahuac, the emperor who replaced Moctezuma after the latter's death in battle, was among the many who died of the virus. After numerous attempts to take the capital city, Hernán Cortés and his cavalry successfully overthrew the people of Tenochtitlan, valiantly led by emperor Cuauhtémoc, in 1521.

THE COLONIAL ERA

Shortly after Cortés's final victory over the Mexica, Spanish settlement of Mexico began. Missionaries and settlers began to arrive in the New World, seeking Catholic converts and worldly fortune. The first Spanish viceroy of Mexico, Don Antonio de Mendoza, took his post in 1535. For the next 300 years, the Spanish crown controlled politics, religion, and trade in the colonies.

To encourage colonization, the Spanish crown doled out land grants to Spanish settlers, authorizing them to begin farming and mining operations in native territory. The Franciscans were among the first groups to settle the states of Michoacán, Querétaro, and Guanajuato, where they opened rural schools and hospitals, hoping to attract native people to the Catholic church. In 1543 Fray Juan de San Miguel founded San Miguel de los Chichimecas on the banks of the Río Laja.

Having heard news of the conquest, the native tribes in the Bajío region were not welcoming to the Spanish settlers. The Chichimeca repeatedly attacked Spanish ranches and raided their donkey trains. San Miguel de Allende and other settlements were temporarily abandoned during a period called the Chichimeca War, a protracted series of attacks against the Spanish, which ran roughly 1550-1590. Despite hostility from the native people and harsh, arid conditions, the thirst for gold and silver created an incredible incentive for Spanish settlers to expand their interests in the northern region. Many Spanish landowners helped fund the war against the Native people, in the absence of sufficient support from the crown.

Spanish efforts quickly paid off. In 1546 a Spanish convoy found a large silver vein in Zacatecas. Shortly thereafter, silver was discovered in both Guanajuato and San Luis Potosí. The mining settlements required enormous resources and, in turn, generated impressive wealth. Throughout central and northern Mexico, mine owners commissioned churches and built lavish mansions, making the "silver cities" some of New Spain's most beautiful settlements. A long highway known as the Camino Real de Tierra Adentro (Royal Inland Route) connected the northern mines to the capital in Mexico City. Both San Miguel de Allende and Querétaro were important protective towns along this route, gaining incredible wealth through auxiliary industries and agriculture. Like the mining towns, they were lavishly constructed in the baroque style of the 17th and 18th centuries.

Although the Bajío was originally divided into large haciendas, or rural estates, it eventually became more developed as the silver trade flourished. By the 18th century, immigrants from across Mexico had come to work in the mines and industries, and the Bajío became one of the most densely populated regions in the world.

Throughout Mexico, the colonial era was a time of great inequity, and the Bajío was no exception. With the incredible wealth gleaned from the silver trade and related industries, ruling families lived in lavish mansions, traveled in horse-drawn carriages, and ate food imported from Spain. At the same time, disenfranchised Indigenous laborers often worked for impossibly low wages (or no wages at all) and lived in inhumane conditions. Divided by ethnicity and heritage, colonial society was highly stratified. In the Spanish colonies, full-blooded Spaniards born in Spain were called peninsulares (for the Spanish peninsula where they were born) or gachupines, and they retained the highest social status. Peninsulares were also appointed to all the most important political posts. Mexican-born people of Spanish heritage were referred to as criollo and, despite their common heritage, had a lower social and political standing. Mestizo people of mixed ethnic heritage held a far lower place in society, only better than the abysmal position of Indigenous people and African slaves.

WAR OF INDEPENDENCE

Among the criollo population, there was already quite a bit of resentment against the peninsular-born Spanish when the Bourbon kings took control of Spain in the 18th century. A self-proclaimed "enlightened despot," King Charles III made major changes to the oversight of Spanish territories in the New World. He quickly established royal monopolies on many important industries, like tobacco, ice, stamped paper, mercury (a key element for silver extraction), and gunpowder. He also declared a Spanish monopoly on profits from cockfights and outlawed church loans, a major source of credit within Mexican communities. For many—especially those in the pious Bajío region—the most outrageous blow was King Charles's expulsion of the Jesuits from Mexico in 1767.

In the Bajío, rich criollo landowners began to hatch a plan against the Spanish governors of Mexico. Independent thinkers like Juan Aldama and Ignacio Allende from San Miguel began to hold secret meetings with other conspirators, including Miguel Domínguez, the Mexican-born governor of Querétaro. Pastor Miguel Hidalgo from the small town of Dolores was among the conspirators' most important allies, a beloved priest with great influence among the Native and mestizo people. When Napoleon invaded Spain in 1807, the conspirators decided to exploit the Spanish weakness and plan their attack against the crown.

Originally, Aldama and Allende were selected to oversee the independence army; however, there was a change of plans when Spanish loyalists in Querétaro uncovered their plot. Alerted to the plan, royalists locked conspirator (and wife of the governor) Josefa Ortiz de Domínguez into her bedroom in the government mansion; however, she managed to get word to co-conspirator Ignacio Pérez, who in turn alerted Allende and Hidalgo before the Spanish forces could arrest them. With no time left, Hidalgo immediately launched the insurgency.

On September 16, 1810, Miguel Hidalgo released the prisoners from the Dolores jail and then ascended the stairs before the city's parish church. There, he gave an impassioned call to arms, rousing the crowd (this is known today as el grito, and reenacted in cities across Mexico with the cry "¡Viva México!"). With a ragtag army and small cavalry, Hidalgo rode from Dolores to the settlement at Atotonilco, where he gave another call to arms. In Atotonilco, Hidalgo seized a banner from the Catholic sanctuary that bore the image of the Virgen de Guadalupe. The banner would become the official flag for the Mexican army and a symbol of independent Mexico.

Hidalgo's army met with easy success in San Miguel de Allende and Celaya but sustained major casualties in taking the city of Guanajuato. Thereafter, a major loss at the Battle of the Bridge of Calderón threw the army into chaos, precipitating 11 years of chaotic armed conflict. The following year, Hidalgo, Allende, and Aldama were ambushed and executed by royalist forces.

After these deaths, José María Morelos took over as head of the army. He in turn was captured and executed. The battles continued haphazardly across the country for almost a decade until the government of Ferdinand VII was overthrown in Spain. As a result of the change in Spanish governance, Colonel Agustín de Iturbide, a fierce royalist, switched sides to join the Mexican army. With Iturbide

Independence Heroes

Many of the most famous figures in the history of Mexico are from the cities of San Miguel de Allende, Dolores Hidalgo, and Querétaro. Today you will see the names of these heroes of the independence movement on statues, on street corners, and in public plazas throughout the region.

- **Miguel Hidalgo y Costilla:** The great leader of the independence movement, Miguel Hidalgo was born in Dolores, Guanajuato; the city was later renamed Dolores Hidalgo in his honor. Hidalgo was a parish priest and an incredibly popular figure with the local population. As the general of the Mexican army, he officially gave the call for the revolution to begin with his famous cry, or el grito, from the steps of the cathedral in Dolores.

- **Ignacio Allende:** A wealthy landowner from one of San Miguel's most prominent families, Ignacio Allende was one of the chief conspirators against the Spanish crown. A high-ranking official in the Spanish military, he hosted secret meetings at his home on San Miguel's central plaza, the jardín. During the war, Allende fought alongside General Hidalgo. His former home on the southeast corner of San Miguel's central square is now the **Museo Histórico de San Miguel.**

- **Josefa Ortiz de Domínguez:** The wife of Querétaro's mayor, Josefa Ortiz de Domínguez was one of the few women to actively participate in the conspiracy against the Spanish crown. When the conspirators' plot was discovered by Spanish royalists, Ortiz de Domínguez was imprisoned. However, she was able to send warning to Allende and Hidalgo, sparing them arrest and thereby saving the independence movement. Though largely unrecognized in her lifetime, she is today celebrated throughout Mexico.

- **Juan Aldama:** When the news of the conspiracy's discovery reached San Miguel El Grande (today San Miguel de Allende), Juan Aldama rushed to Dolores, where he informed independence leaders Ignacio Allende and Miguel Hidalgo that the plot had been uncovered. He fought in the war with Allende and Hidalgo, and today his name graces one of the prettiest streets in San Miguel, **Calle Aldama.**

- **Juan José de los Reyes Martínez:** Popularly known as El Pípila, Juan José de los Reyes Martínez was born in San Miguel de Allende; he worked in the mines of Guanajuato when the War of Independence broke out. He is remembered throughout the Bajío for his bravery in the battle to take the **Alhóndiga de Granaditas** in Guanajuato, an early and important victory for the Mexican army.

- **José Mariano Jiménez:** Though he was not a Bajío native (he was born in San Luis Potosí), Jiménez's legacy is closely tied to the city of Guanajuato. This leader of the Mexican army was executed along with Hidalgo, Allende, and Aldama, and, like his fellow heroes, his severed head was suspended from a corner of the **Alhóndiga de Granaditas** by royalist forces.

at the helm, Mexico achieved independence in 1821 with the signing of the Treaty of Córdoba in Córdoba, Veracruz.

THE NEW NATION AND THE MEXICAN-AMERICAN WAR

The end of the War of Independence was the beginning of a century of political unrest and instability in Mexico. After signing the Treaty of Córdoba, Mexico took its first steps toward establishing autonomy. Twenty-four states were named in the First Mexican Empire, with independence leader Agustín de Iturbide, a staunch monarchist and key figure in the eventual Spanish defeat, crowning himself emperor of Mexico.

Just eight months after Iturbide took control of the government, Vicente Guerrero and Antonio López de Santa Anna led a successful revolt against the new Mexican monarchy.

They established the first Mexican republic, and another hero of the War of Independence, Guadalupe Victoria, became the country's first president. Amid turmoil, Vicente Guerrero assumed the post of president when Guadalupe Victoria stepped down, though the conservative forces of General Anastasio Bustamante quickly ousted him.

It was during this period of unrest that U.S. citizens began to settle in Texas, encouraged by the zealous U.S. expansionism following the Louisiana Purchase in 1803. These settlers had little interest in conforming to Mexico's laws. When Mexico's constitution centralized power and abolished slavery in 1835, Texas declared independence. In response, Santa Anna sent troops to Texas. He sustained a major victory at the Alamo, but the brutality of the fighting galvanized Texans. After numerous confrontations, the Texan army overpowered Santa Anna's forces.

Texas gained total independence, with the support of the U.S. military, and tensions again flared between the U.S. and Mexico when Texas was officially annexed by the United States in 1845. Both sides sent troops to the territory. After battles in Texas, New Mexico, and California, the U.S. Army invaded Mexico from the south, entering via the port of Veracruz, which was defended by both the military and civilians for 12 days before they were overpowered by the U.S. forces, led by Winfield Scott. From there, Scott led his army toward the capital. The U.S. troops defeated the Mexican army at Cerro Gordo, taking the city of Puebla, and then marched to the capital in Mexico City, where the U.S. defeated the Mexican army in a fierce battle at the Castillo de Chapultepec.

While the U.S. occupied Mexico City, the capital was temporarily relocated to Querétaro. In Querétaro, Santa Anna signed the infamous Treaty of Guadalupe, which ceded half of Mexico's territory to the United States, including California, New Mexico, Arizona, Texas, and Nevada. In Mexico, the Mexican-American War is known as the Invasión Estadounidense (U.S. Invasion) and is generally viewed as an aggressive act of warfare in the name of American expansionism.

REFORMATION AND THE PORFIRIATO

Santa Anna was ousted after another coup in 1855. Liberal Oaxacan politician Benito Juárez became president of the republic and took the lead on a series of liberal reforms, including the abolishment of church property and the constitutional recognition of freedom of religion. Juárez's celebrated presidency was interrupted in 1860 when France invaded Mexico under Napoleon III. The French established the Second Mexican Empire as a client state, placing Emperor Maximilian I in charge. In 1867 there was yet another successful upheaval by the liberals, and Maximilian was executed in Querétaro. Benito Juárez returned to the presidency, and he remained in power until his death in 1872.

Not long after Juárez's successor, Sebastián Lerdo de Tejada, had won his second election, army general Porfirio Díaz took over the office in a coup. A powerful leader with a strong military outlook, Díaz was both a dictator and despot; he created a strong central government that favored foreign investment. While the country's wealth increased, social conditions for the poor only worsened under Díaz's ironfisted control. While his legacy is controversial, Díaz did manage to keep Mexico in relative peace during his entire presidency. His rule is known as the Porfiriato.

The Porfiriato was a mixed blessing for the Bajío, where some cities flourished while others withered away in disrepair. San Miguel de Allende was all but abandoned, its churches left to crumble and its tiny population dwindling away. Guanajuato, on the other hand, continued to produce silver and received handsome gifts from the president himself. Porfirio Díaz attended the grand opening of Teatro Juárez, and he commissioned the city's beautiful municipal market in commemoration of the independence movement. The silver town of Pozos was also a favorite of the president, who renamed the city Ciudad Porfirio Díaz.

MEXICAN REVOLUTION

In response to the ongoing dictatorship of conservative leader Porfirio Díaz, wealthy politician Francisco I. Madero announced his intentions to run for the presidency. When Díaz threw him in jail, Madero helped organize a revolution against the government, assisted by General Victoriano Huerta. The great idealist revolutionary Emiliano Zapata joined their efforts in the south, recruiting a troop of peasant soldiers and demanding large-scale land reform on behalf of the people.

Once Madero took the presidency, he proved to be a weak leader, uninterested in enacting the land reforms for peasants that had inspired Zapata to join him. Observing this weakness, Huerta organized a coup against Madero, taking the presidency himself after Madero was executed. Again Mexico's famous rebel leaders joined forces. Together, Venustiano Carranza, Álvaro Obregón, Pancho Villa, and Emiliano Zapata led the revolt against Huerta's government, with additional support from the U.S. Army. They successfully toppled the regime in August 1914, with Carranza at the head of the army.

Carranza took the presidency with initial opposition from Villa and Zapata. However, he won support with the people through promises of land reform, eventually overseeing the writing of the Constitution of 1917. The new constitution was based on the Constitution of 1857, though it included many important land, law, and labor reforms. Carranza was eventually forced out of power and replaced by General Álvaro Obregón. Pancho Villa was ambushed and executed during the Obregón presidency, likely at the president's own command.

THE 20TH CENTURY

Mexico's government began to stabilize in the decades following the revolution, eventually coalescing into a single political party, the Institutional Revolutionary Party (PRI). The postrevolutionary period was a time of great progress, as the country began to flourish culturally and intellectually. During Obregón's presidency, José Vasconcelos served as the secretary of public education and oversaw the establishment of the National Symphony Orchestra and the Symphonic Orchestra of Mexico. He also began the Mexican mural program, through which famous artists like Diego Rivera and David Alfaro Siqueiros were commissioned to paint monumental art on the walls of public buildings. After the 1920s, the Mexican economy began to grow annually.

In a watershed moment in Mexican politics, Lázaro Cárdenas was elected to the presidency in 1937. Unlike his predecessors, Cárdenas enacted land reform and redistribution as laid out in the Constitution of 1917. In a move that would serve as a model for other oil-rich nations, Cárdenas expropriated oil reserves from the private companies that had been running them. He established Petróleos Mexicanos (Pemex), concurrently founding the National Polytechnic Institute to ensure a sufficient engineering force in the country. Among other famous decisions, Lázaro Cárdenas granted exile to Bolshevik revolutionary Leon Trotsky, who lived the final years of his life in Mexico City.

Music and cinema flourished during the 1930s and 1940s, with Mexican movies outselling Hollywood films during World War II. During and after the Spanish Civil War, many European intellectuals took up residence in Mexico, adding to the thriving art and cultural community. In the 1950s, Luis Buñuel, the famous Spanish filmmaker, made some of his most influential pictures in Mexico, eventually naturalizing as a Mexican citizen.

In the early 1980s, falling oil prices and high worldwide interest rates created a massive recession in Mexico. President Miguel de la Madrid was forced to drastically cut government spending, the economy stagnated, and unemployment soared. Recovery was incredibly slow, with the GDP growing just 0.1 percent per year until 1988. Economic recovery began under the next president, Carlos Salinas de Gortari, who renegotiated the country's external debts and embarked on a policy of trade liberalization. By 1994 Mexico was economically stable enough to sign on as a member of the North American Free Trade Agreement (NAFTA).

The same morning that NAFTA went into effect, a small Indigenous army called the Ejército Zapatista de Liberación Nacional (EZLN) took control of three cities in the southern state of Chiapas. This rebellion was small in scope but wide-reaching in consequences, inspiring widespread support for Indigenous people throughout Mexico and the world. The army's leader, Subcomandante Marcos, became a national spokesperson for the Indigenous cause and met repeatedly with Mexican government leaders.

THE 21ST CENTURY

In the 21st century, the PRI began to lose its hold on the unilateral power it held since the Revolution. In the elections of 2000, popular support began to rally around the tall, mustachioed Vicente Fox Quesada, a former Coca-Cola executive. Campaigning on a ticket of change, Fox won a much-celebrated victory over PRI candidate Francisco Labastida. Fox's PAN successor, President Felipe Calderón, was elected in 2006, taking the office after winning by just one percentage point over the Party of the Democratic Revolution (Partido de la Revolución Democrática; PRD) candidate, Andrés Manuel López Obrador, in an election that was mired by controversy.

During his presidency, Calderón declared a war on drugs as a major spike in drug-related violence plagued much of northern Mexico, causing widespread instability and fear along the border with the United States, among other areas. Capitalizing on dissatisfaction with the PAN and the violence in Mexico, the PRI regained control of the executive branch with the election of Enrique Peña Nieto, former governor of the state of Mexico, to the presidency. Like his predecessor, Peña Nieto won over PRD candidate López Obrador, and protests against his legitimacy, though less widespread, were also fierce.

Violence, organized crime, and corruption continued to plague Mexico into the 21st century, with journalists, activists, and ordinary citizens the targets of extortion, murder, and disappearance. On September 26, 2014, university students from the Ayotzinapa teacher's college in the state of Morelos—an activist educational institution dedicated to teaching and advocating for the rural poor—boarded buses to Mexico City, where they planned to attend a political protest commemorating the 1968 student massacre in Tlatelolco. In circumstances that have never been fully uncovered, their buses came under armed attack in the city of Iguala. Six students died and 43 went missing without a trace.

Despite widespread public outrage and years of demonstrations, both national and international, there has never been a full account of what happened to the 43 students. However, the events of Ayotzinapa became a galvanizing moment in Mexican history, sparking massive public protest against Peña Nieto's government and human rights abuses in Mexico.

During his candidacy and controversial loss in the 2012 presidential elections, former Mexico City head of government and two-time PRD presidential candidate Andrés Manuel López Obrador founded a new leftist opposition party, Movimiento Regeneración Nacional, or MORENA. López Obrador, popularly known as AMLO, entered the 2018 presidential race as Morena's candidate and won the presidency.

Government and Economy

As laid out in the Constitution of 1917, Mexico is a federal republic overseen by an elected government. It is a federation of 32 individually governed states (including the distrito federal, or federal district), united by a national government in Mexico City.

ORGANIZATION

Mexico is overseen by a federal government, which is divided into three branches: executive, legislative, and judicial. The president, elected to a single six-year term, oversees the executive branch. The congress is divided into the Senate and Chamber of Deputies, and there is a single supreme court, with justices appointed by the president. Each of Mexico's 32 states has three representatives in the senate. Citizens elect two of the three senators, while the leading minority party appoints the third. There are 500 deputies in the Chamber of Deputies, with one representative for every 200,000 citizens. Of these, the people directly elect 300, while the other 200 are appointed by proportional representation. The federal government operates in the distrito federal in Mexico City.

In each state, power is also divided between the executive, legislative, and judicial branches, with an elected governor overseeing executive activities. States are independent and sovereign. Each has its own laws, though none can enact laws that contradict the country's federal constitution.

Each state in Mexico is further divided into autonomous municipalities. Municipalities are managed differently in each state, but a municipality usually comprises a larger city and all the small towns and ranches surrounding it. In San Miguel de Allende, for example, Los Rodríguez is overseen by the municipality, even though it is about 16 km (10 mi) outside the city and has almost 3,000 inhabitants.

Municipalities are run by a local government, with a presidente municipal (municipal president) elected democratically to a nonrenewable post. In the Bajío, a large percentage of the state and municipal divisions were laid under the Spanish viceroyalty, which divided the country into ayuntamientos (town councils), overseen by local governors.

Both the city of Guanajuato and the city of Querétaro are the capitals of their states of the same name, and therefore home to both the municipal and state government.

POLITICAL PARTIES

From the end of the Mexican Revolution until the year 2000, the Partido Revolucionario Institucional (PRI, Institutional Revolutionary Party) was the dominant party in Mexican politics. Once considered socialist, the PRI upholds more centrist views today. Although the PRI had a fraught relationship with the Mexican people, it remained uncontested for most of the 20th century. In 1988 PRI defector Cuauhtémoc Cárdenas ran against the official PRI candidate but was defeated in a highly controversial election that included an unexplained glitch in the electoral system.

In 2000 Vicente Fox Quesada was elected to the office of president under the conservative Partido Acción Nacional (PAN, National Action Party) ticket. Before his election, Fox was a prominent businessman in the Bajío and the supervisor of the Coca-Cola Company in Mexico and Latin America. He represented Guanajuato in the Chamber of Deputies and then served as governor of the state 1995-1999. His home and ranch are located in the community of San Cristóbal, Guanajuato. Fox was followed by another PAN president, Felipe Calderón, who won the presidential elections in 2006 by a slim margin and amid prominent accusations of fraud from the opposing candidate, Andrés Manuel López Obrador, who was, at that time, a member of the most leftist of the three major parties, the Partido de la Revolución Democrática (Party of the Democratic Revolution), or PRD.

In 2012 Calderón was replaced by PRI candidate Enrique Peña Nieto, the former governor of the state of Mexico. In 2014 López Obrador founded a new political party, Movimiento Regeneración Nacional, or Morena, which is now the most progressive party in Mexico. López Obrador, popularly known as AMLO, became president of Mexico in 2018, and the Morena party has come to dominate politics. Twenty-two Mexican states had Morena governors in 2023.

In the states of Guanajuato and Querétaro, voters tend to elect fiscally and socially conservative candidates, and are considered strongholds for the PAN party. At press time, both were overseen by PAN governors.

ELECTIONS

Elections for both national and regional posts are secret, universal, compulsory, and free. They are overseen by the Instituto Federal Electoral (Federal Electoral Institute). IFE credentials, or voting cards, are the national form of identification, so there is no need to separately register to vote. The president and senators are elected to one six-year term. State and regional elections may or may not be held concurrently with federal elections.

ECONOMY

Mexico has a free-market economy, with energy, agriculture, manufacturing, ranching, fishing, and forestry forming the largest sectors. After Brazil, Mexico is the second-largest economy in Latin America and is among the 15 biggest economies in the world. Nonetheless, the distribution of wealth in Mexico is highly uneven, with widespread poverty throughout the country.

Although Mexico's economy grew robustly throughout the 20th century, it suffered from intermittent crises. In 1982 the country fell into a serious recession, principally caused by poor economic policy, falling oil prices, and high inflation worldwide. Having borrowed extensively from international banks, Mexico's president, Miguel de la Madrid, was forced to reduce public spending. Economic recovery was slow, lasting almost the entire decade. In 1996 the currency was devalued.

During the worldwide financial crisis of 2009, Mexico's GDP dropped 6.5 percent, with remittances from the United States also dropping off as that country suffered economic crisis. Since the crisis, the economy has been rebuilding, with significant foreign investment during 2010. The economy was again affected by the COVID-19 pandemic, when all but essential operations in the Bajío were shut down. Recovery was slow in many areas. In San Miguel de Allende, restaurants, shops, and other small businesses—including some places that had been in business for decades—closed during the pandemic and were unable to reopen. At press time, both the local and the national economy overall had made a significant recovery, with the peso very strong against the dollar.

The state of Guanajuato contributes about 4.3 percent to the national gross domestic product (GDP), with manufacturing, agriculture, cosmetics, chemical products and pharmaceuticals, textiles, medical equipment, and tourism among its biggest industries. Querétaro is a much smaller state, yet also a manufacturing capital. In total, Querétaro contributes about 2.3 percent to the Mexican GDP.

Agriculture

Although a large percentage of Mexico's population is involved in agricultural activities, farming has slowly become less important to the nation's overall economy. Currently, agriculture accounts for less than 3 percent of the GDP.

With its fertile plains and large watershed, the Bajío has traditionally been an important agricultural region in Mexico and remains so to this day. A third of Guanajuato's state land is dedicated to farming, though, like the nation at large, its impact on the state GDP is less profound (it accounts for less than 5 percent).

According to data from Mexico's National Institute of Statistics and Geography (INEGI), the state of Guanajuato a major producer of strawberries, broccoli, barley, lettuce, rye, wheat, asparagus, and sorghum. It is also a major dairy producer. Querétaro is a top producer of roses in addition to significant crops of vegetables, grain, and meat.

In both Querétaro and Guanajuato, there has been an increase in the production of organic fruits, vegetables, and dairy products; both have begun to cultivate grapes for wine. Agriculture accounts for only a small percentage of Querétaro's overall economy.

Manufacturing

Manufacturing is a huge contributor to Mexico's economy, accounting for up to 90 percent of the country's exports and close to 20 percent of the GDP. Though Mexico faces competition from manufacturing giant China, it has managed to continue its growth in this sector by focusing the industry on more specialized products, like automobiles and electronics. Within manufacturing, metal products and machinery account for the largest manufacturing sectors countrywide, followed by food and tobacco, chemicals, petroleum products, and shoes and clothing.

Manufacturing is crucial to Guanajuato, comprising around 28 percent of the state's economy. León, Guanajuato's biggest city, and the suburb of Silao are major manufacturing zones. Automobiles and automobile parts are big contributors; there are five auto manufacturing plants in the state, including General Motors and Volkswagen plants in Silao, and the shoe and leather goods industries continue to grow at a rapid clip in León.

Energy

Mexico built its first oil well in 1896. Today it is among the world's top nations in conventional oil production, and in 2022 the country was the second-largest source of foreign crude oil to the United States. In the 1930s, President Lázaro Cárdenas declared all natural resources state property, including oil, expropriating the assets of foreign companies operating in Mexico. He established Petróleos Mexicanos, Pemex for short, the state-run company in charge of extracting, refining, and distributing oil throughout Mexico.

In 2014 President Enrique Peña Nieto instigated a series of reforms to Mexico's energy policy that were aimed to increase production, lower energy prices, and allow increased foreign investment in industry—a profound change to the sector after nearly 75 years as a state-run entity. Most noticeably for tourists (especially those on the road), since 2016, Peña Nieto's policies allowed foreign companies to operate franchises of their gas stations in Mexico, which now account for more than 60 percent of gas stations across the country.

Tourism

Mexico is one of the world's most popular travel destinations, welcoming almost 25 million foreign visitors every year. The Mexican government invests heavily in tourism, including massive international marketing campaigns designed to attract potential visitors to the country. North American visitors are far and away the largest group of foreign tourists; U.S. citizens constitute about 70 percent of international visitors to the country. While their numbers have remained steady, an increase in visitors from other countries worldwide (like Russia and Brazil) has helped the Mexican tourist sector grow in recent years.

Although Mexico is most famous for its beach resorts, cultural tourism is also a major draw in the country's colonial towns and cities. Tourism, both national and international, is vital to the Bajío's economy, especially in cities like San Miguel de Allende, Guanajuato, Tequisquiapan, and Bernal, which rely heavily on the income from hotels, restaurants, gift shops, tour operators, and other tourist-related activities. Since being declared a United Nations World Heritage Site, Guanajuato has seen a huge increase in tourism; today it is one of the most visited colonial cities in Mexico. Even Querétaro, a state less recognized as a tourist destination, owes 20 percent of its internal economy to tourism and related commercial activities.

Relationship with the United States

Sharing 3,200 km (2,000 mi) of land border (with 47 active ports of entry), Mexico and the United States are neighboring countries with an important political, economic, social, and cultural relationship. The United States has always been Mexico's most important trading partner, and, at press time, Mexico had achieved the same status in the U.S. By early 2023, Mexico had become the United States' top trading partner, with bilateral trade accounting for 15 percent of total U.S. trade. On July 1, 2020, the United States-Mexico-Canada Agreement (USMCA) replaced NAFTA as the free trade agreement for North America. In addition to trade, the governments of Mexico and the United States have cooperative agreements in science, technology, border management and immigration, education, and security.

Census data from the Instituto Nacional de Estadística, Geografía e Informática (National Institute of Statistics, Geography, and Infomatics; INEGI) indicated that there 13.5 million Mexicans living overseas, with virtually all of them residing in the United States. Remittances from Mexicans living in the United States have hit record highs in recent years, with more than $58 billion wired to Mexico from the U.S. in 2022 alone. On the flip side, 1.6 million American citizens are estimated to live in Mexico, according to the U.S. Department of State.

Distribution of Wealth

Mexico is a wealthy nation with abundant natural resources, macroeconomic stability, and a GDP among the world's largest. However, Mexico's wealth is not distributed evenly across its population. Poverty remains a widespread problem nationwide, though numbers have been showing consistent and dramatic improvement across many metrics.

According to data published by the National Council for the Evaluation of Social Development Policy, or Coneval, 43.5 percent of the population in Mexico lived in poverty in 2022. This number represents a notable decline from 2018, when 49.9 percent of the population was living in poverty. (There was simultaneously a slight but not insignificant increase—0.1 percent—in people living in extreme poverty, according to the same study; in 2022, 7.1 percent of Mexico's population lacked sufficient income to cover basic medical care and food.) A number of factors have contributed to the progress nationwide; among them, President Andrés Manuel López Obrador expanded social programs and doubled the minimum wage when he took office in 2018. Remittances from the United States have also hit record highs, helping bolster the economy.

Poverty varies by region. Wealth is concentrated in and around the capital, Mexico City, in Nuevo León (and its prosperous capital city of Monterrey), and along the U.S. border. Through most of the 20th century, the Bajío region was neither the richest nor the poorest part of Mexico, but it has been showing very promising economic growth in the 21st century. According to a 2017 report by INEGI, both Guanajuato and Querétaro rank among the 10 states with the highest average family income.

People and Culture

DEMOGRAPHY AND DIVERSITY

Mexico is a large and multiethnic country. Today the majority of Mexicans are mestizo, or mixed race. Genetic studies have confirmed that most Mexicans are predominantly a mix of Spanish and Indigenous American heritage; however, mestizo implies a mixed ethnic background, and it may include other ethnicities. To a smaller extent than in the United States or the Caribbean, African slaves were brought to New Spain during the colonial era, and they also mixed with the population. Mexicans of strictly European heritage, comprising about 10 percent or less of the population, are generally Spanish descendants, though there have also been other waves of European migrants to Mexico over the course of the country's history, including Irish, German, and French, among others.

In the past decade, Central American migrants fleeing violence in their home countries have begun to settle in Mexico. The Mexican government granted refugee status to over 100,000 of these migrants in 2017, but many more are living in Mexico without refugee status or passing through the country on their way to the United States. There is also a noticeable population of South Americans, mostly from Chile and Argentina, with the largest population residing in the capital. Mexico is also home to small but visible populations of Lebanese, Chinese, Japanese, and Korean people.

Data from the 2020 census registered a population of 6,166,934 in Guanajuato and 2,368,467 people in Querétaro, accounting for 4.9 percent and 1.9 percent of the national population respectively. The vast majority of the people in Guanajuato and Querétaro live in urban environments. In both states, roughly 75 percent live in cities, with almost half Querétaro's total population residing in the capital. These statistics reflect an overall trend in Mexico, where the majority of the population lives in overcrowded urban centers.

INDIGENOUS CULTURES

Indigenous people (indígenas) are direct descendants of the native people of Mexico, and many still speak native languages. According to Mexico's census data, the country's population is about 9 percent Indigenous, though numbers vary greatly by region, and the 2020 census indicated that up to 20 percent of Mexicans self-identify as Indigenous. About 6 million people in Mexico speak one of the country's 62 recognized Indigenous languages; the vast majority of these people also speak Spanish. Relatively speaking, there is only a small Indigenous community in the Bajío region. In the state of Querétaro, about 2 percent of people speak an Indigenous language, with the largest populations of Indigenous communities concentrated in the cities of Amealco de Bonfil and Tolimán. In the state of Guanajuato, less than 1 percent of the people speak an Indigenous language.

EMIGRATION

Although the figures are not exact, an estimated 8-10 percent of all Mexican citizens live in the United States. Mexican emigration to the United States has a major influence on Mexico's economy and culture, especially in states where emigration is high—including the state of Guanajuato. Data shows that remittances from Mexicans living overseas accounted for an amazing US$58 billion in 2022.

According to a study conducted by INEGI in 2020, Guanajuato has the fifth-highest emigration rate in Mexico, after the states of Zacatecas, Michoacán, Guerrero, and Oaxaca. Of the more than 63,000 people from Guanajuato who moved overseas in 2020, 93 percent went to the United States. Querétaro state has one of the lowest rates of emigration nationally.

RELIGION

Spanish missionaries introduced Catholicism to the native population in Mexico during the 15th and 16th centuries. Missionaries were extremely active in New Spain, establishing an abundance of churches, Catholic schools, and hospitals, often with the financial assistance of wealthy Spanish nobles. The largest Catholic cathedral in the Americas is just beside the government buildings in Mexico City's central plaza, indicating the enormous importance of the church to both the state and the people.

During the early Spanish conquest, there were massive conversions among the Indigenous population to Catholicism. Conversions spiked after the apparition of the Virgen de Guadalupe in Mexico City in 1531. While accepting the new religion, many Indigenous communities incorporated their own religious beliefs into Roman Catholic ritual, creating some unique Catholic traditions in the New World.

Throughout Spanish rule of Mexico, the Catholic church had a major influence on governance and society. During the independence era, the image of the Virgen de Guadalupe adorned the official flag of Mexico's first national army. Catholics continued to maintain massive power in Mexico until the 1850s, when President Benito Juárez began to secularize the country's constitution and laws. Among other reforms, he limited church power and appropriated church property for the state. While the relationship between the church and government warmed after Juárez left office, anticlerical forces gained power during the Mexican Revolution. The current Mexican constitution separates church and state. Nonetheless, the Catholic church continues to be an important part of Mexico's national identity. Almost 90 percent of Mexicans identify as Catholic.

Guanajuato and Querétaro are largely conservative and Catholic states, with more than 95 percent of the population identifying as Catholic. Foreigners from any background will quickly be introduced to myriad Catholic holidays, often celebrated with rich tradition and pageantry. The Holy Week festivities in San Miguel de Allende, for example, are among the country's most beautiful and well attended. Every town celebrates its patron saint's holiday with enormous fanfare and parties. Religion also plays an important role in personal and family life, with milestones like baptism, confirmation, weddings, and funerals celebrated in the Catholic tradition.

LANGUAGE

Spanish is the language most commonly spoken in Mexico, including in San Miguel de Allende, Guanajuato, and Querétaro. In addition to Spanish, English is widely spoken throughout the Bajío, particularly in San Miguel de Allende, where there is a large and influential English-speaking expatriate population. In San Miguel, most restaurant menus, publications, and advertisements are printed in both English and Spanish.

THE ARTS

A major cultural destination, the Bajío is an excellent place to immerse yourself in Mexico's artistic and cultural heritage. It's home to several large universities, numerous museums and galleries, and a large population of artists and writers, and there are ongoing cultural events and exhibitions throughout the region.

LITERATURE

Mexico's writers have made a significant contribution to literary traditions in Spanish, including several noted authors from San Miguel de Allende and the Bajío region. Although poems, stories, and legends were passed down orally before the Spanish arrived in the New World, historians point to the descriptive chronicles of the conquest (written by Hernán Cortés, as well as other Spanish and Indigenous writers) as the true birth of Mexican literature. These accounts have been

Helpful Spanish-English Cognates

As an English speaker, you may know more Spanish vocabulary than you think. Spanish and English share hundreds of cognates—words with a similar spelling and meaning. Many words have an easy-to-recognize English equivalent, with the Spanish word taking an *o, a,* or *e* on the end. In other cases, the -tion ending in English is replaced by the -ción ending in Spanish. Sometimes it is just the pronunciation that changes, as some Spanish and English words are spelled exactly the same!

Cognates are especially helpful for travelers to Mexico, where words are constantly incorporated from English (computadora for computer is a good example). If you start paying attention, you are likely to see many words and phrases you understand. As you brush up your español, here are some cognates that may be useful during your travels in the Bajío:

aeropuerto: airport
artista: artist
auto: automobile
balcón: balcony
banco: bank
computadora: computer
consulado: consulate
costo: cost
declaración: declaration
delicioso: delicious
desierto: desert
doctor: doctor
dólares: dollars
familia: family
festival: festival
gasolina: gasoline
historia: history
hospital: hospital
hotel: hotel
local: local
mapa: map
medicina: medicine
menú: menu
monumento: monument
nacionalidad: nationality
periódico: periodical, or newspaper
persona: person
plaza: plaza
rancho: ranch
romántico: romantic
taxi: taxi
teléfono: telephone
turista: tourist
visa: visa

FALSE COGNATES

Before you get carried away, remember that there are a few words that have deceptively similar spelling in Spanish and English, yet different meanings. Tuna refers to the fruit of the prickly pear, not the fish. Librería is not a library but a bookstore; a library is a biblioteca. Fútbol is a true cognate if you are British; for Americans, the translation is soccer.

highly significant to anthropologists' understanding of Mexico's native cultures.

After the conquest, Mexico made a distinguished contribution to literature during the colonial era. Baroque poet Sor Juana Inez de la Cruz holds a hallowed place in Spanish literary history, along with some of her contemporaries, dramatist Juan Ruiz de Alarcón and writer Carlos de Sigüenza y Góngora. (Sor Juana's image is well known to any Mexico tourist, as it adorns the 200-peso bill.) During the 19th century, Mexican writers contributed to the Spanish Romantic movement and, later, to modernism. In San Miguel de Allende, Ignacio Ramírez (also known as "El Nigromante," or The Necromancer) was a celebrated poet, journalist, and political thinker of the 19th century as well as a noted atheist.

During the 20th century, Mexico's national character was more strongly reflected in its literary traditions. Writers like Rosario Castellano and Juan Rulfo began to describe a distinctly Mexican environment, exploring the country's mixed identity and heritage. By the second half of the 20th century, Mexico's diverse writers had become highly recognized and widely translated, including Carlos Fuentes, Elena Poniatowska, and Laura Esquivel. In the 1990s, Octavio Paz was the first Mexican to win the Nobel Prize in literature.

In addition to Mexican authors, many foreign authors have lived in and written about Mexico. English writers Graham Greene and D. H. Lawrence both wrote novels based on their experiences in Mexico. Beatnik poet and novelist Jack Kerouac lived in Mexico City (and is rumored to have visited San Miguel de Allende), while Chilean writer Roberto Bolaño ably described youth culture in Mexico City in his novel *The Savage Detectives*. Colombian Nobel laureate Gabriel García Márquez resided in Mexico City for decades before his death in 2014.

VISUAL ARTS

The colonial cities of San Miguel de Allende, Guanajuato, and Querétaro are excellent places see and learn more about early colonial art and architecture in Mexico. Made wealthy by the booming silver trade, the Bajío region attracted master painters, sculptors, and artisans to assist with the building and decoration of Catholic chapels during the 17th and 18th centuries.

In particular, Guanajuato's churches contain a wonderful collection of colonial painting, including many works by 18th-century master Miguel Cabrera. (While some visual artists from the colonial era are well known, a large number of the existing paintings are unsigned.) After being inducted into the United Nations World Heritage program, Guanajuato undertook a massive restoration project of cultural heritage. Unfortunately, many churches in the Bajío were sacked or destroyed over the course of history. However, original altarpieces, retablos, paintings, and sculpture do remain among the rebuilt interiors of many churches of the region.

While there were some very talented artists in New Spain, it wasn't until after the Revolution of 1910 that the arts began to express an original and distinctly Mexican character. In the postrevolutionary era, the Mexican government promoted varied cultural and artistic programs, including the famous public mural project, overseen by Secretary of Education José Vasconcelos. The muralists, along with other vanguard thinkers of the postrevolutionary era, brought worldwide renown to Mexico's artistic scene. Diego Rivera, one of the most prominent Mexican muralists, was born in the city of Guanajuato; his childhood home is a museum dedicated to his work as well as the work of his contemporaries.

San Miguel de Allende held a modest yet important role in the great intellectual and artistic achievements of the early 20th century. All but abandoned during the late 19th century, San Miguel became a retreat destination for artists, thinkers, and musicians from Mexico City during the 20th century. In 1937 Peruvian writer and art historian Felipe Cossío del Pomar visited San Miguel

de Allende. The following year, Mexican president Lázaro Cárdenas granted Pomar the funds he needed to open a fine art school in one of San Miguel's abandoned convents. Both Mexican and American artists came to study and teach at this school, including (for a brief time) the famed muralist David Alfaro Siqueiros. Though it would go through several incarnations, Cossío del Pomar's art school is still open today as the Instituto Allende.

Two influential early-20th-century Mexican artists, Olga Costa and José Chávez Morado, also lived briefly in San Miguel de Allende; they eventually settled down in Guanajuato, where they made an enormous contribution to city museums and culture.

MUSIC AND DANCE

Mexico's unique musical genres have their roots in the 16th century, when traditional European composition and instruments collided with traditional Mesoamerican music. The result was a wide range of sones (musical genres), most of which are also associated with a traditional style of dance. In any of the Bajío's cities, visitors may have the opportunity to see a traditional music or dance performance in one of the city's public squares.

Mexico's most well-recognized musical ensemble, the mariachi band, dates back to 18th-century Jalisco. Dressed in two-piece charro suits and corbatin bow ties, mariachi bands usually feature an impressive lineup of violins, trumpets, guitars, bass guitars, and guitarrón (a large five-string guitar). Mariachis play traditional Mexican ballads, often singing the chorus in unison. In central Mexico, mariachi music is a fixture at special events, like weddings or birthday parties. However, it is not necessary to await a special event to enjoy mariachi; on any night, you can commission a tune from the mariachis waiting in the central plazas of Guanajuato or San Miguel de Allende.

Some of the most famous names in Mexican music and cinema are originally from the Bajío region, and they are honored in their hometowns. In the 19th century, Juventino Rosas, a famous bandleader and composer of Otomí descent, was born in the small town Santa Cruz de Galeana (today, Santa Cruz de Juventino Rosas). Following the Revolution of 1910, the great singer and songwriter José Alfredo Jiménez was born in Dolores Hidalgo. Today Jiménez is remembered as one of the greatest creative minds of his generation. Jiménez's contemporary, Jorge Negrete, was a native of the neighboring city of Guanajuato and became one of Mexico's most cherished singers and actors during the golden age of Mexican cinema.

1: wedding procession in San Miguel de Allende
2: festival in the Valle del Maíz

Essentials

Transportation

GETTING THERE
Air

Two major airports service the region around San Miguel de Allende, Guanajuato, and Querétaro: the **Del Bajío International Airport** (BJX, Carretera Silao-León, Km 5.5, Col. Nuevo Mexico, Silao, Guanajuato; tel. 472/748-2120), near the city of León, and **Querétaro International Airport** (QRO, Carretera Estatal 200, Querétaro-Tequisquiapan, Querétaro de Arteaga, Querétaro; tel. 442/192-5500; www.aiq.com.mx), just outside the city of Querétaro. If you are

traveling to San Miguel de Allende or Dolores Hidalgo, either airport is appropriate. If you are traveling to Querétaro, choose QRO; visitors to Guanajuato should fly into BJX. Both airports are equipped with customs and immigration offices for international arrivals and departures.

It's also convenient for travelers to Querétaro to fly into **Aeropuerto Internacional Benito Juárez Ciudad de México** (MEX, Capitan Carlos León s/n, Peñón de Los Baños Venustiano Carranza, Distrito Federal; tel. 55/2482-2400; www. aicm.com.mx) in the capital. **Primera Plus** (toll-free Mex. tel. 800/375-7587; www. primeraplus.com.mx) offers hourly direct bus service from Terminals 1 and 2 in the Mexico City airport to Querétaro's main bus station, for about US$20.

Shuttle Service

Reliable transport company **BajíoGo** (Jesús 11, San Miguel de Allende; tel. 415/185-8665, U.S. tel. 202/609-9905; www.bajiogo.com) offers ground transportation to San Miguel de Allende from the airports in León, Querétaro, and Mexico City. Shared shuttles run about US$30 per person from Querétaro and León and $100 per person from Mexico City.

Bus

Mexico's extensive and efficient bus service makes it easy to travel between cities countrywide. The Bajío region, including San Miguel de Allende, Guanajuato, and Querétaro, is serviced by several first-class bus lines, which have extensive routes in the region as well as connecting service throughout the country. The most prominent bus lines servicing the region are **ETN** (toll-free Mex. tel. 800/800-0386; www.etn.com.mx) and **Primera Plus** (toll-free Mex. tel. 800/375-7587; www. primeraplus.com.mx). Both companies allow you to make reservations over the phone, online, at ticket sales desks at the bus stations,

and in the nationwide OXXO convenience store chain.

From Mexico City, all buses to the region arrive and depart from **Terminal Central del Norte** (Eje Central Lázaro Cárdenas 4907, Gustavo A Madero, Magdalena de Las Salinas; tel. 55/5587-1552), also known as Los Cien Metros, one of four bus terminals in the capital.

Bus travel is comfortable and efficient, and departures and arrivals are almost always punctual. First-class buses are equipped with bathrooms, usually offer a snack and beverage to passengers, and show movies during the ride. Because buses are incredibly popular in Mexico, it is a good idea to book bus tickets in advance in any case, but especially during a holiday weekend. Holiday weekends can also cause a bit of delay on popular bus routes, particularly those buses heading to and from the beach or Mexico City, owing to heavy traffic.

Car

Driving across the border has long been a popular choice with U.S. and Canadian visitors to Mexico. In just one long day, you can reach San Miguel de Allende from the Texas border. Driving in Mexico is usually comfortable and easy, with a circuit of well-maintained toll highways running across the country. However, as a result of widespread drug cartel-related violence, travel through northern Mexico has become less safe. That said, thousands of cars and trucks make the drive every day without incident. With a good map and some basic safety precautions, tourists can travel by road to San Miguel and environs, then have the benefit of a car to use while visiting the region.

Car Permits

All foreign residents bringing a car into Mexico must apply for a temporary import permit for their vehicle. You can apply and pay for the permit 10 to 60 days before your trip online at **Banjercito** (www.banjercito.com. mx/registroVehiculos), then you must stop at a customs office to have your paperwork reviewed and the permit ratified after crossing the border. It is also possible to process the paperwork at a customs office at the border; check the website to locate a consulate that can process your paperwork at the border. The permit is good for 180 days. Thereafter, the car must be returned to the United States or Canada. If the car's owner has a resident visa, the car's permit will remain valid for as long as the resident visa is active, for up to 5 years.

The cost of the permit is US$400 for cars manufactured in 2007 or later, $300 for cars manufactured between 2001 and 2006, and $200 for cars manufactured in or before 2000.

Car Insurance

All foreign vehicles must be insured in Mexico. Fortunately, Mexican auto insurance is inexpensive and widely available. You can preregister for insurance online, or you can sign up for insurance at one of the many insurance agents located along the U.S.-Mexico border. **Qualitas** (www.qualitas.com.mx) is one of several large companies that cover foreign cars, and it is a popular insurer throughout Mexico. **Sanborns** (www.sanborns.com) has locations along the U.S.-Mexico border and specializes in insuring foreign cars. Neither U.S. nor Canadian automobile insurances are valid in Mexico.

Highway Information

The government bureau **Caminos y Puentes Federales** (Capufe; Federal Roads and Bridges) can provide toll costs and road conditions for Mexican highways at tel. 074. You can also call 074 for help requesting a tow truck or medical assistance on the road. For information on road conditions or to inquire about unexpected traffic or accidents, you can call the **Guardia Nacional** (National Guard) at tel. 088 (information is provided in Spanish).

Most places you'll be visiting on a trip to the Bajío can be located using a GPS app on your phone. Waze and Google Maps both offer real-time traffic conditions throughout Mexico. They are most reliable along major highways and in big cities than in more rural areas.

Choosing Safe Routes

Driving in and around San Miguel, as well as between San Miguel and the destinations covered in this book (Guanajuato, Querétaro and the Querétaro countryside, Dolores Hidalgo, and Mineral de Pozos) is generally safe, though road conditions will vary depending on the routes you choose. Avoid driving in south and central Guanajuato state, particularly Highway 45D and south of Highway 45D, including Celaya, Irapuato, and Salamanca, due to the high incidence of violent crime in these areas.

To ensure your safety on the road, travel only during the day, and always choose toll roads rather than free highways when the option is available (note that there are no toll highways between San Miguel and Dolores Hidalgo, Mineral de Pozos, and Guanajuato). Toll roads are well maintained, well lit, and patrolled by police. On most Mexican toll roads, the toll also includes insurance coverage for any accidents you may be involved in while on the highway.

If you are driving from the U.S. to San Miguel de Allende, be aware that widespread violence related to the drug trade in northern Mexico and along the border has made travel more precarious than it was in the past. Near the city of Monterrey and in the state of Tamaulipas there have been an increased number of illegal roadblocks and carjacking. Along Highway 57, which connects Mexico City to Piedras Negras, there have also been widespread reports of violence and extortion around Matehuala in the state of San Luis Potosí.

While drivers should certainly be aware of the hazards of driving through northern Mexico, many Americans and Canadians continue to drive through Mexico with little problem. Drive during the daytime, always take toll roads, and don't pull off the highway in places you aren't familiar with.

Mexican highways are patrolled by **Los Ángeles Verdes** (the Green Angels), a fleet of emergency responders and road mechanics operated by the Mexican Secretariat of Tourism. The Green Angels can offer tourist information for visitors, assist with medical emergencies, and attend to mechanical problems 8am-6pm daily (and 24 hours during popular holidays or long weekends). Dial 078 from a telephone to reach the Green Angels.

Driving Etiquette

On smaller two-lane highways, such as the highway between San Miguel de Allende and Dolores Hidalgo, slower traffic often drives totally or partially on the shoulder to allow faster drivers to pass. This arrangement usually works well, but can lead to dangerous situations when motorcycles, tractors, and pedestrians are on the shoulder, or when two cars are trying to simultaneously pass on opposite sides. Stay alert and drive defensively.

On larger highways, faster traffic travels in the left lane and slower traffic in the right lane. On two-lane highways, often a slower car will put on its driver's side turn signal to indicate that it is safe to pass. The passing car will then put on its driver's side blinker and pass to the left. *Do be aware* that a driver's blinker can also indicate the intention to turn to the left, rather than safety to pass. Always use precaution when passing slower cars.

GETTING AROUND

Walking is the most popular mode of transportation for most tourists to San Miguel de Allende, Guanajuato, and other hilly cobblestone cities. In the pretty and compact centro histórico of most colonial cities, you can easily visit major sights on foot. When you need wheels, there are several other options.

Bus

While national bus lines are efficient and comfortable, intracity buses can be rather baffling—and noisy! In the cities of the Bajío,

most buses do not run on exact schedules, nor are there published route maps for tourists. In most cases, learning to use the bus systems in a city comes down to trial and error.

In San Miguel de Allende or Guanajuato, the majority of sights are located in the city center and do not require bus travel. If you would like to take a bus to a neighborhood or sight outside the city center, head to one of the city's larger bus stations. Each bus will have its destination posted in the window. When in doubt, you can always ask the bus driver where the bus is headed. When you get on, pay the driver directly for the cost of your ticket, unless the driver indicates that you should sit down (someone may then pass through the bus to collect your fare).

In every major Bajío town, there are buses from the first-class bus terminal to the city's downtown district. Look for the buses marked "Centro."

Car

In San Miguel de Allende, Guanajuato, and Querétaro, driving a car is generally safe and easy. San Miguel de Allende's drivers are particularly courteous, even giving pedestrians the right-of-way (which is rarely the case in other Mexican cities). Big cars and SUVs can be more difficult to navigate through the city's narrow streets. Otherwise, the biggest nuisance you'll face is some weekend traffic or the not-uncommon practice of drivers stopping to talk to their acquaintances in the middle of a busy street. Don't get exasperated; in a few weeks, you may find yourself doing the same.

Foreign plates are not uncommon in San Miguel de Allende, and they rarely warrant extra attention from authorities. As long as you have your paperwork in order (see "Car Permits," page 237), you will rarely have problems with law enforcement.

Taxis and Ride-Hailing Services

There are inexpensive taxis circling throughout San Miguel de Allende, Guanajuato,

Querétaro, and other cities in the region. Except for in the city of Querétaro, where cabs have a meter, taxis charge a flat rate for travel around town. Outlying neighborhoods may cost more than a trip within the city center. To be sure, ask the price of the ride when you get in. It is safe to hail taxis in the street, though you can also call a cab if you are in a more remote location. If you need to call a cab, San Miguel de Allende, Guanajuato, and Querétaro all have radio-taxi companies, which are listed in this guide.

Uber operates in the cities of San Miguel de Allende, Guanajuato, and Querétaro.

Because of the low cost and efficiency of taxis, Uber is less competitive in San Miguel de Allende and not commonly used. It is also uncommon to use Uber in place of regular taxi service in Guanajuato city. However, for travel to the airport from Guanajuato city, or for late-night rides, Uber is a good option.

Querétaro is a larger city, with some sights of interest outside the central districts. Although taxis are inexpensive, efficient, and ubiquitous in Querétaro, Uber can be handy and cheap when you need a pickup outside the city center, where there are fewer taxis, or when traveling late at night.

Visas and Officialdom

ENTRY REQUIREMENTS

To enter Mexico, all foreign citizens (including children) must have a valid passport and an official permit to travel (called an FMM), or tourist card. Note that children under age 18 who are traveling to or from Mexico without a legal parent or guardian must carry an official notarized letter from the absent parent authorizing the minor to travel in the company of a designated adult. You can find more information about tourist cards, nonimmigrant visas, immigrant visas, and unaccompanied minors at the **Instituto Nacional de Migración** (Mexican Immigration Service; www.gob.mx).

If you are arriving in Mexico by airplane, you will be directed to immigration and customs checks on the ground. In Mexico, you pass through immigration at your final destination, not your first port of entry; for example, if you arrive in León via a connecting flight in Mexico City, you will pass through immigration in León.

If you drive into Mexico, it is your responsibility to locate the immigration office closest to the border crossing and complete the necessary paperwork. Most immigration offices are open 24 hours a day and located just a few yards from the border checkpoint. Note that some immigration offices are farther from the border; check with the border agents when you enter.

TOURIST CARDS

Every foreign visitor must have a permit to travel in Mexico. Visitors from most countries will be automatically issued a temporary permit, or "tourist card," at the port of entry. Technically called the **Forma Migratoria Múltiple (FMM),** tourist cards are good for up to 180 days of travel in Mexico. If you are arriving in Mexico via airplane, the flight staff will usually provide the FMM form to fill out while in the air, which will then be validated and stamped by an immigration official on the ground. On the form, you need to list the address where you will be residing in Mexico or the name of a hotel. The cost of the visa is included in the taxes and fees of your airfare. If you are traveling to Mexico by car and intend to visit the Bajío, you will need to stop at an immigration office at the border to request your FMM and pay the fee, about US$25.

After you have received your stamped form from immigration, keep it in a safe place until your departure. You will be asked to return the form when you leave the country. If you lose the form, you will be required to pay a fee at the airport.

RESIDENT VISAS

Foreigners who wish to reside in Mexico may apply for a resident visa at a Mexican consular agency in their home country; after approval via the consulate, the visa is processed in Mexico. All visa applications for residents of San Miguel de Allende and Guanajuato are processed at the **Instituto Nacional de Migración** (Mexican Immigration Services Guanajuato Branch, Calzada de la Estación de FFCC s/n; tel. 415/152-8991; 9am-1pm Mon.-Fri.) in San Miguel de Allende. There is a separate immigration office in the city of Querétaro (Calle Francisco Peñuñuri 15, Fracc. San José Inn, Delegación Centro Histórico; tel. 442/214-2712; 9am-1pm Mon.-Fri.), which serves immigrants and visitors in that state.

There are two types of resident visas, residente temporal (temporary resident) and residente permanente (permanent residents). Temporary resident visas are intended for long-term nonimmigrant residents of Mexico who do not intend to naturalize; a permanent resident visa is intended for those who plan to make a permanent move to Mexico and, most likely, pursue citizenship. In most cases, temporary resident permits are granted to those who can demonstrate investments or a source of foreign income that will support their life in Mexico (retirees or professionals who work remotely often fall into this category), though qualified professionals, artists, or investors may also apply for the right to legally participate in lucrative activities, such as giving art classes or opening a business. Both documents must be renewed annually.

Once the process is complete, you will receive a printed identification card with your photo and a Clave Única de Registro de Población (CURP), a number that you can use to open a bank account, buy property, or take advantage of public services.

If you are offered a job in Mexico, your employer must sponsor your visa application. In most cases, employment visas are only extended to foreigners who have special skills not generally available within the local population. For example, native speakers of a foreign language, like English or French, can seek employment as language teachers. If you receive a visa through your employer, the paperwork is nontransferable: If you leave your current job, your next employer must sponsor the visa's extension.

The **Secretaría de Relaciones Exteriores** (www.sre.gob.mx) maintains a list of Mexican consulates overseas as well as up-to-date information on visa requirements.

CUSTOMS
Basic Allowances

Customs (aduana) allows visitors and residents of Mexico to bring personal effects into the country as well as duty-free gifts valued at no more than US$500. Personal effects may include two photographic or video cameras, up to three cell phones, and one laptop computer. You cannot enter the country with most animal-derived food products, including homemade foods, pet food or dog treats, fresh or canned meat, soil, and hay. Other food products are allowed, including tobacco, dried fruit, coffee, and fruit preserves. Note that pseudoephedrine (including the brand-name Sudafed) is prohibited in Mexico, and there are severe penalties for carrying firearms to Mexico. A full list of permitted items appears on the official customs form produced by the **Secretaría de Hacienda y Crédito Público** (www.sat.gob.mx).

If you are arriving by air, you will be given a customs declaration form on the airplane and will pass through the customs checkpoint right after immigration. You may choose to have your luggage reviewed by customs; otherwise, customs checks are performed by random selection. After collecting your luggage, you will be directed to a stoplight and asked to press a button. If you get a green light, you can pass. If you receive a red light, customs officials will open your luggage to inspect its contents. In larger airports, luggage is often passed through an X-ray machine, and passengers may be asked to open their luggage if a possible contraband item is detected.

If you are entering Mexico by car or on foot at a border crossing, you will be asked to choose the voluntary review line or the "nothing to declare" line. If you choose to declare nothing, you must come to a full stop at the border and wait to receive a red or green light. If you receive the red light, customs officials will ask you to pull over and will check the contents of your car, including the trunk.

Pets

Dogs, cats, and other common pets may enter Mexico with their owners. To be admitted, a pet needs an original and a copy of a certificate of health issued by a licensed veterinarian (on letterhead with professional certification) no more than 10 days before entering the country, proof of vaccination against rabies, administered at least 15 days before entering the country, and proof of external and internal parasite treatment within the previous six months. Double-check that all your pet's information, including name and address, is correctly noted on the forms. If you have all the paperwork, you will receive a Certificado de Importación Zoosanitario for the animal, which has an associated cost of about US$95. Animals may be given a physical exam at the border to confirm they are healthy and match the description on the paperwork. Sick animals may also be detained at the border or at the airport. You can get more detailed information about bringing your pet at www.gob.mx/senasica.

Dogs and cats are the most commonly imported animals and usually pass through customs with little problem. More unusual animals like lizards or rabbits can also be imported to Mexico, but owners should check with customs and immigration officials to determine what paperwork is necessary before making the trip.

Cars

If you are driving a foreign-plated car to Mexico from the United States or Canada, you must acquire a temporary import permit. You can apply for a permit online via **Banjercito** (www.banjercito.com.mx/registrovehiculos) one week to 30 days before your trip, then send supporting documentation to Banjercito to complete the process. However, most drivers find it's easier and more efficient to simply apply for a temporary import permit at the Vehicular Control Module desk at the customs and immigration offices at the border. To apply, you must present proof of citizenship (a passport), an immigration form (a tourist card or temporary resident visa), valid registration for your car, the leasing contract (if the car is rented), a driver's license, and an international credit card or debit card in the driver's name. Bring two copies of each document as well as the originals. You will be charged the cost of the permit (about US$50), plus a deposit, which may range from US$200-400 depending on the age of your vehicle.

Your temporary import permit includes a sticker, which must be affixed to your car's windshield, just above the rearview mirror. Do not remove that sticker until you are returning the car to the United States and are in the presence of a customs agent at the border. If you bring a car into Mexico, you are not permitted to sell it in Mexico, and it must be returned to its country of origin. If you have a temporary resident visa, your car is legal in Mexico for as long as your visa is valid. However, the car's temporary permit must be renewed at a local transit office. If your car's permit is not valid, the car can be confiscated by Mexican authorities. If you have a permanent resident visa, you are no longer permitted to operate a foreign-plated car in Mexico.

EMBASSIES AND CONSULATES

All foreign embassies are located in the capital in Mexico City. Most embassies are near the city center, with the majority of embassies concentrated in the Polanco and Cuauhtémoc neighborhoods, including the **United States Embassy** (Paseo de la Reforma 305, Col. Cuauhtémoc; tel. 55/5080-2000; https://mx.usembassy.gov), **Canadian Embassy** (Schiller 529, Col. Bosque de Chapultepec, tel. 55/5724-7900; www.canadainternational.gc.ca/mexico-mexique), **Australian Embassy** (Ruben Dario 55, Col. Polanco; tel. 55/1101-2200; https://mexico.embassy.gov.au), and **British Embassy** (Paseo de la Reforma 350, 20th floor, Col. Juárez; tel. 55/1670-3200). If you have trouble with the law while you are in Mexico, or your citizenship papers have been lost or stolen, you should contact your embassy right away.

In the Bajío region, there is a **U.S. Consular Agency** (Plaza La Luciérnaga, Libramiento Jose Manuel Zavala No. 165, Locales 4 y 5, Col. La Luciérnaga; https://mexico.usembassy.gov; 9am-1pm Mon.-Thurs.) in San Miguel de Allende. The consular office is a branch of the U.S. embassy in Mexico City and can assist with lost or stolen passports, apostilles (certificates of notarization authenticity), and other services. For all other nations, the closest field offices are in Mexico City.

POLICE

Protección Civil (Civil Protection) is the local police force. They respond to emergencies, break-ins, or other complaints within the municipality. Throughout Mexico, you may see Civil Protection officers in blue fatigues patrolling the streets in cars or on foot. In addition, transitos (transit cops) patrol the roadways around town. They are principally involved in preventing traffic infractions, like speeding, and assisting at the scene of accidents. Throughout Mexico, calling 066 will summon emergency services.

In 2018 President Andrés Manuel López Obrador, in a sweeping reform of public safety, eliminated the federal police and reformed the role of the National Guard, a hybrid of the armed forces, naval police, and federal police that is now directed by the military. In addition to city police, the **Guardia Nacional** (National Guard; www.gob.mx/guardianacional) patrols cities throughout Mexico, as well as intercity highways. They are a visible presence, and tourists will likely see them rolling through town in blue pickup trucks and in blue fatigues, usually heavily armed.

Food

One of the world's great cuisines, Mexican food is diverse and delicious. Typical Mexican dishes are as basic as the ubiquitous quesadilla (a warm tortilla filled with melted cheese) or as elaborate as mole negro (a Oaxacan sauce prepared with chocolate, chiles, almonds, spices, and dozens of other hand-ground ingredients). Food is essential to Mexican culture, and eating well is something enjoyed throughout the country, at every price point and in every type of establishment—from food stalls, bakeries, and markets to cafés, cantinas, and restaurants.

BASICS

Since the pre-Columbian era, corn, squash, chile peppers, and beans have formed the base of the Mexican diet. In addition to these key staples, Mexican food makes ample use of other native American foods, including tomatoes, green tomatoes, avocados, potatoes, prickly pear cactus, chocolate, and turkey. In the 15th century, Spanish settlers introduced new culinary techniques to Mexico, along with new ingredients like wheat, onions, rice, cheese, chicken, pork, and beef. Throughout the country, European traditions began to fuse with indigenous recipes. The result was a new and wholly original cuisine.

A staple at most Mexican meals and a key ingredient in many traditional dishes, tortillas are round flatbreads made of corn or wheat flour. A warmed tortilla wrapped around seasoned meat or vegetables is a taco, while a tortilla filled with melted cheese is a quesadilla. In addition to tortillas, corn flour is used to make a variety of flatbreads. Sopes are thick corn discs topped with beans, crumbled cheese, sour cream, and salsa, whereas huaraches are torpedo-shaped flatbreads, usually topped with beans, guisados, and salsa. Gorditas, a specialty of the Bajío region, are thick, round corn flatbreads, which are cooked on a griddle and then stuffed with cheese, meat, or other fillings.

Beyond tortillas and other flatbreads, corn is an essential ingredient in a wide range of traditional foods, many of which have roots in pre-Columbian cuisine. One of the oldest and most popular foods in the Americas, tamales are made of corn masa (dough) steamed in a corn husk or banana leaf and stuffed with chile peppers, meat, cheese, or fruits. Tamales are often accompanied by atole, a warm corn-based drink flavored with chocolate or fruit and sugar. Pozole, a hearty hominy soup, is another corn-based dish with pre-Hispanic origins, popular throughout the country, and made regionally with a variety of broths and additions.

As anyone who's spent time in Mexico knows, chile peppers are fundamental to the Mexican palate. Salsa picante, which refers to any sauce made of ground chile peppers and condiments, is served as an accompaniment to almost every meal in Mexico, formal or informal. There are seemingly infinite types of salsa, from the ubiquitous salsa verde (typically made with green tomatoes, cilantro, onion, and green chiles) to pico de gallo (a fresh salsa of chopped tomatoes, onion, and serrano chile peppers) to the dark charred-habanero salsa from the Yucatán Peninsula.

Aside from salsa, chile peppers are used to season meat, beans, and sauces or are served whole and stuffed with cheese in a chile relleno. There are hundreds of varieties of chile pepper cultivated in Mexico, some of which are incredibly spicy (the habanero being Mexico's spiciest traditional variety), while others are mild but flavorful, like the poblano or the chilaca.

Like chile peppers, many varieties of beans are cultivated and prepared in Mexican cooking. Beans are generally served as a side dish to a meal or as part of a soup. In addition to beans, rice is a common accompaniment to a meal in traditional Mexican restaurants.

Mexico has a large ranching industry, with a variety of meats and cheeses produced throughout the country, including in the Bajío region. Pork and chicken are popular, and northern Mexico is known for its large ranches raising grass-fed beef. Traditional Mexican cuts of beef include the lean arrachera and norteña. Thanks to long and abundant coastlines, fish and shellfish are popular at Mexico's beach resorts as well as across the country.

Mexico also produces several varieties of cheeses, including panela (a smooth, low-fat fresh cheese), cotija (a dry and salty cheese used for crumbling on top of dishes), and queso oaxaca (a mozzarella-like cheese, rolled into balls), also called quesillo. Mennonite communities in the north of Mexico make queso chihuahua (chihuahua cheese), which resembles a mild cheddar. There are many locally produced cheeses in the Bajío, which you can find in specialty shops and delis throughout the region.

MEALTIMES

Mexicans typically eat three meals each day, though there are few hard-and-fast rules when it comes to eating. Breakfast (desayuno) is usually a light morning meal, often accompanied by hot chocolate or coffee. A larger breakfast or brunch is called almuerzo, typically eaten a bit later than a regular breakfast. Almuerzo is often more substantial than a typical breakfast, though the term refers more to the hour it's eaten (around 11am) than the content.

The comida, or midday meal, is traditionally the largest and most important meal of the day, eaten around 2pm. A traditional comida begins with soup, followed by a pasta or rice course and finally a main course, served with tortillas or a basket of bolillos (white rolls). While you might not always find that exact lineup on the table, the Bajío region remains fairly traditional with regards to lunch. Families usually eat comida together, and there are still a number of small businesses that close 2pm-4pm to accommodate an afternoon break. On Sunday afternoons, it is typical to plan a large comida with friends and family.

Dinner is eaten late in the evening, typically around 8pm or 9pm, and is usually a lighter meal than comida. Traditional dinners include tamales with atole, sweet breads with milk or coffee, or tacos. That said, in cities like Querétaro, San Miguel de Allende, and Guanajuato, going out for a big dinner is a popular activity.

REGIONAL FOOD

With its varied terrain and diverse local traditions, it's not surprising that Mexican food is highly regional. Certain states, like Oaxaca and Puebla, are known for their spectacular cuisine, but every state in Mexico distinguishes itself through local dishes and ingredients. Although it is an important agricultural center, the Bajío region has not been historically known as a culinary destination in Mexico.

Nonetheless, there are a few dishes typical to the states of Guanajuato and Querétaro as well as ingredients that are produced locally and consumed more widely here than in other parts of Mexico. Notably, enchiladas mineras is a hearty dish of tortillas rolled around cheese, covered in a mild chile sauce, and then smothered in fried potatoes and carrots. A very similar dish called enchiladas queretanas is served in Querétaro, sans vegetables. Gorditas, stuffed corn flatbreads, are also traditional to the region.

Many restaurants in San Miguel de Allende, Guanajuato, and Querétaro prepare traditional food from other states, giving the visitor an opportunity to sample Mexico's most iconic dishes. Some of Mexico's most interesting culinary traditions can be found in the southern states of Veracruz, Puebla, Oaxaca, and Yucatán. If you are interested in trying specialty foods, look out for popular Mexican dishes like cochinita pibil (shredded and seasoned pork from the Yucatán), mole negro (a chocolate-based sauce from Oaxaca), and chiles en nogada (poblano chile peppers stuffed with almonds, raisins, apples, dried fruit, cinnamon, and meat, then bathed in a creamy walnut sauce).

There is also a growing organic and artisanal food movement in both Guanajuato and Querétaro states, where small-batch cheese, local wine, and organic fruits and vegetables are becoming increasingly common.

DRINKS

Delicious and refreshing, aguas frescas or aguas de fruta are a cheap and ubiquitous beverage throughout Mexico. Usually these drinks are made with fresh fruit, water, and sugar, blended together with ice and then strained. The most popular aguas include tamarind, mango, lime, lemon, jamaica (hibiscus), and horchata (rice water with cinnamon). Fresh juice is sold at informal stands in the morning, as are licuados (shakes made with milk, sugar, and fruit).

Both coffee and chocolate are cultivated in Mexico and widely consumed as hot beverages. A popular option at many casual fondas and restaurants, café de olla is boiled coffee mixed with cinnamon and piloncillo (unrefined sugar). Atole is another popular beverage for the morning or evening, a hot drink made of cornstarch, sweeteners (like sugar or piloncillo, a type of unrefined sugar), and fruit or chocolate, often served alongside tamales.

Corona is the world's top-selling beer and one of a ubiquitous roster of national brews. Most Mexican beers are, like Corona, light lagers, though León and Negra Modelo are both amber. Mexican beers are often served with a lime in foreign countries, but they are rarely so embellished in Mexico. If you like the lime taste, you may want to try a michelada (a beer served in a glass with ice, lime juice, Worcestershire sauce, hot sauce, and a salt rim) or a cubana (beer, ice, and lime juice with a salt rim).

Mexican beer was formerly dominated by two major conglomerates: Grupo Modelo (makers of Corona, Negra Modelo, Modelo Especial, León, Pacifico, and Victoria, among others) and Cervecería Cuauhtémoc Moctezuma (makers of Sol, Dos Equis, Bohemia, Carta Blanca, Indio, Tecate, and Superior). Smaller breweries have since gained tremendous momentum, however. Today many bars and restaurants carry small-batch beers as part of their bar menu—or exclusively. If you're a craft-beer aficionado, look for local producers like Dos Aves or Cervecería Allende from San Miguel de Allende, Chela Libre from Celaya, Hércules from Querétaro, and Serrana from the Sierra de Guanajuato.

In addition to beer, Mexico is famous for tequila, a distilled liquor made from the sap of the agave cactus. Fine tequila is best sipped slowly from a tall shot glass, rather than downed in a single gulp. Casa Dragones, a well-known tequila producer, has its headquarters in San Miguel de Allende. In many traditional bars and cantinas, you can order your tequila with sangrita, a popular chaser made of tomato juice and spices.

A cousin to tequila, mezcal is a spirit made from distilling maguey cactus. Unlike tequila, mezcal can be produced in any region and is rapidly gaining popularity throughout Mexico as well as overseas. While mezcal from the state of Oaxaca remains the gold standard, there are several popular mezcal producers in the state of Guanajuato, as well as many mezcal-centric bars throughout the Bajío. Mezcal is often sipped, like tequila, accompanied by wedges of orange and salt, though you'll also find lots of mezcal cocktails on San Miguel de Allende and Guanajuato's drinks menus, rivaling the still-ubiquitous margarita.

Over the past couple of decades, vineyards in Baja California, Coahuila, and Aguascalientes have begun to produce some very nice and widely acclaimed wines. Today, the Bajío has begun to make inroads into the industry, with a number of vineyards operating in the states of Querétaro and Guanajuato. Cuna de Tierra, La Santisima Trinidad, Dos Buhos, Rancho Toyan, and Viñedos San Lucas are some of the nascent producers operating near San Miguel de Allende, with tasting rooms on-site; their bottles are becoming more widely available at restaurants or shops in town.

DESSERT

The most ubiquitous Mexican dessert is the famous flan, a thick egg custard that seems to be offered in every restaurant in the country. Other popular Mexican desserts include pastel de tres leches (three-milks cake) and ate (fruit paste) served with cheese. On the street, you'll often find ice creams (nieves) for sale in cups or cones. Nieves are made from a cream or water base and often incorporate fresh tropical fruits like mango or coconut. In addition to nieves, paletas (popsicles) made from real fruit, sugar, and, in some cases, milk are sold in small shops or on street corners throughout the country. A popular treat in San Miguel de Allende, churros are deep-fried pastry sticks doused in sugar and cinnamon, which you can buy from street vendors, at markets, or in cafés.

MARKETS

Since the pre-Columbian era, Mexicans have bought their food in mercados (markets). Throughout Mexico, markets are almost always the best place to buy fresh produce, artfully displayed in neat stacks and sold at the lowest prices available. In addition to fruit and vegetable stands, food markets can be a good place to buy inexpensive grains and legumes, like dried beans, rice, hibiscus, lentils, and garbanzos, as well as Mexican cheeses and dairy products. Adventurous eaters may want to try some of the food prepared at a market's fondas and food stands.

Many visitors believe that bartering for a lower price is customary in Mexican markets; this is not necessarily the case in San Miguel de Allende and the surrounding region. Merchants will often offer a reasonable price for their goods, and it is unnecessary (and sometimes rude) to bargain. This is especially true for foodstuffs that are often very inexpensive to begin with. However, if you buy in bulk, a merchant may offer you a lower rate for the entire lot, or they may give you a papaya, fresh herbs, or another extra on the house.

Conduct and Customs

GREETINGS

When meeting someone for the first time or greeting acquaintances in Mexico, it is customary to make physical contact, rather than simply saying hello verbally. A handshake is the most common form of greeting in Mexico. Between male and female friends, or between two women, Mexicans will often greet each other with a single kiss on the cheek. Male friends may also give each other a quick hug. The same gestures are repeated when you say good-bye. When greeting a group of people, it is necessary to greet and shake hands with each person individually, rather than greeting the group together.

When speaking to an elder or to someone with whom you will have a professional relationship, it is customary to use the formal pronoun "usted" instead of the informal "tú." Spanish language classes will often spend quite a bit of time explaining the difference between usted and tú, though most English-speaking tourists find themselves baffled by the distinction. Err on the side of caution by using usted when speaking to most people you don't know well or anyone older than you.

MANNERS

Mexicans are generally very polite when interacting with people they do not know well. Throughout the country, good manners are still practiced and appreciated. Most Mexicans appreciate those who make an effort to be polite but are nonetheless very forgiving

of foreign tourists who aren't familiar with the country's customs.

When you sit down to eat in Mexico, it is customary to wish other diners "Buen provecho" before you dig in. Buen provecho is similar to the well-known French expression bon appetit and means "Enjoy your meal." In small towns and even big cities, it is not uncommon to greet other diners when you enter a restaurant or to wish them buen provecho as you come in or are leaving. Likewise, it is common courtesy to make eye contact and greet the salesperson when you enter a store.

When greeting someone, it is common practice to speak to that person using a polite title, such as señor for a man, señora for a married or older woman, and señorita for a young woman. When speaking with a professional, Mexicans may also use the person's professional title, such as doctor or doctora (doctor), arquitecto (architect), or ingeniero (engineer). The title licenciado or licenciada is often used to address a college graduate, as a term of respect. In addition, the term maestro (master) can be used when addressing a skilled tradesman or a teacher.

On San Miguel de Allende and Guanajuato's narrow sidewalks, two pedestrians cannot always fit side by side. It is customary to step into the street to allow someone else to pass, especially when that person is elderly or carrying a child. If you have to squeeze past someone, you can say "con permiso," which functions like "excuse me" in English.

PUNCTUALITY

The famous Mexican penchant for putting things off until mañana (tomorrow) does have an element of truth. Time is a bit less structured in Mexico, and it is common practice and not considered excessively rude to arrive a bit tardy for a social engagement. In a professional setting, however, punctuality is required.

TIPPING

In Mexico, tips are essential wages for workers in service industries. In many cases, tipping is required, and in every case it is appreciated.

In a restaurant, it is customary to tip the server 15 percent on the bill. In San Miguel de Allende, it is customary to tip 15-20 percent of the bill at a restaurant, especially in a sit-down restaurant. In bars, a 10 percent tip is standard. Though a customer may choose to leave a bit more or less based on the quality of the service, tipping is obligatory. European tourists who do not tip at home should be prepared to conform to Mexico's tipping standards.

In most cases, it is not necessary to tip a taxi driver when traveling within city limits, though tipping is always welcomed. If a taxi or shuttle service is taking you to the airport or to another city, a tip is customary and can be given at the passenger's discretion. Likewise, tour guides and transport services can be tipped at your discretion; in most cases, around 10-15 percent is appropriate.

At service stations, a small tip of about 5 percent is customary for gas station attendants (all gas stations are full service in Mexico); 20 to 50 pesos is usually sufficient. It is customary to tip porters at an airport or hotel US$5-10, depending on the size of your load. Throughout Mexico, it is becoming increasingly common to tip the cleaning staff in a hotel. In San Miguel de Allende, it is common and usually expected.

DRINKING LAWS

Throughout Mexico, the legal drinking age is 18. Although it is not legal to drink on the street, you may see people take drinks outside during citywide parties and festivals. Drinking and driving is a serious offense in Mexico, though it remains a largely uncontrolled problem on the roads, where driving under the influence and drunk-driving-related accidents are not uncommon.

Dry laws (ley seca) are sometimes enacted on election days or, occasionally, during major holidays, like Independence Day (Sept. 16). In that case, liquor stores and bars may close early (or not open at all). The decision to enact dry laws is up to each municipality.

SMOKING

In 2008 smoking indoors at both restaurants and bars was prohibited throughout Mexico. While the law was heavily enforced when it first went into effect, it has become a bit looser with time. Usually restaurants and bars do not allow their customers to smoke in enclosed spaces (patios and sidewalks are still fair game), but some bars and music venues may be more lenient.

Health and Safety

There are few serious health and safety risks for visitors to San Miguel de Allende, Guanajuato, and Querétaro. With sensible precautions, visitors can enjoy a safe and comfortable trip to the region.

DOCTORS AND HOSPITALS

There are plenty of doctors, dentists, and hospitals in San Miguel de Allende, Guanajuato, and Querétaro, many of whom have extensive experience working with foreigners. It is usually fairly easy to locate competent, English-speaking doctors in the region.

In almost all cases, Mexican doctors and hospitals do not accept U.S. insurance. Medicaid is also not accepted in Mexico. If you will be in Mexico for an extended period and are concerned about health care, you can explore the options for international coverage. Fortunately, medicine in Mexico tends to be far less expensive than in other developed countries; in many cases, tourists can pay for their medical exams, associated lab tests, and prescription medication out of pocket. Hospitals will usually accept cash and credit cards, though private doctors may be cash-only.

PRESCRIPTIONS AND PHARMACIES

Visitors to Mexico are permitted to carry prescription medication for a pre-existing condition among their personal effects. They can bring no more than three months' worth of medicine with them, and it should be accompanied by documentation from a doctor. (There can be strict penalties, including incarceration, for tourists who are suspected of drug abuse.) Most common over-the-counter medication is available in Mexico. Drugs in Mexico are regulated and safe; there are also generic brands. Note that pseudoephedrine, the active ingredient in Sudafed, is illegal in Mexico; leave it at home.

If you need to purchase medication while you are in Mexico, you can visit a doctor who will write you a prescription. Not all drugs require prescriptions. However, it is usually a better idea to get a prescription for medication, as the brands may differ in Mexico and there can be penalties for those carrying medication without a doctor's prescription. Prescription medication is often a bit cheaper in Mexico than in the rest of North America or Europe.

Many pharmacies (farmacias) are open 24 hours a day, while others close in the evening. In smaller towns like San Miguel de Allende and Guanajuato, there is always at least one pharmacy open through the night to attend to emergencies.

COMMON CONCERNS
Altitude Sickness

The Bajío's average elevation is 2,000 m (6,500 ft), and for some visitors, the altitude may require a short adjustment period. Altitude sickness, though rarely serious, can include symptoms like shortness of breath, dizziness, headaches, and nausea. If symptoms are severe or persist past a few days, see a doctor.

Gastrointestinal Distress

Some tourists experience gastrointestinal distress when traveling in Mexico for the first time. Changes in your eating and drinking habits, as well as a new overall environment, can cause unpleasant diarrhea, nausea, and vomiting. Because it often affects Mexico newcomers, gastrointestinal distress is called turista, which translates to "tourist" (it's also known as "traveler's diarrhea" in English). In many cases, turista can be effectively treated with a few days of rest, liquids, and antidiarrhea medication, such as Pepto-Bismol, Kaopectate, or Imodium. Although you cannot necessarily prevent turista from striking, you will have a better chance of faring comfortably through your vacation if you eat and drink in moderation, get plenty of sleep, and stay hydrated. Many visitors to the Bajío do not experience any stomach discomfort.

More serious gastrointestinal problems can also occur in Mexico, though less frequently. If you are experiencing serious nausea, vomiting, and diarrhea, consult a doctor who can test and treat you for parasites or other gastrointestinal maladies.

Water Quality

Mexican tap water is treated; however, it is generally considered unsafe for drinking. Bottled water is readily available throughout Mexico and, like any bottled beverage, is safe to drink. If you will be staying in Mexico for an extended period, you can purchase large plastic jugs of purified water, called garafones, to be delivered to your home. You can also make tap water safe for drinking by boiling it for five minutes to kill any bacteria or parasites. Most grocery stores sell droplets to sterilize fruits and vegetables; these can be used to purify water, though the flavor may be affected.

Tap water is not served in restaurants. Ice is made with purified water. Likewise, coffee, lemonades, and other drinks are made with purified water.

Food Safety

When eating raw fresh vegetables and some fruits, it is common practice to disinfect them before consumption. In some cases, leafy vegetables may contain residual bacteria from watering or handling. For raw consumption, supermarkets sell several varieties of food sanitizer, the most common of which are made with chloride bleach or colloidal silver. If you plan to cook your vegetables, you do not need to disinfect them; just rinse them in water. The heat will kill any potentially harmful substances.

Most restaurants in the Bajío will sterilize raw vegetables served for salads or other dishes. Nonetheless, some visitors experience gastrointestinal distress after consuming raw

vegetables. If you are in the Bajío for a short vacation, you may want to err on the side of caution and avoid raw vegetables or only consume vegetables that have been sterilized.

There is always more risk associated with food stands located outdoors or in marketplaces, where hygiene is more difficult to maintain. Some people consume street food with no incident; others become ill after eating in markets or on the street. Use your discretion, and introduce new foods into your diet slowly.

Infectious Disease

Hepatitis A affects the liver and is contracted from food or water infected with fecal matter. Vaccines are available to protect against hepatitis A infection. Symptoms may resemble the flu, though they are severe and may last several months.

There has been a recent surge in cases of dengue fever in Mexico, though mostly along the coast; it remains a very limited problem in the central highlands. Nonetheless, the government has launched an extensive campaign against mosquito proliferation, which includes a periodic check of residences and their water storage systems as well as occasional insecticide spraying. The best way to prevent dengue infection is to avoid mosquito bites.

At time of writing, coronavirus was not a major health concern in San Miguel de Allende and the Bajío region. Wearing a facial covering is no longer required in indoor spaces or on public transportation, and there are no other current COVID-related restrictions in place in San Miguel de Allende or the Bajío region.

Creepy Crawlers

Mosquitoes are a common nuisance during the summer months, especially close to bodies of water or large gardens. Most serious mosquito-borne illnesses (such as malaria or dengue) are unusual in the areas around San Miguel de Allende. However, their itchy bite makes this pest a serious nuisance.

Situated atop a wide plain in the central Mexican plateau, the Bajío region doesn't feel like the mountains. There are no pine trees and granite peaks, just sun and cactus. However, at almost 2,000 m (6,500 ft), San Miguel is as high as Lake Tahoe, California. In some cases, tourists forget that they are at altitude and may blame that queasy feeling on last night's tacos.

Altitude sickness can affect both young and old people, even those who are in good physical shape. Symptoms may include nausea, dizziness, loss of appetite, and fatigue. Keep an eye out for altitude sickness, and take a few simple steps to increase your body's chances of a smooth acclimation.

- **Drink Lots of Water:** Bodies tend to lose water more quickly at higher altitudes. Stay hydrated throughout your trip.

- **Limit Coffee and Cocktails:** It's best to avoid drinks that can dehydrate you, especially alcohol and caffeine.

- **Don't Push It:** Take it easy during your first few days in the Bajío. Let your body adjust to the altitude before heading off on a horseback riding adventure or a hike in the countryside.

- **Eat Light:** Doctors recommend avoiding heavy foods when you first arrive at a higher altitude. Have smaller meals and stick to lighter foods and carbohydrates.

- **Stay Alert:** Altitude sickness is rarely serious; however, if symptoms don't improve after a day or two, see a doctor.

Scorpions live in the Bajío, and they occasionally turn up indoors. In most cases, scorpion stings are painful but not fatal. The exception is in and around the city of León, where a highly venomous scorpion can be found. Under any circumstance, consult a doctor if you are stung by a scorpion. Most scorpions are reclusive and avoid human contact. To avoid encountering them, shake out your shoes in the morning before you put them on, and use care moving bookcases or other furniture with its back to the wall.

Spiders are also common in the Bajío, including the poisonous black widow. Black widows are shiny black with a red hourglass on their abdomen. Like scorpions, black widows are generally reclusive. They may hide in wood piles, fields, or quiet corners. Though they rarely kill healthy adults, they can be a risk to children, the elderly, or pets. If bitten by a black widow, consult a doctor.

CRIME

San Miguel de Allende, Dolores Hidalgo, the city of Guanajuato, and Querétaro city and state are generally safe and welcoming destinations for travelers. That said, visitors should take the same precautions when traveling here as they would in any foreign country: Avoid traveling alone at night, don't carry excessive amounts of cash, and remain aware of your surroundings.

Tourist areas are rarely affected by violent crime. Even so, visitors should take the time to familiarize themselves with the political and social situation before they visit. The state of Guanajuato, particularly the south and central regions, has become notoriously violent since drug cartels began moving into the area around 2018. The U.S. Department of State recommends against travel to these areas, which include Celaya, Irapuato, and Salamanca, citing the high number of murders associated with cartel-related violence. At press time, the city of Celaya, located about 45 minutes from San Miguel, was one of Mexico's most violent. For updated information, the U.S. Department of State (www.travel.state.gov) publishes up-to-date travel advisories for each state in the republic.

Though things are generally quiet in San Miguel, there have been a few high-profile crime stories in recent years. In 2014 there was a flurry of news when cartel leader Hector Beltran Leyva was apprehended at a seafood restaurant in San Miguel de Allende, and there have been some notable organized-crime-related kidnappings in the region. The leader of the criminal ring associated with these kidnappings (which was, incredibly, tied to a group of Chilean fugitives, not the drug trade, as many had assumed) was apprehended in 2017.

In the case that you have been arrested for a crime in Mexico, contact your embassy. International law requires that the Mexican government contact a foreigner's embassy at their request. However, foreign citizens may still be tried and held accountable under Mexican law for any crimes committed in Mexico.

Practical Details

WHAT TO PACK

San Miguel de Allende has a year-round temperate climate, which doesn't call for any special clothing or gear. The one exception is footwear. San Miguel de Allende, Guanajuato, and Querétaro have colonial-era downtown districts crisscrossed by uneven cobblestone streets. They can be quite slick, especially in the rain, and it is not unusual for visitors to slip or sprain an ankle while momentarily distracted by a beautiful 18th-century bell tower. For sightseeing, bring comfortable shoes that are good for walking.

When packing, keep in mind that the dry, semiarid climate means that temperatures fluctuate significantly from morning to midday to evening. In the winter months, temperatures can drop below freezing at night. Bring layers and, if you are visiting in the summer, an umbrella and waterproof shoes.

Dress code is generally casual, even at the nicest establishments. At the same time, the Bajío is not the beach, so tourists in excessively summery outfits (shorts, bathing suits, sarongs, and the like) may stand out.

If you plan on doing a little shopping in San Miguel de Allende, bring along your checkbook in addition to bank cards and credit cards. Surprisingly, many small businesses will accept checks from U.S. banks, even if they don't accept credit cards.

MONEY
Currency

Mexico's currency is the peso. However, in San Miguel de Allende, some shops, hotels, and restaurants may accept U.S. dollars. In most cases, prices are listed in pesos, though on occasion, you will see prices listed in dollars; both currencies are denoted with a $ sign. Clearly, the arrangement can lead to confusion for San Miguel's shoppers, who aren't sure if an item is surprisingly cheap or incredibly expensive. (Restaurant menu prices are almost always listed exclusively in pesos.)

Exchanging Money

For most visitors to Mexico, the most common and efficient way to change money is by using a foreign bank card at an ATM. Banks and credit unions generally offer the day's best exchange rates (usually posted at the bank's entrance). Most international bank cards are accepted at Mexican banks, though it is always advisable to call your bank at home before attempting to withdraw money or use a credit card in a foreign country. When using your ATM card, it's best to choose an official bank rather than a stand-alone ATM in a shop or mall; there have been reports of ATM and credit card numbers being stolen and used for illicit withdrawals in Mexico.

You can also change foreign currency to pesos at a casa de cambio (exchange house). There are casas de cambio in the centro histórico in both San Miguel de Allende and Guanajuato. Be aware, however, that the Mexican government is attempting to reduce crime and fraud by limiting the amount of money that a customer can change in a single day. If you might need a large sum of money, plan ahead or use travelers checks.

Travelers Checks and Credit Cards

Until recently, Mexico was largely a cash culture. Nowadays it's far more common for businesses to accept credit cards. That said, some small hotels and restaurants, especially those of the budget variety, do not take credit cards. At traditional markets or street stands, cash is the only form of payment. At the same time, credit cards are widely accepted for large purchases, at gas stations, in shops, and in upscale restaurants. (In some cases, shop owners will give you a discounted price if you pay with cash or, conversely, charge you a bit more if you pay with a card.) To rent a car, a credit card is required.

Travelers checks are an alternative to cash and can be useful if you need to change a lot of money in a single day. The drawback is that travelers checks cannot be changed everywhere and may not be accepted at restaurants or shops in Mexico.

SHOPPING

When shopping for home goods, art, craftwork, clothing, and other souvenirs, it is not common practice to bargain or ask for lower prices on goods. In some stores, vendors may offer a small discount for bulk purchases or for cash payments, but these are offered at the shop owner's discretion. In general, shoppers should not expect employees at a brick-and-mortar store to lower prices on their goods.

However, you may be able to negotiate the price on an expensive antique or a work of art, particularly in San Miguel de Allende. This is particularly true if you are buying multiple pieces from a single store or artist. In that case, it is acceptable to inquire about flexibility in the price. That said, prices are rarely

marked up significantly, so don't be too insistent after you've reached a vendor's limit.

In an artisan or craft market, such as the craft market in central San Miguel de Allende, prices for goods may be more flexible. It is customary to ask the vendor for the price of the item (they are rarely marked with price tags), and the vendor may then offer you a lower price as you think it over. This is particularly true for large purchases. In general, these discounts are not significant (don't expect to pay half of the price initially quoted) and aggressive haggling is not common, nor is it particularly fruitful. If you do wish to bargain on a price, do so politely.

Do not bargain at food markets, even if you are buying a substantial quantity. Usually the prices at food markets are very low to begin with, and few vendors can afford to drop their price further. In some cases, a vendor will offer a something extra (say, a papaya or a pineapple) to a buyer who makes a large purchase at their stand.

COMMUNICATIONS
Internet Access

Mexico is wired. For smartphones and laptops, there is Wi-Fi at most cafés, restaurants, hotels, public libraries, and even public plazas and parks in Guanajuato, San Miguel de Allende, Dolores Hidalgo, and Querétaro. Local wireless carriers, like Telcel and Movistar, have extensive networks that make it easy to connect your smartphone via roaming if you've signed up for an international plan. You may find fewer services in very small towns, like Pozos. Otherwise, getting connected is rarely a problem.

Shipping and Postal Service

The Mexican post office will ship letters, postcards, and packages to any location in the world. They offer insured as well as expedited shipping services. The Mexican post is by far your cheapest mailing option, but it is not renowned for its reliability—use it for nonessential communication and never for time-sensitive documents. For

By the Numbers

- **Time Zone:** The hours in San Miguel de Allende, Guanajuato, and Querétaro correspond to the Central Standard Time zone in the United States, six hours behind Greenwich Mean Time.

- **Electricity:** Like the United States and Canada, Mexico uses 110 volts 60 cycles. It can be useful to bring a socket adapter with your computer, since many Mexican outlets only allow for a two-prong plug.

- **Weights and Measures:** Mexico uses the metric system for all measurements, including temperature, distance, weight, and volume.

- **Climate:** Average high temperatures range 21-29°C (70-85°F) year-round. Average lows run 7-14°C (44-58°F).

- **Population Distribution:** In the states of Guanajuato and Querétaro, 70 percent of the population lives in cities; 30 percent is rural.

expedited shipping, **MexPost** (www.portal. correosdemexico.com.mx/portal), a division of the government-operated postal service, will offer faster service at a higher (but still accessible) price. MexPost's services are generally more reliable than the standard post.

In addition, many major shipping companies offer shipping services within Mexico and internationally, including Estafeta, DHL, Redpack, UPS, and FedEx. Of these, DHL is the most reliable and widely used in the Bajío region.

Media

Large media conglomerates control the majority of Mexico's communication channels. Televisa Group is the largest and most powerful media company, operating several television stations, radio stations, sports teams, and record labels. In addition to privately owned stations, the government runs two public television stations available on a limited basis throughout the republic.

In San Miguel de Allende, taxi drivers will often tune in to XESQ (103.3 FM), a local radio station that broadcasts local news and special programming. The excellent **Radio Universidad** (www.radiouniversidad. ugto.mx) covers news and cultural events, as well as music, at 970 AM or 100 FM in Guanajuato. From San Miguel de Allende, Radio Universidad is on the dial at 91.3 FM.

Local and national newspapers and news magazines cover current events. In the Bajío, there are several papers published in the cities of Guanajuato, Celaya, León, and Querétaro, which cover local news and politics. Published in the city of Guanajuato, the Spanish-language newspaper **Correo** (https:// periodicocorreo.com.mx) covers news, arts, and culture for the entire region. You can also get news about the state of Guanajuato from newspapers **El Sol del Bajío** (www. elsoldelbajio.com.mx), published in Celaya, and **am** (www.am.com.mx) from León. In Querétaro, *El Diario de Querétaro* is among the largest papers, though the city also has special Querétaro-specific editions of the national newspaper *El Universal*. In addition, national dailies are distributed in all of the Bajío's major towns, including the Mexico City papers *El Universal, Reforma,* and *La Jornada*.

TIME ZONE

San Miguel de Allende, Guanajuato, and the Bajío are on Central Standard Time. Since October 2022, Guanajuato and Querétaro states, along with all but four Mexican states along the U.S. border, no longer participate in the daylight saving time program.

Traveler Advice

OPPORTUNITIES FOR STUDY AND EMPLOYMENT

San Miguel de Allende, Guanajuato, and Querétaro are all excellent places for beginners to learn Spanish. The region is friendly and safe, and there are many language schools in Guanajuato as well as several schools in San Miguel de Allende.

In addition to Spanish-language programs, San Miguel de Allende is a great place to take art classes. Many working artists in San Miguel de Allende give classes in disciplines like watercolor, ceramics, oil painting, printmaking, and jewelry-making. There is also the well-reputed Centro Cultural Ignacio Ramírez, where students can take classes in a variety of disciplines (though the school does not confer certificates or degrees). The Instituto Allende confers undergraduate degrees in art to Mexican students and offers continuing education classes for adults.

Students who plan to take classes in Mexico for six months or less can use a standard tourist visa. If you will be studying for more than six months at an accredited school, it may be easier and more efficient to apply for a student visa. Student visas can be processed either at a Mexican consulate overseas or at a local immigration office in Mexico.

Self-Employment

Many foreigners work and own businesses in San Miguel de Allende and Guanajuato, where you'll find a slew of American- and Canadian-owned restaurants, bars, galleries, bookshops, and boutiques, as well as a smattering of business owners from Europe and Asia. Mexico will also extend self-employment benefits to temporary resident visa holders who wish to open their own business. In many cases, it is easier to open your own business—or give independent language or art classes—than to find employment

through another source. To be eligible for this type of visa, foreigners must have proof of foreign income in addition to demonstrable skills in the field in which they plan to work (such as a degree in English or a TOEFL certificate for a language teacher).

Foreign Employers

Foreigners may be employed by a Mexican- or foreign-owned business; however, foreign employees must be sponsored by their employer, who will assist with the visa application process at immigration. In most cases, Mexico will extend employment visas to foreigners with special skills that are not available within the local population. For example, native speakers of English can seek employment in a bilingual school. In order to be eligible for an employment visa, foreigners must present all necessary documentation for a tourist visa as well as documentation of their skill, such as a university diploma or a certificate in teaching English as a second language. In most cases, a school or other business that routinely employs foreigners will be familiar with the visa application process.

Volunteer Work

There are many opportunities for rewarding volunteer work in San Miguel de Allende and Guanajuato, whether you like working with people, animals, or the environment. Several U.S. universities operate rural assistance programs for college-age volunteers, and there are several summer programs operated by international charities.

For students, several of Guanajuato's Spanish-language schools operate volunteer programs at local charities, which can be an excellent way to learn more about the local culture and continue improving your Spanish skills. Cacomixtle, an adventure and tourism company based in Guanajuato, also runs volunteer programs.

Kid-Friendly San Miguel

With its bright colors, festive atmosphere, and kid-friendly attitude, San Miguel can be a wonderful place to visit with your family. If you are bringing tots to San Miguel, here are some ways to spend your time.

- In the **jardín** in San Miguel de Allende, life recalls an older and more wholesome era. Throngs of kids bounce balls along the cobblestones, long lines await the ice cream vendor, and police officers on horseback snap photos with wee ones. In **Parque Juárez,** there is always a crowd of tots on the playground in the afternoon.

- San Miguel de Allende is a wonderful place to introduce children to Mexican culture. For a diverting look into the history of Mexican toys, take the family to **La Esquina: Museo del Jugete Popular Mexicano,** which features a wonderful collection of antique handmade toys, like rocking horses, whistles, and dolls. Kids can pick out their own classic toys in the museum gift shop.

- At the **Biblioteca de San Miguel de Allende,** a nonprofit cultural center and library, kids can find books in English and Spanish, or participate in one of the many children's programs or movies (often in Spanish).

- Ford streams and explore canyons on a horseback ride with **Rancho Xotolar** or **Coyote Canyon Adventures,** wonderful family-oriented experiences in the beautiful countryside around San Miguel.

- There is no better place to spend a summer afternoon than at one of the many swimming spots around town. With numerous warm spring-fed pools, big lawns, and an on-site restaurant, **La Gruta** is an excellent place to spend a day relaxing with the kids. For waterslides and big swimming pools, take the family to **Xote,** on the highway toward Dolores Hidalgo. Go on a weekday to avoid the massive Saturday and Sunday crowds.

- Children can buy fish food for the koi pond or climb into the on-site treehouse at **Mama Mía Campestre,** a family-friendly outdoor restaurant in Atotonilco. The other branch of **Mama Mía,** in San Miguel's centro histórico, is also a top pick for kids, with cheesy pizzas, live music, friendly service, and an upbeat atmosphere. Get double scoops of Mexican-style ice cream at **Nieves Las Monjas** or take a trip to Dolores Hidalgo, where nieves are served in wacky flavors like shrimp or avocado.

The Mexican Constitution prohibits foreigners from participating in political activities, including demonstrations. Breaking this law can result in deportation. If you are volunteering in Mexico, refrain from attending political demonstrations.

ACCESS FOR TRAVELERS WITH DISABILITIES

San Miguel de Allende and Guanajuato can be difficult places for travelers with disabilities, particularly those with limited range of movement. The colonial cities of the Bajío were built hundreds of years ago, and their streets are often narrow and uneven. There are few sidewalk ramps or elevators in old colonial buildings, even at the entrance of public institutions and museums. The situation is changing, slowly. During renovations, most public buildings will simultaneously make entryways more accessible, and some newer luxury hotels, like the Rosewood Hotel in San Miguel de Allende, are equipped with elevators to all floors.

If you are in a wheelchair or have trouble walking, the easiest place to visit is Querétaro, where the city center is flat, most sights are at ground level, and the government has made a more visible effort to accommodate travelers with physical disabilities.

People in this part of Mexico are ceaselessly friendly and courteous, and most are willing to lend a hand as necessary. Many senior citizens with limited range of movement are able to comfortably visit San Miguel de Allende, and many others make their home there.

TRAVELING WITH CHILDREN

San Miguel de Allende, Guanajuato, and Querétaro are wonderful places to travel with your family. On the whole, children are well-loved members of Mexican society, and they are generally treated kindly in restaurants, museums, and other public places across the region. Mexico's many urban parks and public squares are a bonanza for little ones, who are often free to run wild amid trees and crowds. There are plenty of family-friendly activities in the region, like horseback riding and swimming, as well as plenty of places to take classes in the Spanish language. If you are planning to stay in a hotel with your children, be aware that some bed-and-breakfasts in San Miguel de Allende do not allow children under a certain age.

Many foreign children, mostly from the United States and Canada, live in San Miguel de Allende. In San Miguel there are several bilingual private schools that have significant foreign enrollment. Over the summer, there are several day camps for local and international kids as well as Spanish classes for children at local language schools. The library and municipal government often host events and movies for children in San Miguel de Allende; however, most of this programming is in Spanish.

Remember that, like adults, children must have a valid passport to be admitted to Mexico, even if they are accompanied by a parent. In order to combat child trafficking and kidnapping, Mexico requires that a parent accompany a non-Mexican minor when leaving the country. If the child is traveling with a relative or other adult guardian, he or she must have an official letter of consent from the official parent or guardian authorizing the child's travel plans.

TRAVELING WITH PETS

Dog and cat lovers will meet many like minds in Mexico, where pets are popular and beloved parts of the family. That said, traveling with a pet can be more complicated, especially if you are planning to stay in hotels. There are several inns, hotels, and bed-and-breakfasts that welcome pets, so you should make reservations for yourself and your pet in advance. In San Miguel de Allende, the Rosewood Hotel, Hotel Matilda, and L'Otel all accept pets, though note that these are high-end establishments; in many cases, it can be harder to find a place for your pet in budget accommodations. If you have trouble locating a pet-friendly hotel, consider a rental house or apartment, which may have a more liberal pet policy.

Pets are generally not permitted in the coaches of Mexico's bus lines, though hardy canines may travel in the luggage compartment below the bus, an unpleasant but practical option for some pet owners. Many rental car companies and tour operators will permit an animal in their vehicles, though they may charge an additional fee. Airport shuttles and taxis will also often allow pets. Travelers should check individually if they plan to bring their dog or cat on the road.

WOMEN TRAVELING ALONE

San Miguel de Allende, Guanajuato, Querétaro, and environs are generally safe for solo female travelers. A lone woman rarely warrants any special attention from locals, and most people treat women with respect. Hundreds if not thousands of women travel unaccompanied to San Miguel de Allende each year, and even more foreign women live alone in town. At the same time, a woman traveling alone should take basic precautions, especially when out at night.

SENIOR TRAVELERS

The whole Bajío region, especially San Miguel de Allende, is a welcoming place for older travelers. The cobblestone streets and many hills in San Miguel can make the city a bit more challenging to traverse on foot for anyone with limited mobility, and all visitors to San Miguel must be careful not to twist their knee or ankle on the uneven streets. Beyond these small problems, many senior travelers have a comfortable and rewarding experience visiting San Miguel.

LGBTQ+ TRAVELERS

Despite its reputation as conservative and devoutly Catholic, the Bajío is generally a socially tolerant and accepting region. LGBTQ+ travelers are unlikely to experience discrimination from locals, especially in larger cities. In the cosmopolitan small towns of San Miguel de Allende and Guanajuato, the population is markedly more open-minded than the region's conservative reputation would lead you to believe. There is a relatively large and visible gay population in San Miguel, made up of both local and foreign residents. While public displays of affection between same-sex couples are relatively uncommon, same-sex and queer couples will rarely experience negative reactions from locals.

TRAVELERS OF COLOR

In central Mexico, most people are from a mixed-race heritage, predominantly Spanish or European and Indigenous American. On the whole, other ethnic or racial groups are in the minority and less visible. The country's demographics are slowly changing as more immigrants from the United States, Canada, Africa, Asia, and Central and South America move to Mexico. Mexico has a long history of racial inequality running all the way back to the conquest and enslavement of the native people by the Spanish. Issues of racial discrimination and prejudice persist, which travelers may or may not witness or experience.

In some cases, Mexican customs and attitudes toward race may differ from what you've experienced in your home country. One noticeable example is that terms that would be considered derogatory in the United States are still somewhat commonly used (without overt derogatory intent) in Mexico, such as addressing someone who is Asian (of any background) as "chinito/chinita."

Resources

Glossary

adobado: chile seasoning or marinade
aduana: customs
aeropuerto: airport
agave: large Mexican succulent plant
agave azul: blue agave, used in tequila production
agua: water
aguas frescas or aguas de fruta: cold fruit drink
alebrije: hand-painted copal wood animals and figurines from Oaxaca.
almuerzo: meal eaten around midday
andador: pedestrian walkway
antigüedades: antiques
antojitos: snacks or appetizers
arquitecto: architect
arrachera: Mexican skirt steak
arte: art
artesanía: traditional handicraft
atole: a sweet and hot beverage made with corn flour
autobús: bus
autopista: highway
ayuntamiento: town council
azulejo: tile
Bajío: a geographical region that encompasses the states of Guanajuato and Querétaro, as well as segments of the states of Jalisco and Michoacán
Ballet Folklórico: a traditional Mexican dance troupe from Mexico City
banco: bank
baño: bathroom
barbacoa: pit-cooked lamb
biblioteca: library
bolillo: white roll

bomberos: firefighters
botana: appetizer
buen provecho: an expression meaning "enjoy your meal"
burro: donkey
caballo: horse
café: coffee
café con leche: coffee with milk
café de olla: boiled coffee with unrefined sugar and cinnamon
caldo: broth
caldo tlalpeño: chicken and chipotle soup
calle: street
callejón: alley
callejoneadas: famous traveling minstrel shows in Guanajuato
calzada: road
camión: bus
cantina: traditional bar or drinking establishment
capilla: chapel
carnitas: braised pork
carretera: highway
casa: house
casa de cambio: exchange house
casita: small house
castillo: castle
catrina: skeleton figurine or drawing dressed as an aristocrat; originally invented by artist José Guadalupe Posada
cempasúchil: marigold
centro histórico: historical district
cerveza: beer
chal: shawl
charro: traditional Mexican cowboy or horseman

Chichimeca: name used by the Spanish during the early colonial era to describe the nomadic tribes of northern Mexico

chilango: Mexico City resident

chilaquiles: fried tortilla strips bathed in salsa, cream, and cheese

chiles en nogada: poblano pepper stuffed with meat, dried fruit, and nuts, covered in creamed walnut sauce, and sprinkled with pomegranate seeds

chiles rellenos: stuffed chile peppers

chipotle: a smoky dried chile pepper, derived from fresh jalapeño pepper

chorro: spring

churro: a tube-shaped sweet bread, deep fried and dusted in sugar

clínica: clinic

cochinita pibil: Yucatecan-style pulled pork

comida: the large midday meal in Mexico, typically eaten around 2pm

comida corrida: an economical, set-price lunch served in restaurants

concha: a sweet roll topped with sugar

consulado: consulate

convento: convent

corregidor: magistrate, in the colonial era

correo: postal service

corrida de toros: bullfight

cotija: an aged Mexican cheese

criollo: a term used in New Spain to describe a Mexican-born person of Spanish descent

Cruz Roja: Red Cross

cuaresma: Lent

cuatrimoto: all-terrain vehicle (ATV)

cultura: culture

cumbia: a traditional musical style from Colombia

desayuno: breakfast

Día de Muertos: Day of the Dead

Distrito Federal: Federal District, former official name of Mexico City

dulces: sweets

dulces típicos: traditional Mexican sweets

El Gran Chichimeca: colonial-era name given to the northern Mexican region, including the Bajío, by Spanish settlers

embajada: embassy

enchiladas mineras: cheese-stuffed tortillas in guajillo sauce with sautéed potatoes and carrots

enchiladas verdes: stuffed tortillas bathed in green salsa

enmoladas: tortillas in mole sauce

entrada: appetizer

equipal: traditional wood and pigskin furniture style from Jalisco

escuela: school

español: Spanish language

farmacia: pharmacy

feria: fair

festival: festival

fiesta: party

fiestas patrias: patriotic holidays

flan: egg custard dessert

flauta: deep-fried and stuffed tortilla, topped with cream and salsa

FMM: Forma Migratoria Multiple (tourist card)

fonda: casual restaurant

gachupín: Spanish person

galería: gallery

gomita: gumdrop

gordita: stuffed corn cake

gringa: a flour tortilla filled with melted cheese and meat

gringo: American

guanabana: soursop, a tropical fruit

guayaba: guava

guisado: stew or side dish

hacienda: estate

hojalatería: tinwork

horchata: traditional drink made with ground rice, sugar, and water

huarache: torpedo-shaped corn flatbread; also, a sandal

Huasteca: Mexican region comprising northern Veracruz, southern Tamaulipas, a portion of San Luis Potosí, and the Sierra Gorda in Querétaro

huevo: egg

huevos a la mexicana: eggs scrambled with tomato, onion, and chile pepper

huevos rancheros: fried eggs in tomato-chile sauce

huipil: traditional women's tunic from southern Mexico

huitlacoche: corn fungus

iglesia: church
indígena: Indigenous person, or Indigenous (adj.)
ingeniero: engineer
instituto: institute
jamaica: hibiscus
jamoncillo: flavored milk-fudge
jarciería: shop selling home and cleaning products
jardín: garden
joyería: jewelry
Las Mañanitas: Mexico's birthday song
lavandería: laundry
La Vía Dolorosa: Stations of the Cross
ley seca: dry law
librería: bookstore
licenciado: college graduate
licuado: milk or fruit shake
longaniza: a type of sausage
maciza: in carnitas, pork shoulder or leg
maestro: master; teacher
maguey: large succulent plant common in Mexico
majolica: tin-glazed pottery, originally from Italy
mañana: tomorrow; morning
manta: lightweight cotton fabric frequently used in traditional Mexican clothing
mantilla: lace or silk scarf
maquiladora: manufacturing plant
mariachi: a traditional Mexican music ensemble
menudo: beef stomach soup
mercado: market
mesquite: mesquite tree
mestizo: a person of mixed ethnic heritage
mezcal: distilled spirit made from the maguey plant
mezcal de gusano: mezcal distilled with the maguey worm
michelada: beer served with lime juice, salt, hot sauce, and Worcestershire sauce
migajas: pork drippings
migración: immigration
milagritos: small tin ornaments
mixiote: lamb steamed in agave leaf
mole: flavorful sauce made of ground nuts and spices

mole negro: ground sauce made of chocolate, nuts, and spices from the state of Oaxaca
momia: mummy
montalayo: lamb stomach
mordida: literally, bite; slang for bribe
museo: museum
Navidad: Christmas
nevería: ice cream parlor
nieve: ice cream
norteño: northern
novena: nine days of prayer or worship
órgano: organ
oro: gold
Otomí: indigenous ethnic group of central Mexico
palenqueta: honey-covered disc of nuts or seeds
paleta: popsicle
pan: bread
pan dulce: sweet bread
panela: a variety of fresh cheese
panteón: cemetery
papadzules: Yucatecan tacos stuffed with hard-boiled egg
papel picado: decorative cut-paper adornments
parque: park
parroquia: parish church
partido: political party
Partido Acción Nacional: National Action Party
Partido de la Revolución Democrática: Party of the Democratic Revolution
Partido Revolucionario Institucional: Institutional Revolutionary Party
pascua: Easter
pasilla: a mild but flavorful dried chile pepper
pastor: taco preparation using chile pepper and spices
Pemex: Petroleos Mexicanos (Mexican Petroleum)
peña: rock
peninsular: colonial-era term for a person born in Spain
peso: Mexico's currency
petate: woven rush mat
picadillo: spiced ground beef

pico de gallo: salsa made of chopped tomatoes, onion, cilantro, and chile peppers

pipián: a sauce made of ground pumpkin seeds and spices

plata: silver

plaza: plaza or public square

plaza de toros: bullring

plazuela: small plaza

poblano: from the state or the city of Puebla

Porfiriato: historical period during the presidency of Porfirio Díaz

posada: inn

pozo: well

pozole: hominy soup

presa: reservoir

presidente municipal: municipal president

priista: member of the PRI political party

Protección Civil: Civil Protection, or police

pueblo: small town

pulque: alcoholic drink made from fermented maguey sap

puntas de filete: beef tips

querétense: something or someone from Querétaro

quesadilla: a warmed tortilla stuffed with cheese

queso: cheese

queso de tuna: prickly pear cheese, a regional sweet

queso fundido: melted cheese

ranchera: musical style from Northern Mexico

raspado: shaved ice

rebozo: shawl

reggaeton: modern musical style based on reggae

rentistas: visa designation for foreigners who live but do not earn money in Mexico

requesón: ricotta-style cheese

residente permanente: immigrant visa

residente temporal: nonimmigrant resident visa

restaurante: restaurant

retablo: devotional painting

río: river

salsa roja: condiment made with red tomatoes and chile peppers, or red chile peppers

salsa verde: condiment made with green tomatoes, chile peppers, and spices

sangrita: a tomato-based chaser for tequila

santa escuela: a Jesuit school in the colonial era

Semana Santa: Holy Week

señor: Mr.; sir; man

señora: Mrs., madam; woman

señorita: Miss; young woman

serape: traditional Mexican wool shawl or cloak

serrano: variety of green chile pepper

siesta: nap

sombrero: hat

sopa: soup

sopa azteca: tortilla soup

sope: thick, round corn flatbread

surtido: mixed

taco: seasoned meat or vegetables enclosed in a warm tortilla

tacos dorados: deep-fried tacos

Talavera: hand-painted majolica-style pottery from Puebla, Mexico

tamal: tamale, or steamed corn cake (plural: tamales)

tarifa: fee, cost (as in the cost of a night in a hotel)

teatro: theater

templo: temple, church

Tenochtitlan: capital city of Mesoamerica at the time of the Spanish conquest

tequila: a Mexican distilled spirit made from blue agave

tintorería: dry cleaner

tlayuda: a large Oaxacan tortilla stuffed with beans and cheese

torta: hot sandwich served on a white roll

transito: transit

tranvía: trolley

tú: you (informal)

tuna: prickly pear fruit

turismo: tourism

turista: tourist or traveler's diarrhea

universidad: university

usted: you (formal)

verano: summer

viceroy: colonial governor

Viernes Santo: Good Friday

vino: wine

vino tinto: red wine

visa: visa
xoconostle: sour prickly pear fruit
zapote: sapodilla, a tropical fruit

ABBREVIATIONS

Col.: colonia (neighborhood)
esq.: esquina (corner)
Gto.: Guanajuato (state of Guanajuato)
IMN: Instituto Nacional de Migración (National Institute of Immigration)
nte.: norte (north)
ote.: oriente (east)

PAN: Partido Acción Nacional (National Action Party)
pp: por persona (per person)
PRD: Partido de la Revolución Democrática (Party of the Democratic Revolution)
PRI: Partido Revolucionario Institucional (Institutional Revolutionary Party)
prol.: prolongación (prolongation, usually of a city street)
pte.: poniente (west)
Qro.: Querétaro (state of Querétaro)
s/n: sin número (without number)

Spanish Phrasebook

Your Mexican adventure will be more fun if you use a little Spanish. Mexican folks, although they may smile at your funny accent, will appreciate your halting efforts to break the ice and transform yourself from a foreigner to a potential friend.

Spanish commonly uses 30 letters—the familiar English 26, plus four straightforward additions: ch, ll, ñ, and rr.

PRONUNCIATION

Once you learn them, Spanish pronunciation rules—in contrast to English—don't change. Spanish vowels generally sound softer than in English. (*Note:* The capitalized syllables receive stronger accents.)

Vowels

a like ah, as in "hah": *agua* AH-gooah (water), *pan* PAHN (bread), and *casa* CAH-sah (house)

e like ay, as in "may": *mesa* MAY-sah (table), *tela* TAY-lah (cloth), and *de* DAY (of, from)

i like ee, as in "need": *diez* dee-AYZ (ten), *comida* ko-MEE-dah (meal), and *fin* FEEN (end)

o like oh, as in "go": *peso* PAY-soh (weight), *ocho* OH-choh (eight), and *poco* POH-koh (a bit)

u like oo, as in "cool": *uno* OO-noh (one), *cuarto* KOOAHR-toh (room), and *usted*

oos-TAYD (you); when it follows a "q" the **u** is silent; when it follows an "h" or has an umlaut, it's pronounced like "w"

Consonants

c like k as in "keep": *cuarto* KOOAR-toh (room), Tepic tay-PEEK (capital of Nayarit state); when it precedes "e" or "i," pronounce **c** like s, as in "sit": *cerveza* sayr-VAY-sah (beer), *encima* ayn-SEE-mah (atop)

g like g as in "gift" when it precedes "a," "o," "u," or a consonant: *gato* GAH-toh (cat), *hago* AH-goh (I do, make); otherwise, pronounce **g** like h as in "hat": *giro* HEE-roh (money order), *gente* HAYN-tay (people)

h occurs, but is silent—not pronounced at all

j like h, as in "has": *jueves* HOOAY-vays (Thursday), *mejor* may-HOR (better)

ll like y, as in "yes": *toalla* toh-AH-yah (towel), *ellos* AY-yohs (they, them)

ñ like ny, as in "canyon": *año* AH-nyo (year), *señor* SAY-nyor (Mr., sir)

r is lightly trilled, with tongue at the roof of your mouth like a very light English d, as in "ready": *pero* PAY-doh (but), *tres* TDAYS (three), *cuatro* KOOAH-tdoh (four)

rr like a Spanish r, but with much more emphasis and trill

Note: The single small but common exception to all of the above is the pronunciation of Spanish **y** when it's being used as the Spanish word for "and," as in "Ron y Kathy." In such case, pronounce it like the English ee, as in "keep": Ron "ee" Kathy (Ron and Kathy).

Accent

The rule for accent, the relative stress given to syllables within a given word, is straightforward. If a word ends in a vowel, an n, or an s, accent the next-to-last syllable; if not, accent the last syllable.

Pronounce *gracias* GRAH-seeahs (thank you), *orden* OHR-dayn (order), and *carretera* kah-ray-TAY-rah (highway) with stress on the next-to-last syllable.

Otherwise, accent the last syllable: *venir* vay-NEER (to come), *ferrocarril* fay-roh-cah-REEL (railroad), and *edad* ay-DAHD (age).

Exceptions to the accent rule are always marked with an accent sign: (á, é, í, ó, or ú), such as *teléfono* tay-LAY-foh-noh (telephone), *jabón* hah-BON (soap), and *rápido* RAH-pee-doh (rapid).

BASIC AND COURTEOUS EXPRESSIONS

Most Spanish-speaking people consider formalities important. Whenever approaching anyone for information or some other reason, do not forget the appropriate salutation—good morning, good evening, etc. Standing alone, the greeting *hola* (hello) can sound brusque.

Hello. *Hola.*
Good morning. *Buenos días.*
Good afternoon. *Buenas tardes.*
Good evening. *Buenas noches.*
How are you? *¿Cómo está usted?*
Very well, thank you. *Muy bien, gracias.*
Okay; good. *Bien.*
Not okay; bad. *Mal or feo.*
So-so. *Más o menos.*
And you? *¿Y usted?*
Thank you. *Gracias.*
Thank you very much. *Muchas gracias.*
You're very kind. *Muy amable.*
You're welcome. *De nada.*
Good-bye. *Adios.*

See you later. *Hasta luego.*
please *por favor*
yes *sí*
no *no*
I don't know. *No sé.*
Just a moment, please. *Momentito, por favor.*
Excuse me, please (when you're trying to get attention). *Disculpe or Con permiso.*
Excuse me (to apologize). *Lo siento.*
Pleased to meet you. *Mucho gusto.*
What is your name? *¿Cómo se llama usted?*
My name is ... *Me llamo ...*
Do you speak English? *¿Habla usted inglés?*
Is English spoken here? (Does anyone here speak English?) *¿Se habla inglés?*
I don't speak Spanish well. *No hablo bien el español.*
I don't understand. *No entiendo.*
How do you say ... in Spanish? *¿Cómo se dice ... en español?*
Would you like ... *¿Quisiera usted ...*
Let's go to ... *Vamos a ...*

TERMS OF ADDRESS

When in doubt, use the formal *usted* (you) as a form of address.

I *yo*
you (formal) *usted*
you (familiar) *tú*
he/him *él*
she/her *ella*
we/us *nosotros*
you (plural) *ustedes*
they/them *ellos* (all males or mixed gender); *ellas* (all females)
Mr., sir *señor*
Mrs., madam *señora*
miss, young lady *señorita*
wife; husband *esposa; esposo*
friend *amigo* (male); *amiga* (female)
sweetheart *novio* (male); *novia* (female)
son; daughter *hijo; hija*
brother; sister *hermano; hermana*
father; mother *padre; madre*

grandfather; grandmother *abuelo; abuela*

TRANSPORTATION
Where is ... ? *¿Dónde está ... ?*
How far is it to ... ? *¿A cuánto está ... ?*
from ... to ... *de ... a ...*
How many blocks? *¿Cuántas cuadras?*
Where (Which) is the way to ... ? *¿Dónde está el camino a ... ?*
the bus station *la terminal de autobuses*
the bus stop *la parada de autobuses*
Where is this bus going? *¿Adónde va este autobús?*
the taxi stand *la parada de taxis*
the train station *la estación de ferrocarril*
the boat *el barco*
the launch *lancha; tiburonera*
the dock *el muelle*
the airplane *el avión*
the airport *el aeropuerto*
I'd like a ticket to ... *Quisiera un boleto a ...*
first (second) class *primera (segunda) clase*
round-trip *ida y vuelta; viaje redondo*
reservation *reservación*
baggage *equipaje*
Stop here, please. *Pare aquí, por favor.*
the entrance *la entrada*
the exit *la salida*
ticket *boleto*
the ticket office *taquilla*
(very) near; far *(muy) cerca; lejos*
to; toward *a*
by; through *por*
from *de*
the right *la derecha*
the left *la izquierda*
straight ahead *derecho; directo*
in front *en frente*
beside *al lado*
behind *atrás*
the corner *la esquina*
the stoplight *la semáforo*
a turn *una vuelta*
right here *aquí*
somewhere around here *por acá*
right there *allí*
somewhere around there *por allá*

road *el camino*
street; boulevard *calle; bulevar*
block *la cuadra*
highway *carretera*
kilometer *kilómetro*
bridge; toll *puente; cuota*
address *dirección*
north; south *norte; sur*
east; west *oriente (este); poniente (oeste)*

ACCOMMODATIONS
hotel *hotel*
Is there a room? *¿Hay cuarto?*
May I (may we) see it? *¿Puedo (podemos) verlo?*
What is the rate? *¿Cuál es el precio?*
Is that your best rate? *¿Es su mejor precio?*
Is there something cheaper? *¿Hay algo más económico?*
a single room *un cuarto sencillo*
a double room *un cuarto doble*
double bed *cama matrimonial*
twin beds *camas individuales*
with private bath *con baño*
hot water *agua caliente*
shower *ducha*
towels *toallas*
soap *jabón*
toilet paper *papel higiénico*
blanket *cobija*
sheets *sábanas*
air-conditioned *aire acondicionado*
fan *abanico; ventilador*
key *llave*
manager *gerente*

FOOD
I'm hungry *Tengo hambre.*
I'm thirsty. *Tengo sed.*
menu *carta; menú*
order *orden*
glass *vaso*
fork *tenedor*
knife *cuchillo*
spoon *cuchara*
napkin *servilleta*
soft drink *refresco*
coffee *café*

tea *té*
drinking water *agua pura; agua potable*
bottle of water *botella de agua*
bottled carbonated water *agua mineral*
bottled uncarbonated water *agua sin gas*
beer *cerveza*
wine *vino*
milk *leche*
juice *jugo*
cream *crema*
sugar *azúcar*
cheese *queso*
snack *antojito; botana*
breakfast *desayuno*
lunch *almuerzo*
daily lunch special *comida corrida* (or *el menú del día* depending on region)
dinner *comida* (often eaten in late afternoon); *cena* (a late-night snack)
wine list *lista de vinos*
the check *la cuenta*
tip *propina*
eggs *huevos*
bread *pan*
salad *ensalada*
fruit *fruta*
mango *mango*
watermelon *sandía*
papaya *papaya*
banana *plátano*
apple *manzana*
orange *naranja*
lime *limón*
fish *pescado*
shellfish *mariscos*
shrimp *camarones*
meat (without) *(sin) carne*
chicken *pollo*
pork *puerco*
beef; steak *res; bistec*
bacon; ham *tocino; jamón*
fried *frito*
roasted *asada*
barbecue; barbecued *barbacoa; al carbón*
spicy, hot *picante*

SHOPPING

money *dinero*
money-exchange bureau *casa de cambio*
I would like to exchange travelers checks. *Quisiera cambiar cheques de viajero.*
What is the exchange rate? *¿Cuál es el tipo de cambio?*
How much is the commission? *¿Cuánto cuesta la comisión?*
Do you accept credit cards? *¿Aceptan tarjetas de crédito?*
money order *giro*
How much does it cost? *¿Cuánto cuesta?*
What is your final price? *¿Cuál es su último precio?*
expensive *caro*
cheap *barato; económico*
more *más*
less *menos*
a little *un poco*
too much *demasiado*

HEALTH

Help me please. *Ayúdeme por favor.*
I am ill. *Estoy enfermo.*
Call a doctor. *Llame un doctor.*
Take me to ... *Lléveme a ...*
hospital *hospital; sanatorio*
drugstore *farmacia*
pain *dolor*
fever *fiebre*
headache *dolor de cabeza*
stomachache *dolor de estómago*
allergy *alergia*
burn *quemadura*
cramp *calambre*
nausea *náusea*
vomiting *vomitar*
medicine *medicina*
prescription *receta*
antibiotic *antibiótico*
pill; tablet *pastilla*
aspirin *aspirina*
ointment; cream *pomada; crema*
bandage *venda*
cotton *algodón*

sanitary napkins *toallas,* or use brand name, e.g., Kotex
birth control pills *pastillas anticonceptivas*
contraceptive foam *espuma anticonceptiva*
condoms *preservativos; condones*
toothbrush *cepilla dental*
dental floss *hilo dental*
toothpaste *crema dental*
dentist *dentista*
toothache *dolor de muelas*

POST OFFICE AND COMMUNICATIONS

long-distance telephone *teléfono larga distancia*
I would like to call ... *Quisiera llamar a ...*
collect *por cobrar*
station to station *a quien contesta*
person to person *persona a persona*
credit card *tarjeta de crédito*
post office *correo*
general delivery *lista de correo*
letter *carta*
stamp *estampilla, timbre*
postcard *tarjeta*
aerogram *aerograma*
airmail *correo aereo*
registered *registrado*
money order *giro*
package; box *paquete; caja*
string; tape *cuerda; cinta*

AT THE BORDER

border *frontera*
customs *aduana*
immigration *migración*
tourist card *tarjeta de turista*
inspection *inspección; revisión*
passport *pasaporte*
profession *profesión*
marital status *estado civil*
single *soltero*
married; divorced *casado; divorciado*
widowed *viudado*
insurance *seguros*
title *título*
driver's license *licencia de manejar*

AT THE GAS STATION

gas station *gasolinera*
gasoline *gasolina*
unleaded *sin plomo*
full, please *lleno, por favor*
tire *llanta*
tire repair shop *vulcanizadora*
air *aire*
water *agua*
oil (change) *aceite (cambio)*
grease *grasa*
My ... doesn't work. *Mi ... no sirve.*
battery *batería*
radiator *radiador*
alternator *alternador*
generator *generador*
tow truck *grúa*
repair shop *taller mecánico*
tune-up *afinación*
auto parts store *refaccionería*

VERBS

Verbs are the key to getting along in Spanish. They employ mostly predictable forms and come in three classes, which end in *ar, er,* and *ir,* respectively:
to buy *comprar*
I buy, you (he, she, it) buys *compro, compra*
we buy, you (they) buy *compramos, compran*
to eat *comer*
I eat, you (he, she, it) eats *como, come*
we eat, you (they) eat *comemos, comen*
to climb *subir*
I climb, you (he, she, it) climbs *subo, sube*
we climb, you (they) climb *subimos, suben*
Here are more (with irregularities indicated):
to do or make *hacer* (regular except for *hago,* I do or make)
to go *ir* (very irregular: *voy, va, vamos, van*)
to go (walk) *andar*
to love *amar*
to work *trabajar*
to want *desear, querer*
to need *necesitar*

to read *leer*
to write *escribir*
to repair *reparar*
to stop *parar*
to get off (the bus) *bajar*
to arrive *llegar*
to stay (remain) *quedar*
to stay (lodge) *hospedar*
to leave *salir* (regular except for *salgo*, I leave)
to look at *mirar*
to look for *buscar*
to give *dar* (regular except for *doy*, I give)
to carry *llevar*
to have *tener* (irregular but important: *tengo, tiene, tenemos, tienen*)
to come *venir* (similarly irregular: *vengo, viene, venimos, vienen*)
Spanish has two forms of "to be":
to be *estar* (regular except for *estoy*, I am)
to be *ser* (very irregular: *soy, es, somos, son*)
Use *estar* when speaking of location or a temporary state of being: "I am at home." *"Estoy en casa."* "I'm sick." *"Estoy enfermo."* Use *ser* for a permanent state of being: "I am a doctor." *"Soy doctora."*

NUMBERS

0 *cero*
1 *uno*
2 *dos*
3 *tres*
4 *cuatro*
5 *cinco*
6 *seis*
7 *siete*
8 *ocho*
9 *nueve*
10 *diez*
11 *once*
12 *doce*
13 *trece*
14 *catorce*
15 *quince*
16 *dieciseis*
17 *diecisiete*
18 *dieciocho*
19 *diecinueve*
20 *veinte*
21 *veinte y uno* or *veintiuno*
30 *treinta*
40 *cuarenta*
50 *cincuenta*
60 *sesenta*
70 *setenta*
80 *ochenta*
90 *noventa*
100 *ciento*
101 *ciento y uno* or *cientiuno*
200 *doscientos*
500 *quinientos*
1,000 *mil*
10,000 *diez mil*
100,000 *cien mil*
1,000,000 *millón*
one-half *medio*
one-third *un tercio*
one-fourth *un cuarto*

TIME

What time is it? *¿Qué hora es?*
It's one o'clock. *Es la una.*
It's three in the afternoon. *Son las tres de la tarde.*
It's four in the morning. *Son las cuatro de la mañana.*
six-thirty *seis y media*
a quarter till eleven *un cuarto para las once*
a quarter past five *las cinco y cuarto*
an hour *una hora*

DAYS AND MONTHS

Monday *lunes*
Tuesday *martes*
Wednesday *miércoles*
Thursday *jueves*
Friday *viernes*
Saturday *sábado*
Sunday *domingo*
today *hoy*
tomorrow *mañana*
yesterday *ayer*
January *enero*
February *febrero*
March *marzo*

April *abril*	**December** *diciembre*
May *mayo*	**a week** *una semana*
June *junio*	**a month** *un mes*
July *julio*	**after** *después*
August *agosto*	**before** *antes*
September *septiembre*	
October *octubre*	*Courtesy of Bruce Whipperman, author of* Moon
November *noviembre*	Pacific Mexico.

Suggested Reading

HISTORY

Brading, David. *Miners and Merchants in Bourbon Mexico.* Cambridge, U.K.: Cambridge University Press, 2008. Widely recognized as one of the preeminent scholars of early Guanajuato and the Spanish colonies, David Brading offers a fascinating look at life in colonial Mexico.

Coe, Michael D. *From the Olmecs to the Aztecs.* London: Thames and Hudson, 2008. Yale anthropologist Michael D. Coe has written extensively about Mesoamerican civilizations. In this volume, he introduces the great cultures of pre-Columbian Mexico.

Collier, George. *Basta: Land and the Zapatista Rebellion in Chiapas.* Oakland, California: Food First Books, 1994. An excellent introduction to Indigenous communities and the 1994 Zapatista uprising in Chiapas.

De las Casas, Bartolomé. *Short Account of the Destruction of the Indies.* London: Penguin Books, 1992. A Dominican friar and humanitarian, de las Casas recounts his firsthand observations about Spanish abuse of Indigenous Americans during the colonial era.

Krauze, Enrique. *Mexico: A Biography of Power.* New York: Harper Perennial, 1998. A general history of Mexico, written by one of the country's preeminent intellectuals.

Riding, Alan. *Distant Neighbors.* New York: Knopf, 1984. Though written in the 1980s, this book still offers an insightful perspective on the differences between U.S. and Mexican culture with striking accuracy.

Thomas, Hugh. *Conquest: Montezuma, Cortés, and the Fall of Old Mexico.* New York: Simon & Schuster, 1995. An exhaustively researched and beautifully written account of one of the greatest events in history: the meeting of the New and Old Worlds in Mexico in 1519, and the war that followed.

Womack, John. *Emiliano Zapata and the Mexican Revolution.* New York: Vintage, 1970. A wonderful, well-researched history of the great hero Emiliano Zapata, written by Harvard's Mexico expert, John Womack.

FOOD AND CULTURE

Franz, Carl, and Lorena Havens. *The People's Guide to Mexico.* Berkeley, California: Avalon Travel Publishing, 2012. A cultural handbook to travel in Mexico, the *People's Guide* offers hard-won and well-placed advice for adventurous Mexico travelers.

Kennedy, Diana. *My Mexico.* New York: Clarkson Potter/Publishers, 1998. More anthropological tome than practical cookbook, this book offers detailed regional recipes from across Mexico, accompanied by the author's personal observations and stories.

GENERAL INTEREST

Cohan, Tony. *On Mexican Time: A New Life in Mexico.* New York: Broadway Books, 2000. Cohan's best-selling memoir vividly recounts his first years of life as an expatriate in San Miguel de Allende.

De Gast, Robert. *Behind the Doors of San Miguel de Allende.* Petaluma, California: Pomegranate Communications, 2000. De Gast's follow-up to his successful photography book about San Miguel shows you the courtyards and gardens behind the town's distinctive doorways.

De Gast, Robert. *The Doors of San Miguel de Allende.* Petaluma, California: Pomegranate Communications, 1994. A wonderful photographer and writer, Robert de Gast captures the unique culture and color of San Miguel through photos of its beautiful doorways.

Simeone, Riccardo, and Archie Dean. *The Insider's Guide to San Miguel.* Self-published, 2013. You will have to seek out this classic guide to San Miguel de Allende in one of the city's local bookshops. Originally written and published by Archie Dean, it offers a comprehensive and annotated list of restaurants, hotels, and other businesses in San Miguel.

Internet Resources

SAN MIGUEL DE ALLENDE
San Miguel de Allende Official Site
www.sanmiguelallende.gob.mx
The official website of San Miguel de Allende offers information about the city and city services, like education and the police force, in Spanish.

Don Day in SMA
http://dondayinsma.com
An entertaining blog about food and drink in San Miguel de Allende authored by an opinionated resident.

Cupcakes and Crablegs
www.cupcakesandcrablegs.com
A food-centric San Miguel de Allende blog, Cupcakes and Crablegs also covers shopping, artists, and places to stay in the city.

GUANAJUATO
Festival Internacional Cervantino
www.festivalcervantino.gob.mx
The official site for Guanajuato's renowned Cervantino festival offers complete programming information.

Guanajuato Official Site
www.guanajuato.gob.mx
The official website of Guanajuato's state government offers general information about state programs as well as links to tourist information.

Universidad de Guanajuato Cultural Extension
www.extension.ugto.mx
This website offers updated information about the numerous concerts, film screenings, and art exhibitions produced by the University of Guanajuato's cultural extension. You can also read an online version of *Polen,* their monthly arts magazine.

QUERÉTARO
Asomarte
www.asomarte.com

The online version of Querétaro's free art and culture magazine features events listings, cultural news, and travel-related podcasts as well as restaurant and hotel reviews.

Travel Querétaro
www.queretaro.travel

Maintained by the Querétaro state government, this informative website details major sites in Querétaro city and state, lists upcoming events, and offers maps, photo galleries, and cultural articles. The Spanish version contains more detailed content than the English version.

Index

List of Maps

Photo Credits

All photos © Julie Meade except; page 5 (top) © Emattil | Dreamstime.com; (right middle) © Devon Lee; (bottom left) © Egomezta | Dreamstime.com; (bottom right) © Elovkoff | Dreamstime.com; page 8 © Ibrester | Dreamstime.com; page 10 © Mardzpe | Dreamstime.com; page 11 © (top) Elovkoff | Dreamstime.com; (bottom) © Devon Lee; page 13 © Ibrester | Dreamstime.com; page 14 (top) © Afagundes | Dreamstime. com; page 16 © Jennifer Posner; page 22 (bottom) © Devon Lee; page 23 (top) © Bpperry | Dreamstime.com; page 24 (top) © Elovkoff | Dreamstime.com; page 26 (bottom middle) © Mathes | Dreamstime.com; page 34 © Shane Adams | Dreamstime.com; page 35 (top left) © Devon Lee; page 50 (top) © Devon Lee; (left middle) © Devon Lee; (right middle) © Ibrester | Dreamstime.com; page 60 © Rancho Xotolar; page 72 (top right) © Devon Lee; page 75 © Arturoosorno | Dreamstime.com; page 103 © Devon Lee; page 104 © Winston Lee; page 120 (top left) © Elovkoff | Dreamstime; (top right) © Egomezta | Dreamstime.com; page 131 (top) © Egomezta | Dreamstime.com; page 132 © Elovkoff | Dreamstime.com; page 165 © Jcfotografo | Dreamstime. com; page 167 © Jerl71 | Dreamstime.com; page 168 (top left) © Leoncioruiz33 | Dreamstime.com; (top right) © Christophertp | Dreamstime.com; page 176 © Roberto Galan | Dreamstime.com; page 180 © (right middle) Jerl71 | Dreamstime.com; page 205 (left middle) © Girnyk | Dreamstime.com; page 211 © Bpperry | Dreamstime.com; page 234 (bottom) © Kobby_dagan | Dreamstime.com

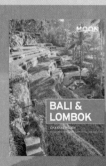

MOON

BALI & LOMBOK

CHANTAE REDEN

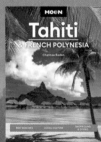

MOON

Tahiti
& FRENCH POLYNESIA

Chantae Reden

BEST BEACHES · LOCAL CULTURE · SNORKELING & DIVING

MOON

Japan

Jonathan DeHart

PLAN YOUR TRIP · AVOID THE CROWDS · EXPERIENCE THE REAL JAPAN

MOON

NEW ZEALAND

JAMIE CHRISTIAN DESPLACES

MOON

Baja
TIJUANA TO LOS CABOS

Jennifer Kramer

ROAD TRIPS · SURFING & DIVING · LOCAL FLAVORS

MOON

BELIZE

LEBAWIT LILY GIRMA

MOON

CARTAGENA
& COLOMBIA'S CARIBBEAN COAST

OCEAN MALANDRA

MOON

CHILE

STEPH DYSON

MOON

Costa Rica

BEST BEACHES · WILDLIFE WATCHING · OUTDOOR ADVENTURES

MOON

Galápagos Islands

LISA CHO

WILDLIFE · SNORKELING & DIVING · TOUR ADVICE

MOON

ECUADOR
& THE GALÁPAGOS ISLANDS

BETHANY PITTS

MOON

TRIP OF A LIFETIME

MACHU PICCHU
WITH CUSCO, CUZCO & THE INCA TRAIL

RYAN DUBE

MOON

OAXACA

NICK GORDON

MOON

TRIP OF A LIFETIME

PATAGONIA
INCLUDING THE FALKLAND ISLANDS

WAYNE BERNHARDSON

MOON

Puerto Vallarta
WITH SAYULITA, THE RIVIERA NAYARIT & COSTALEGRE

Madeline Milne

BEACH GETAWAYS · SURFING · LOCAL FAVORITES

MOON

YUCATÁN PENINSULA

LILIANA FIGUEROA & GARY CHANDLER

DOMINICAN REPUBLIC

JAMAICA

MOON
Puerto Rico

BAHAMAS

Caribbean

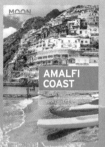

AMALFI COAST

AMSTERDAM
BRUSSELS & BRUGES

EGYPT

MOON
Greek Islands
& ATHENS

Europe, Middle East & Africa

Iceland
WITH A ROAD TRIP ON THE RING ROAD

MOON
Morocco

NORMANDY & BRITTANY

WITH MONT-SAINT MICHEL

MOON
Portugal
WITH MADEIRA & THE AZORES

MOON
Croatia & Slovenia
WITH MONTENEGRO

MOON
Rome, Florence & Venice

MOON
Scotland

MOON
SOUTHERN ITALY

SICILY, PUGLIA, NAPLES & THE AMALFI COAST

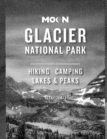

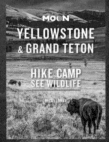